# Ruth Gordon

*Myself Among Others*

*Billy Day*

*13 March, 1975*

# RUTH GORDON

# MYSELF AMONG OTHERS

New York  *Atheneum*  1971

Portions of this book were first published
in *Vogue* and *The New York Times*

*Designed by Harry Ford*
*First Printing April 1971*
*Second Printing May 1971*

*Ruth Gordon*

*Myself Among Others*

# Woollcott Speaking

W AKE UP, Blossom, Northern Lights."
By the way, are the Northern Lights still doing it? After Woollcott died I never saw them, but before that his friends did. Charlie MacArthur said an invite of Woollcott's was like a call to the jury panel. And if the summons was to his Vermont island in August, you saw the Northern Lights.

"Wake up, Blossom. Northern Lights! Slip on something indecent, you're going to have competition."

"I don't—"

"Do you want me to tear this door down with my bare hands and make suet of you?"

"What?"

"Two minutes flat or Dr. Crippen will be in there with his bag of lye."

"Oh God!"

"That's my dated ingenue!" He knocked next door. "Stout Cortez?"

Bea Kaufman groaned. "I'm asleep, Dream Boy."

"Get that upstate charm into something shapeless not to bedazzle poor sensitive Howard Bull."

There was a sound of feet on the floor.

3

Woollcott called up the stairs. "Myra, throw Harpo out and be down before I can count your age! Thirty-three, thirty-five, thirty-eight—"

People stumbled out in anything from a raincoat to a Charvet dressing gown or an Emma Maloof or Boué Soeurs.

"We're going out in the gondola."

"Oh, no!"

"Acky, no!"

"Please, Acky!"

"Why go *out?* Can't we see the goddam Northern Lights through the window?"

Woollcott took Alice Duer Miller's arm. "Turn the hose on anybody who lags behind, Bull," he told his helper. "Come, Alice, class will tell, *we* get the cushioned seats." They started down the dark path. "Bull, drench any renegade not aboard in two minutes."

Bull propelled the gondola gently to left, to right. Everybody sulked in different positions, but Alec saw only fierce beauty play over the Vermont forest and from time to time light up the zinnia placed rakishly back of Howard's ear. In the prow a shivering Ross muttered imprecations. "It looks like goddam doomsday," he said through clenched teeth. "And that's how *you'll* look, Woollcott, if I can find the matches and get you to drink a cup of kerosene."

If you never saw the Northern Lights, did you ever see Woollcott lecture? Across the whole country, crowds turned out. When he was announced for Mecca Temple in Newark, Moss Hart requested to be allowed to sit on the platform with him. "I don't have to be introduced, I don't have to do anything but just sit there. It will mean a lot."

"Sure," said Woollcott.

Success was fairly recent and brought Moss pain, pleasure and trips to the analyst. Wearing an impeccable dinner jacket, impeccable shirt, tie, shoes, socks and cufflinks, Moss rode with Woollcott to Newark. He was given a chair on the platform to the left of the podium.

Applause followed Woollcott as he strode down Mecca Temple's center aisle. He kept them laughing and applauding for an hour and a half, then went off to bigger applause. He came back, stepped to the edge of the platform, held his hand up for silence. "Thank you. Today the question period will be omitted since the obvious question would be, who is this ridiculous figure sitting on the platform? Goodnight." He walked off and, convulsed with laughter, watched handsome Moss wend his way offstage.

Woollcott could give and he could take. Which summer was the Chicago World's Fair? Whenever it was, Woollcott ordered his friends to go. Nobody knows how many times *he* went and always with friends he curved into line. On one trip, he left a deposit on a jinricksha and a gondola to be sent to Neshobe Island when Chicago had no further use for them. Howard Bull punted the gondola around Lake Bomoseen and pulled the jinricksha with Woollcott in it to the croquet game where, if Woollcott loved you, you could sit in it and watch.

What he admired most in the Chicago World's Fair was the Chalice of Antioch, softly lit and reverently arranged on the manqué Last Supper table. The public admired, worshipped, fell down and prayed or wept at a discreet distance, according to how affected they were. It affected Woollcott most of anybody. He wrote about it, spoke about it on the radio, off the radio, saw to it that magazines photographed it. "Rush to Chicago," he urged, "and count yourself blessed to stand before the Chalice of Antioch."

Then one hateful day came a wire.

ALEXANDER WOOLLCOTT

BOMOSEEN, VT.

THINK YOU SHOULD BE TOLD BEFORE STORY BREAKS STOP
CHALICE ANTIOCH SORRY HAVE TO INFORM YOU IS FAKE PIECE OF
POTTERY MADE BY SKILLFUL EMPLOYE AVONDALE POTTERY
WORKS OUTSIDE CINCINNATI STOP THOUGHT YOU SHOULD BE
GIVEN CHANCE THINK OF SOMETHING BEFORE CHICAGO TRIBUNE
PRINTS NEWS STOP REGARDS

MAYOR KELLY

Woollcott turned dark red. "It's that goddam Maud Hutchins," he shouted. "She never liked me. She's snooped around till she ferreted this out."

Fortunate for Charlies MacArthur and Lederer, their telegram didn't bring on the stroke that years later struck Woollcott down on the radio program saying "The people of Germany are just as responsible for Hitler as the people of Chicago are for Colonel Mc-Cormick." His face went dark red and half an hour later he lay dead at Roosevelt Hospital.

One winter, the love of his life was Eleonora Mendelssohn, among other things goddaughter of Duse. She told Alec that as a little girl her mother and Duse took her on a golden Venetian afternoon to play by the Grand Canal. She let her toy pig fall in. As it disappeared in the dark water, she burst into tears.

"Les adieux commencent," sighed Duse.

Another adieu was when Duse parted with a long string of massive gold beads. Had they been mined and smelted for Duse personally? If beads could look grief-stricken, these did. Duse gave them to her goddaughter and generous Eleonora gave them to Woollcott. He admired them, but said they must belong to an actress. Who among his loved ones? Nobody made it till Ethel Barrymore accepted his invite to the Island.

Her train was due late afternoon and Howard Bull's motorboat brought Alec across the lake for the hour's auto ride to where the Montreal express paused at Whitehall. For no one else had Woollcott ever made this trip. Rather shaken by his gesture, he climbed fully dressed into Bull's boat and something made him think of the beads. He called back to Mrs. Robert Emmet Sherwood, "Put Duse's beads on Ethel's bureau, Puss."

Put Duse's beads on Ethel's bureau, but *how?* Do you throw Duse's beads on a huckabuck bureau scarf? Do you drop them on a sweetgrass pin tray? Puss didn't. She searched the Island for what flowers she could find. Her own gardens at Witley would have been a better place to look, but Surrey was too far from Vermont. Undaunted, she came back with two black-eyed Susans, four small ferns, two chickweed stalks, a bouncing Bet, the last of the nasturtiums rather measly and both red, a twig with four blueberries and three blades of ribbon grass.

Ethel admired Duse's beads, but blew her mind over Mrs. Sherwood's arrangement.

One evening Woollcott and Ethel and I leaned back against the cushions in the Chicago gondola while Howard Bull punted us round the lake. "Can you remember the Arch Street Theatre well?" asked Alec.

"Of course. We lived with our grandmother at her house not far away."

"Did you like her?"

"*Like* isn't the word to use. She was good to us, but she was a stiff lady. She sat in a stiff chair in a stiff parlor and wore a stiff black dress no matter what the weather. She was old and I suppose lonely, no one was left to call her by her first name. She and Mr. Jefferson went one week each summer to a hotel in the Catskills where they'd been with their families. They sat and rocked on the piazza and called each other Joe and Louisa."

"Why did you stay with her?"

"Oh, our parents went off on a tour. Or Father would play a season in London where they criticized him for his American accent or he'd act in the United States with Modjeska where they said he sounded British. He said, 'A concert on an ocean liner is the only place I'm accepted.' "

"Did you go to school in Philadelphia?"

"No. It wouldn't have been practical with all the coming and going. Our grandmother engaged a governess for us and we slogged away. Lionel and I weren't very interested in learning out of books and Jack was too little. To us, learning was what you did with a part. Once Lionel took action. The governess marched him down the hall to the stiff parlor. 'Ma'am,' she said, 'Master Lionel kicked me in the shins.'

"When Lionel told us about it, he made us roar. He could take off our grandmother perfectly. He reported she stared at our governess, then boomed forth, '*Shins*, woman? What are *shins*? Leave the room.' "

At breakfast, Woollcott sat behind his twelve-cup coffeepot, gift of Lewis and Conger. "Rebecca's brilliant young man gets here about now."

"Why does he have to come up *here*?" whined a guest.

"Because it's his first trip to this country and Rebecca West asked me to ask him up and I like *her* a goddam sight better than I like *you*."

Bull's motorboat hit the dock and a tall young man with flaming

7

red hair got out and followed his luggage up the path to the breakfast table.

"Livingstone, I presume," said Woollcott and turned to the table. "This is David Ogilvy. David, these are spongers."

"Good morning," said the new guest, "is there a writing table?"

"What kind of goddam unnatural question is *that?*" asked Woollcott. "Sit down and drink some coffee, better than you or any subject of your government deserves."

"Thanks, but first I must write the President of the Central of Vermont Railroad about that *disgraceful* trip."

Woollcott's interest was caught. "What disgraceful trip was that?"

"This country must *do* something about that roadbed. May I have a sheet of paper? I wish to register my complaint."

"Do you write letters about everything that annoys you? If you're going to spend time in this country, you'll need more pens than the late James Boswell."

Are you organized? Woollcott was. He also organized his friends. It might be to rent a house for the winter in Salem, N.Y., whereupon he'd tell his steward Joe Hennessey to figure out the monthly cost, then bill Harpo, Bea Kaufman, Alice Miller and Dan Silberberg for their share and send them the address, phone number and key.

Once the house was on West 47th Street and Harold Ross was one of the organized. Ross was trying to organize some dental problems along with the new magazine he'd thought up.

One spring it was to rent the Villa Ganelon at Antibes.

One September he rented the third floor of the Atlantic City Ritz and notified such disparate sojourners as S. N. Behrman and Eddie Cantor to show up and pay their share.

In October he booked a drawing room to Philadelphia for the *Animal Crackers* matinee. Alice Duer Miller, Neysa McMein, Ellin Mackay and I went with him and at Broad Street Station Irving Berlin met us with his limo.

We loved the show, we loved Harpo and after the matinee and a chat we went back in another drawing room except for Ellin, who stayed to have dinner with Irving.

As the train pulled out of Broad Street, we waved to them and agreed *that* romance wouldn't amount to anything. She was pretty in her bois-de-rose suit from Thurn, her conversation held up, she also listened, but she was *not* Irving's type. Imagine our surprise when a month after, they eloped. Have they celebrated their forty-fifth? Or their forty-sixth? Woollcott had us organized wrong.

High on his long list of accomplishments was his gift of enraging people. At the Durand-Ruel Gallery, he wanted to smoke. The attendant said he couldn't. Woollcott put an unlit cigarette in his mouth. "*You're* an amusing fellow!" he said, then turned to me. "Always remember a great way to enrage someone is put it in the form of a compliment."

Who was more enraged? The attendant or Woollcott not allowed to smoke?

"Come to Princeton," urged Heywood Broun, "there's a medium there that's in contact with Clara Bloodgood."

Clara Bloodgood is the only stage star who killed herself. She made a big hit in Clyde Fitch's *The Truth*, then planned to take London by storm, but Marie Tempest got the part, and in Baltimore Clara Bloodgood said, "That's it!" Or words to that effect, and that *was*.

Woollcott and Broun hired a car and said, "Princeton." Before long, they sat waiting for the seer to take off.

"Why did you do it?" asked Woollcott.

"The play was *written* for me and I had every right to play it in London, but they gave it to Marie Tempest."

"Didn't you feel another play might come along you could play in London?"

"It might, but I was so discouraged by losing this one, I couldn't go on. All I wanted was to give up."

"Did Marie Tempest make a hit?"

"Yes she did, but I'd have made a bigger. The part was written for *me*."

"Who wrote it?"

Princeton's Clara didn't reply.

"Who wrote the play?"

The medium looked like *she* might kill herself. "I know, but it slipped my mind."

Woollcott reached for his hat. "A star that doesn't know who wrote a play she made a hit in *should* kill herself." He stormed out of the room.

When *you* had been on the stage twenty-five years, did people make a fuss? December 21, 1940, over Chicago's station WBBM after the second act of *Here Today* the curtain stayed up and a bell rang. "Hear ye!" said the announcer, then another bell rang. "Hear ye!" The bell rang. "Hear ye! Alexander Woollcott—the Town Crier."

We up on the stage and the audience heard, "This is Woollcott speaking. This is the Town Crier coming to Chicago by parcel post —I do hope they haven't classified me as third-class mail—coming to Chicago to celebrate an anniversary, to speak in memory of something that happened twenty-five years ago tonight. Something I saw happen with my own eyes on the night of December 21st, 1915.

"Twenty-five years ago. Do you know how long ago that was? A quarter of a century. That's easy enough to say, but to get a real sense of that distance in time calls for a little more effort. Perhaps we'll come nearer the mark if we stop a minute and try to recall just what was going on then. And what has happened since. Where were *you* twenty-five years ago? In your prime or in your pram? More specifically, I wonder how many of you now listening to me would be ready with an answer if called to the witness stand and the district attorney were to ask, 'Where were you on the night of December 21st, 1915?' Could you answer that question? *I* could. I had a seat on the aisle at the Empire Theatre in New York. I had gone to see Maude Adams in *Peter Pan*.

"At that time my years on this earth had been twenty-seven and ever since my college days I had been toiling as an ink-stained wretch on the staff of *The New York Times*. Nearly two years before, that great newspaper, to the unflattering surprise and considerable annoyance of the theatrical managers, had made me its drama critic. In fact, some of the managers were so annoyed that in 1915 one group was excluding me from their theatres, throwing me out at every first night with stubborn regularity. Besides considering me a viper, they pointed out I didn't know anything. It dawns on me now, they had something. Indeed, when I try now to recall what I was like, I'm impressed with the number of things I didn't know.

"In 1915 I'd never seen a cement road nor a tomato-juice cocktail nor an electric icebox nor a radio nor a one-piece bathing suit nor a dial telephone nor a lipstick. I'd never heard of a microphone nor a loudspeaker nor an inhibition nor a complex nor a tabloid nor a vitamin nor a G-Man nor a jitterbug. I'd never heard of mah-jongg nor midget golf nor contract bridge nor cellophane. I'd never heard of a Soviet nor a Nazi nor a Fascist and I didn't know there was such a person as Adolf Hitler. Well, this was the ignoramus *The New York Times* employed as its drama critic and twenty-five years ago this very evening going off buckety-buckety to the Empire Theatre to see Maude Adams in *Peter Pan*.

"How much more vividly I remember it than many a play I saw last season. That breathless moment when Peter flew in through the high nursery window? The clash of cutlasses in his mighty fight with Captain Hook? Captain Hook! Remember that somewhat different pirate? Across the years I can see him moping on his quarterdeck, hear him muttering to himself: 'I should be feeling deevy but a disky spirit broods over me, threatening to enclose me like a folding um-ber-ella.' I remember, and shall remember while I live, the last glimpse of Peter as he waved goodbye from his house in the treetops—waved goodbye to you and to me and, perhaps, to a gentle world that soon—so soon—might be no more.

"At that time Maude Adams had a greater hold on the affections of the American playgoers than any other actress. But she had been playing *Peter Pan* off and on for ten years and the mere fact she was bringing it back to Broadway the week before Christmas didn't strike the older members of the deathwatch as an event worth their attention. But I was a new broom with no inclination to rest in the corner. Therefore mine was, I think, the only account of the revival—except for routine notices—which was printed in New York next day. Being a devotee of all Barrie's plays, I had hoped to write a Peter Panegyric, but it was not so easy to find pleasant things to say about that revival. I remember dimly suspecting that, with one shining exception, the actresses engaged by Miss Adams to play the lost boys had been chosen because they'd gone to school with her mother. I even intimated as much next morning in the *Times*. 'But,' I said, 'Ruth Gordon was ever so gay as Nibs.'

"She was the shining exception. Ruth Gordon. She's still an exception and still shining.

"In my mail on the following day was a rapturous letter, my enjoyment of which was slightly dimmed by the fact it was addressed to Mr. Roger Woollcott. It was signed Ruth Gordon and from it I learned that that performance of Nibs which so delighted me had been her first on any stage.

"Down she'd come from Wollaston, Mass., to attend dramatic school and look for a job. In the daytime she'd make the endless rounds of the managers' offices, in the evening she lugged home volumes of Shakespeare from the public library and in her room at a theatrical boardinghouse rehearsed herself for Juliet and Lady Macbeth. Then came the news Miss Adams was recruiting a cast for *Peter Pan* and next, the overwhelming moment when she was sent for. Her first night on any stage was excitement enough, but a notice in the paper next day! She had thought of notices as something that would come later. She hadn't dreamed she'd get one her first try. In her letter to Roger Woollcott she ventured to predict that, whatever the years might bring, no words in print would ever seem so magical as 'Ruth Gordon was ever so gay as Nibs.'

"Well, the Ruth Gordon who made her first appearance on the stage twenty-five years ago is now heading her own company in Chicago in the comedy called *Here Today*. And I wish with all my heart I were, too. I don't mean heading my own company. I mean I wish I were here today. Then my evening would present no problem. I would be going off to the Selwyn Theatre—buckety-buckety—to see Ruth Gordon—Ruth Gordon, as ever was.

"You may ask me how I remember all this? How, after attending more than three thousand first nights in theatres all the way from Moscow and Berlin to Tokyo and Pekin, could I recall that minor episode of a far-off December? How do I happen to know that the celebrated Ruth Gordon here today was the ambitious kid who wrote so rapturously to Roger Woollcott? It's because I have the manual dexterity of a hippopotamus. I can do nothing with these old hands. I'd rather be horsewhipped than change a shoelace. I'd rather be shot than change a typewriter ribbon. Whenever I'm faced with the disaster of *having* to change one, I yell for help. But one day—it was New Year's Eve in 1926—the ribbon broke when I was marooned in my apartment and no help within earshot. Copy would be due down at the office before midnight. Apprehensively I got out the old repair kit which hadn't been molested in years. It proved difficult to take the top off. Something was wedged under the lid. It was a letter which, from among the mess of papers always on my desk, must have got stuck there. It was addressed to Roger Woollcott, dated December 22, 1915, and signed Ruth Gordon —Ruth Gordon, who by this time was among the foremost of our actresses and who in that very season was giving an enchanting performance in *Saturday's Children.*

"Next day—January 1st, 1927—I telephoned her and asked to pay a New Year's call, promising her something that would start her New Year with a smile. She took the letter, read it, saw all the ghosts of her first struggles come thronging, and burst into tears.

"That was nearly fifteen years ago. Since then—since *Saturday's Children*—Ruth Gordon, like Mrs. Fiske before her, has become something of a cult. There be those here and in England—I might name the great Charles Laughton as one, for example, and your own Lloyd Lewis as another and your occasional Thornton Wilder as a third—who think there is no actress in the English-speaking world quite so fascinating as Ruth Gordon. To this cult I belong.

"From the likes of us she has had extraordinary tributes. London rang with praise of her when she gave her dazzling performance in *The Country Wife* at the Old Vic, to my mind the most richly comic performance I have ever seen given by any actress in any country at any time in any play.

"Then I seem to recall considerable critical ecstasy by all and sundry when she toured as Nora in *A Doll's House,* and some appropriate dancing in the streets after her two movie performances last year. She was the Mrs. Lincoln in *Abe Lincoln in Illinois* and the Mrs. Ehrlich in *Dr. Ehrlich's Magic Bullet.* And for real ringing hosannas in the press I give you the piece Lloyd Lewis wrote for the *Chicago Daily News* when first he saw Ruth Gordon do *Here Today* in the East. Indeed, when I think of all this I could wish that

I might hang around the stage door of the Selwyn Theatre tonight to ask her a question as she comes out. Does she still remember when she was pretty pleased with a single sentence? 'Ruth Gordon was ever so gay as Nibs.'

"Now I still have time to clean up some odds and ends of unfinished business. It goes against the grain with me to assemble an audience without recommending so much as a single book. Out of my browsing among the new titles I come up with one suggestion. The new novel by the woman who is, I suppose, the foremost American writer. Willa Cather. Her latest work, a story of Virginia just before the Civil War, is called *Sapphira and the Slave Girl*. I've already read it twice. You might do worse—and probably will.

"Then there is the matter of 1944. 1915 is all very well, but what about 1944? I mean who shall succeed Franklin Roosevelt in the White House. The other day Sinclair Lewis as he passed through Chicago gave out an interview in which he nominated President Hutchins of the University of Chicago. I second that nomination.

"All of which is respectfully submitted as a Christmas card. This broadcast is intended to carry season's greetings—to Ruth Gordon from Roger Woollcott. And since this *is* the Christmas season, let me wind up by quoting one of my betters. I shall close this broadcast by repeating the shortest and best after-dinner speech of which there is any record. It consists of five words. 'God bless us every one.' "

Up at the Island, Woollcott and Thornton sat talking. Thornton looked off toward Rutland. "I'd like to wander round the world and never put on a tie, wear old shoes, old clothes, just be a bum."

Woollcott studied him. "You wouldn't have far to go."

Do you believe the one about the hare and the tortoise? Or is that what Thornton calls a visceral myth? Woollcott *had* to believe it. He was working late at the *Times* the night that news of the *Titanic* came in. Jack Binns tapped away and in the confusion Woollcott was hustled onto a train which took its time to pull into Halifax. The seaport was alive with reporters, sober, drunk, old, young, big, not so big. The star was the *New York World*'s dashing Swope. "I'll give you the signal, boy," he told Woollcott. "As soon as they land the bodies, they'll let me in ahead and I'll say you're working for me. Keep your mouth closed and your bowels open."

Word spread that the first bodies had arrived. Swope shook his head. "Keep your eye on me, boy, didn't a *Times* reporter ever hear of a red herring?"

Woollcott watched crowds pour into the building.

"Wait," said Swope, "what's time to a hog?"

Woollcott was born nosy and also could never bear to be alone. Swope was away up in the rarefied circles, but Woollcott had nobody to talk to. He tagged along with the others. Inside, they were identifying the bodies. *The New York Times* scooped the *New York World*. Who said, "The race is not always to the swift"? Was it Swope? Whoever it was must've been up in Halifax. And, Thornton, *is* that a visceral myth?

At the Villa Ganelon, breakfast was served on the terrace. Woollcott drank coffee and read the *Nice Matin.* "Shaw's here."

"Shaw's where?"

"At the Beau Site. The Du Cap is full of the Dwight Wimans and the Wiman kids and their nannies. They turned down Shaw and Mrs. Shaw, so they descended at the Beau Site."

"It says that in the *Matin?*"

"No, Blemish, it says, 'Mr. and Mrs. George Bernard Shaw are sojourning at the Beau Site,' but I don't need to live on Baker Street to know they didn't leave Adelphi Terrace to taste the pleasures of the Beau Site."

"Let's ask them to lunch."

Woollcott looked interested.

"Don't you know him? You must."

"I met him, but only once and there were a lot of—"

"Write him a letter. If he's at the Beau Site, he'll love a good meal and we have the greatest food."

"Write him, Alec," said Harpo.

"Do it."

He did. It had personality, but not too much.

Woollcott gave it to Guy. "Pour Monsieur Bernard Shaw au Beau Site."

Guy got into Harpo's quatre chevaux and tore down the drive.

The heat and my efforts made me sleepy.

"Wake up." It was Harpo. "He's coming."

"Who is?"

"Shaw." Harpo looked like he must have when and if he read the notices for *I'll Say She Is*.

"How do you know?"

"He came over to say so."

That woke me! "Shaw's been here!"

"Just now. My God, we're laying on the rocks—when *you're* not there, we don't wear trunks—and I look up and I see somebody come down the steps with a big black umbrella that keeps opening every step and every time it opens he stops and closes it—" Harpo acted it out. "And up on the edge of the rocks is a dame with her hand over her eyes looking out to sea." He acted it. " 'Could this be Shaw?' I say."

"God damn it," I said.

"*You'll* meet him. He's coming to lunch. But get a load of *this!* When I said, 'Could this be Shaw?' Woollcott jumped and his glasses fell in the water, so he couldn't see a goddam thing." If there was trouble, Harpo laughed. "He had to crawl crab-fashion back over the rocks." When he could stop laughing at Alec's afflictions, Harpo acted it out.

"I'll probably never meet him, what did he come for?"

"To say he'll come Thursday. He'll come! Acky crawling on his back!" He gave another performance.

We told our friends that on Thursday we were off to Hyères, back around six. We didn't want any drop-ins. At one o'clock precisely, our quatre chevaux, sent to fetch them, rocked into the drive. "Sorry about the car," said Woollcott. "How did you get into it?"

"With a shoehorn," said Shaw. He unfurled his six feet whatever and helped out Mrs. Shaw—no Lilliputian, she.

Did you ever see a beautiful man? Was it Bernard Shaw? Blue eyes like your sapphire, white zesty hair and an Ultima Thule complexion. Shaw accepted the fact that it was hot and left his jacket at home, but wore a white boiled shirt with a wing collar and wide crocheted mauve tie. At our suggestion he took off collar and tie.

Our menu offered everything the Côte d'Azur did, except meat or fowl. Does a vegetarian eat seafood? We had it. Does a vegetarian eat cheese? We had every kind. Pasta? You bet. The chef was from Menton or Mentone depending on if you're Italiano or Franco. Veg? All the primeurs from all around. Salad? California could learn. A confident Woollcott led Mrs. Shaw into luncheon. Guy passed the langoustine mayonnaise and Mr. Shaw helped himself generously. "A vegetarian eats fish" registered in the minds of Shaw's hosts. As Guy disappeared for the next dish, Mrs. Shaw leaned across the table. "De-ah."

Shaw, fork poised, looked up.

"That is *fish*."

Shaw dropped his fork with a clatter.

Do you think if Big Mouth hadn't opened up he would have eaten it? We thought so. To serve himself, he had to see it, didn't he? Does a baby lobster look like a carved beet? It looks like a baby lobster. Draw the veil and goodnight, Mrs. Shaw, where*ever* you are, and maybe you shoulda stood in bed.

Woollcott slid Mrs. Pat's name into the conversation.

Shaw ran with the ball. He told of the *Pygmalion* rehearsals.

What was that dreadful clatter? Why did Mrs. Shaw drum on her plate with her fork? Shaw had a voice that could reach the gallery, but she drowned out *some* of the words.

"Did you write *Major Barbara* for Ellen Terry?"

"Oh, that wicked woman," he sighed. "She never played it. One of yours did."

"Annie Russell," said Alec.

"She was good, except for her entrance. *Major Barbara* was the day when a star on her entrance might or might not stop and acknowledge her round. Mrs. Kendal did and Lady Bancroft, but the new ones at the Royal Court scorned it. Your Annie Russell was of two minds."

He disappeared out the French window, beyond the hortensias, then came striding in, one eye resting on his public as he went stage center to start the scene.

"Are you a Marxist?" he asked Harpo.

"No," said Harpo, "are you?"

17

Dorothy Parker was the only American he wanted to know about. "What's she like?" were his very words. We gave him three versions, mine, Woollcott's, the non-Marxist's.

"Oh," he said. "I thought of her as an old maid."

Draw the veil.

We'd agreed not to ask for his autograph, but Woollcott weakened and shoved a book at Shaw. Harpo, too. Harpo had sneaked over to Nice and now offered its author *The Perfect Wagnerite*. Shaw looked at it, made a face and wrote "G. Bernard Shaw."

They were leaving. "Do you have a good press agent?" he asked me.

"I don't have one at all."

He looked shocked. "Oh, an actress must have a press agent. That's a first requisite."

Without shoehorn, they got back into the quatre chevaux. Guy drove off. In a happy daze we just stood on the steps he'd left. The quatre chevaux whizzed back, Guy stepped out and came and stood with us. "Il est très presentable," he said.

Did anybody ever save a show for you? After two weeks *A Doll's House* was going to close, then one night on station WOR at 7:15 the announcer rang the bell. "Hear ye!" He rang a bell again. "Hear ye!" He rang again. "Hear ye! Alexander Woollcott, the Town Crier."

"This is Woollcott speaking. This is the Town Crier dropping back onto the air—almost without warning. This year in radio I don't belong to the regulars. Will I give away my age when I quote a song hit of the Spanish-American War? 'I Don't Belong to the Regulars, I'm Only a Volunteer.' Until October—at the earliest—I shall broadcast only when I have something on my mind. Well, I *have* something on my mind and everything was set for me to spill it on a broadcast on one of the great sponsored programs next Sunday or the Sunday after, but now it seems I'll be leaving New York before Sunday—leaving on a job that will keep me away and keep me busy for at least four weeks. If I want to get this thing off my chest, it must be now or never. All right, then, let it be now. Let's go!

"I might as well stop at this point and confess to the activities which are going to keep me busy for at least the next four weeks. You may have seen some reference to them in that lesser and waning form of journalism—the printed page. Yes, I've gone back on the stage. It's now more than six years since I made my first appearance—my debut as a promising young actor of forty-five. At the close of that play—this was back in March '32—I murmured to the sky as I walked out the stage door for the last time, 'Never again.' And now look at the darned thing!

"Well, we've been playing in Philadelphia and Pittsburgh. Now we've laid off for a week of rehearsals and revisions. We're getting a new set of scenery, a new first act and a new leading woman. The play—for reasons which escape me—is called *Wine of Choice* and will open next week in Baltimore. It will then play Wilmington, Delaware—Princeton, New Jersey—New Haven and Hartford, Connecticut—and then go into the Wilbur Theatre in Boston for two weeks. After the middle of February—if ever—it will come to New York.

"I read in *The New York Times* yesterday—that exasperating but essential newspaper, which I could no more dispense with at breakfast than I could with coffee—I was somewhat startled to read in the advertisements and posters of *Wine of Choice*, I was one of the actors to be featured. Featured. This was news to me and in my nervous state I couldn't help remembering the English actor who, after playing season after season in *Peter Pan*, went to the author of that immortal comedy and suggested that *he* be featured. The late J. M. Barrie—the strangely gifted man who wrote *Peter Pan*—was a Scot by birth and by nature. He received this actor's proposal cautiously. He began by asking just what featuring would mean. Well, said the actor, of course he couldn't expect to be starred. His role wasn't important enough for that. But he did think that in some way his name should be separated in the programs and posters from the rank and file of the company. It should be printed so that it would hit the eye. The whole company could be listed, and just before *his* name there could be in big type the word 'and.' All the rest and So-and-so.

" ' "And"?' asked Barrie, puffing thoughtfully at his pipe. 'Why not "but"?'

"You know, Barrie was like that. The legend is, he was mild and benign. He was nothing of the sort. He had a sharp tongue and the most disconcerting pair of eyes I ever wriggled under. The first time I went to see him—it was back in 1914—those frightening eyes of his unnerved me completely. I had meant to drink in and preserve for posterity every word he said, but he made me so nervous I talked for two hours. He never got a word in. I'm sorry.

"There suddenly comes back to me what Barrie did to an actor who made him the very kind of announcement I'm now making to you. Perhaps I should explain that when *Wine of Choice* opened its season early in December I wasn't in the cast, I joined the company in Chicago. The play picked me up the way a person picks up a cold. I was injected into it like adrenalin—or snake venom. I accepted the part with a tremendous show of reluctance, explaining I was doing so only because the author was an old friend of mine I couldn't bear to refuse. This may have fooled *him*, but it wouldn't have fooled anyone with a grain of sense. Anyone who really knew me would have realized I was playing the part because I suspected —and rightly—that I'd have the time of my life. I am. Well, I can't help recalling another actor—he shall be nameless in this anecdote —who, in somewhat the same way, joined the cast of a comedy then playing at the St. James's Theatre in London. But all the critics and managers and playwrights of importance must have seen the play on its first night. Great grief! They would none of them see *his* performance in it. So to fifty such gentry he sent telegrams announcing he was to join the cast Monday night. Of the fifty recipients, only one answered. Barrie wired, 'Thanks for the warning.'

"So, good people of Baltimore, Wilmington, Princeton, New Haven, Hartford and Boston, don't say I didn't warn you.

"However, that's not what's on my mind. What I shall do in this broadcast before it's finished is something I've done only twice before in my life as a speaker on the radio. The first time was five years ago, when, in my retreat from Moscow, I lingered for Christmas in England. There had been a suggestion from the BBC I toss a few thoughts onto the airwaves which Britannia rules, but the payment offered was what is called an honorarium, a flossy term for 'not much money.' I had no interest in the offer until one night, quite by chance, in a small theatre in a side street, I saw a beautiful play, beautifully acted. The house was only half full. I'd been dining out in London for a month and no one had even mentioned it. Plenty of people had said it was a dull season, there was nothing to see in the theatre. They always say that at dinner in London. No one mentioned *Children in Uniform* nor the exquisite performance with which it was being blessed. Filled with a passion to run up and down the streets telling everyone about it, I realized the best way to do that is to broadcast. Next morning I was around at the BBC, hat in hand, offering to reconsider. They were willing enough until they found out what I wanted to broadcast about. At that they were truly shocked. They simply couldn't permit it. I could understand their hesitancy to let me go on the air and denounce a play, but who, I asked, could object to a burst of applause? They said every other management in town. Every one of them would be on the telephone the next morning complaining that the BBC—which is a government monopoly—was playing favorites. I was about to give up discouraged when an idea occurred to me. Why shouldn't they let me make this broadcast and pretend they hadn't known what I was going to say? When all the other managers in London swarmed around next day like angry bees, the station could say it agreed with them, I was a base fellow and should never be allowed to broadcast again. This would be all right with me, because I was sailing home the following Saturday. As it turned out, they fixed the broadcast on a day I would have to be in Dublin. This seemed to present no difficulties. The broadcast was transmitted by wire, first to Belfast, then across to Liverpool, then down to London, and out to the whole British Isles. When I came off the air, the manager of the Dublin studio, while helping me into my overcoat, said, 'Your remarks amused me. And it may interest you to know that due to a slight heterodyne interference from Cork, your entire discourse on the London theatre was accompanied by a faint sound of distant Irish bagpipes.' When I passed through London on my way home to America, I called up the BBC to get my fan mail. In my hurry, I offered to send a truck for it. I was the more embarrassed when I learned it consisted of one letter. But they were impressed. It seems in England that's considered a lively response. However, at its next matinee *Children in Uniform* turned away three hundred people. It ran in London for ten months.

"Having thus tasted blood, you might have thought I'd be hot to do the same thing again, but one is not inspired to such an effort more than once in a blue moon. The impulse didn't revisit me until nearly four years had passed. Then, one night last November, in a New York theatre, I saw a great play greatly acted. And the theatre was only half full. At the same time, I wasn't broadcasting nor writing on any paper. If I'd been mayor, I'd have declared a public holiday and called meetings in the parks. As it was, I did what I could. The following Monday I burgled my way for four minutes into a morning program sponsored by a pickle manufacturer. I used the four minutes to say with all my heart what I thought of the new production of *Hamlet* with Mr. John Gielgud as the sweet prince. In forty years of theatregoing I had seen nothing better.

"In forty years of theatregoing, I thought it unlikely—not impossible, of course, but improbable—that anyone then listening *would* see anything better. I said as much to those who just happened to have tuned in. Enough of them responded. That night *Hamlet* sold out. That night and thereafter through all the weeks Mr. Gielgud played in America, he never knew the embarrassment of a vacant seat.

"Now, don't think I'm suggesting for one moment that I made John Gielgud's *Hamlet* into a success. *He* did that. It would be ignorant, silly and self-important of me to pretend otherwise. I didn't even turn the tide. It would have turned anyway. Perhaps I advanced that turn by a day or so. If so, I am both pleased and proud. That's my function. If I have any job in the world, that's it.

"All of which brings me to my point. It takes your Town Crier a long time to pass a given point, but now I've come to the reason for doing this broadcast. Once again in a theatre in New York I've seen a great play greatly acted. Every impulse within me bids me tell as many people as possible about it as soon as I can. This is the easiest way to do it. In my younger days, when I was not merely an amateur actor but an amateur playgoer, too, it was my custom on such great occasions to rush from the theatre to the nearest telegraph office and wire everybody I knew. The trouble was I didn't know enough people and I didn't have enough money. This way is better.

"This time, in a sense, however, I'm too late. The tide has already turned. By the only kind of advertising that's really worth anything—I suppose, if this were a sponsored program, it would be indiscreet of me to say this—by the word spreading down the street, one neighbor telling another, the news is already abroad of how fine a thing this is at the Morosco Theatre in New York: this performance by Ruth Gordon as Nora in that early Ibsen masterpiece, *A Doll's House*. So I'm merely adding my word to a word already spreading. Yet I wish I could add it so effectively that everyone listening at this minute who has not yet seen the play—everyone, that is, who lives in New York—would start out now for the theatre. There's still more than an hour before the curtain goes up. What if, when you get there, you find the seats all sold? You can then buy seats ahead, can't you?

"Here, if ever I saw one, is a night in the theatre which many people throughout the country would remember all their lives. It is so right, so true, so devastating that it knocks at the door of every human heart.

"Ruth Gordon in *A Doll's House* at the Morosco—one of the really great nights in the theatre of the world in our time. Suppose it sells out tonight and tomorrow night and for weeks ahead. Will the management be satisfied? I suppose so. Will I be satisfied? Not me. I won't be satisfied until they turn hundreds *away* every night —till the line at the box office stretches for blocks and blocks. Here, for once in a way, on a lighted stage, is something beautiful and true. It is part of the music of the spheres that such a thing should come into its own.

"Well, that's off my mind. Goodnight. (Bell) Goodnight. (Bell) Goodnight."

The first anyone knew of the broadcast was a little before eight when a man came up to the Morosco Theatre box office and said, "Have you got a seat?"

"Yes."

"I'll take it. I never saw an Ibsen show I liked, but if Woollcott says it's good I'll try it."

The show didn't close. *Our Town* opened at the Henry Miller on a ten-day booking, made history and moved into the Morosco. The same author's adaptation of *A Doll's House* moved over to the Broadhurst and broke all records.

Woollcott said of all the actresses, Ada Rehan was the greatest. He was in Germantown High when he saw her at the Chestnut Street Opera House. Ed Wynn was a boarder and Ed and Woollcott went to see her. "I'd studied *The Taming of the Shrew* in school, but when I saw Ada Rehan I didn't need to study any more. She didn't rant and rage, but just arranged her life so that she got a lot of wishy-washy people out of her way. Watching her, you thought why the hell shouldn't she? When Petruchio's servant fell on his knees and crawled away, Kate, every bit as exhausted as he was yet still on her feet, summoned up some last scrap of energy and ground her heel into his hand as the weakling crawled past."

How would *she* be for Women's Lib?

Woollcott didn't favor guests disappearing from the Island for the day. "Where'd you go?" he asked Thornton.

"I went to Rutland."

"You *ate* in Rutland?" asked the employer of Vermont's best cook.

"Yes."

"Where?"

"I don't know the name of it."

"Well, do you know what you had?"

"Oh yes. Lobster Newburg, peach shortcake and cocoa."

"My God," groaned Woollcott, "that's the most unnatural meal since the Bordens sat down to a breakfast of lamb stew and sugar cookies. If you ask me, their hired girl was as suspect as Lizzie. Mrs. Belloc Lowndes is looking into it."

Woollcott couldn't understand why George and Beatrice Kaufman's house in Bucks County showed no signs of being theirs. "Early American furniture and strawberries on the wallpaper! Why no record of *The Royal Family?* Why no record of *Dulcy?* Why none of *The Butter and Egg Man?* And all the other lives they've lived? Why do they let a decorator erase their life?"

No one could say that Woollcott had. At Bomoseen under a glass case was the small knife Dickens carried in his pocket when he lectured. A glass bowl of water held a single pumpkin blossom, the bowl turned upside down. It was the gift of Howard Bull. A charcoal drawing of me by William Auerbach-Levy took a back seat to a Ralph Barton poster of Mrs. Fiske. Duse's gold beads were on Woollcott's bureau till he passed them along to Ethel. His dogs were gifts from the Seeing Eye people, Pip, a French poodle. Duchess, a black German Shepherd dog. Japanese prints were from Frank Lloyd Wright, given *him* by the Japanese government when he built the Imperial Hotel. In the corner stood Sir Henry Irving's gold-knobbed cane. The broad-brimmed black hat on the hook was made from shearings of Graham Robertson's poodle dogs.

Woollcott wasn't well and he wouldn't look after himself. "What for?" He sat up and received in bed, then got dressed and went crosstown to Voisin's for Mr. Mueller's Apple Charlotte. "I have one kind of life I live and am not interested in another."

People dropped in to see him at the Gotham. "I'm like the Sage of Ferney," he said, then got weary, which wasn't like him. All of a sudden he drooped.

Sometimes he sat up in bed. Sometimes he sat out in the sitting room and looked out the big windows down Fifth Avenue.

One afternoon I brought my son, Jones.

"Hello, Jones, sit down. Does your mother get in your hair?"

Jones was turning over a reply.

"Well, tell her not to. Parents are necessary, but keep 'em in line." He leaned back on the cushions and his pajamas came loose.

"Aren't you going to pull your pajamas together?" I asked.

Woollcott looked down at the big white rotunda framed by his crumpled Sulka pajamas. "Why should I?"

It was the last time Jones ever saw Woollcott. The big white belly and Woollcott's disdain of it and parents stayed in Jones' mind.

Katharine Cornell and Guthrie McClintic and my husband Garson Kanin and I stood at the foot of the iron stairs going up to the dressing rooms. Everybody else had gone home. After a triumphant week of sellout, we were loath to leave the theatre. Kit and Guthrie were driving up to Sneden's Landing. Garson had a weekend leave pass and we were going to "21" to join David Selznick's party. Gert Macy came in ecstatically from the box office to brag about the week's gross. She'd been over the figures with the house manager and joy reigned out front. She interrupted her own excitement. "Did anyone hear that radio report that Woollcott is ill?"

"What?"

"I heard it, but it wasn't clear. I heard it, then it didn't continue. It probably isn't anything."

"Call up Dr. Devol," said Kit.

Gert went to the pay station by the stairs.

"He was on that broadcast tonight," said Garson. "That debate on the air."

"Dr. Devol . . ." said Gert.

Garson looked at the backstage clock. "The news is on now, Johnny," he said to the night doorman. "Turn up your radio. We want to hear the news."

"Alexander Woollcott died of a massive heart attack at Roosevelt Hospital. He had been on the 'Question of the Hour' program and when one of the participants had said, 'Well, after all, the people of Germany are not responsible for Hitler,' Mr. Woollcott lost his temper. 'The people of Germany,' said Mr. Woollcott, 'are just as responsible for Hitler as the people of Chicago are for Colonel McCormick.' Then Woollcott stopped and motioned to the moderator. An ambulance rushed him to Roosevelt Hospital. He never regained consciousness. His doctor, Edmond Devol, declared him dead twenty minutes ago. In Montreal the Rangers scored a—"

"We'll go up there," said Garson.

He and I got in the limousine. "Roosevelt Hospital."

It all went black. At Roosevelt Hospital Garson said something at the desk. What? Everything was black. Or blurred? Or black. I could hear all the hospital sounds. In the elevator was an intern in a dingy white crumpled suit. A nurse got in with a book under her arm and a glass of milk with a saucer with a cookie on top of it. What was it? Was it clear? Was it blurred? Was it—

They got out of the elevator and Garson spoke to a floor nurse. On her desk was a toy tiger. The nurse pointed down the hall. All the doors were half open, some with lights on, some with lights off. What was in those rooms? Which was Alec in? Which had he been taken to? Did he know? Did he hate it? Was he frightened? Was he furious? Was he furious? Garson's hand on my arm slowed me. He looked in a door. Joe Hennessey was there and Dr. Devol. We all just looked at each other. We looked, then I went over to the bed. How could anyone look so tired? And as though he'd lost. So tired. Eyeglasses off didn't seem right. Had I ever seen him with his eyeglasses off? Was the reason I didn't marry him because his glasses weren't clean? Was I looking at Alec? That wasn't Woollcott with all the fun and fierceness, all the excitement, the demolishing hate. Alec lying here in an ugly place on a Saturday night? Alec?

Joe and Dr. Devol and Garson went out in the hall. I stood alone with him. He had loved me and I had loved him. I hadn't been in love with him, but I loved him. With him were a lot of my secrets.

Why did I choose Woollcott to tell secrets to? At first it was to rivet his interest. Capture the *New York Times* drama critic's attention. Make him see I was someone. Then it went deeper. There was excitement in telling him things. The unbearable things I told Thornton. With Alec I shared the devious, dangerous excitements. The risks. The private, private things.

*The New York Times* of December 22, 1915: "—but Ruth Gordon was ever so gay as Nibs." My letter thanking Mr. Roger Woollcott. The first time I saw him was the Algonquin lobby. Gregory Kelly and I were showing off, staying at such a great address. "Where are you staying?" "The Hotel Algonquin," as though it was nothing.

Someone came by in a corporal's uniform. Woollcott had come back from the war.

"Hello, Kelly. I'm Woollcott."

No wonder people went without, to stay at the Algonquin. Woollcott was shaking hands with Gregory and Gregory was introducing me.

"Oh, Mr. Woollcott, you gave me a good notice in *Peter Pan* and I wrote you a letter."

"Probably," he said and stared at me through his thick glasses that were dirty.

A pretty lady flung her arms around his neck.

27

Woollcott beamed. "What you do for our boys, Blossom! It's St. Cyr all over again."

Garson was beside me, his arm around me. "We'll go back with Joe to the Gotham." We stood for a minute.

Goodbye. Goodbye, a part of my life.

At the memorial service at McMillin Theatre I had to speak because George Kaufman couldn't, Moss Hart couldn't and Edna Ferber couldn't.

"What are you going to say?" asked Garson.

I told him.

"You're just telling his accomplishments."

"Well?"

"They *know* all that. What they want is somebody to bring him back."

The day of the service a snowstorm raged. New York was thick white and Mayor La Guardia ordered all private cars off the street, but up at McMillin Theatre every seat was full. Beatrice sat between George and Moss. Nearby sat Ross. Woollcott hadn't spoken to him since the profile of David Lamson. Ross wasn't the only one. There were others Woollcott had stopped speaking to. What there wasn't any of were latecomers. And at ten A.M. in an automobile-less blizzard.

"The Island must look lovely today," I said. Did that bring him back? "I was his dearest friend." George looked sore. So did Bea and Moss and Edna. Harpo looked surprised. Did that bring him back? It brought *me* a lot of bad feeling. After time for everybody to hate me, I said, "And so were all of *you*." Did that bring him back? It made them laugh.

"Alec's gone and I wish he'd come back, the way he did from that other trip. That one during World War I?" A lot of them remembered. "He was on a troopship that set out from Jersey City. Leaning on the rail talking to somebody, a ship seemed to be coming straight at them. 'Wouldn't you think that ship was going to run into us?' he said, and it did. They put back into Jersey City and Alec came home and waited for another troopship. I wish he'd come home from *this* trip."

We all thought about that.

"Can you imagine what he'd say to me, up here trying to explain him? 'Why, you withered ingenue, what do you think you're doing? Sit down, Blemish, this is Woollcott speaking.' "

The *Tribune* headed its piece, "Laughter at Woollcott's Service."

A service but no funeral was what he'd stipulated. Gert Macy thought he should have had a funeral. She thought we should override his wishes. She thought it should be at the Little Church Around the Corner whose story Alec wrote so beautifully. And so often. Irving Berlin should play and sing like he did at Nigger Mike's, and when he tired, the Hamilton choir should scream out an anthem from the wings or whatever they call those shadows on each side of an altar.

A three-sheet of Mrs. Fiske would lead the procession down the church aisle borne by Alfred Lunt and Lynn Fontanne in their *Guardsman* costumes, followed by Kit in her *Bill of Divorcement* dress worn for a year's run at the George M. Cohan, due solely to Woollcott's efforts. MacArthur and Harpo and Charlie Lederer should follow with the Chalice of Antioch borne by Harpo, out of whose *I'll Say She Is* costume silverware from Voisin's should drop.

Instead of litany, the radio would broadcast *Goodbye, Mr. Chips*, which Woollcott had broadcast into the unheard-of sale of over a hundred thousand copies even though that number of the *Atlantic Monthly* had gone off the stands. During this, Woollcott's first-grade teacher, Miss Lucy Drage, would march with Joe Cook and the Four Hawaiians and Ruth Gordon dressed ever so gay as Nibs followed by a well-known somebody with a newly issued passport and college diploma, the latter won through Woollcott sending him to Hamilton, the former ripped by Woollcott from the State Department with words by Franklin Delano Roosevelt written by hand on a sheet of paper. Howard Bull would lead Pip and the Duchess, briefly down from the Island. Will Bull would carry John trout in a small tank. On a float with George pacing, Moss would set down *The Man Who Came to Dinner*. Behind them, Gus Eckstein, holding Red the canary and a box with Father cockroach, would help Mr. Mueller of Voisin's, with his police dog, carry a plate of Apple Charlotte. Ethel Barrymore being Ethel Barrymore and Paul Robeson being Paul Robeson would precede Mrs. Roosevelt and Charlie Chaplin chatting about a Seeing Eye dog, each leading one on loan from Montclair where Woollcott did so much for them. Behind them the hundred old people with glasses that Woollcott got away from other people due to his radio request. All this enthusiasm would weave down the aisle, split at the altar and halt while Ada MacLeish sang Woollcott's favorite song, which was any song Ada sang.

Too bad we didn't listen to Gert. How gutless can you get, but some of us believe in the hereafter and until we found out if Woollcott still has the same amount of clout in the Great Beyond, why not follow instructions?

"There are thirty-four policemen in this room, but I would rather have you, my dear."

In *A Kiss for Cinderella,* the policeman wrote that in his letter to Cinderella and that's what Woollcott wrote in his letter to me.

❊   ❊   ❊   ❊   ❊

Are you getting it right? I am. Last year I took up lying, but this is the truth. I also know what I'm talking about. Woollcott told me, "If you want to make sure you know what you're talking about, talk about yourself."

I'm seventy-four and I'm a Scorpio, so I'll only cite a few excerpts.

Twenty-eight years ago this December I started getting it right when I married the best man in the world. And after twenty-eight years he's *still* the best man. Is *that* getting it right? And last October I celebrated my seventy-fourth birthday. At seventy-four don't a lot of people think of retiring? I asked Ethel Barrymore if she ever thought of it.

"God, no."

"But won't you hate playing all those supporting parts?"

"God, no, but what I *will* hate is walking up five flights of stairs to my dressing room."

She never had to. Nor I. I'm still in Dressing Room Number

One. And speaking of dressing, I just bought an original Valentino and am still solvent. Is *that* getting it right?

Something *else* I'm getting is not any older. On my seventy-fourth birthday I dreaded looking in the glass. I didn't want any surprises, but I got one. At seventy-four I look better than seventy-three. If you make it through seventy-four years, can it be that things shape up?

Think it over.

The government wrote me saying that check for $149 they'd been sending wasn't enough and raised it to $184.50. Then wrote again and raised it to $202.40, saying next month's check would be for $341, due to something retroactive.

Do they pick up *your* doctor's bills? They do mine.

Do *you* pay Equity or do they pay you? They mail me $70.79 every first day of every month and I only send them $18 the first day of May and November. If you don't have your Equity pension, hurry up. Don't let the grass grow.

"Throw away all your Blue Cross and other stuff," AFTRA wrote, "because here's a *new* policy, gift of AFTRA. We defray all expenses." No wonder I can get a book published, there must be *something* to me!

There's also something to the New York Mets. When they had their great day, one of them was asked how it happened. "We're a hustlin' team," he said, "and we make our *own* luck!"

Well, some of mine I make, and some I was born with. To get it *right* you have to have luck. Mine came from Quincy, Mass., where I lived for my first seventeen years, and when I chose to leave home and become an actress, Quincy gave me a send-off at our Old Colony Railroad station and put a note in the *Quincy Patriot Ledger*, "Miss Ruth Gordon Jones, daughter of Mr. and Mrs. Clinton Jones of 14 Elmwood Avenue, is leaving for New York to go on the stage. She will appear under the name of Ruth Gordon, named after Dr. John Alexander Gordon of 42 Hancock Street."

Shall we say Quincy, Mass., got it right?

What *didn't* get it right was the Old Colony Railroad station. It got it in the neck. Made of bricks, Quincy granite, slate roof with a weathervane, but it got torn down.

31

Anything strike you?

Bricks and Quincy granite didn't make it, but notice who's writing this?

Critics tore me down from time to time, but unlike the Old Colony I pulled myself together.

Someone else who got it right was my father, foreman of the Mellin's Food Company at $37 per week. When I told him I wanted to go on the stage he gave me his confidence, plus $50 to pin to my corset cover, plus a one-way train ticket to New York.

I still have the confidence. I still have the $50. The corset cover joined the Old Colony Railroad station among things that are no more.

I went to New York to become an actress and sometime during the next fifty years it was conceded I was. Fifty years is a long time, but is it the how *long*, O Lord? Or the *how?*

Think it over.

Fifty years at the same stand and I got restless, I got thinking about stout Cortez and Balboa and thought *I'd* go out and discover the Pacific. So with nothing pinned to nothing I got on TWA and went.

I'm a native of Massachusetts, I'm a legal resident of New York, but California is the land I choose. I'm not a daughter, but they make me feel I belong.

When the late great Justice Frankfurter was still professor of law at Harvard, he lived in a house in Cambridge and one day Mayor Curley crossed the Charles and came over to pay him a call. As the mayor walked into the library, his attention was caught by a Zorn etching of a nude woman. He looked at it intently, then turned to the professor. "Daughter of the house, I presume?"

I'm not a daughter of the house, but I'm an adopted daughter. Isn't that getting it right?

To get it right, be born with luck or else make it. *Never* give up. Get the knack of getting people to help you and also pitch in yourself. A little money helps, but what *really* gets it right is to *never*—I repeat—*never* under any conditions face the facts.

If I had, would I have gotten out of 14 Elmwood Avenue? Did anybody want an actress five feet high? In 1914, actresses were tall and willowy and beautiful. Or at least pretty. In 1914, everybody didn't hightail it into the movies. All the beautiful people went on the stage in New York City, where I didn't know anyone except the Ketcham family who lived in Brooklyn. Look at pictures of Billie Burke and Marguerite Clark and tell me if I should face the facts. I look better now than I did then and what did I have to offer? No looks, no singing voice, and for dancing I was just able to hold my own in the pageant where I danced like Dorothy Quincy was supposed to during the Revolution. What market was there for that? Or for my dance as Evening Star done to Edward MacDowell's "To a Wild Rose" at Mrs. Faxon's lawn party. Did Edward MacDowell invent camp? Did you ever hear "To a Wild Rose"? What's *wild?* Maybe *he* didn't face the facts.

Where did *I* learn not to? Was it that afternoon? Was it that costume? Long, Grecian-style, cheese-colored cheesecloth with a wand finished off by white cotton roses on loan for that afternoon by Miss Eleanor Jones (no relation), one of the Beach Street Joneses. Was it those cotton roses taught me never face the facts? Instead of kissing George Segal's ass in *Where's Poppa?*, I might be loaning *my* white cotton roses.

Think it over.

I'm doing OK at getting it right and for New Year's I may take up vindictiveness. Last year I took up lying, this year selfishness, but it's not so easy. From childhood you're stunted with "Do unto others" and so forth. Next year shall I do it *to* others? Or is that too much work?

Is a visceral myth "The exception proves the rule"? I'm getting it right, but what happened at Sardi's? Garson stopped to talk to Jack Gilford sitting with Michael York, then we ordered and after an eternity came the best welsh rarebit in the business.

"Don't you want some Worcestershire?"

I shook the bottle, hit my water glass, it smashed and glass went in my rarebit. I waited another eternity.

Over to our table came tall blond good-looking Michael York. "I'm sorry, Garson, I didn't know who you were when you spoke to me."

"Oh, that's all right."

33

"Hello," I said. "You and I met last night."

He looked surprised.

"Don't you remember the party for Princess Grace? You told me you live at 58 West 58th Street?"

"Hey, I'm not who you think I am."

"You aren't? Who are you?"

"I'm Jon Voight."

What good luck! "I want to send you my script of *Heaven's My Destination*."

Jon Voight looked blank.

"Didn't you ever read Thornton Wilder's novel?"

He shook his head.

"How's Lucy?" asked Garson to get things moving again.

"Lucy who? Oh, you mean that column stuff. I never met Lucy Saroyan and I'm sore! It's caused a lot of trouble for me." He turned to me. "Is this *Heaven's My Destination* script a play?"

"No, it's a movie."

"Oh. I want to go on the stage."

"You do? I know you were with the William Ball company, what plays did you do?"

"I was never with the Ball company."

"Oh, you weren't? I thought John Schlesinger said that's where he discovered you."

"No, I never was."

"What *were* you in?"

He named something.

I hadn't heard of it.

He named some others.

I hadn't heard of them either. "Well, I'll send you the script of *Heaven's My Destination*. Maybe after you go on the stage you'll want to come back and do another movie."

He left.

"I'll ask him for his address as we go out." I got up and as I cleared the table, I knocked the Canada Dry bottle across the red leather banquette. It stopped an inch from the girl in the pink crepe dress being served chicken à la king from the chafing dish, a flame flickering beneath it. Her companion motioned to me. "Don't knock these flames over," he urged.

Thornton Wilder's father says don't tell stories against yourself and I don't. This is the exception to the rule. And what about an evening like that? Is it the exception that proves the rule or is that another of Thornton's visceral myths?

What *isn't* a myth is that in *spite* of that evening I really am getting it right.

\*     \*     \*     \*     \*

What do you make of the Sitwells' father? He said, "*Such* a mistake to have friends." Could he have meant fish?

Will Bull didn't think so. Down on his dock where he rented boats to summer people, Will made big circular motions over the deep lake water and pretty soon a handsome trout surfaced. Will Bull tossed some bait out, the trout got it and went down to the watery deep.

Some people didn't believe it was the same trout each time, they thought it was just any old trout that happened to respond to Will's gestures.

"No, it's John trout," said Will. To end the argument he beckoned John trout up and plucked two scales off, like a branding mark, then put John trout back and tossed him the bait.

Now when John surfaced, everybody could see where the two scales had been.

One afternoon some summer people rented a boat to go out and fish.

"Any luck?" asked Will's boy on the dock.

The summer visitor showed his hamper. On top gasped John trout.

"That's Mr. Bull's trout," said the dock boy.

"No it's not, it's mine." The summer people got in their brown Plymouth and drove up the road.

The dock boy ran for Will. His Ford tore up the road and stopped the brown Plymouth at Greencastle. He got John trout out, but the two-mile ride had John gasping something fierce. Will got over that dirt road quicker than anything this side of the Memorial

35

Day Classic at Indianapolis. He ran down to the dock and eased
John into the water. John plopped out of sight.

Three or four times that afternoon Will went to the pier end
and made his gesture.

No John.

Will was up at four-thirty and went out. Four-thirty is a good
time for fish.

No John.

Will made the gestures a lot of times that day, but no John.

The sun went down behind Woollcott's island and Will went
down to the dock. A flash of silver and John surfaced. After that,
John trout was even more of a celebrity. Where else but Lake Bomoseen was a trout that had ridden two miles in a brown Plymouth
to Greencastle?

"Summer people most of the time aren't used to nature," said
Will, "and don't know what in hell to do with it."

\* \* \* \* \*

Do you know who Mrs. Calabash is? The last words on any
show Jimmy Durante is in are "Goodnight, Mrs. Calabash, wher-
*ever* you are." Who is Mrs. Calabash, Jimmy, wherever *you* are?

\* \* \* \* \*

Vivien Leigh thought nobody was going to enjoy *The Matchmaker*.

"Have you *read* it, darling?" she asked, doubt coloring that
lovely voice.

"Yes."

"Have you *really*, Ruthie? All your friends are *terrified* you'll
make a balls-up. Oh, *please* don't do it, darling."

"*You're* going to do *Elephant Walk*," I said, "and that's dreadful."

"Oh, darling, *Elephant Walk* will be shot in Ceylon. It'll be
beautiful."

What if I'd listened to her? What would have happened to
*Hello, Dolly!?* Could they have made *that* out of *Elephant Walk?*

36

René Clair says nobody listens to anybody and wasn't it a good thing I didn't, Carol, Ginger, Betty, Bibi, Martha, Phyllis, Pearl and Ethel?

✳   ✳   ✳   ✳   ✳

And wasn't it a good thing Raoul Fleischmann *did?* He listened to Harold Ross and footed the bills for Ross's new magazine and just as Raoul was getting sick of it, things took a turn for the better and Eustace Tilley started footing Fleischmann's bills. Do *you* listen or don't you? Maybe both ways are good.

✳   ✳   ✳   ✳   ✳

Someone else who doesn't go in for too much listening is Sinatra. "Is this going to take long?" asks Frank. He'd have liked Woollcott. Woollcott didn't take long. When he was on *The New York Times* he reviewed a show called *Number Seven*. Next morning along with all the news that's fit to print was Woollcott's review.

*Number Seven*<br>by<br>Alexander Woollcott

*Number Seven* opened last night at the Republic Theatre.
It was misnamed by five.

People knew how to raise eyebrows long before isometric exercises.

✳   ✳   ✳   ✳   ✳

Do you stand in line to get into shows? Diana Wynyard got out of her taxi at the stage door of the Globe. "Oh, you must be so cold," she said to the shivering line.
"Oh, we don't mind."
"But it's freezing."
"Oh, we don't mind."
Diana smiled her beautiful smile. "I suppose you love the theatre."
A woman looked troubled. "Oh, Miss Wyn-yard, we *dread* it."

37

# *Garrick*

H<small>E CAME</small> to New York as Garrick Golden, but soon changed
back to John. Next time *you* feel cold, go in Sardi's and look
at the bronze plaque on the column, center aisle and to the rear:

J O H N   G O L D E N ' S

T A B L E

Will a plaque say where your table was?

Well, that's show business.

While you get warm, think it over and maybe work a little
harder on adding to the gaiety of nations. That's what John Golden
did. On St. Patrick's day he wore a handsome suit he'd had tailored
in London, it was the color of a shamrock and so was his tie and so
were his cufflinks. He wasn't Irish, he just liked to wear green.

He'd made millions and enjoyed it. "I'm a very rich man," he
reminded you. He could also have reminded you that he was very
smart because when the Depression hit, everybody else's money
seemed to disappear and John Golden had all his. But now he *didn't*
enjoy it. Everybody was low-spirited. Even the Lambs' Club was
gloomy. When he came in, a brother Lamb looked miserable and
said, "John, I hate to do this to you, but could you—"

John could and they had lunch.

A sad-eyed chum looked embarrassed. "I don't like to trouble
you, John, but—"

38

John took care of it and they finished the game of pool.

A comic that always came up with a good one mumbled, "Could you help me out—"

John could, then went over to the window marked CASHIER. "I'm goddam sick of being asked for dough every time I come here. Tell anybody needs it, use this and get the hell off my tail." He made out a check to the Lambs' Club, marked *Loans to Members*. It was for a hundred thousand dollars. He was rich and he'd remind you he was. "I'm very rich and I like to be."

Arthur Hopkins said when money was scarce, John Golden sent several hundred thousand down to Wall Street on loan at some hair-raising rate.

Did he? He didn't charge his brother Lambs interest, he didn't even ask to be paid back. He didn't ask interest from a performer he'd known when they worked at the Hippodrome, where the sign now says Hippodrome Garage and cars from Jersey and Pennsylvania and South Carolina pull in out of 44th Street's one-way traffic. When traffic went *two* ways, the Hippodrome's elephants filed out into it to go to supper, then filed back among all the cars to work the night show, their backs glistening in the rain, horns honking. Till traffic started to edge along, they shifted feet, then stopped shifting and started the tread they picked up in the jungle and curved through their stage door.

How did the whole country know how to sing the Hippodrome's "Poor Butterfly" that John wrote the lyrics for to the music of Ray Hubbell? No TV, no radio, but Omaha and South Bend and Pasadena had the string quartet play it in the hotel dining room.

> *The moon and I*
> *Know that he be faithful—*

Do you know when you drank your first cocktail? I drank mine adding a tear to the nation's for "Poor Butterfly 'neath the blossoms waiting."

John gave up writing lyrics and took a partner. He and Winchell Smith produced a lot of hits. Vaudeville went on the blink. The Hippodrome made way for the Hippodrome Garage and its at-liberty dog act asked, "Could you help me out?"

John could.

"I'm short on security."

"I don't want any." Could Arthur be wrong?

The dog act didn't want charity from Poor Butterfly's lyric writer, he sent a letter to John, c/o Smith and Golden office up that long flight of stairs beside the Hudson lobby. "I'm putting Yippy up as security. He's the best Boston Bull in the business, but there's no demand. I'll drop him off at your house. I got the address, John Golden Lane, Bayside, Long Island. He's well behaved and worth something as soon as vaudeville comes back. When I repay you, I'll collect him."

The last thing John Golden Lane needed was a vaudeville dog, but the day the letter got left was the day John's accountant unlocked the money room and from ten A.M. to closing time he and John talked investments, deals, propositions, expenses and prospects. You think a producer's life is all producing plays?

John's car pulled up at John Golden Lane, John's chauffeur opened the door, John breathed the salt air off the bay, John's butler greeted him. "A dog has been delivered, sir."

"What the hell do I need a dog for?" growled John and glared at the one on the landing.

Between the newel post and the dark green wallpaper, a Boston bull looked at John, then shifted position, lifted his right paw to where a Boston bull's heart is and bowed to the floor.

Did you ever ask John for a loan? I'm sure he didn't refuse you, but I bet he loaned you just half.

"Can you lend me five hundred?"

John looked dark, stared hard at me, "I'll lend you two fifty" and did.

Only once did he go the other way. The American Theatre Wing needed a hundred and fifty dollars for some emergency. The Wing's president knew where to go. John got out his checkbook and wrote, then stopped and looked exasperated. "Oh, damn it," he said and started to tear up the check.

"What's the matter?" asked Rachel Crothers.

"I wrote *two* hundred and fifty. Wait, I'll write another."

"No, you won't!" shouted the president of the American Theatre Wing and clung to John's hand. "You sign *that* one!"

"She really thought I'd made a mistake!" John enjoyed his money.

"Would you lend me five hundred, John?" Charlie Dillingham stood in front of Golden's desk. Charles Bancroft Dillingham had been Broadway's most dashing producer. How had Charlie been squeezed out of show business? Was it Klaw? Was it Abraham Lincoln Erlanger? Was it the Shuberts? Mr. Lee knew and John Golden knew and Marc Klaw and Abe Erlanger, but none cared to say how Dillingham lost his Globe Theatre now called the Lunt-Fontanne, lost his elegant town house later owned by George S. Kaufman, lost his Long Island estate with the fuzzy gray sheepdogs, lost his beautiful ex-show-girl wife, later Mrs. Gillespie.

"I'll give you two-fifty, Charlie." John peeled off a fifty-dollar bill, then four more.

Dillingham thanked him as though it were a loan at Belmont and tomorrow his accountant would send a check.

John went to lunch at the Astor.

"Good morning, sir," said Fred, then handed the cigar-stand girl a fifty-dollar bill and the girl handed him four long black cigars. John watched the girl ring up his fifty.

"Perhaps you'd go up to see him, sir? He's about to have his lunch." Dillingham lived in an inside single, but his manservant came every day to look after him. And sometimes lend him a little something?

They got off the elevator and started down the hall, but were blocked by white damask-covered tables agleam with silver, a bottle cooling in a frosty bucket, and waiter following captain, busboy following waiter. John and Fred followed busboy and all pulled up in front of Charles Bancroft Dillingham's inside single.

"Come in."

Embarrassment? None.

"Delighted. Will you have something?"

"No, I'm lunching downstairs."

"Forgive me?" Dillingham took the white linen napkin from his manservant. Fred poured a glass and prepared to serve.

It was John who felt odd. He looked around the little room. "Charlie, what the hell do you *do* all day? What the hell do you do with your *time??*"

Charlie, who'd hopped on ocean liners when he felt like it, stepped into his Hispano-Suiza, produced the Astaires' show, the Gaby Deslys show and all those other unforgettable evenings, tasted the wine and approved. "Well, I walk around. A *lot* of people are walking around, it's the Depression, y'know. I walk, I look, I see what's going on. Everywhere around town, people are lined up. Sometimes *I* get on the line. This morning before I came in to see you, I got on a *long* line. A long line's not easy to find, but this morning I found one. It was the damnedest thing! I stood, then I moved up, then I stood, then I moved up, then I got to the end and what do you think? They handed me a cup of coffee."

Wauseon, Ohio, was where John Golden came from. It used to be a one-nighter and he ushered at the Opera House to see the shows. He was going to New York to become an actor, but till he got the money to get there, he saw all the road attractions. He didn't have the money, but he had his stage name. He'd leave Wauseon as John, lose the John on the Baltimore and Ohio and hit Broadway as Garrick Golden.

An earlier Garrick left home and headed for London. He had a chum go with him by the name of Johnson. They both made it and so did the Garrick from Wauseon, though the name didn't. OK for the Lichfield breakthrough, but on a Broadway sign Garrick Golden? John looked better than Garrick.

Any money he could pick up bought him gallery seats at Daly's where Ada Rehan was the greatest leading lady of her day, John Drew the greatest leading man, Otis Skinner the greatest second business, James Lewis unequaled in characters, Mrs. Gilbert the top old lady in the business or anywhere else. At three score and ten, she walked through the blizzard of '76 to find the show called off on account of weather.

Great people, great nights and the greatest was when John Drew drew back the blue velvet curtain and led forward the Katharine, the Rosalind, the Peggy, all played by Ada Rehan who had come to Broadway as Ada Crehan but the print on the program slipped and came out Ada C. Rehan. She bowed to fate, dropped the C. and did fine with the Rehan. Well, that's show business.

In John Golden's office over the St. James Theatre hung a dingy blue square of velvet framed in a gold frame and in the center was the smudge made by Drew's hand holding back Daly's curtain for Ada. When Judge Daly put his brother's effects up for auction, John bought the curtain, had the smudge cut out, had the curtain repaired and sent to Saranac for the Actors' Sanitarium where it went in their theatre and the smudge went in John's gold frame.

"Did you ever go to French Lick? All the managers used to. Oh, hell, those days we had some fun," said John. "Autumn and spring Sam Harris, Arthur Hopkins, Charlie Dillingham, Arthur Hammerstein, Winchell Smith, Willie Collier, Martin Beck, a whole bunch of us would light out for French Lick and take the cure. That goddam water! We'd drink it and exercise, and drink it and sweat, and drink it and get rubbed down, have a dandy dinner with just time for a game or two of Bingo before turning in. When Willie Collier won, he'd remember that damn water and holler 'Pluto!' "

Up the elevator to John's office came show business, politicians, tycoons. Among the latter was Albert Lasker, not just handsome, though that's not a bad thing to be, but Lasker also looked like the good person he was. The St. James elevator, run by an actor waiting for the start of the season to free him from being at liberty, moved slowly upward. "Hey, don't waste time at the Golden office," he advised Lasker. "Go down the hall to Maurice Evans, they're casting for a priest."

Another to use the elevator was Mrs. Roosevelt. Once John brought her into our office on their way down to Sardi's.

"What's eating you, Garson?" he asked.

"I'm trying to think of a funny line."

John turned to the wife of the President of the United States. "Do you know a funny line?"

"I believe I do." Her mission in life was to help. "Two vaudevillians were standing outside the Palace when Franklin was running for the third term. 'Who are *you* going to vote for?' asked one.

" 'I'm going to vote for Roosevelt.'

43

" 'Roosevelt! What's the matter with the one in there *now?*' "

When the war began, she flew off with a bag of oranges and other things to see how she could help England. John, both fearful and proud, told the newspapers, "She's the first lady of the world."

At Sardi's he told us, "The papers used my title," then motioned us to lean closer. "She's 'the first lady of the world,' but I want her to feel like a woman. I went over to Arnold Constable's and bought her a mess of silk underwear to take."

He sent me a play. "Fine part for you." Around the envelope was an inch-wide blue elastic band.

"Don't like the play," I wrote back, "love the elastic band."

He produced the play at the Booth.

"Why is *Claudia* such a hit?" I asked him.

"Because Rose Franken believes every goddam word."

*He* may not have believed every word of his plays, but he believed in not letting them die. "When I had *Three Wise Fools* over at the Criterion, they rapped it. I hired extras to line up and buy tickets. A line at the box office looks good. Pretty soon people I *didn't* hire joined the line and bought. Do you know what Criterion means? Something to go by. Why is *that* a good name for a theatre?"

One morning we met in the elevator. "I've been up at the Jolson," he said. "Muni received the Italo-American Award. The newspapers were all up there snapping pictures."

Garson asked, "What's the Italo-American Award?"

John beckoned us into his office, now David Merrick's. "The Italo-American Award is to show friendly relations with the foreign element. This is its first year. I'm going to see they give it annually."

"How did they choose *your* play?"

John closed the door. "Oh hell, *I* chose it. Business is rotten, so I told Tony to wear his good suit and meet me at the Jolson and read this scroll." He reached into his desk. "Here's my rough draft I wrote coming in from Bayside, Clarence typed it."

The buzzer buzzed. "Tony's on the way in, Mr. Golden."

In he came, white coat, white trousers and carrying a suitcase. "Hot towels today?"

44

"You did fine, Tony."

The bestower of the Italo-American Award bowed and disappeared into John's private barber shop, complete with chair and bootblack stand.

At twelve-thirty once a week John and Mr. Lee Shubert and Garson and I showed up at Lindy's. All punctual, we filed in, welcomed by Mr. Lindy, who seated us in a booth and left us to the glories of his menu. Across the table, John glared at Mr. Lee. "Well, Leona, you're stuck with the check."

Outside a business deal, Lee Shubert was a generous man. Was it the Leona or anticipation made us laugh?

We ordered and John took off, "Did you ever know Uncle Joe Cannon? He played poker with us at French Lick. Nothing serious, we'd just sit around playing, gassing. Willie Collier asked, 'Can you remember the first time you ever did it?' Winchell Smith told, Sam Harris told, Willie, Charlie Dillingham, then it got to Uncle Joe. Charlie nudged him. 'Joe?'

" 'What?'

" 'When was the first time you ever did it?'

"Uncle Joe looked blank. 'Hell,' he said, 'I can't remember the *last* time.' "

Once the luncheon was at *our* house.

"Did I ever tell you about all the managers getting together to make a gift to Broadway? Lee remembers."

Mr. Lee nodded and looked grim.

"Lee contributed the 44th Street Theatre. Our motto was 'Do something great!' We chose Gus Thomas to guide us. Gus was the most distinguished playwright-director and he recommended we do *As You Like It*. The consent was unanimous. For Rosalind he chose his girl friend, who was also a Broadway star, a wonderful actress, a beaut and a drinker. Gus's production was just as lush. The cast he assembled was the public's dream and their salaries a manager's nightmare.

"The opening was white tie and evening dresses. Lee remembers. What did you want to sell the 44th Street for, Lee? The 44th Street was a good house."

Mr. Lee shrugged.

"Nobody came late, everybody was seated when the curtain went up. But before the girls got to the forest, it was clear Rosalind was soused. She'd outsmarted Gus and put gin in her water cooler. Lee remembers. Hell, why wouldn't he? It was his theatre! The evening was a disaster and sinking lower and lower in his last-row seat was Gus, the color of his tie. Beside him sat his wife trying to comfort him. 'Don't you care, dear,' she said, 'just be thankful you didn't write it.' "

After lunch I went to tell Suzanne they'd enjoyed it.

"Yes," she said. "One came out and said, 'I'll give you double what *they* pay you.' "

I went back. "John."

"What can I do for you?"

"Did you tell our cook you'd pay her double?"

"Certainly. What the hell is money *for?*" Every first of May he sent her a cartwheel of lily of the valley and on a summer day his chauffeur might drive up with a bucket of clams sent from John's beach at Northport, "For Suzanne."

Our office door flew open. "What the hell's your play closing for, Garson?"

"It's in its fourth year."

"What the hell's that got to do with anything?"

"The last two weeks it only broke even, Max doesn't want his backers to have a loss."

"They made a goddam lot on it, didn't they? Don't close till there *is* a loss." He sat down at Garson's desk. "Take five thousand dollars just for the hell of it, let's see how far *that* goes!" He blotted the check.

*Born Yesterday* ran seven months more.

A big hit of John's was *Lightnin'*. Frank Bacon wrote it, then Winchell Smith helped him with the rewrite, Smith and Golden produced it at the Gaiety, now the Victoria, 46th and Broadway. It was a sensation and so was Frank Bacon. New York had never seen him, but he'd kept busy in about every stock and tank town and jerkwater anywhere west of the Mississippi till Broadway gave him rave reviews. Some people make it younger, but Frank Bacon was seventy when he won the hearts of all show business and anybody else that had one.

Those were the days when a playwright could call a character Lightnin' to show he was slow. Today to show he's *not* slow, a character goes bareass. Well, that's show business. And look what's playing at the Victoria!

On the stage there in 1918, Lightnin's wife was divorcing him because he didn't amount to anything. He didn't go for that and claimed he did amount to something. "I brought a swarm of bees across the desert," he boasted, "and never lost a *bee*." He won. The show ran right through the dog days. No air-conditioning, but people lucky enough to get in had to be told it was hot. In August, humidity increased and so did differences between Equity and the managers. Equity stood up for what *they* thought and non-members formed another outfit. Fidelity actors stuck by the managers and made accusations about Equity members, Equity members broke off old friendships and nobody was on the fence.

At the meeting, Equity voted to go out. Not many shows were playing through August. *Lightnin'* was. Stock and tank towns and jerkwaters and now they'd laid down the red carpet for Frank and he was selling out, but he had his own ideas. "Mama, we cooked over a Sterno, we can do it some more." He marched his troupe out of the Gaiety. LIGHTNIN' HAS STRUCK! was on his banner. They headed down Broadway, the band playing George M.'s

> *Give my regards to Broadway,*
> *Remember me to Herald Square.*
> *Tell all the boys on 42nd Street*
> *That I will soon be there.*

They soon were, but George M. was over at Fidelity urging the boys and girls to stay in line.

After the battle, mother, and the shows lighted up again, *Lightnin's* author came up to Smith and Golden's. "I'm writing a new one."

John beamed. "Good for you. What's it about?"

"There's this feller goes out West to look for gold and that's all he *does* look for, he doesn't think about anything else. That's all that's in his heart, he's *crazy* for gold. And he struggles and fails and struggles and fails. *Ambition* has him half crazy. Fear drives him the rest of the way. But no stopping him, he struggles on, obsessed with the craze for gold, that's all he cares about. It's all he knows. Then one day there comes into his life a fine, pure girl. Through her he learns 'Failure is *nothing*. Failure depends on what you fail trying to *do*.' The girl makes him *see* that. And through her *purity*, he sees his struggle was unworthy. His craze for gold was not worth ruining life for. The girl has made him believe that and he changes. We *see* him change. We see he *does* believe it. We see him take her in his arms and weep. 'You saved me,' he cries. 'Marry me,' and he kisses her and when they come out of the embrace she's weeping, too, but hers are tears of gladness and she says, 'Look, dear,' and points down at the earth they're standing on. In the earth that had been so barren, now are nuggets of gold. And there on the spot they first kissed, they dig and discover their gold mine. That's the curtain."

"And I got the title for it," said John. "*Kiss Mine*."

❋  ❋  ❋  ❋  ❋

Did you ever notice everybody isn't rich? Living at the Hotel Seville down on 28th Street and Madison, Mrs. Pat Campbell was up against it. Financially the times were "out of joint" for her and Moonbeam, the white Pekinese.

She went up to see her goddaughter. Sara and Gerald Murphy and Mrs. Pat and Moonbeam sat down with the mound of unpaid bills, carried in the same bag with the letters Shaw wrote her, but wouldn't consent to have published.

Gerald and Sara wanted to help. How could they do it delicately? "What do you suggest?" asked Gerald.

Mrs. Pat glanced up from a letter of Shaw's. "Well," she said, "I always say money is for those that need it."

❋  ❋  ❋  ❋  ❋

Next time you see *Madame Butterfly*, thank Miss Ginty. You'd never be hearing "Un bel dì vedremo" if she hadn't picked up the pieces.

*Madame Butterfly* was a play by David Belasco made from a

short story by John Luther Long. And between the Madame and oblivion stood the great Miss Ginty, secretary to David Belasco. "And collaborator," said some.

Draw the veil!

One day Mr. Belasco, raging around in a good old-fashioned show-business tantrum, picked up the newly finished script of *Madame Butterfly* and started tearing it to pieces.

Miss Ginty shrieked, got down on her knees, pleaded, implored, wept. (Does that sound like *your* secretary?)

Mr. B. just kept on tearing it to pieces, then to smaller pieces. He had a carbon copy in his cupboard, so he tore up the little pieces into littler ones as Miss Ginty fainted dead away. (Did Katherine Gibbs' school discontinue that course?) There was no carbon in the cupboard. Miss Ginty had knocked over an ink bottle. No page was unsoaked.

Miss Ginty came out of the vapors and kept pasting little bits of typed scraps together, day and night, night and day, and that's why "Un bel dì vedremo" floats out over the Met. They'd be singing something else except for unsung Miss Ginty whose middle name had to be Never Give Up.

❋ ❋ ❋ ❋ ❋

How do you get your pretty blue eyes open in the morning? Robert Benchley's man leaned over Benchley's sleepy head and said, "The man is here for the trunks."

Would that rouse you? It roused Benchley. Now there's no more Benchley. Also no more trunks.

❋ ❋ ❋ ❋ ❋

Talk about thorough! In my Holt Spoken Language series, Spoken Italian, Book One, on page vii under B:

> bad    CATTIVO (KAT-TI-VO)
> Baltimore    (BOL-TI-MOR)
> bank    BANCA (BAN-ka)

Can we blame this on Spiro?

49

❊   ❊   ❊   ❊   ❊

Ever stay at Mrs. Brown's in Boston? The only way you could board at her house was if you dressed somebody at the Colonial, Majestic, Plymouth, Shubert, Wilbur, Tremont, Boston Theatre, Park, Park Square, or B. F. Keith's. She assigned rooms by the cast system. If you dressed Marilyn Miller, you got a front with a bay window. If you looked after Fred Astaire, you got the other front with the other bay. My Selena Joiner drew a back room looking over the garden. I was starred, but I didn't rate like Fred or Marilyn.

# *Kaufman and*

Mrs. Brown was a friend to dressers and George Kaufman was a friend to the people the dressers dressed. Why did he never say anything nice to them? When he was directing *Over Twenty-one*, I asked him, "Don't you *ever* pass a compliment?"

"No, you're supposed to be good. When you're not, I'm supposed to tell you."

(No one gets a swelled head from *that*.)

But he was our friend. The best friend an actor can have is somebody who writes good parts in good plays. George and Marc Connelly wrote *Dulcy*. They opened it in Indianapolis at Captain English's Theatre, sometimes known as English's and sometimes known as English's Opera House, but always owned by the Captain and always managed by Ad Miller, another good man. Ad decided Columbus, Ohio, was too slow and came up to Indianapolis to get into things.

The opening night of *Dulcy*, Ad counted up and came out to see what was causing all the laughs. It was Lynn Fontanne as Dulcy, Gregory Kelly as her brother, Howard Lindsay as a movie director and Elliott Nugent as Elliott Nugent. Ad saw that and also saw someone pacing up and down the center aisle. He'd left Columbus to get into things and he got right into the question of who that goddam blockhead was. When the blockhead got up to where Ad could grab him, he asked what the hell he meant by taking a stroll in the center aisle. "I'm worried about that last exit of Lynn's," said stroller George S. Kaufman. "We've got to get her a laugh to go off on."

*Dulcy* was his and Marc's first play and when it settled in for a run they thought how they could write some more good parts. They remembered how good Helen Hayes was and wrote a good part for her. Did they also write the notices? They were so great that *To the Ladies!* and Helen became the talk of the town.

Then they noticed Glenn Hunter was going to be at liberty, so George and Marc wrote him a good part. Over the title *Merton of the Movies* Glenn Hunter's name shot up in lights. Why not? Down on his knees in his bedroom back of Gashweiler's Department Store, Merton prayed, "Oh God, make me a good movie actor, for Jesus' sake, amen." Cheers and hurrahs and hosannas. No one ever had a better Act I curtain. Harry Leon Wilson had it in his book and George and Marc knew an actor should say it just before the curtain came down.

*Merton of the Movies'* dress rehearsal was at the Shubert Montauk or Werba's Shubert or whatever was the good theatre in Brooklyn, and Gregory and I went over to see it. The first act was great, Act II needed a scene change and we sat and waited. And waited. And waited. George, Marc, director Hugh Ford, producer George C. Tyler and Gregory and I waited. And waited. An hour went by. Another. It was one A.M. And tomorrow they were going to open.

"What will you do?" I asked.

"Oh," said Marc, "tomorrow for this intermission we're booking in *Orphans of the Storm.*"

It's the first and last time I ever heard George S. Kaufman laugh out loud.

"What's the S. for?" I asked him.

"Nothing."

"Then why do you have it?"

George screwed his face up and looked aggressive. "Listen, if Al H. Woods, Charles B. Dillingham, Henry B. Harris, George C. Tyler, William A. Brady, Sam H. Harris, George M. Cohan, J. J. Shubert, A. L. Erlanger, B. F. Keith, Sam S. Shubert, H. H. Frazee need a middle initial, why not me?"

When George was second-string critic on *The New York Times*, he reviewed a play that wasn't very good. Neither was the acting. "Guido Nadzo," wrote George, "is nadzo guido."

It made everybody laugh and when you didn't like something, you said, "It's natso guido."

George called up Guido Nadzo. "Do you think it has hurt you?" he asked.

"Well, I haven't been in a play since."

"Oh dear," said Kaufman. "Let's have lunch and see what can be done."

They did and George said he'd try to get him something. He tried, but when he spoke to Sam Harris or Arthur Hopkins or George Tyler about this actor he'd like to place, they asked, "Who is he?"

"Guido Nadzo."

"Oh, natso guido," said Sam and George and Arthur, and sometime after that Guido Nadzo left the stage.

Was it George's fault? Some of us thought it was tempting fate to go on the stage with Guido Nadzo for a name. When you go on the stage, choose a name critics can't make a joke out of. And also will look good in lights. Sometimes it's hard to know what *will* look good.

What if your name is Paddy Chayefsky? He wasn't thinking about his name in lights, but when would he get out of the army hospital. Garson liked the way he talked and said, "Write some scenes for us?"

"I don't write."

"Try."

When the war was over, Garson asked what he was going to do.

"Go in my uncle's factory."

"You should write. Take five hundred dollars, see how far you get."

He wrote a play that was good but didn't get put on. He wrote another.

"Great," said Garson.

"I've got all the money for the production."

"So he gave the play to someone else?" asked pessimist Kaufman.

"No, he's giving it to *us*."

"Very unusual."

Next day George read in the *Times* that Josh Logan was going to direct *The Middle of the Night* by Paddy Chayefsky for the Theatre Guild. "I feel better," said George.

And Paddy Chayefsky looked fine in lights for a long time at a lot of theatres.

"Want me to come over and read a play to you?" It was a Sunday night. George tried out several chairs and found the one. I stretched out on the sofa.

George screwed his face up in knots and read, "Act One," then sighed, uncrossed his legs and crossed them left to right. "It's called *The Royal Family*."

He'd written it with Edna Ferber and the grapevine said it was about the Barrymores. It was. And it was great. The best part was old lady Drew who ran the great Arch Street Theatre where Booth and Modjeska played and where she put her son John and her daughter Georgie to work. Years later Georgie's children Lionel, Ethel and Jack went to work, too. Not in Grandma Drew's Arch Street Theatre, but in about everybody else's. George and Edna wrote about them in the new play.

He finished and I raved.

A day or two later Ethel called up. "Has George read you his new play?"

"Yes. It's great."

"Is it about the Barrymores?"

"Yes. You'll love it."

Click.

"Ethel?"

That click was on the level.

George rang up. "Did you tell Ethel the play's about the Barrymores?"

"Oh yes."

"Oh my God!"

"Well, isn't it?"

54

"Of course. Ethel just rang up and said, 'Send the script.' Click."

"Max Steuer is handling the suit," Ethel told me.

"But it's so *great!* Your grandmother—"

"It's a disgrace. We'll forbid it. It's— How can you say it's good? It's a—"

"Ethel, you *asked* me what I thought."

"Sorry." Click.

A week later she got into the elevator, looking fraught.

"What's happened?" I asked.

"Max says the only one that has a suit is Jack and he won't answer the phone. Max says without him we haven't a case."

The play was a riot, the Barrymores became ever more beloved and Ethel never forgave George or Edna. Did she forgive Jack?

She always forgave her family.

Another play George wrote with Edna was *Stage Door*. Another big hit. Morrie Ryskind wrote the screenplay. "It's changed a lot, George," he said. "You better look at it."

George did. "It certainly is changed. Maybe you should change the title. What about calling it *Screen Door?*"

New at directing, Abe Burrows went to George for advice. "I want to use a treadmill. What do you think of a treadmill, George?"

George screwed his face up and gave it his thought. "Well," he said, "a treadmill's all right. It's what you *do* on a treadmill."

Why do I remember what Lucille Gleason said as the producer's wife in *The Butter and Egg Man* and don't remember a line from a show I wrote? At the Act II after-the-tryout conclave upstairs in the Syracuse Hotel the property man served soggy club sandwiches and cups and cups and cups of coffee. Everybody had a flask of booze. The girl on the switchboard was brought in and her opinion asked. "Well, it's this way, Syracuse either likes you or it doesn't." She was shown out.

Out of a silence as soggy as the sandwiches, Lucille Gleason said, "Well, I *like* the show. And that'll give you a rough idea of *my* condition!"

Down in Cherry Lane they opened a theatre. The name was pretty, but the seats were bare wooden benches. Midway through

*The Way of the World*, George whispered, "What this bench needs is a long felt want."

Can you believe there was a time when a play was called *Pigs* and pigs was what it meant? John Golden opened it at the Little Theatre. Very short skirts were just coming in. Always a problem for the stage, before the days of show-everything. Chic Ina Claire solved it, she had Kayser silk pants dyed the same color as her dress. That was resourceful, Ina, but the character lady in *Pigs* didn't have your know-how. In Act II her dress worked up higher and higher. The audience got nervous and laughed. Beverley Sitgreaves hadn't thought of a laugh in that scene, but didn't George M. say, "Give them what they want"? Encouraged, she went after the laughs, flipped around and her dress went higher. The audience gave out shrieks.

Kaufman whispered, "For the rest of the run she'll try to get those laughs and wonder *how* she did it tonight."

George had been away. Back in town, he dropped in to *Of Thee I Sing* and was troubled by William Gaxton putting in lines and doing new things. He went next door to Western Union and wrote Gaxton a wire: AM STANDING IN THE BACK OF THE THEATRE WISH YOU WERE HERE.

George and Ring Lardner got together. They wrote *June Moon*. Then they rewrote it. Then they rewrote it again. That rewrite looked hopeful enough to make them tackle another one. That new one was good. "Good isn't enough on today's Broadway," counseled George. Ring looked even gloomier than usual and they pitched in to another rewrite. It was better. "Let's try one more and make this one the *one*," said George. They did another. And another. It was too late for another, the show opened.

*Variety*'s notice started, "This one wrote itself."

Sam H. Harris booked the Apollo Theatre in Atlantic City for the first performance of *Here Today*. George, co-author and director, watched the curtain go up, then whispered to Bob Sinclair, "See how quick the curtain went up?"

His assistant nodded.

"That's how quick Charlotte Granville is going to go up."

She came on with her script rolled up and sticking out of her

56

downstage coat pocket. Sometimes it seems as though you can't count on anybody.

George didn't eat onions, he didn't eat cheese, so when you went to the Kaufmans', you didn't look for onions or cheese. Bea ran things to suit George. They were married, but they both had a lot going. George was crazy about Myra, who liked him but only had eyes for Harpo, who liked her but that was all. And Evelyn had her friends worried she'd jump out the window because she was crazy about George.

On the distaff side, things went about the same. Then Bea died and George went into melancholia. Stayed home, didn't work, forsook the world. When we came to see him he showed us a list of the friends who'd sent flowers and messages. He knew all the ones that didn't.

After a time he started going out again. "Oh, hello," he said to Peg Pulitzer. "I thought we were both dead."

A while had gone by since I'd called George. I rang him up.

"Yes?" he said.

"It's Ruth."

There was a pause. "What's the matter, did you get the wrong number?"

At the play George was reviewing there was a lot of forgetting. "The prompter was in good voice," wrote George, "I look forward to a time when he gets some better material."

All the prizes went to *Oklahoma!* Then they all went to *South Pacific.* Now Dick and Oscar were opening a new one.

Our phone rang. "*The King and I* opens tonight in Boston," said George. "What are you prepared to do if Rodgers and Hammerstein come up with another hit?"

George and Leueen MacGrath were married. One day they went shopping at Bloomingdale's on the furniture floor. Leueen, expert in such matters, discussed with a salesman just what sort of table she wanted.

George wandered around.

"Can I get you anything?" asked a saleswoman.

"Yes," he said. "Have you got any good second-act curtains?"

Leueen acquired a Siamese cat named Adam. He had to take a

trip to the vet. "Shouldn't we change his name to Hadam?" asked George.

George wasn't feeling well. In fact, he was dying. George Oppenheimer went up to see him. "Do you eat honey?" asked George O.

"Yes."

"Do you eat *much?*"

"Well, some."

"No, George, that's not good enough, you must eat a *lot*. You must eat it every time you think of it."

"All right, I will."

"And *think* of it. And eat as much as you possibly can. I had an uncle and he ate honey every day all day long and he died at *ninety-two.*"

"Too much honey," said George.

Later that afternoon I came to visit.

"Did you ever take a bath?" he asked.

"Yes."

"When you took the bath, did the phone ever ring?"

"Yes."

"When you took the bath and the phone rang, did you ever get out and answer it?"

"Yes."

"Did it turn out to be George Oppenheimer?"

❊   ❊   ❊   ❊   ❊

I guess Burt Bacharach and Hal David should pay me royalty. "Do You Know the Way to San Jose?" they wrote. Well, that, or words to that effect, is said to *me* wherever I am. Wherever I am, I look like someone that lives there.

"Where's Broadway?"

"Where's Sunset Boulevard?"

"Où est l'avenue Kléber?"

"Where's Charing Cross Road?"

I look like a native of everywhere and I found that out just one year after I went on the stage. I came back to Wollaston made up

like an actress, acting like an actress, in a dress from Fifth Avenue's
Franklin Simon, an actressy hat on my head, shoes from Slater's
with French high heels that sank into Wollaston's tar sidewalks.
Tar is for chewing, not for Slater's enamel-buckled patent-leather
pumps worn with taupe silk stockings when everyone in Massachusetts wore black. I was a New York actress and looked like
one, but as I got off the train a lady said, "Where's Brook Street?"
In Wollaston if I didn't look like a New Yorker, I never will. I
bowed to fate. I look like a native of everywhere.

"Do you know the way to Brook Street?"

"To Broad Street?"

"Do you know the way to Nagasaki?"

Hal? Burt? Did you think up "Do You Know the Way to San
Jose?" or were you chasing around behind me?

\* \* \* \* \*

In Philadelphia old Mrs. Drew's theatre on Arch Street got torn
down and so did the Adelphi, the Garrick, the Chestnut Street
Opera House, the Lyric and the Broad, but one they didn't tear
down is a rakish-looking burlesque house. A big banner featured

THE GREAT HUNGARIAN STAR
COUNTESS BARASSY

Who says Philly doesn't swing?

# London Guide

W HAT'S YOUR RULE for choosing a present? Mine is would *I* like it? Who knows what anyone else likes, but if *I* like it, that at least is something. I also have to like what I *get*. Did you ever give a present back? When I got married, Lillian Gish gave me an opal necklace set in silver and I don't like silver jewelry. "*You* wear it," I said. Opals are lucky for her, too, she has an October birthday.

A present that *I* liked was my going-away present to Susan Strasberg. Susan had finished playing Anne Frank and was going on her first trip abroad. I wrote her a London Guide. "London, here I come! Where's the greatest coffee and chocolate ice cream? At Claridge's. Go to lunch there. Costs the world and is worth it. Ask Ernest for his Pauline Frederick dessert. Chocolate cake in chocolate goo with whip cream. I saw Pauline Frederick in *Joseph and His Brethren* before I left Wollaston and sometime after that she got to be a big movie star. When she came to London, she stayed at the Savoy, sent for Ernest who was maître d' there. 'I don't want to go out and have a lot of publicity,' she told him. 'I want to stay in and eat. Here's a cake recipe, always have it on the menu,' and he always has.

"For lobster, go to Driver's. Willie Maugham sent me there. Sit at a table or up at the counter. *Great!* Look it up in phone book. It's just off Regent St., go! Also go to Scott's, Piccadilly Circus.

Great lobster up at counter or at table. It's got several restaurants all under the same roof, but turn left into the one that looks out on Piccadilly and a side street.

"Also drop in for lunch at Chez Victor. Binkie Beaumont, John Gielgud, Peggy Ashcroft, lots of show folk sit at the ten tables. Cheap, dandy and interesting! Biftek, pommes frites? Salade saison? The best!

"Swell Soho restaurant that Princess Margaret goes to is the White Tower. Look it up. Gorgeous food and bring money.

"Gunther's for tea on Curzon Street right by the Dorchester. It used to be on Berkeley Square and used to be gorgeous, but still good. Take it in.

"For real English, go to Brown's Hotel, sit in lounge and have high tea. All the county folk are there. Take a look, you'll know you're not at Sardi's. Take a slice of their pink frosted cake, also a hunk of their Dundee.

"Are you aiming for a little class? Tea at the Ritz.

"Elizabeth Arden is on Bond Street. Hair done, manicure, nice bits and pieces to buy, bags, dressing gowns. Poke around, but first ask for Mrs. St. John to arrange about hair tint, set, manicure. Also foot fixer. Gr-reat!

"Asprey's? To die! Combination Bergdorf-Tiffany-Paradise. Fabulous bags, fabulous cashmere shawls to throw over your dressing room couch, fabulous everything. It's a must. Bond Street. Corner of Grafton? Upstairs, Sir Henry Irving used to live. Was *he* crazy about Asprey's, too?

"Walk up and down Bond Street and look and look! Fritter away some time, then fritter over to Hill Street. 35 is where Nancy Astor lives. Don't be so above it all, it's nice to see where.

"Queen Mum lives at Clarence House, just back of St. James's Palace. Walk through St. James's courtyard, then left and you'll know it by the guards. Be a tourist, what do *you* care?

"Take a taxi to Pelham Place. Adorable! Cecil Beaton lives at 8. Oliver Messel at 17. Next to it in Pelham Crescent lives Emlyn Williams, number 15. Eric Ambler, 16.

"Sweaters? Cashmere? A *must!!* W. Bill, Ltd., 12 South Moulton St., W. 1, one block from Claridge's. Ask for Miss Fitzgerald and have her send stuff to boat or plane, then no tax. Save while you're young!

"Gorgeous tweed? Pink tweed? The Cuchullin Handloom Co., Ltd., 31 Beauchamp Place, S.W.3 and leave time to walk around there. If your soles and heels are on the blink, Thackeray Shoe Repair, 6F, Knightsbridge. 2 minutes from your hotel, whatever hotel. Why is that?

"Cyclax is across from W. Bill's at 58 S. Moulton St. Wonderful cold cream, gorgeous soap, toilet water called Gay Chiffon. Queen uses their stuff. Would you hate to have skin like hers?

"Wonderful dentist I hope you don't need. Mr. George Cross, Eastman Dental Hospital, Gray's Inn Road, W.C.1.

"Another. Mr. Arthur Sturridge, 29A Wimpole St., W.1. Dentists are called Mister.

"Another. (Everybody goes away in August.) Mr. A. Garrow, 72 Harley St., W.1.

"Great throat doctor. Looks down Queen's. Dr. John Musgrove. 34 Wimpole St., Welbeck 3593.

"Edith Evans lives at Albany, Piccadilly. Byron lived there and Macaulay and God knows who else. Don't refer to it as 'the.' It's just Albany.

"Take a taxi to Kensington Palace Gardens. It's a road with an open gate at each end. Look at old mansions. Some are closed up. Some are embassies. French Embassy is Number 11. A good Sunday pastime when most of London shuts down. Princess Margaret lives here and Princess Marina, Duchess of Kent.

"Fortnum and Mason? Paradise on all floors. You can have lunch there and take snacks back to hotel to eat in the room. Don't be swell. Fortnum's is on Piccadilly near Ritz.

"Walk along Oxford Street to Holborn District. Go to Lincoln's Inn. Ask for 23 Old Buildings. It's Tony Guthrie's address. Nice to see where the great live. Also look at the rest of the place. Try it by moonlight. Or at dusk.

"John Gielgud is 16 Cowley St. Right by Westminster Abbey. Old streets with snug houses. See it.

"The Silver Vaults? Ask any taxi man. Chancery Lane, W.C.2. Vaults full of silver they give away. Go! It's stores and stores and stores all underground. Go!

"Tower of London? Crown Jewels? Beefeaters? Take it in.

"And take the Brighton Belle (a train) from Victoria Station. Buy a 1st-class ticket. And look out both sides. The scenery is equally adorable right and left. In an hour you're at Brighton. Go to the Hotel Royal Crescent by taxi and from there go down and walk along the shore. When you come to the Toonerville Trolley get in. Five minutes later at Black Rock get out and walk beneath the great cliffs. It's four miles to Rottingdean, adorable village. Have a great tea in the garden of the tea room. (You can't miss it.) Rottingdean is that kind of a place. A beautiful home on the green is where Enid Bagnold lives. 'Burne-Jones' it says on the plaque. Rudyard Kipling's house is across the green. Ring Enid's bell and if she's home say hello for me. Go back to station on top of the bus. Scary, but great. Want to look at Brighton Pavilion? Fabulous home of George IV, and opposite is the Theatre Royal where we all play on the world's most uneven stage. Don't miss tea at Fuller's. Don't miss their choc layer cake. Wow! Lunch at Wheeler's. Dover sole. Wow! If it's a weekday eat at English's. Wow! Ask anybody. Also ask for the antique district. Little twisted lanes full of gorgeousness of just what you want to buy. Also if you like to, go for a swim.

"Back in London? Harvey Nichols Dept. Store, Knightsbridge, 2 minutes taxi from hotel. Adorable everything, like Bonwit's. Further along, by a block or so, is Harrod's Dept. Store, paradise in all departments. Food store? Men's store? Junior Miss? You name it, they've got it. And *great!* Go!

"You want an adorable skirt? Wooland's. Look around. Floris is on Jermyn St. back of Fortnum and Mason's. Gorgeous soap. All their perfumes are great, but Sandalwood!!! Gorgeous true lily of the valley, bath oil number something. It's the popular one. *They'll* know. Is it Number 127?

"Great hats? You don't wear them? Maybe you should. Simone Mirman's, 9 Chesham Place off Belgrave Square, makes Princess Margaret's.

"Go to Mary Lee Fairbanks' foot fixer for when you walk too much, Arthur Mock, Regency House, 1 Warwick St. Gerard 4497. Never say four four 97, say double four nine seven.

"Look at Cheyne Walk, Chelsea, lovely row of houses! Sargent had one. And Carlyle. And Laurence Olivier. And Whistler. And maybe his mother.

"If you buy big things, they can be freighted or crated to take home. Pitt and Scott, 1–3 St. Paul's Churchyard, London E.C.1. City 6474. Buy a lot. It's nice.

"Cameo Corner. Look in the phone book. It's one block from Oxford St. and one from the British Museum. Antique jewelry all the way from a canary diamond to a safety pin! Look around and see if Edith Sitwell is in. Or Queen Mary. The owner calls her H.M.

" 'Why?' asked Garson.

" 'Because she asks "How much?" all the time.'

"Charing Cross Road for second-hand book stores. It's between Shaftesbury Avenue and the Strand. Or between Shaftesbury Avenue and Oxford St. You'll find them.

"Eat some potted shrimp. Eat Gooseberry Fool (dessert)! Drink Stone Ginger (ginger ale).

"Jaegers? Tartan pleated skirts? Regent St.

"Greatest gloves outside Paris? At the White House, a department store. Bond St.

"Did I put down Lyon's Corner House, Piccadilly Circus? Have Swiss roll and their tea. The greatest! Bath buns? Eat one for me. Their ice cream? Grand.

"Nice pink linen sheets? Selfridge's, Oxford St. Grand department store. Very cheap and *great!*

"Lovely personal maid? 7 shillings sixpence the hour. Catherine Shaw, 16 Deyburgh Road, Putney, S.W.15. (That's London.) You call her Miss Shaw. She's great. Presses, packs, shops.

"Do you use Leichner's makeup for stage or off? The greatest! What more can I say? Go to tiny shop on Leicester Square next to Warner's Cinema. Frizell's is the name. Just get some, you'll never go back to pancake. Use their greasepaint base, rouge, the works.

"Want a great cook? Scottish are the best. Mrs. Massey's Agency, 100 Baker Street, London W.1. Welbeck 6581. Our cook was Mrs. Ball. Believe it or not, she was six feet tall. And great. Garson thought she was a man. Who knows?

"Fabulous perfume? J. N. Taylor, 67 Mortimer St. Get Verveine Water, Nicotiana, Heliotrope. Try all their very different kinds at the shop, then choose them all.

"Need a wig? Nobody in the world is like Stanley Hall. For on stage or off. Makes them for Vivien Leigh, Elizabeth Taylor. Wig Creations, 22 Portman Close, W.1. Hunter 0771. 4 lines. Give my love to Stanley. Keep some for yourself.

"I wish I was going every place with you, except the doctor and dentists.

"When you leave London (and how can you?) take the Golden Arrow to Paris. It goes from Victoria Station where you took the Brighton Belle. Go early and look at the names of trains going all the places. Don't eat much on English train. On the channel boat get a cabin de luxe on deck. It costs 1 pound or $2.80. Great! Have a glass of champagne, and a ham sandwich. *No more!* Wait for grand lunch on French train. Through Cook's, demand 'first sitting.' In Paris have car meet train. Write or cable to 'Garage Quillet, 11 rue Mesnil, Paris XVI, Phone: Passy 62-12,' ask for Paul as chauffeur, but all their chauffeurs are great. M. Quillet is a dear man and his cars cost no more than a taxi. Sight-see in one, his chauffeurs are English-speaking. Say you're friends of M. Kanin. Pronounce it Can-Ann. That's how *they* do. When they say Maugham, they say Mog-Um, but that's for my South of France Guide."

Where are the snows of yesteryear? A lot of it's melted, but *some* is still there!

❈  ❈  ❈  ❈  ❈

Did you know Arthur Macrae? I hope so. Charles Laughton got Paramount to bring him over to help write *Ruggles of Red Gap.* Charles told me about him, then forgot him. Arthur and I met on a blind date.

"How will I know you?" I asked him.

"I'll be humming a snatch."

During the war he was in the Royal Air Force. He wrote, "You do know the ENSA tour was responsible for the breakthrough at Caen. The chaps saw Ivor and Diana in *Love from a Stranger.* That did it."

65

# *Friend*

I F YOU DIDN'T KNOW Arthur, did you know Charles?

"Are you going to Scarborough Fair?" sing Simon and Garfunkel. Charles Laughton came from there. Up in the north of England, on the coast. We have Scarboroughs, too, in our country. Up the coast of Maine. And in Rhode Island. Charles came from the English one. His people had the hotel there. They wanted him to be in the hotel business and sent him to London with a note to Claridge's. Claridge's made him a desk clerk, but some of the guests took fright, so he was sacked. Good for Claridge's. They barreled him out of the business and along his remarkable course.

"Scarborough where I was born. Like *A Trip to Scarborough*."

"What's a trip to Scarborough?" I asked.

"You don't know it? Sheridan's great comedy?"

Most people don't know *A Trip to Scarborough*. They know *The School for Scandal*. Charles knew that *and A Trip to Scarborough*. The things he *didn't* know, he was inclined to dismiss. The things he *did* know, he was astonished at his friends' ignorance. "You don't know *A Trip to Scarborough?* You don't know 'Here run in adoors quickly; get a Scotch coal fire in the parlour, set all the Turkey work chairs in their places, get the brass candlesticks out, and be sure stick the socket full of laurel—run.' You don't know that?" *He* knew it.

Nothing in Charles' life was simple, including his New York debut. *Payment Deferred* was announced to open one hot September night in 1931. That night the Lyceum Theatre was hotter than hell in the Old Testament. Laughton postponed his debut. Did anyone in theatre history ever do that? Do *you* know anyone that postponed his opening for better weather? When *Payment Deferred did* open, it was a cool night and New York saw an actor worth waiting for. A great actor. Not only for our day, but for all days. Unique in his talent, unique in his looks, unique in his approach to life. His knowledge wasn't something he learned at an academy, it was learned from the tune in his head.

After a performance of *Payment Deferred*, Jed Harris brought me to meet the Laughtons at the Chatham Hotel on East 48th Street. Small, elegant, formal, expensive and didn't look it. It might have been in Mayfair.

Why is it a surprise to be liked? The Laughtons liked me and I liked them. Was it based on admiration? Mine for them was boundless. They came to see me in *A Church Mouse* and praise flowed.

Our liking lasted through New York and strengthened in Hollywood where Charles and Elsa lived at the Garden of Allah, once the estate of the great Nazimova and now a cluster of rented bungalows around the pool that had been Alla's. There, Benchley and Dottie Parker and all the bright people sat and told stories for then and now and always. And when they couldn't think of anything else to do, wrote them down and sold them.

One night Charles sat watching twilight color the Hollywood hills. "Actors couldn't think up this place if they tried," he said. "I want this to be my home."

Inside the Laughtons' bungalow, their English cook served boiled fowl and bread sauce for dinner and whatever veg seemed reminiscent of marrow. It was as English as Scarborough, but beside the pool Marc Connelly told his new play to Pare Lorentz and Charley Butterworth and sometimes wrote it and more often didn't. And Donald Ogden Stewart said funny things that would be repeated at New York's "21." Charles felt at home.

He also felt he was going to make film history. And did. He was going to play Marmaduke Ruggles, a gentleman's gentleman won at a Paris poker game when the Honorable George lost his shirt plus his manservant to a big noise from Red Gap, Montana. Charles knew a great event was about to take place and wanted to curve me in. "You must be the Widow Judson," he said and told Paramount I was the greatest. Paramount, not as hasty as Charles, arranged for a test.

I'd made movie tests before, but I'd never gotten the part, so for this test Charles supervised my costume, hairdo and makeup, meanwhile telling everybody I was the funniest, the most original, the most unusual, the most.

What could have happened between those days and the day we saw the test? Nothing much was on the screen, ZaSu Pitts got the job and I got the message. Whatever else I was great at, it wasn't making movie tests. Thank you, Charles. Thank you, Paramount. No tests and I got into pictures.

"Actors couldn't think up this place if they tried." I wondered if he was right.

"The Theatre Guild wants me to do *The Country Wife*," he said. "By the way, it has a good part for you."

Margery Pinchwife has been a good part since sixteen hundred and something, but it was Charles that told *me* so in Hollywood's Garden of Allah.

A year later in New York, Thornton Wilder and I sat on my 60 West 12th Street front steps. "Be part of the great world, go out, meet people, be at parties—" urged Thornton.

"We could be at a party now. Tony Perry invited me to one at her apartment up on Park Avenue."

At supper Lawrence Langner sat on my right. "Westport opens a month from tonight with *The Country Wife*, dear."

I looked at him astonished. "You're going to do that without *me?*"

"I didn't know you wanted to do summer stock, dear."

"How can you do it *without* me?" Thornton brought me to the party, Charles supplied the ideas.

"Would you want to come to Westport, dear?"

"Send me the script, I don't remember the play." How *could* I? I'd never read it.

During the week at the Westport Country Playhouse, Helen

Hayes came. She went to work on Gilbert Miller to give me the chance to do *The Country Wife* on Broadway and told Gilbert she'd be his partner. Until this generous idea took shape, she invited me to go to London with her on the new *Normandie* to meet Rex Whistler, designer of the beauteous scenery and costumes for *Victoria Regina*.

Claridge's phone rang. "We want to give a party for you." It was Charles and Elsa. They were living in Thackeray's Bloomsbury at their house in Gordon Square. "Who shall we ask?"

"Every actor and actress in London and H. G. Wells," we said.

They were there. Plus Virginia Woolf, plus David Garnett. Theatre great, men of letters, ladies of letters climbed the Gordon Square stairs. Charles and Elsa lived up a flight and rented the downstairs to a wholesale Hay, Grain and Feed. Or Corporate Solicitors. Or something. But *up* the stairs past Hay or Corporate, Gordon Square was alive with ideas.

Helen was also alive with ideas. A year later she and her partner Gilbert booked me to sail on the *Queen Mary* heading for Southampton. Again Gordon Square made me welcome. *The Country Wife*'s American leading lady was given comfort and confidence to open at the Old Vic, where a few seasons before, Charles had tackled Macbeth and Henry the Eighth and Prospero among others. He'd also finished *Rembrandt* and would soon start another for Korda.

The Vic was opening its 1936 season with *Love's Labour's Lost* followed by *The Country Wife*, both of them directed by Tyrone Guthrie. Elsa said we must go to *Love's Labour's Lost*'s first night. "Not to might make a bad impression," she said. We went and the play made a bad impression. I didn't like it.

"Oh dear, what would I do if you were Charles?" moaned Elsa. "When Charles is miserable he tries to learn something. Would you want to practice laughter?" She and I laughed and laughed till Dodie Smith, sitting next to us, asked why? We explained, and before the evening was over, all three of us were laughing quite skillfully. Elsa had plenty of practice how to prevent people from making a bad impression.

At rehearsals I worried about myself, but even more about Mr.

Sparkish, a fop of seventy acted by a nineteen-year-old. When I told Charles, he worried, too. Like me, he could see all that Leichner's Healthy Old Age greasepaint and painted wrinkles. Tony Guthrie didn't worry about the nineteen-year-old septuagenarian, but he worried about me being worried and fired the actor. His name was Alec Guinness.

I also worried about young Michael Redgrave playing Mr. Horner. Charles, wanting everything to go right for my first London appearance, offered to play the part at no salary.

"You were a nice little Macbeth, dear," said Lilian Baylis, "but you don't look like Mr. Horner."

As opening night got closer, I forgot about Sparkish and Horner and worried about myself. I made Charles and Elsa promise not to come. The evening went off to bravos and as I stepped from the stage into the long stone passage, back of the scenery, there was Charles, open arms. And Elsa. They'd stood in line for the standing-room privilege, afraid if they booked seats I'd hear about it.

We went back to Gordon Square with old friend Arthur Macrae and new friend Edith Evans, *The Country Wife*'s great Lady Fidget. We supped on the Cornish basket that arrived biweekly from Cornwall, brown Cornish loaves, cream so thick it didn't pour, sweet butter, and chicken. A memory! Charles knew about food and admired it.

The weekend after the opening, Charles and Elsa drove me to the cottage in Surrey. It didn't have a proper bathroom, only a septic-tank arrangement. Was there ever a colder place? They loved it because a tree grew through the roof. And they loved their land that bordered on a dukedom. The duke's deep forest was like Arden. Maybe it was Arden.

"Put a log on the fire," said Charles and launched into an enraptured description of André Obey's *Noah* which the Compagnie des Quinze had made memorable on a Paris stage. "Put on a log," he said. Did Charles ever do anything manual? He could have. It didn't occur to him.

> "*When icicles hang by the wall,*
> *And Dick the shepherd blows his nail*

*And Tom bears logs into the hall,*
*And milk comes frozen home in pail—"*

Charles stopped.

"—milk comes frozen home in pail." He tasted the words. "—blows his nail." He laughed his inaudible laugh.

"Do you know *Love for Love?* Congreve. 'The jut of her bum would stir an anchorite!' " He fell in love with language.

"Methinks a college education is a thought too pedantic for a gentleman—" Did Charles laugh? He appreciated.

The Old Vic engagement was closing. Charles came to say good-bye to me at Claridge's where once he'd frightened the guests. A friend from Paris was with me. Charles talked to her in flowing French.

"Where did you learn?" I asked.

"The army." He was surprised at the question. Didn't everybody?

At the Comédie Française his performance was received in awe. Awe, followed by salvos. Was it *Le Malade Imaginaire?* Whatever it was, "La Tradition Laughton" was included in ensuing performances.

The September hot spell of 1939 topped the *Payment Deferred* weather and found Charles and Elsa fanning themselves in Allah's Garden and me searching for an electric fan to temper the Chateau Elysee. By day I was Mary Todd Lincolning at Gower Street's RKO Studio. At RKO's ranch in the valley Charles, as the Hunchback, debated with director William Dieterle.

"It was unbearable today," Charles said happily. "The putty noses all ran off. Notre Dame was 136 ° in the shade." It pleased him that when *he* worked, even the heat was legendary.

"Bill, this is Ruth Gordon, a very great actress."

Dieterle bowed and took off. He had had plenty of trouble with Laughton. Was a very great actress five foot nothing with her hair in a braid pinned round her head? No makeup? Yellow cotton dress and rope-sole shoes? Dieterle had put up with a lot from Laughton. "Tell them I want to see some out-takes on *Abe Lincoln in Illinois*," he said.

7 I

Most of us get aggravated and cool off. Or get aggravated at something *else*. Dieterle's aggravation took him to the projection room to see that infuriating Laughton's idea of "very great."

The day after came an offer to play Edward G. Robinson's wife in *Dr. Ehrlich's Magic Bullet*, directed by the very great Dieterle. Charles looked at me with loathing. "God damn it!" he said. "Why can't I do that for *Elsa?*"

Charles loved the West. The air. The grandeur. One weekend we drove up to Lake Arrowhead. Somewhere this side of San Bernardino we stopped to see the Padua Hills players. What were they doing, was it a play or a happening? It was going on when we arrived. The sun started down. It was going on when we left. And through the whole thing, chickens wandered around underfoot wherever the actors were acting.

"That's what's lacking in the West End, do you follow me? And on Broadway. The plays all have form and the dressing rooms are urinals, do you follow me?" This was the year of "Do you follow me?"

Goodbye to the Garden of Allah. The Laughtons bought the house at Pacific Palisades. It was a grand house. Renoir's *Judgment of Paris* hung over the mantel. But not center. Skewed off a little.

In the hall a Rousseau hung left of center as you came in. "You never heard of the Customs House man that became the greatest—"

And in the small room, askew, was the black man Horace Pippin. "You never heard of Horace Pippin? The great American primitive—"

Years after when everybody *had* heard of him and he won an award at the Pennsylvania Academy, I bought Pippin's *The Milkman of Goshen*. It hangs in our New York dining room. Over the mantel. But not center. Skewed off a little.

"Do you know Andrew Marvell?"

I didn't know *A Trip to Scarborough*, I didn't know *The Country Wife*, I didn't know Rousseau or Pippin or Andrew Marvell.

> *"The grave's a fine and private place*
> *But none, I think, do there embrace—"*

After that, I read Andrew Marvell. Mar*vell* he called it. Does everyone?

When Bosley Crowther reviewed *The Hunchback of Notre Dame* in *The New York Times*, he wrote, "Laughton overdoes."

I said to Crowther, "A careful, sincere performer does *not* overdo, but then you get a careful, sincere performance. Laughton is the grand style. Laughton paints big. Sometimes big goes *over*. Didn't it with Kean? A red wig for Shylock. Didn't it with Booth? His deep, deep, deep melancholy. How did Salvini reach the rafters? Was he careful to trim off the edges? With Laughton you get the great range and you also get some scaffolding. Look around it. There's a work of art inside."

Faraway Meadows. He came to our house in the Connecticut country. He said he *must* come, he needed our advice. "I'm going to do a one-man show and I want to do it for you. Then you tell me what you think about it."

"But films?" said Garson.

"The offers come slower. And they're not very good."

He would do his one-man show that evening, in the afternoon we walked through the woods. The wild flowers weren't very different from those in the Surrey woods. Charles knew them and ours. Cinquefeuille and Solomon's seal, lady's tobacco, red columbine, wild geranium, jack-in-the-pulpit, cowslip, lady's-slipper—he gathered them and damp moss from the brook to wrap around them to last the journey home.

Coming out of the wood onto a back country road, a car stopped. It was Gilbert Miller and Kitty with their maid, valet and chauffeur en route to their house up the hill from ours. Gilbert greeted Charles warmly. Some small talk and off sped the Miller car.

Charles and I walked on. "I don't like Gilbert Miller," he said.

My turn to be Elsa. "You think of Gilbert as if he were a friend, but everybody doesn't fall into that category. Gilbert is a Restoration character. Fascinating, informed, a brilliant storyteller, a—"

"You're right," he said eagerly. "Gilbert *is* Restoration, I was wrong to say I don't like him—"

At Southdown Farm, Gilbert was talking to his shepherd.

Anxious to make amends for misjudging him, Charles was all warmth. "What a fine flock you have, Gilbert," he said, looking over the meadow full of curly gray faces.

Gilbert glared at his shepherd. "I wish he'd get me a better price for them, instead of all these damn blue ribbons."

Charles and I walked up the hill toward the woods. "I don't like Gilbert Miller," he said.

The flowers stood the trip. Charles looked at them admiringly. "I must have a Chablis bottle to put the columbine in."

"We have all kinds of vases," said Garson.

"I need a Chablis bottle."

"Would this do?" Our maid offered him a slender green vase.

"No," said Charles. "A Chablis bottle."

"Open one," said Garson.

Red columbine in the Chablis bottle. Try it. You'll think of Laughton.

At the far end of the white parlor, he stood with his pile of books. In front of our white curtains came to life the Boy David, Nebuchadnezzar, Launce the servant of *Two Gentlemen of Verona*, Bottom the weaver—they filled the white parlor. And the Young Men's Hebrew Association. And auditoriums from one end of the world to the other. Charles. His pile of books. The tune in his head.

Hotel St. Moritz. New York. He had come home from Memorial Hospital. Elsa said I might go in. It was hot weather. Not as hot as at the RKO ranch, but hot as the time he postponed his debut at the Lyceum. He lay on the white sheet, another drawn over him, one bare arm along the edge of the bed. He was thinner. And whiter. Eyes deeper and very blue. He looked like one of his beloved French Impressionist paintings. On the bed table were twigs from Central Park he'd asked Elsa to pick. He wanted something growing.

We talked. We said things. We even laughed. We knew. A long chain of events, a long admiration, a long love lay between us. The visit ended. Tomorrow Charles would go on the plane to his beloved Hollywood "where an actor could not dream it up for himself."

I went down in the elevator. Picked up life again on 59th Street. Upstairs a great actor grappled with his fate.

Behind him he would leave great memories. Can anyone ask for more?

*   *   *   *   *

Anything that begins "I don't know how to tell you this" is *never* good news.

# 1970

D O YOU NOTICE much change?" people ask me. I wish Saturday nights I was seeing them at the Sixty Club. Saturday night if you were in show business you put on your Madam Frances or Lucille or Milgrim ballgown, your guy put on his tux, paid ten dollars and you walked down eight steps into the Ritz-Carlton's crystal ballroom. The Prince of the Asturias couldn't get in, if he wasn't in show business. Or with someone that was.

Ziegfeld danced with Billie Burke and married her. That was exceptional, but every manager was there with his wife, girl, or both. Jeanne Eagels, Alice Brady, Blanche Bates, Grace George, George M. Cohan, Clifton Webb, Clifton Crawford, Al Jolson, the Dolly Sisters, the Fairbanks Twins, Marilyn Miller, Charlie Dillingham, Gus Thomas, Edgar Selwyn, Arch Selwyn, Emma Haig, Emma Carus, Emma Dunn, Fannie Ward, Fanny Brice, Hazel Dawn, Mitzi Hajos, Flora Zabelle, Raymond Hitchcock were there eating chicken à la king or lobster Américain. It was Prohibition, so you brought your wine in under your wrap. One Saturday Pola Negri came. And Ernst Lubitsch. One Saturday we saw Mae Murray. And one Saturday there was Rudolph Valentino. Why was that a drag? Next Saturday night would you hate to shag around with Natalie Wood or Mia Farrow or Ali McGraw or Barbara Harris or Betty Bacall or Mike Nichols or Hal Prince or Steve Sondheim or Irving Berlin or Doc Simon or Jerry Orbach or Robbins? What's David

Merrick doing, he's too busy to walk down those eight steps next Saturday night and swing with show business? Etan, what did you and David do *last* Saturday that was better than that?

❄   ❄   ❄   ❄   ❄

I'm glad we're fliers. On Super Chief, Garson turned on me. Cecil Beaton was making the trip with us and Super Chief hadn't passed Pasadena when Cecil said, "I want to tell you about my engagement to Greta and why it was broken off, but you must *promise* you won't tell a soul."

"Don't tell us," said I.

"No, I want to, but I want it to go no further."

"Don't."

"Pinkie," said Garson, "Cecil *wants* to tell us."

"Don't," I said.

"No, I know I can trust you."

"Don't."

"What's the matter with you, Ruth? Cecil *wants* to."

"Don't. If it's no good, I don't want to hear it and if it is, I'll have a problem."

Garson was cross and so was Cecil, but could *you* keep secret why Garbo and Cecil broke off their engagement? I'm weak as water and thank God, I know it!

# On!

W HEN YOU CAN FIND HIM, do, but there's nothing predictable
about Tyrone Guthrie. His guiding motto is "On!" It took
him to Swansea to stage Emlyn Williams' play *Pen Don* with the
Swansea Acting Society. The cast was newsboys, schoolteachers
and people of Swansea, the only professional was Tyrone Guthrie,
not yet Sir.

"We'll come to see it," said Garson.

Tony wrote out the date and the place, the Natural History Museum, Swansea, Wales.

Did you ever take the train to Swansea on a February day? No
idle gesture that! Euston Station? Or is it Paddington? And once
the train leaves, it goes and goes and goes. On our trip a wild-eyed
young man got restless, came and stood in the carriage door.
"You're all no good and God should destroy you *all*," he shouted at
us. "He ought to end all your bloody, useless lives and He will."

Well, don't blame that on Tyrone Guthrie, he didn't stage *that*.

"Caswell Bay Hotel," we told the taxi.

"I don't know if I want that long a fare."

"Where is it?"

"Caswell Bay."

"Where's that?"

"Five miles yonder, on the cliffs." Why did Tyrone Guthrie
have to reserve us a room way out there?

Have *you* ever been to Swansea? It gets bleaker the further away you get. More black cliffs, more black windy clouds, then the road opens and you get a load of the bay churning itself to soapsuds down below. Up above, with a good view of all that cold water down below, is the Caswell Bay Hotel.

They led us to a room on the front.

"Have you one without the window broken?" I asked.

The boy looked at me as though I was a kook. "Don't you like fresh air?"

"Not this time of year."

"Here's one, but it's got no towels."

"Might we move some in from another room?"

"I shouldn't do that if I were you."

We took the one with no towels. Deal with that later.

A note said Tony and Judy could be reached at Oystermouth.

"Where's Oystermouth?"

"Three miles yonder." He pointed back to town.

We drove it. The bell to the Guthries' digs didn't answer. "On," we told our driver. "Natural History Museum."

Judy was on her knees in a room lined with glass cases of priceless Swansea china. She was turning up the hem of a slip on a member of the Acting Society. "What are you doing here?" she screamed.

"Tony invited us."

"Tomorrow! The opening is *tomorrow*."

We showed our letter.

"Tonight is dress rehearsal for the Curator, but of course you're welcome to come."

The Guthries gave us tea and lava bread.

Draw the veil on that latter.

At seven-thirty we filed in. Around the walls were the treasures, in the center was a big oblong platform. The Curator and lady sat through the show under his umbrella, due to inclement weather. The elements found a leak in the roof.

Did it matter? You can always find a theatre where the roof doesn't leak, but in Swansea's Natural History Museum we saw a great event. Tony's miracle of staging, the newsboys' and schoolteachers' unforgettable performance and Emlyn's great play.

"Excuse me, I'm not going," said the young boy when his folks were forced to leave their mountain. "Excuse me, I'm not going."

What will *you* remember all your life? I'll remember the people having to leave Pen Don and the young one reiterating, "Excuse me, I'm not going."

When next we went to see Tony, we didn't. We walked up the twisting stone steps to his flat in Lincoln's Inn, Old Buildings. "Gone to Holland to see the tulips. Back next week" was scribbled on a slip of paper glued to his door. No "Excuse me," like the young one said, just "Gone to Holland" and so forth and so on. When you can find Tony Guthrie, do.

\* \* \* \* \*

"Did you see *Applause?*" asked the interviewer.

"Yes," said Ina Claire.

"Well, Miss Claire, did girls have to sleep with the director or the author or the manager to get a job?"

"Of course not," said Ina. "Unless, of course, they didn't have any talent."

\* \* \* \* \*

Dottie Parker called it fuff, but in the crevices of my handbag there's not only fuff, but sugar. It came off the Meggazones. Do you use Meggazones? Sir Robert Helpmann said, "I wouldn't act Hamlet without one stuck in my back teeth."

Well, it's Judy Anderson doing Hamlet but I have Meggazones in my handbag in case anybody asks me. Today is bag-cleaning day, everything out and there's all that sugar and fuff. I emptied it out my bedroom window. Fuff blows away, but sugar looks good on red bougainvillea. The way it sparkles makes me think of Christmas. Do you shop early? Why not buy some to sprinkle on the bougainvillea? I don't think saccharin will do it, better stick to sugar. Maybe it'll catch on and people will scrap those silver paper icicles. Weirder things have happened.

# At the Age of 91

"THERE WAS A TIME there when it seemed like every Saturday somebody died," said Angela.

She and I sat at her tea table in Ridgewood, New Jersey, the only ones left of the great Maude Adams Company, the others have joined the majority.

"It was a Saturday night that Alan Faucett died."

"Angela, should you live alone here?" I asked. Angela is ninety-one.

"This is my older sister Clara's house," she said as though it was the answer. "She and her husband built it sixty years ago. Nothing is changed."

The house was as impersonal as if Angela had rented it for the day.

"Do you remember when we stood in Wendy's house, Michael and John fighting for the smoke pot?" she asked.

Did I remember! *Peter Pan* was my start.

" 'It's always so,' Miss Adams told me. 'I couldn't play Peter if Michael and John didn't fight for the smoke pot.' "

At the 39 John Street tea table sat the only two who remembered.

"Do you remember how nobody could go backstage at the Empire? George the doorman saw a little man in the shadows by the stacked-up flats. 'Who are you?' asked George.

" 'Abe Erlanger.'

" 'Well, you'll have to go. Miss Adams doesn't like people back-stage.' Of course, Abe was the candy butcher at the stock company in Cleveland where Papa acted and Granny Erlanger lived across the street from us. The boys came to visit her often, they were good boys."

"Is that where you started, Angela? The Cleveland stock?"

"Oh, no, dear. Canada. When I was three I acted the little boy in *Miss Moulton* with Clara Morris. My *first* part was when I was two, but I don't really think that counts. That was in *Uncle Tom*. I played the little slave boy. The little boy engaged to play it was afraid of the gun going off. My mother asked me would I be afraid? 'No,' I said, 'I like the gunshoot.' Did you know Miss Adams thought of going over to entertain the troops?"

"No, I didn't."

"She asked would I go with her? I thought hard before I answered. If I said no, I was sure it would end my engagement with her. I said no. Miss Adams looked at me a long time. I could read 'the end.' 'I've always respected you,' she said at last. 'My respect has doubled.' "

What a wonderful person I started my career with! "Did she know when Grant Stewart used to sneak backstage at the Empire to talk about Equity?"

"Oh, Miss Adams knew. She knew Grant was coming up to David Torrence's dressing room. 'It's what *I've* always stood for,' she said. 'Extra pay for extra matinees, ladies given seats in the Pullman, cabs from the station to the hotel. I've always had that in my company, I never want to have an actress carry her bag into a trolley car, but I can't come out for it.'

" 'You know they are against the long hours,' I reminded her.

" 'What do you mean?'

" 'Our dress rehearsal at the Broad Street was called at eight at night and went on till eight-thirty in the morning.'

" 'Oh, but we were *opening*, we had to get it right. You can't *unionize* getting it right.' "

The dining-room table had a white cloth and embroidered doilies, a plate of little cakes frosted pink, a plate of Dundee cake, a plate of cookies. The Scottish lady looked in from next door. "Your kettle's not a-boil," she said.

Angela reproved her. "We were talking."

The Scottish lady made the tea, but wouldn't join us.

"Angela, did *you* believe in Equity?"

"Oh, yes. You know, my sister Vivia was a suffragette and she was one of the starters of Equity. I came in from a tour and saw the Equity parade marching down Broadway. One of them waved to me. It was my sister Vivia. I'd been away all season, so I stepped in beside her and marched. I thought it was as good a way as any to see her."

"Did that make you want to join Equity?"

"Not necessarily."

"When we played *Peter* in New York, Miss Adams lived at the Hotel Manhattan. Did she always live there?"

"I think we all lived at the old Buckingham Hotel, Miss Adams, Phyllis Robbins and me."

"What street was that?"

"Oh, I don't know, dear."

The Scottish lady stood and listened. Angela and I drank our tea facing each other. "I've never been to Europe, Ruth. I can't tell you how that surprises me."

I took a slice of the Dundee cake. Angela pointed to the frosted ones.

"No thank you."

"Want to take them home? That's what I always did when I went to a party."

Her neighbor for over thirty years asked when had we seen each other last?

We thought. "After Indianapolis stock," thought Angela.

"When was that?" asked Mary.

"1921. Did Angela tell you we dressed together in *Peter Pan?*" Angela nodded.

"Did you think I was going to be an actress, Angela?"

The ninety-one-year-old blue eyes looked off across the state of New Jersey. Finally they looked back at me. "I couldn't tell, dear," she said gently.

Isn't honesty a surprise?

"Do you think Miss Adams enjoyed life?"

"No."

"Never?"

"She didn't enjoy life. Only a part of it."

"When she was working on lighting?"

Angela nodded. "She enjoyed it when it didn't have anything to do with acting."

"Even when Mr. Frohman was alive?"

"He was very opinionated, you know. Once he and Miss Adams disagreed about how she read a line. It was in *The Legend of Leonora*. Mr. Frohman said, 'I'm going to get on a boat and ask Barrie,' and sailed that night.

" 'How does *she* read it?' " Barrie asked.

" 'She reads it to get a laugh.' "

" 'That's the way I wrote it.' "

I played Nibs in 1915 and now it was 1970. Angela went to the parlor and brought back a book. "I've saved this for you. It belonged to De Wolf Hopper's aunt. Her scrapbook." Angela's father had been with Mr. Hopper in *Bluebeard's Wives* and Mr. Hopper's aunt's book had wound up in the Ogden family. Now it was going home with me, brown paper leaves crinkled, edges broken off.

"Do you go out much, Angela?"

"Not much. I was the youngest of nine children, so I had to run all the errands."

"I'll come back for another tea party."

That night after dinner I thought I'd just glance through De Wolf Hopper's aunt's book. Why did my back hurt? The clock told me I'd been glancing nearly three hours. My table was snowed over with small crinkled bits broken off from old pages full of pictures of people I loved and admired and had read about and acted with. What surprises from those brown pages! Clara Blandick as Kyrle Bellew's leading woman at the Empire in *The Night of St. John?* Clara Blandick played the small part of Mr. Wheeler's snippy secretary in *Clarence* when we toured out to the Coast. "Constipated Clara" was how Grace Filkins referred to her. A

84

brown page for Grace Filkins? Young, dazzling, sexy, playing leads at the Empire and the Knickerbocker so many years before the tour of *Clarence*. Long before South Bend, Washington, where we waited for a listless train. No parlor car, a day coach with the windows open and cinders pouring in to join cinders already on board. The conductor stood on the car steps and barred the way. "Where are you going?" he asked Grace Filkins.

"I have *no* idea!" she said in her perfect Clyde Fitch voice. "Will someone please give me a kick in the behind to help me up these steps?"

At my apartment on West 59th Street, around from where the Jolson Theatre had been, I spent the evening with Angela and Vivia and sister Clara and Granny Erlanger and the Erlanger boys and the Empire Theatre's George and Mr. Hopper and his aunt and Michael and John and the irresistible smoke pot and Clara Morris and Grant Stewart sneaking Equity backstage where the great lady gave so many of us a chance. "You can't unionize perfection," she said and paid for our Pullman fare, paid for extra matinees and taxis to and from the train.

Darling Angela, you and I ate the Dundee tea cake, but how many came to our party!

# The Lady

I N THE Maude Adams company everybody behaved themselves.
Even Wally Jackson who knew when to take a discreet nip.
Never before the performance, but, the show over, Wally was
known to enjoy a something. Things didn't quite work out and one
matinee of *Chantecler* the duck that quacked had a hangover. He
quacked in the wrong place. Nothing was said, he'd been with the
company so long, but two nights later, as they waited after the final
curtain for the Lady to say goodnight, she walked over to Wally
Jackson. "Thank you so much for the beautiful silver ice pick you
gave me for my birthday, I think perhaps *you* need it more than
me."

The company laughed and applauded as she left the stage.

Do things like that happen at your show?

When Willard Barton came to deliver something to her at San
Francisco's St. Francis Hotel, Mary Murray, her personal maid,
took it into the bedroom. "Thank you," said the Lady's voice and
just as Willard started to say, "You're welcome, Miss Adams,"
around the bedroom door wagged a black-silk-stockinged leg en-
cased in a black Kayser silk bloomer.

Willard said he was so stunned he never told about it until four
years afterward, then wondered if it had ever happened. "It *must*
have," he insisted and lowered his voice. "How would *I* know the
Lady wore black silk bloomers?" He looked thoughtful. "It *had* to
have happened, I *saw* it."

86

Mr. Frohman engaged Richard Bennett to be the Lady's leading man. Dick Bennett was a great actor. Everybody knew it. They also knew he was a handful. A handful, a devil, a however-far-your-vocabulary-went, but for his acting the word was "great."

In *What Every Woman Knows* his part was John Shand, the young student who breaks into the Wylie household to read their books after the Wylies have gone to bed. The Wylie brothers catch him and are about to clap him into jail till they think of offering him the choice of marrying their old-maid sister.

Onstage Dick Bennett was a great John Shand, but backstage he and Miss Adams clashed. They clashed quite often. And quite loud. When the season was over, it was a pleasure to them both to say goodbye.

The next season when Maude Adams opened in *Chantecler* playing the part Coquelin played in Paris, she got an opening-night wire from Dick Bennett. "How happy you must be to be your own leading man."

(*Players' Guide*, omit.)

On tour, Miss Adams' laundry was sent back to West 40th Street to the English Hand Laundry opposite the stage door of the Empire. Traveling with her were her personal maid and her theatre maid, both named Mary, but twice a week the laundry boxes were mailed back to New York. From Philadelphia or Detroit or Ishpeming, Michigan, they went to West 40th, opposite the stage door of the Empire. Once Sophie Eggert showed me a handkerchief. M.E.A.K. was embroidered in the corner. Some of the company said it stood for Maude Elizabeth Adams Kiskadden, some said it stood for Maude Ewing Adams Kiskadden. Like most things about the Lady, nobody actually knew. Not even Wally Jackson who'd been with her how long? Nor Freddie Tyler who'd been in *The Legend of Leonora* nor R. Peyton Carter, so often her Captain Hook.

Sophie showed me a nightgown. It was white nainsook with little tucks and hemstitching and fine Valenciennes lace and where most ladies have pink or blue satin ribbon run through the entre-deux, the Lady's nightgown had narrow moss-green velvet. Why was that so indescribably charming? Why did it make you think of Peter Pan?

Sophie said the nuns made all her lingerie and handkerchiefs and embroidered the M.E.A.K. on everything. They were in a convent in France where Miss Adams had passed a season. Or was it a year? No one was sure how long, but everyone was sure that one season the stage's biggest star didn't appear. Some said she had tuberculosis, some said she had twins. But twins or tuberculosis, she was cured of the latter and did anyone ever see the kids?

She never married, or if she did, no one ever knew about it. Mr. Frohman didn't marry either. Well, that's their business. The legend of his love persisted, without evidence, unless you count his dedication to her career. He managed Billie Burke and Ethel Barrymore and John Drew and others, but for Maude Adams came *Romeo and Juliet*, extravagant beyond dreams and a failure. *L'Aiglon*, extravagant and a failure. *Chantecler*, the *most* extravagant and a failure. Frohman cast them with only the best actors to be hired. Did it matter if the plays failed? Maude Adams' triumphs in *Peter Pan*, in *The Little Minister*, in *Quality Street*, in *What Every Woman Knows*, brought full houses for as long as she chose to play them in Philadelphia, New York, Norfolk, Norwalk, Atlantic City, Mason City, Bridgeport, Hancock, Boston and Chicago. At every box office MAUDE ADAMS on the houseboards made the cash pour in.

Inside the house that the lost boys built for Wendy stood Peter and Nibs and Second Twin and John and Michael Darling, the way Angela remembered, and outside sat Wendy and Slightly and Curly and First Twin playing the scene. Nightly Michael and John wrestled over who should hold the smoke pot that made smoke curl out of Wendy's chimney and give the place that lived-in look.

John pushed Michael. Michael shoved John. Was this the way to behave in front of the Lady? She saw us worrying. She shook her pretty head. "Michael and John *always* fight over who should hold the smoke pot," she whispered. "It started in 1905 and is one of the few things to remain constant. I should miss it."

Yes, Angela, I do remember.

The Lady closed her 1915–1916 season July 5th in hot Springfield, Illinois. The company's last evening together was on the sleeper. One by one we were bidden into the drawing room. Miss

Clarens first, Miss Ogden second, old Mrs. Ada Boshell, Miss Gillen, Mr. Tyler, Mr. Carter, Mr. Torrence, Mr. Jackson who'd quack like a duck when asked to, Mr. Carhart who asked for a room with running water, two windows and a rocking chair for a dollar a day, our Rob Dow, Lady Babbie's Gavin Dishart all went in in the order of their importance and all called Mr. Mrs. or Miss after how many years for some of them? I was the newest to join and the least important, so I was the last to say goodbye. Would the Lady ask me to stay with the company and play in *A Kiss for Cinderella?* She'd asked some people. Tonight would she ask me?

"Miss Gordon," called Willard Barton, then whispered, "Hurry up, she's tired." He opened the door, Miss Adams sat riding backward. After years of touring does an actress know the difference? All in black: black flowing skirt, black high-collared blouse, black hat though she'd been on the train all that hot July 5th day and soon was going to sleep. The high collar set off her adorable face with curtains drawn except when acting. "Do you know what you will do?" she asked.

"I wish I might stay with you."

"I'm sorry there's no part."

That hope went out the open window. "I wish there was, but I'm going to be an actress."

"You don't think of going home?"

"Oh heavens, no."

She held out her hand. "It was nice having you. The best of luck."

"Thank you for giving me the chance." We shook hands. Was she embarrassed by my feeling? She'd been an actress since she was six weeks old. Was staying on the stage all that important?

"I hope I can be with you again."

"I hope so."

Willard Barton had the door open. That was as long as I should take up the Lady's time and I was out. The Maude Adams season had ended. We hugged, shook hands, exchanged addresses, promises, wishes, but epilogue was her handshake. With that the season closed.

All of us were going back to New York with money that we'd

saved and memories. On a train between Cedar Rapids and Daven-port Mr. Tyler might tell the story of when the Lady was going to do *The Ladies' Shakespeare* for the first time and Mr. Barrie came to Atlantic City. "Watching rehearsals at the Apollo Theatre on the Boardwalk, Barrie thought a new scene was needed. He went back to the Traymore, wrote it and sent it over.

"The director looked at it. Then looked at it some more. Miss Adams was in her dressing room, so he had time to look again. The Lady was still in her dressing room, so he called the stage manager over. 'Read me this.'

"Stage manager, flattered, took the pages, looked at them, then looked some more.

"A rustle of admiration meant the Lady was coming onstage. 'Has Mr. Barrie sent the scene over?'

" 'We were just looking at it, Miss Adams.' Director snatched it from stage manager's hands and offered the pages to his star. Stage manager slid up a chair for her.

"She didn't sit, just looked at the pages. Then looked some more. Then looked again. 'I can't read this,' she said. 'Can you?'

" 'No, Miss Adams.' He turned to stage manager. 'Can you?'

"No, sir."

" 'Ask Mr. Barrie if he would please come over,' said the pretty, pretty voice.

"Mr. Barrie was pleased to speed down the Boardwalk in a chair. Past the saltwater taffy, past the pier the horse jumped off every afternoon at four, past grand hotels, Mr. Barrie rolled up to the stage door.

" 'We're so sorry we weren't able to read your writing. Be a dear and read it to us.'

"Stage manager and assistant and assistant's assistant whisked a circle of kitchen chairs in place, an armchair facing the circle for Miss Adams, armchair for Mr. Barrie.

"A hush.

"Barrie looked at the pages, cleared his throat, looked at the pages, looked some more, looked again, looked at Miss Adams. 'I can't either,' he said."

(Dramatists' Guild members, does that ever happen to you?)

In places like Hancock, Michigan, Miss Adams lived on her private car. Riding over to the Opera House, she saw Gladys Gillen and me. On the callboard that night it said, "The ladies of the company are requested to wear hat and gloves in public."

On one-nighters Miss Adams invited the ladies to sleep on her private car and in the morning, coffee and rolls were served by her steward. The men had to leave a five A.M. call at the hotel.

(Men's Lib, copy.)

The Lady, of course, was in the drawing room. She never came out. Nor did any sound. Only when Miss Phyllis Robbins arrived from Boston looking like she had, did we hear anything in the drawing room. Miss Robbins walked through the car glancing nor left nor right, knocked, went in, the door closed and laughter rang out almost continuously as the train rolled to St. Joe.

Before each performance of *Peter Pan*, wearing a black satin negligee with wide flowing sleeves and a slit between the shoulders where the wire could hook onto the harness, the Lady gave the signal and the German flyman who'd flown her since the first performance started the machines. She flew in through the window of the Darlings' nursery, across to the mantelpiece, where a plush monkey fastened at the right place on the wall was there for her to steady herself before she flew down to the center of the room to look for Peter's lost shadow. When she gave the signal to fly away through the window the long black satin robe with the wide sleeves spread out in the breeze, looked like a big black bird leaving the Darlings' nursery.

After the matinee at the Empire, most of the audience moved around to the stage door on 40th Street. "Stand back," warned stage doorman George. "Let Miss Adams get to her carriage." It was shiny black with a fine brown horse, the coachman standing ready by the door.

When George was satisfied the sidewalk had a wide enough path, he swung open the stage door and stood respectfully waiting. Out came the awaited long dark skirt, long gray silky moleskin fur coat, small black hat with its long black chiffon veil reaching down to the wearer's waist, front and back.

A quiet murmur of love and admiration came from the crowd as the carriage door was opened by Willard Barton, San Francisco Beau Brummell who through an acquaintance had become her stage manager and also lieutenant of the Scottish Guards.

No one in the crowd thought of speaking. No one thought of asking for an autograph. Her presence was all they asked. The carriage drove east on 40th and everybody went off to Mary Elizabeth's for tea and cake or for ice-cream soda at Huyler's. They'd seen a great matinee and a great lady. What a great city where this could happen!

West 40th Street was empty when another shiny black carriage pulled up. Another long dark skirt, long gray silky moleskin fur coat, small black hat with long black veil, got in with Willard Barton's help, drove east on 40th to rest and dinner in her suite at the Hotel Manhattan, corner of 42nd Street and Madison. The wearer of the first moleskin served it to her. That was Miss Adams' personal maid, Mary Murray.

Ten years passed since the goodbye on the train. I had finished dress rehearsal in Rochester's Lyceum Theatre. Crossing the hotel lobby, I passed a group, then I looked back. Who was that? "Miss Adams," I said, as shaken as I was that last night in her drawing room.

"Yes?"

"I'm Ruth Gordon. I played Nibs."

"Ah yes." She put her arm around my shoulders and turned to those with her. "This is Miss Ruth Gordon. We were together in *Peter Pan.*"

❋   ❋   ❋   ❋   ❋

Are you superstitious? I am and I'd be a lot more scared today if I didn't remember a sea gull flew in a suite at the Ritz in Atlantic City, circa 1928.

"When a bird flies in a room, one of the people is supposed to die that year," my mother warned me. Today when Garson was helping a yellowbird get out the window of my writing room in Beverly Hills I'd have worried, except that that year of the sea gull neither Jed Harris nor I died.

92

❊   ❊   ❊   ❊   ❊

Who was it having a romance with Irene Castle? Whoever it was, among other things, he and Irene liked a game of chess. Cartier was told to make a super chessboard of gold and ebony and in the center a wreath to twine around I.C. That wasn't the work of a moment and before Cartier finished, love cooled. The board was delivered and its owner was asking everybody, "Do you know Ina Claire?"

# Fellow American

Down in the King Cole Bar of the St. Regis, Sherwood stayed too long. Upstairs, their suite had two doors, one to the grand sitting room and master bedroom, one to the smaller bedroom the other side of the sitting room. Madeline got tired of waiting, took Sherwood's set of spares, hung them on the doorknob of the small bedroom next to the sitting room and went to bed.

Dinner at the White House had been the same as usual, nothing very good. "What do *you* eat most of the time, Archie?" asked the President.

"Well, tonight Ada had fried chicken."

"Fried chicken!" The President's face melted into one big joyous look. "Do *you* like fried chicken, Bob?"

"Yes indeed."

"Was it brown, Archie?"

"Oh yes. Ada knows just how to do it."

"Small birds?"

"Oh, broilers."

"Fried chicken! You can't beat a good piece of fried chicken. Don't you think so, Bob?"

"I do indeed."

Archie hesitated, but the look on two faces encouraged him. "There's some left. Would you—"

The President's face was like sunrise at Campobello. "You think Ada has some?"

"Oh yes, we didn't finish it."

"Do you think if we sent over?"

"Oh yes indeed, let me call her."

President Roosevelt was a man who took action. "I'll start the fellow on his way." He pushed a button.

"Ada, the President is sending over for our fried chicken. Have it . . . What?"

"What?" asked the President.

"Ada ate it."

A knock at the door and the aide looked in. "Yes, Mr. President?"

"Never mind."

"Yes, Mr. President." The aide left.

"The President was a good loser," said Sherwood, "considering he didn't get much practice."

Sherwood offered his speech. Roosevelt read it. "This whole front page there's not one laugh, Bob. Would you do that to Alfred Lunt?" He read on. "It's still too inside. Nobody likes to feel left out, Bob."

The President knew what he was talking about. When I first lived at the Algonquin, I felt left out and didn't like it. How could I get in with the Algonquin crowd? I rode up and down in the elevator with them, but knew them only from reading F.P.A.'s Saturday column, called "Mr. Pepys' Diary." It told what Swope and Broun and Woollcott did, along with the social activities of Neysa Mc-Mein, Dottie Parker and Alice Duer Miller. It reported where Benchley and Sherwood went, what Don Stewart said, how Jascha Heifetz, Sascha somebody, Mischa Elman, Toscha Seidel went to a party and played and sang,

> *"When Jascha, Sascha, Mischa, Toscha*
> *All go fiddle dee dee—"*

Mr. Pepys reported on Reinald Werrenrath, Mr. Otto Kahn, Edna Ferber, Kathleen and Charles Norris, Irving Berlin, Ralph Pulitzer and everybody else I'd be glad to be in with. In the Algonquin elevator, restaurant and lobby, I saw them all, but how was I going to meet them? Then Bob Sherwood married Mary Brandon. That was the gossamer thread. Mary had scraped up an acquaintance with me when I played summer stock in Indianapolis and though no longer trying to get into stock, she remembered the old days and invited me to Bob's birthday party at their apartment somewhere up Madison.

She also invited a lot of Mr. Pepys's list including Mr. F.P.A. Pepys himself who was susceptible and said shortly after meeting me he'd like to see me home. Triumphant, I smiled at Pearl Swope, Neysa McMein and a beauty from Philadelphia named Peggy Thayer. All three just stared back at me from the sofa.

"Who is that?" asked Neysa, not lowering her voice.

Pearl Swope appraised me with those cool hazel eyes. "I haven't the *faintest* idea."

I *still* wasn't in. Roosevelt was right, Bob, nobody likes to be left out.

The President reached for a pencil. "Dammit, wouldn't you think the President of the United States would have a sharp pencil?"

Heads will roll, thought Bob.

"Things are going to change around here!" threatened the President.

The door opened.

"Yes, Mr. President?"

"May I have this pencil sharpened?" He smiled his warm smile.

"Yes, Mr. President."

"Thank you so much." He turned to Bob and pointed to a place midway on the manuscript page. "How would Lunt read *that* line?"

Two menus at Faraway Meadows were dedicated to Bob and Madeline Sherwood. Fried chicken and banana ice cream was the Aunt Lena Jones special. She served that in Federalsburg, Maryland, when she wanted to put on airs.

The Readville Special was for Sherwood. When he went to Milton Academy and felt the urge, he bypassed what Milton had to offer and walked over to Readville for their coffee ice cream with hot chocolate sauce. If it was like ours, so would you.

The first plays Sherwood started writing didn't go. He decided he'd quit trying for success and write something to please himself.

Hannibal and his elephants seemed likely to appeal to no one, so he went over to the Harvard Club and wrote about them. With his record for plays failing, managers weren't welcoming any more, but with Delphic prescience he took his script to Brady and Wiman whose record was worse than Sherwood's. They'd had sixteen bombs in a row. Sherwood gave them *The Road to Rome* and to their and everybody's amazement they had a hit. So amazed was Sherwood that during the second-act intermission he stood on the 48th Street sidewalk opening his first-night telegrams, tearing up the messages and folding the envelopes into his pocket. When his wife Mary pointed this out, he hauled off and hit her, bringing comfort to scads of friends. Years later when they got the divorce Sherwood said he almost felt sorry for her when his friends told him how they disliked her. Goodnight, Mary Brandon Sherwood, where*ever* you are, and wherever it is, stay there.

After Milton Academy and the Readville Specials, Sherwood went to Harvard. From there he joined the Black Watch. He'd tried to get into our army, but got turned down for being too tall.

"Why didn't you give up?" I asked him.

He looked rattled and kicked his feet around. "Well, if truth be told," he said, "I wasn't doing all that well at Harvard."

In England at Great Enton, the Sherwoods had a Scottie, brooding with melancholia. He'd been to the vet. There was no cure. He sat by the corner of the great stone house written up in the Domesday Book and brooded. When anyone came near, he gave a mournful growl and looked off beyond the edge of Surrey into another time. One day he left home and went down past Sweetwater Pond, crossed by Mrs. Stent's boiled-sweet shop and on to where the British Southern railroad occasionally stopped at Milford Station. Duncan waited and when the London-bound express sounded its whistle over by Hindhead, Duncan made his decision.

The stationmaster at Milford rang up. "Sorry, sir, your little doggie caught it. The 5:02 to Waterloo got him."

Graham Robertson lived near Great Enton. They said sometimes he paid a call. How could I meet him? I'd dropped hints to the Sherwoods to no avail.

One warm afternoon Sherwood and Madeline and I went up to

the croquet lawn. I stretched out in the big hammock. Madeline did the same in the other. Sherwood stretched out in a chair. Then from a million miles away something sounded like, "Why, Graham! Delighted to see you."

I opened an eye. Madeline opened one of hers. We somehow marshaled our appearances and I was shaking hands with the great Graham Robertson. Then, so suddenly called from our sleep, we all became tongue-tied. Madeline rallied first. "I'm terribly hot," she said.

Why let my friend bear all the burden? I rallied, too, "Why don't you shit in the sade?" I asked in precise, clear tones.

Either you're going to become friends or you're not and Graham became my friend.

It was a wrench when Sherwood had to leave Great Enton. He did so as seldom as possible, but it was always a wrench. He postponed the day he must go to see René Clair at St. Tropez. Then the calendar moved up to the date to go. Better bring something to swim in. "I'd like bathing trunks," he said to the man at Fortnum's.

The frock-coated attendant bowed. "With or without ball trap, sir?"

※  ※  ※  ※  ※

Willie Wyler was running *Dead End* for Mr. Goldwyn. Mr. Goldwyn was pointing out the mistakes. Willie and Lillian Hellman were listening. In the picture was Humphrey Bogart, so over in the corner sat Sammy, Junior.

On screen, Bogart told the bartender to get him a drink. The bartender put down a bottle and a glass, then took a pencil from behind his ear, made a mark on the bottle and walked away.

Bogart gave him a dirty look, then poured.

"What the hell is *that?*" asked Sam.

"It's a gag," explained Willie. "As a rule the bartender could set up a bottle and a glass, but he takes a look at our boy and doesn't trust him, so he gets his pencil and makes a mark and Bogart does a take."

"Who the hell can understand *that?*" shouted Sam.

98

"What're you talking about! Any child can understand it."

Sam noticed his son in the corner. "Sammy, do *you* understand it?"

"Yes, Daddy. The man puts a mark on the bottle because he doesn't trust Humphrey Bogart to tell him how many drinks he will have."

Sam thought about it. "Oh, what the hell does a child know!"

That one knew enough to produce *Cotton Comes to Harlem*.

※　※　※　※　※

"The main thing in my job," said General Marshall, "is you have to learn to see the other fellow's point of view." He saw the other fellow's point of view about the Atom Bomb, but Burpee's Seeds floored him.

He said he was working on his bills one day when General Groves was announced. The Burpee Seeds bill for his farm in Virginia was for $182! *How* had he spent $182?

General Leslie Groves was ushered in and presented the check for expenses for the Atom Bomb. It was for $800,000,000.

General Marshall looked at it. "Oh yes," he said and signed.

"Thank you, General," said Groves and went out.

"Dammit," thought Marshall, "how did I spend $182?"

# The Fuchsia Plant

M ARLENE got off the plane at Orly, her friend Ginette Seid-
mann rushed to hug her. Marlene looked at the gray streaks
in Ginette's hair. "What are *you* trying to prove?" she asked. That
afternoon Ginette was over at Alexandre's having her gray streaks
colored.

I didn't wait for gray streaks. At twenty I thought I could go far
as a redhead. I didn't go as far as I thought I should and tried out all
the colors. When I was in *A Doll's House*, I had sort of amber-
colored hair. Mr. and Mrs. Harrison did it. They were British, but
hadn't been home for thirty years. Their shop had been in Sloane
Square, then the weather got too bad for Mr. Harrison, so they
came over here.

Business was excellent and they had a fine clientele. Mr. Harrison's health improved. The New York climate did for him what the
London doctor said it would. Thirty years had passed since the
closing of the Sloane Square shop and Mr. Harrison had a heart
attack. Now both he and his wife said he was recovered.

My hair was long. To color it took an hour and three quarters.
All that time Mrs. Harrison stood beside him. "Would you like me
to take over?"

"No," he said.

She was holding some porcelain flowers she'd made for a friend.
Purple and yellow pansies, blue morning glories, white violets that

had grown along a marshy brook, pink columbine and purple tulips in an ugly square dish. "I want it to look like fieldstone," said Mrs. Harrison. "It's Japanese, but I put acid on and sandpapered it."

Mr. Harrison looked at the flowers. "In the spring we get on the train at Botanical Gardens and ride to Inwood where the Inwood Golf Club is, then turn left down a path to the Bronx River and walk along its bank to Hartsdale."

Mrs. Harrison nodded. "It's really lovely."

"Really woodland, except where it opens up a little at Scarsdale. There are violets growing and buttercups. Some dogwood. You might be in the real country, the noise of automobiles on the other bank is hardly to be noticed. A friend of ours is particularly fond of it. Our friend comes all the way from Brooklyn."

"She gets on the train at Grand Central," said Mrs. Harrison.

"Mrs. Harrison and myself get on at Botanical Gardens, then together we ride to Inwood. The end of the day we take the train at Hartsdale and we get off at Botanical Gardens and our friend continues on till Grand Central and thence to Brooklyn."

"Along the path I gather models for these porcelain flowers. Of course they're not really porcelain, actually they're three thicknesses of Dennison's crepe paper painted with crayon and water color."

Mr. Harrison's brush stopped tinting my hair. "Mrs. Harrison treats them with a 'process' Mrs. Harrison has been developing for some time. It permits the flowers to be washed."

"Pity I couldn't have invented it in time for the fuchsia plant! The fuchsia plant has been such a lot of trouble and now it's got dusty. Mr. Harrison was so fond of it, but of course now it's a sight, yet there was nothing one could do about it. Pity!"

"I'm still fond of it."

"We had one at home. I remember how it looked, still remembering in one's mind's eye is quite different to remembering enough to reproduce it. We went to several florists, but New York florists, while they know them perfectly, say they have little or no call for them and had none on hand."

Mr. Harrison brushed the tint onto my hair. "A fuchsia is a fine plant."

"They say they have no call for them out here."

"One day walking through Botanical Gardens, we came upon one. Mrs. Harrison studied it and I, too."

"At home I started to work."

"Next Sunday we went again and that Sunday I noticed a fuchsia flower had dropped off. I just picked it up and put it in my pocket."

"Then I had that to work from. When the plant was all finished, with leaves and buds and full blossoms and half blossoms, I set it in a flowerpot. It was exactly like we'd always had at home."

"Now it's gotten dusty." Mr. Harrison went out to their room and brought it in. "It's ingrained, you see. Oh, it's had its day." Mr. Harrison sounded discouraged. "You finish her hair," he said and went with the fuchsia plant to the room they kept for their use.

Mrs. Harrison didn't say anything, just brushed the tint on. She put a towel over my head and set the timer for twenty-five minutes. "Mr. Harrison comes from Yorkshire. Scarborough way, a little place called Driffield." Her voice was gently unemphatic. "I'm from Norfolkshire. Lowestoft is a beautiful place. You'd have liked my uncle's house. When he died he left it to the Coast Guards, because it has a lookout and the Coast Guards have right of way across the shore his property was on, but of course no one may own a beach in Europe. I wonder do the Germans know that?"

✻ ✻ ✻ ✻ ✻

Ambassador and Mrs. Aldrich were sitting around at the Embassy. The radio was on.

"Who's that talking German with a Yankee accent?" asked Mrs. Aldrich. "Oh, that's Jim Conant."

He came to the opening of *The Matchmaker* at the Berlin Festival.

"You have the best New England accent," I said. "Where are you from?"

"Boston."

"Oh, nobody's from Boston. Where did you really come from?"

"Dorchester." There he was, down from Bonn on his own private train that had been Hermann Goering's own, and he was from Dorchester. Mrs. Conant said she came from Cambridge. That picked things up.

❊  ❊  ❊  ❊  ❊

Don't get funny with Walter Matthau. "I'll have some sturgeon," he said.

"It's six dollars and thirty-five cents a pound," said the deli man and kept on going.

"I'll have thirty-four pounds," said Walter.

He got attention.

❊  ❊  ❊  ❊  ❊

"Never act in no place where they serve hard liquor," warned my father when I left Wollaston to go on the stage. He was thinking of his early days in Frisco where he went to see Lotta light up some rough places, but the places I hoped to light up were the Booth and Lyceum and Empire where they didn't even serve hard candy. Twenty-one years later I acted at London's Old Vic, the one theatre in Great Britain where I could still heed my father's warning. The Vic had a temperance bar. Clinton Jones and Lilian Baylis saw eye to eye on what was needed to enjoy a play.

❊  ❊  ❊  ❊  ❊

"Oscar Wilde set the style," said Ernest Thesiger as though discussing yesterday. "One Sunday morning he strolled in Hyde Park, a yellow calla lily in his buttonhole. The following Sunday yellow calla lilies were in our buttonholes."

"Why don't you wear one now?" I asked.

"Ah no, it required flair and I regret dreadfully that I never had any."

He had a lot of other things. At the Needlework Show, Ernest won all the worthwhile prizes, and from time to time when he wasn't in a play, Queen Mary invited him over to Buck House to do needlework with her.

Before a matinee he stormed into my dressing room. "Oh dear, I'm in a tantrum!" He flung himself down on a chair.

"What happened?"

"Why can I never learn to mind my business! Driving over here, I was sitting beside my chauffeur and as we went round Piccadilly Circus I held out my hand to show we were making the turn and my beautiful amethyst slipped off my finger! Oh, *why* did I help my chauffeur!"

It was thanks to *my* help he joined *The Country Wife*. The part of eighty-year-old Foppish was being rehearsed by that actor in his teens.

"Will he be good?"

"Yes."

"Will he be good?"

"Yes."

"Will he?"

Tony Guthrie fired him and hired Ernest.

"Oscar Wilde had flair and so have you," said Ernest. "*You* can do what you want because you're the rage of London."

Of course, it's the least Ernest *could* say after what I did for *him*. I wonder what Alec Guinness said after I did for *him*. Goodnight, Alec, wher*ever* you are, you're the only one in fifty-five years I ever got fired. Put it down to the account of Ernest or the Importance of Being Eighty.

# "Devotedly Your Friend, Helen Keller"

W<small>E ALL MAKE MISTAKES.</small> Or is that one of Thornton's visceral myths? Anyway there must be *something* to me. Don Rickles is my friend and so was Helen Keller. And even before she was my friend I thought about her every time the train passed that old brick building. "Blind people are taught to read and write there," my mother told me. "It's where Mrs. Keller brought her little girl Helen."

That was when I was a little girl in Wollaston. New York City was where I met her. The phone rang. It was Alexander Woollcott. "What are you doing this afternoon and whatever it is get out of it. Come up here at four. Something *great!*"

"What are we going to do, read Braille?" I asked. What did *that* mean?

Silence at the other end of the phone.

"Alec?" I asked. "Alec, are you there?"

"Why'd you say that?"

"I don't know. Didn't you ever say anything silly?"

"Rarely. Why *did* you? You must've had *some* idea."

"No," I said. "What's going to be so great at four?"

There was a pause, then he said, "Helen Keller's coming to tea."

When I said what are we going to do, read Braille, it startled Woollcott and when he said Helen Keller was coming to tea, you can bet that startled *me*.

A little *before* four, I got to the Hotel Gotham. Woollcott could turn on you if you weren't on time. And even more important, I didn't want to miss a moment of Helen Keller.

"How could you know Helen Keller and not talk about it?" I asked.

"Known her for years," he said and there was a knock at the door. He certainly *had* known her for years, he planted a big kiss on Helen Keller's cheek, then one on Polly Thompson's and sometime after that, remembered me. "Helen, this is Ruth Gordon. Polly, Ruth."

Do *you* know when a great moment is going on? I think it makes itself felt. This winter afternoon at the Hotel Gotham I knew was a great moment. Part of it was the total surprise. Sitting on that Gotham Hotel sofa was a legend in a terribly pretty dress. An immortal with lipstick and powder and just a touch of eyeshade. She and her companion Polly Thompson could have been two charming anybodies, except for their terrific gaiety. And except for Helen's clouded speech that Polly made clear to us. When *we* talked, she tapped out on Helen's hand what we said. Except for that, they were two adorable ladies hellbent on having a good time.

"Tea?" asked Woollcott.

Polly tapped. Helen didn't look very interested.

"Something stronger?"

Polly tapped. Helen brightened up.

"Old-fashioned?"

Polly tapped. Helen made enthusiastic sounds.

That afternoon in 1941 we all laughed a lot and Helen laughed hardest when the joke was on her. To remember Alec's face, she patted it all over. Then she patted his mustache. Then she patted it again and made sounds. "Helen says she thinks your mustache has gotten smaller, Alex."

Woollcott leaned over and patted Helen's face. "Tell her hers hasn't." Polly tapped, Helen laughed more than anybody.

The next time I saw her was also due to Woollcott. He died. His last will and testament said, "No funeral service," but once he was no longer with us, his friends got out of line. They didn't go so far as to arrange a funeral, but did arrange a memorial service. McMillin Auditorium at Columbia University, on a January morning at 10 A.M.

10 A.M.! Most of Woollcott's friends were late sleepers, but 10 A.M. was when McMillin Auditorium was available, so that January morning a lot of new alarm clocks went off in a lot of unaccustomed ears. And just that morning New York chose to have a blizzard. The Mayor looked out the window and ordered all private cars off the streets. A hush fell on New York City except up at McMillin where Woollcott's sleepy, exasperated friends filled every seat in the big auditorium.

Only Guthrie McClintic, great director that he was, was wide awake enough to direct his yellow taxi to wait, and after the ceremony and after we'd buckled on our galoshes, after we'd pulled on our warm coats and mufflers and mittens, Guthrie directed his wife Katharine Cornell and Helen Keller and Polly Thompson and me into his yellow taxi. *I* was only included because I was playing in his production of *The Three Sisters* and he didn't want me lost in a snowdrift and have the understudy go on.

Well, that's show business. Sometimes it's rough and sometimes you get the breaks and that morning I got the break of being squeezed into Guthrie's yellow taxi along with Helen and Kit and Polly and off we skidded down Morningside Heights.

As we lurched around icy curves, feelings got less serious. Things became more informal when we kept falling all over each other. Once we all landed on the taxi floor in a woolly heap and as Helen untangled herself she spoke. "Wouldn't Alec be delighted," repeated Polly, "at how much trouble he is causing his friends?"

The next time I saw Helen Keller, she was my guest at *The Matchmaker*. I remembered she always came to the plays Kit was in and I invited her to the Royale Theatre. Polly wrote that Helen would be delighted. A Wednesday matinee would be best and might they have five tickets and a script of the play for them to read in advance? The script and the five tickets were sent to Helen's house, Arcan Ridge, in Westport, Connecticut. Back came a check. Well, that wasn't the idea. Back went the check to Arcan Ridge and a few days later there arrived a big luxurious bottle of Gardenia Bath Oil from Henri Bendel's with a message from Helen that she was looking forward to Wednesday. One knows great moments. Who do *you* know that bathed in gardenia-scented bath oil, the gift of Helen Keller!

That Wednesday matinee was the best performance we ever did. *The Matchmaker* had played in London, Berlin, Edinburgh, but we never played it as well as that Wednesday. When the curtain fell, the stage manager went out into the theatre to bring our great lady and her friends backstage. Nobody had arranged it, but the whole *Matchmaker* company stood to see her pass. Distinguished people had come backstage in the course of the run, but only for Helen Keller did the *Matchmaker* company stand and wait.

And then she was in the dressing room. With Polly Thompson. With her three friends from the Lighthouse, the great charitable organization for the blind—and again *such* a sense of somebody having a good time, *again* her radiant smile. And her lovely clothes. That spring afternoon an Alice-blue suit, a hat with flowers and a ribbon. Such a surprise for an immortal to look chic! "Helen," I said, "anyone who walked in here would take *you* for the actress."

To remember just what I looked like, she patted my face, my Mrs. Dolly Gallagher Levi wig, my period costume, the bodice, the sleeves, the 1880 taffeta bustle. Then her hand stopped and suddenly she looked moved. She spoke and Polly looked moved. "Helen says she hasn't thought of a bustle since she was a little girl. Her mother wore one."

The train, the old brick building. "That's where Mrs. Keller brought *her* little girl Helen."

I asked if she had followed the play. Polly tapped. Helen nodded enthusiastically. Polly said, "When you got to the monologue in the last act, which Helen had so admired when we read the manuscript, she pushed my hand away. She didn't want me to tap it out for her. She knew every word as you came to it. Laughed when the audience did. Was moved when they were."

The great moment was over. We spoke briefly of Woollcott and I held out to her a picture I kept of him in the jinricksha from the Chicago World's Fair.

Arthur Hill was waiting to show her to her car. "Oh, we don't have a car," said Polly. "Every taxi driver knows Helen and stops."

Outside on 45th Street, the whole matinee audience waited to see her. Arthur Hill, not as confident of New York taxi drivers as Polly, rushed ahead. He beckoned to a taxi. It dove out of sight into the after-matinee crush. Then Helen came through the matinee ladies, stood at the curb in her Alice-blue suit, smiling her radiant confident smile, and a screech of brakes let Arthur Hill know that life *can* be beautiful. *Two* taxis pulled up to the curb.

A few days later a letter arrived.

DEAR RUTH GORDON,

While the memory of Wednesday's matinee sparkles in my mind, I want to write you grateful thanks. Whenever Polly and I recall "The Matchmaker," the imps of laughter dance in our hearts. Also you were a darling to let us see you after the play when you must have felt tired. It was good to see Alec's picture.

> *Devotedly your friend,*
> HELEN KELLER.

It was typed—beautifully typed—by her. And soon after, a package was delivered. Her book, *Teacher*. Here is what she wrote in her own hand. With a lead pencil. Each word perfectly spaced.

To RUTH GORDON
who is loved not
only for her dramatic art
but also for her sunny
sweetness and her heart of
gold.
> *Affectionately*
> HELEN KELLER
*February 17, 1956*

Whether it's so or not, that's what Helen Keller, with her love of people, her confidence in the human race, that's what Helen Keller thought of me.

❊   ❊   ❊   ❊   ❊

Riding back from Hyères, I said, "I hope I haven't forgotten my key."

"Why should you?"

Mme. René Clair was right, why *should* I? I'm not a person who goes around forgetting keys, but today am I so sure about that? Is anything the way it *should* be? "Why should it?" you say and then it does. So then you wonder. *Can* you use the old yardstick? What do *you* make of things?

❃   ❃   ❃   ❃   ❃

When *Seventeen* played Columbus I stopped at the Neil House because that's where Sister Carrie worked as a chambermaid and I loved Dreiser's novel, it made me cry so. The Neil House was sad, too. And so was the movie. Larry Olivier had lost his job, had run out of money, had to take a place as a waiter, had to press his own pants and burned a hole in the seat and Jennifer Jones had to make hats for a living and the boss got tough because she used too much thread. We followed Korda out of the projection room, looking ready to cut our throats. Nobody said anything, then discouragedly the press agent asked, "What is your advertising campaign slant?"

"I don't know," said Korda.

"How would *this* be?" suggested Garson. "A big poster and on it: YOU THINK YOU GOT TROUBLES."

❃   ❃   ❃   ❃   ❃

Thornton talks about the shrinking world of this and that. What about the shrinking world of show business? When I left home to go on the stage, there were a lot of them. On Broadway were the Empire, Wallack's, the Knickerbocker, the Casino, George M. Cohan's George M. Cohan, the Criterion, the Astor, the Gaiety, the Globe, the Central and the Winter Garden. On 39th Street were the Princess, the Maxine Elliott, the 39th Street Theatre. On 41st was the Comedy. 42nd Street had the New Amsterdam, Sam H. Harris' Sam H. Harris, the Liberty, Al H. Woods' Eltinge, Harry Frazee's Frazee and across the street the Selwyns' Selwyn, also their Times Square and Apollo, somebody else's Lyric and somebody else's Republic. We don't know where the snows of yesteryear are, but we know a lot of the ice got lost on 42nd Street.

On 43rd, Mr. Miller built the Henry Miller, 44th was where Mr. Belasco built the Belasco and Mr. Henry B. Harris had the Hudson. Cross Broadway to the Shuberts' Shubert Theatre, their 44th Street Theatre, their Broadhurst, their Nora Bayes, Mr. Ames' Little Theatre where coffee was served at intermission and maybe David Frost still does.

On 45th Street they tore down the Avon where Kit played her first New York part. What's at the Bijou? Helen Hayes made a zonking hit there in a revival of *What Every Woman Knows*. Now what has it turned into? On 48th, the Vanderbilt, the Playhouse, the Belmont and the 48th Street Theatre all went west. On 49th, Mr. Charles Hopkins' Punch and Judy now runs Nudies instead of a long run featuring Long John Silver.

Up at Columbus Circle was that vari-named big one where little Ernie Truex played *Androcles and the Lion*. Al Jolson drew us up to the Jolson. So did *Kiss Me, Kate*. Around on 58th was the John Golden Theatre number one, where this evening number one Dick Cavett adds to the gaiety of the laity.

Past Columbus Circle on Central Park West, Winthrop Ames built the cavernous Century to house the greatest repertory ever to be seen. He took a beating, then he sent for Granville Barker to come from London and Barker took some more of the same, plus tycoon Huntington's wife. Barker had left his beautiful Lillah McCarthy in London. What happened? Did he feel he wanted something to show for the trip?

After repertory became a memory, Morris Gest imported Max Reinhardt's *Miracle* for the Century and up on the roof Ned Wayburn staged a revue where a young charmer from Federalsburg, Maryland, marked time till she became Ben Turpin's leading lady and, later, Robert Sherwood's.

Around the corner on West 61st, *Shuffle Along* moved down from Harlem. Wish you'd been there?

That was the New York stage, but the world didn't end at West 61st Street. There were stages to go on all over the country. A lot of places had great stock companies whose stars never hit Broadway. Ever see Emma Bunting in Des Moines? That was reason enough to go there. Ever see the Dubinsky Brothers in Kansas City? Sue MacManamy in Albany? Jessie Bonstelle in Buffalo and Detroit? John Craig and Mary Young at Boston's Castle Square where Alfred Lunt got his start playing fifth business? Ever see Oza Waldrop in Syracuse?

On rare occasions some of them made it on the main stem. Alfred Lunt did. So did Maude Fulton. She said goodbye to California and surprised Broadway with an unlikely-sounding show called *The Brat.*

Minneapolis' darling became Will Harris' darling and won the New York critics in *Arms and the Girl.* In our Empire Theatre second-floor dressing room Angela Ogden stated, "Fay Bainter has just about everything." The critics thought so, too, and continued to rave about her in Benrimo's *The Willow Tree* and Colonel Savage's *The Kiss Burglar,* but the gen. pub. held out until *East Is West,* then they caved in, too. The Astor Theatre became the Minneapolis stock all over again with Fay Bainter's adorers lined up as far as the corner and around on 45th.

Leo Carrillo and Grace Valentine were the rage of Oliver Morosco's Coast stock and did fine in New York, but what happened to Belle Bennett? With San Francisco at her feet, she chose the silent movie *Stella Dallas,* then what happened?

San Francisco gave its heart to Bert Lytell at the Alcazar, then he gave it back and became a silent movie star. On Broadway he was Gertie's leading man in *Lady in the Dark* and when Moss thought of replacing him, Gertie said, "You can't."

"Why not?" asked Moss.

"He's president of Equity," said the lady of *Lady in the Dark.*

Reports from the Washington stock company about their little Helen Hayes Brown drove all us ingenues mad. The word was, "She's the best thing going." Everybody breathed easier after the company staged *Kick In.* For that bill the director tried to grow Helen up. That's tough to do in a week. Child actresses ran and skipped and Helen couldn't stop doing it as the sexy *Kick In* ingenue. Back in New York, Edna Hibbard and Dorothy MacKaye and Lotus Robb and a lot of the rest of us heaved a sigh of relief.

Marjorie Rambeau and Willard Mack risked the East Coast and after a shaky start *she* made it in *Eyes of Youth.* He gave up on the acting and did it only when he felt like it and just wrote hits.

Seattle's idol came to town and did all right. In Seattle she had played leads in her husband's stock and Guthrie McClintic's twenty-five cents went into a ticket a week. He also had the presence of mind to swipe a lot of her posters. They looked great in his and Kit's house at Sneden's Landing.

CHARLES TAYLOR REPERTORY CO.
OFFERING
LAURETTE TAYLOR
IN
THE GIRL ENGINEER

Her first part on Broadway was as H. B. Warner's leading lady in *Alias Jimmy Valentine*. Her notices were raves. Later in stock a lot of us thought that must be a good part, but when we looked at the script we couldn't find it. The part was included, but how could it make a hit? Laurette knew the answer. I wish I'd seen her play it. *The Bird of Paradise* was her next. She used dark oil on her face to make her look Hawaiian and every night three Hawaiians came to the West 59th Street apartment that she and her mother rented. Two Hawaiians strummed on their ukuleles and the other one showed Laurette the routine. She could shake her grass skirt, but she didn't keep her hands level, so the instructor fille four walnut shells with water, put two on each of her hands. "G ,," he said, "and if you don't spill any water, you're doing it right."

(*Players' Guide*, copy.)

She did it right.

In New York, Mr. Taylor didn't stay in the picture. She kept his name for the stage, but in private life became Mrs. Hartley Manners. Her new husband wrote *Peg o' My Heart*. The New York wise guys turned it down, but out of the West came rescue. Oliver Morosco said he'd do it and John Cort, owner of a lot of Western theatres, built himself a New York theatre and let it open with *Peg o' My Heart*, but just to let people know who he was, he named it the Cort. It's the last one left on West 48th Street. Where's the block of gold John Cort had engraved and presented to its first star?

FOR A GREAT PERFORMER
IN A GREAT PLAY
THEREBY BRINGING PLENTY OF
BUSINESS TO THIS HOUSE
JOHN CORT

The greatest stock was Milwaukee's. Lowell Sherman was the leading man. Pauline Lord was their leading lady. Henry Kolker played characters. The ingenue was sixteen-year-old Ruth Chatterton. The soubrette was Leonore Ulrich, whose name Belasco rewrote to suit the bright lights of Broadway:

LYCEUM THEATRE

LENORE ULRIC
IN
THE HEART OF WETONA

LYCEUM THEATRE
LENORE ULRIC
IN
TIGER ROSE

BELASCO THEATRE
LENORE ULRIC
IN
THE SON-DAUGHTER

BELASCO THEATRE
LENORE ULRIC
IN
KIKI

BELASCO THEATRE
LENORE ULRIC
IN
LULU BELLE

What happened? It became Lenore Ulric in the Rockland County Hospital.

Up there she was looking at TV. "That's me," she said.

They thought she'd had a relapse.

"That's me talking to Garbo."

Where are the snows of yesteryear? Where the big house at Ossining? Where the town house in the West Seventies? Why did Wetona and Kiki and Tiger Rose and Lulu Belle wind up in Rockland County? Was the Sitwells' father right? Will the sands of time tell? Is the sand running out of show business?

If you think that, you shoulda stood in bed.

❋  ❋  ❋  ❋  ❋

Ever have a day when it doesn't work out for you? Houdini was ready to do his great swallow-the-needle trick. "Step up here," he said to one of the guests. "Look in my mouth and tell me what you see there."

"Py-ree-ra."

Too bad the great Houdini with all his magic got his new year off to a wrong start. He could have chosen anybody at Rube Goldberg's party and he chose Groucho. What use are all those tricks if they don't help you pick out a straight man?

❋  ❋  ❋  ❋  ❋

Are you interested in what you *did* or what you're doing?

Think it over.

At the Sporting Club when Rainier and Princess Grace entered, the room stood up, except for two.

"Who's the girl and man that won't stand?"

Maugham looked where I was looking. "They don't have to, he's the King of Yugoslavia and she's his Queen."

# Mr. Collins

O N A CUNARD LINER," said Marc Connelly, "if you ask for a
glass of water, the steward says 'Yes, sir, thank you, sir, I'll
fetch it, sir.' On an American ship, the steward points and says
'Right over there' and keeps going."

One afternoon in London, after I'd made too many dates for the
same weekend and agreed to move into Ruth Chatterton's Mayfair
house, I thought I better go back home where I had no trouble with
popularity. "Have you a cabin on the *Washington* tonight?" I
asked.

"Yes."

My bill paid at 20 Chesham Place, Vuitton trunk strapped to the
back of a cab, I boarded the boat train at Waterloo. Next day, staring at the luncheon menu, I read, "Commander Giles C. Stedman
welcomes you aboard." Could that be good-looking Chet Stedman?

"Does the Commander hail from New England?"

"And how!"

I thought of Marc, ordered lunch and wrote on the menu, "We
were in the class of 1914 at Quincy High. My name was Ruth
Jones."

A note slid under my cabin door. "The Commander requests the
pleasure of your company for cocktails in the forward lounge."

A crowd milled around our Commander. He greeted me politely.

"At Quincy High—"

"You're from Quincy High?"

He hadn't seen my note.

"Come up after dinner." Chet got out the *Quincy Ledger*'s report of our 1914 graduation. " 'The Worst Class' is the name they choose for themselves." Chet flipped a page. "Remember Miss Dawes?"

He flipped another. "Remember Miss O'Neill?"

And another. "Remember Ramah Baker?"

And another. "Remember Ted Rollins?"

"Remember the boat, Chet, it's rolling."

"Have a drink."

I had a brandy and soda. Chet reached for the Poland Water bottle and poured something browner than water in Maine. "Do you ever see Mr. Collins?"

"No. It's rolling some more, Chet."

"Drink that and have another. He's still principal of Quincy High. I had him on a voyage last summer. He wrote me that he'd never been to Europe and could I find a spot for him to work his way over and back? I told him to come ahead. This ship goes to Southampton, Cherbourg and Bremen and I told him to plan to come on the voyage that calls for us to lay over ten days in Bremen and I mapped out how I could show him Rome, Venice, Paris, London and be back to take the ship home.

"A berth in the Post Office is the soft spot, so I arranged for Mr. Collins to work in there. Till we drop off the pilot and clear Sandy Hook, I'm fairly busy, but I made sure Mr. Collins was aboard. We dropped the pilot over, I called for full steam and my orderly said, 'Mr. Collins has to see you.'

"He came in looking as if he had to expel me. 'Chet, it's not what I thought. I'm at a desk job, I want a *deck* job.'

" 'That means hard work,' I explained.

" 'That's all right, Chet, I *want* that.'

"Well, I'll fix *him!* I thought. He'll be glad to get back where it's easy. I told him all right and sent word below to transfer Collins from P.O. worker to common seaman. I knew I'd hear from him in no time and didn't give the matter any more thought.

"Next morning when the passengers were being served a cup of broth, I took a turn on Main Deck and I was taking it with a damn good-looking widow from Philadelphia when a sailor polishing the brass said 'Hello, Chet' and before I thought, I said 'Hello, Mr. Collins.' The widow must've thought I was cuckoo. All the gold braid and all the World War I ribbons and one for the rescue that got me the Carnegie Medal and a sailor calls me Chet and I call *him* Mr. Collins? I sent for him and asked how he was doing.

" 'Fine, Chet, just what I wanted.'

" 'You don't want to go back to the Post Office?'

" 'No, Chet, but I want to talk over the plans. That's a fine trip, Chet, but I've got to disappoint you, the ten days the ship's laid up, I want to stay in Bremen, Chet.'

" 'You know people there?'

" 'No, Chet, but if I look over Bremen for ten days, I'll know all about it.'

"For ten days we never left Bremen. I could berth the ship blindfolded in the dark. The ship sailed for home, Mr. Collins on deck swabbing and polishing and singing out 'Hello, Chet' and me saying 'Hello, Mr. Collins.' I was glad when we came up the Narrows. You can't explain a thing like that to a crew, there's no way according to nautical terms to have a sailor call the Commander by his first name and the Commander address a common seaman as Mister."

✻　✻　✻　✻　✻

When Maugham died he'd have been ninety-two the next month. That means I've still got eighteen years to write *The Summing Up*. What have *you* got time to do?

Think it over. And do it!

✻　✻　✻　✻　✻

Are you scared to go in a plane? I always went to California on Super Chief and to Europe on the *United States* or the *Queens*. Then one day I had to go alone. Garson had to stay in New York with *A Gift of Time*, I had to go to London to do a play for Tyrone Guthrie, still not a Sir. Such is my good fortune I didn't want to be parted from Garson after twenty years of married life.

Think it over. *I* did and let the last boat go. I *had to* go by air. How would I face it?

The Sitwells' father was wrong, my friends weren't a mistake, they were a help. Should I go Pan Am? Should I go TWA? Should it be a night flight? Should it be day?

"Day or night, BOAC treats you like a nanny," said Gert Macy.

"Air France is the greatest food," said Nela Rubinstein.

"No contest, go Pan Am," said Jones.

"TWA has movies," said Leonard Lyons.

"Go any goddam way there is, but stop *asking* people," said Hank Fonda. Was that what the Sitwells' father meant?

It could be, so I shut up. TWA? Pan Am? BOAC? Air France? Everybody else could go on them, but would I scream as they took off? Would I beg them to let me out?

Paul at Elizabeth Arden's said, "Take a 200-gram Equanil a half hour before takeoff, have red wine with dinner, then another 200 Equanil. That's what I take on Swissair and so does my little dog."

I swallowed a 200-gram Equanil. Could I say goodbye? I seemed to say it through a coat of Portland cement. At my seat, the table was already in place. On it the wineglass had a tall slender stem. Could that tall slender stem stay steady for the red wine? Out the window was Garson. Slim, blue overcoat, alone. In the plane? Me alone. What was going to happen? I looked at that tall slender stem. The glass and I swooped up in the air, the red wine swooped into the glass, "Just below is Nantucket Light Ship," said Pan Am's Captain.

Nantucket? Why, from Woods Hole to Nantucket the *Uncatena* rocks more than this!

Next day in the *Evening Standard* my picture at London Airport smiled on page two. I was a flier! Goodbye Equanil, goodbye red wine, hello white, but only for kicks. In a year and a half I've flown TWA across our country sixty-seven times. And some flights I don't get off at Kennedy, I look at the tall slender stem and keep going to London Airport.

Goodnight, Henry Fonda, wher*ever* you are, I never asked again.

❃   ❃   ❃   ❃   ❃

I wish the Sitwells' father had had *my* friends. What about when I was in big trouble and Thornton left New Haven to help? He didn't know how long I'd need him, so he got off at Grand Central carrying a big suitcase. He'd packed it in such a hurry, one shirt sleeve was hanging out. "First we'll drop my bag at Columbia University Club," he said, "then we'll go to a bookstore." He bought me a paperback in French. "It's by Keyserling. Read it some time."

I did. "Are you generous to your friends? Are you sympathetic? Are you patient when they despair? Then why don't you be generous with *yourself?* Forgive *yourself* when you fail. Be as understanding as you are with your friends. Be *nice* to yourself, you are with *them*."

That's all on page one and would you believe this? It's the only page I've ever read. Would you believe I don't know the name of the book? It meant so much to me and I don't know what it's called. If *you* know, write and tell me. Be as nice to *me* as you are to yourself.

I talked about the book on the Joey Bishop show and next day I went to Boston to do publicity for *Whatever Happened to Aunt Alice?* I was booked to go on the Dave Garroway Show. Elaine Stritch was on it and Dizzy Gillespie. His band was on just ahead of me. I said to the producer, "Please let me just talk by myself. Dizzy and I don't know each other and if I'm on with Elaine, she'll have to say 'I loved you in *The Matchmaker*' and I'll say 'I loved you in *Sail Away*' and New England will turn the knob."

Dizzy Gillespie and his band finished. I was on maybe two minutes when Dizzy Gillespie dashed on. "I know you don't want anyone on with you, but I gotta tell you something. Night before last I was up shavin' and my wife was lookin' at Joey Bishop and she hollered, 'Come down here, Dizzy, there's a lady says she's older than Mama. You come down and look at her.' And I came down and I said, 'That lady ain't older than your mother,' and she says, 'Yes, she is, too. She *says* she is. She just now said so.' And I keep on looking and Joey Bishop says, 'How do you stay so young, Ruth?' And you say, 'Because I'm nice to myself, I treat myself *nice*.'

"I'm never goin' to forget that! 'Be nice to yourself,' you said to everybody. I sure like *that*."

❊　❊　❊　❊　❊

Did you ever get a legacy? We did. From Moss Hart. He'd asked to come to dinner. Kitty was away and Moss said, "Just the three of us." After dinner we sat and talked. It was twelve-thirty when he gave us the legacy.

"Who's playing the girl?"

Garson told him.

"Is she good?"

Garson said the author wanted her.

"Why?"

"Well, she's skinny and dark and looks like his wife."

"Do *you* think she's right?"

"No."

Moss jumped up and leaned over Garson. "Don't have her! Don't say *yes! Don't!* Garson, listen to what I'm saying to you. DO NOT SAY YES. All the mistakes I ever made in my life were when I wanted to say NO and said YES."

Thanks, Mossie. Are you ever right!

❊　❊　❊　❊　❊

Away off in a sandy desert in a Country Club gift shop we were looking at trinkets, souvenirs, postcards, scarves, beads, cactus fudge. "What's this?" asked Leonard. He held up a can that looked like a Yuban coffee can.

Mia and I looked. On it it said, "Instant Jewish."

"What is it?" I asked the saleswoman.

"Oh, just a novelty."

"What do you do with it?" asked Mia.

"Oh, I don't know."

"It must be for *something*."

"You could pack a scarf in it," said the saleswoman.

❋   ❋   ❋   ❋   ❋

Know how to get tired? Be against things. Of course, if Hitler comes back and settles in Glen Cove, you have to be against that, but do you have to be against all the things you *are* against? Henry James said, "Don't let's be such good bookkeepers and enter every stub." Or words to that effect. He wrote it in *The Bostonians*, but couldn't New Yorkers work on that, too? And Californians?

❋   ❋   ❋   ❋   ❋

A lot of people are cross. Is it because they're not getting it right? Jerzy Grotowski is. He's the hit of the Polish theatre and kindly brought his troupe to New York. Only a comparative few got in, because he doesn't believe a show should play to more than forty, so probably you didn't make it. The Dramatists' Guild thought dramatists should and requested a special performance.

"Forty only," said Jerzy.

"Couldn't you stretch it for the Dramatists' Guild?"

"Only forty."

The Guild has hundreds of members, so the members drew lots. Garson and I drew lucky numbers and came from California.

From Kennedy we hurried downtown. At the theatre they said, "Sit on the steps and wait, he doesn't like people to straggle in, everybody crash through at once." Garson and I sat by Paddy Chayefsky, but the signal came and we got separated in the squeeze. I sat half on Murray Schisgal and half on Marc Connelly. Marc is an old friend and Murray became one. The play was in Jerzy Grotowski's native language and quite a lot of it was in the dark. As we drifted out, Marc asked me, "Did you get much? My Polish is only fragmentary."

# Gentleman from Indiana

Too BAD the Sitwells' father never met Booth Tarkington. When *Seventeen* was playing Boston, Mr. Tarkington invited the whole cast to come to Seaward for Sunday. The rest of the company took the Boston and Maine train to Kennebunk, but Gregory Kelly and I went in a hire car, because the night before, walking home after the show along Boylston Street in front of the steep broad granite steps of Lotta Crabtree's Brunswick Hotel, Gregory said, "When I get my family straightened out, let's get married."

"Was the moon beautiful driving up?" asked Mrs. Tarkington. "I didn't see it," I said.

I didn't see the moon, but I did see Mr. Tarkington who, with no perceptible effort, put the moon in the shade. When we strolled out after dinner into its inferior light, Mr. Booth Tarkington's light shone on gray-shingled Seaward's gardens, its pines and the white cabin cruiser *Susannah* riding at anchor and the black schooner *Zantee* tied up in permanent retirement.

Helping him shine was the former Miss Susannah Kieffer, belle of Dayton, who after several misses became Mrs. Tarkington.

To marry a celebrated novelist was in his favor. To marry a celebrated drinker was not, so Tarkington quit, and after six dry weeks Susannah and her sister Miss Louisa took the train to Indianapolis to celebrate the engagement.

Tarkington's friend Will Hodge also took a train to Indianapolis and arrived at 1100 North Pennsylvania Street with a good supply of whiskey, all of it inside him. His host got him to bed in a darkened guestroom and advised the Man From Home to sleep it off. "Do *not* come downstairs," he told him and, to make sure, turned the key in the lock.

Up North Pennsylvania Street clattered the station hack and down his front walk came Tarkington just as his guest jumped out the window, having it on his mind not to come down the stairs.

The old wygelia bushes broke the fall, so Hodge was only stunned, and not half as much as the Dayton ladies, who clattered back to Union Station, convinced Tarkington was as soused as his friend.

But he wasn't. Nor would he ever be. All that remained of those days was disapproval of the bottle and those who indulged. Souvenir of the discarded good times was a tremor in his hand that held the extra-long, made-to-order cigarettes initialed N.B.T. in black on each cigarette paper.

Before he disapproved of liquor, he and his chum Roy Atwell enjoyed it at the Lambs' Club. "This is good," said Atwell, finishing a Pink Lady Cocktail, "but not as good as they make at the Bellevue Stratford. I'd give anything to have one."

"Let's," said Tarkington and helped his friend outside. "Bellevue Stratford Hotel. Broad Street, Philadelphia," he told the astonished taxi. Astonished, but responsive, the taxi drove to the Hudson River Ferry, rattled across the Jersey salt marshes, through busy Newark, through busy Elizabeth, past the towers of Tarkington's Alma Mater off to the right, through busy Trenton, across the Delaware where Washington threw that dollar, sped out of New Jersey across the Schuylkill River and down Broad Street to the high-columned Bellevue Stratford. "Pink Lady," said Tarkington, motioning to his friend and himself.

"Wasn't I right? Next one's on me."

"*One*," said Tarkington and handed a bill to the bartender. "You said you'd give anything to have *one*." He turned a deaf ear to his distressed friend. "Lambs' Club," he told their jehu and back across the Schuylkill, through less busy Trenton, past Alma Mater's towers now off to the left, through deserted Elizabeth and Newark, across dark salt marshes onto the brightly lit ferry. "Pink

Lady," said Atwell just as the Lambs' Club bar was closing.

"Pink Lady," said Tarkington.

In the beginning, Tarkington had a slow start. His sister Terre Haute Tarkington went from publishing house to publishing house, getting only turndowns. Years went by before Hautey landed *Monsieur Beaucaire,* but the firm she landed it with also published *Penrod, Alice Adams, The Gentleman from Indiana, Gentle Julia, The Magnificent Ambersons, Seventeen* and all the rest.

When *Seventeen* was made into a play, I played Lola Pratt, the Baby Talk Lady with whom seventeen-year-old William Sylvanus Baxter is smitten. Him and nobody else. *Smart Set's* George Jean Nathan wrote, "Let us get down on our knees and pray for this poor girl who seems to be copying May Vokes." May Vokes played batty servant girls.

The *Tribune* felt the same. "Ruth Gordon plays Lola Pratt, and anyone who looks like that and acts like that must get off the stage," wrote Heywood Broun.

Did *you* ever cry all Sunday?

And even after a season at the Booth, critics roasted me as far west as St. Louis. The week after was going to be Indianapolis where for the first time Mr. Tarkington would see the dramatization of his novel, now in its second year. If I couldn't do something about my acting, could I do something about my looks? When May Parcher introduces Willie and Joe and Johnny to Lola Pratt and she calls them Ickle Boy Baxter, Big Bruvver Josie Joe and Johnny Jump-up, what could I do to smooth out *that?*

New dress for Act I? I couldn't afford it. New Act I hat? "I'd like a very beautiful pink straw," I said to the astonished millinery clerk at Scruggs, Vandervoort and Barney.

"We don't get our straws till Easter, is it snowing yet?"

That store didn't appeal to me and I went over to Stix, Baer and Fuller. "I'd like a very beautiful pink straw hat, preferably off the face, because people in the balcony—"

"Why straw? It's snowing."

"Next week I'm playing Indianapolis and Booth Tarkington—"

"Excuse me," said a pretty lady with a pretty daughter. "We saw the play and you won't find what you want in St. Louis, but my daughter and I had two pink straw hats made in New York for

Palm Beach. We'd be so pleased if you'd accept one. Where are you staying?"

When Lola Pratt fluttered through May Parcher's door, was it that pink Italian straw with its flutter of tulle and velvet streamers?

"I'm going to write a play for you and Gregory," said Mr. Tarkington. "And you won't talk baby talk. Nobody's amused by it but me."

He had just finished one for Alfred Lunt, whom he happened to see while changing trains in Boston on the trip from Kennebunkport to Indianapolis. Alfred was a road replacement in Tarkington's *The Country Cousin*, starring Alexandra Carlisle. When the matinee ended, Tarkington introduced himself and said he'd write Alfred a play. The play was *Clarence*. It made Alfred a star.

It did well for two other people. The upcoming young Helen Hayes, who was triumphing in Barrie's *Dear Brutus* at the Empire, and the unknown Glenn Hunter, whose only triumph was he'd gotten back from the war.

*Clarence* was produced first at the Apollo Theatre in Atlantic City, where Alfred and Helen were a smash, but young Hunter worried everybody. Too different. Ran all his words together. Slouched into a chair and seemed to sit on the back of his neck. The juveniles in everybody else's show sat up straight, why did *he* have to be so original?

"Fire him, Tark, it's your play," said producer George C. Tyler and headed up the Boardwalk to the Shelburne. The worried author went up a lot of flights of backstage stairs.

"Come in." Glenn was taking off his makeup.

Tarkington offered him a cigarette with the black N.B.T. on the cigarette paper and lit one for himself. The tremor in his hand was more noticeable. "Hunter," he began, "this play means a lot to me."

"Oh, yes," said Glenn, "it must." Did he run those words together?

"It does. How do *you* feel about it? Is this play important to *you*?"

Glenn put down the tin of Albolene and his makeup towel. "I guess it's the most important thing ever happened to me." He didn't run those together.

Tarkington inhaled a lot of smoke and blew it out. "Good," he said. "You're so good, I wanted to make sure you feel comfortable."

Mr. Sitwell dear, you'd have had to like Tarkington, even for a friend.

Goodness was rewarded, Glenn made a hit and the next season all juveniles ran their words together and for a while the only place to sit was the back of the neck.

"Actors have a hard time," said Tarkington, "they're subject to so many whims. When Richard Mansfield played *Beaucaire*, the actors had to be shorter than he was. If they were right for the part but as tall as Mansfield, he wouldn't engage them. The shortest actor in the profession was A. G. Andrews, Mansfield could look right over his head. A lot of good actors couldn't get into the company, but Mansfield looked right over Bogie Andrews' head, season after season after season."

In the second company of *Clarence*, Gregory was featured in Glenn's part and I played Cora. "Why name an adorable part Cora?"

Mr. Tarkington looked astonished. "When I lived in Paris, the two most seductive actresses were Cora La Parcerie and Cora La Pearl."

When we played English's Opera House, Mr. Tarkington invited us to North Pennsylvania Street. At lunch he said he had an idea for the play for us and Harry Leon Wilson liked it. They might write it together, no date mentioned.

Just back from New York where his new play, *The Intimate Strangers*, was going to star Maude Adams, he'd gone to meet A. L. Erlanger whom she'd chosen to manage her. "Klaw and Erlanger own half the theatres in this country," said Tarkington, "but in the outer office all his clerks refer to Erlanger as 'that old goat.'

"Waiting for Maude Adams to arrive, Mr. Erlanger didn't have much to say.

" 'Maude Adams is such a remote figure, yet wouldn't you say she engages the affection of the American public to a greater extent than any other actress?'

" 'Yes,' said Erlanger. 'Maude Adams is our most affectionate actress.' "

Our most affectionate actress decided not to play *The Intimate*

*Strangers* and Ziegfeld bought it for Billie Burke. As the other intimate stranger he co-starred Alfred, fresh from his *Clarence* triumph.

"We invited the Ziegfelds to Seaward for the weekend. Their big gray Minerva drove up, followed by a shiny truck filled with luggage. Did they plan to stay a month? Worried, but cordial, Susannah welcomed them. 'Oh, Miss Burke, we're delighted to have you.' Then a man stepped up behind Billie. 'Oh, Mr. Ziegfeld, we're so pleased—'

" 'Excuse me, I'm not Mr. Ziegfeld, I'm Mr. Ziegfeld's man—'

" 'Oh, how nice! Booth, this is Mr. Ziegfeld's *manager*.'

" 'Excuse me, I'm not Mr. Ziegfeld's manager. I'm Mr. Ziegfeld's man.' It was the famous Sidney, come to unpack Billie's luggage for the weekend."

At Kennebunkport, Tarkington's crony was Kenneth Roberts. "Ken's on the mend, but he's had an awful time. 'Same old vegetables, spinach, string beans,' he complained. 'Why not boil up elm leaves? Why not steam some jack-in-the-pulpit?'

"Anna Roberts didn't know why not.

" 'What about skunk cabbage?' asked Ken and went foraging in the Kennebunk woods.

"Anna served roast lamb for dinner with boiled skunk cabbage. It was a fresh green color and tasted all right. Two hours later Anna turned a fresh green color herself. Ken hurried to the phone. 'Operator, give me Portland Hospital . . . Portland Hospital, this is Kenneth Roberts at Kennebunkport. Send two ambulances to my house.'

"When the ambulances got there, Ken was as green as Anna and could just crawl into his, but a New Englander looks ahead. Out West we turn green first, *then* order the ambulance."

His day began with breakfast in bed. Only the maid who brought his tray saw him start the day. "Oh, I *wish* she wouldn't say good morning so loud. I have to brace myself a *long* time before I ring. If I didn't dread that loud 'Good morning,' I could start the day earlier."

He wrote all morning, then we saw him at lunch. At table his poodle, Figaro, sat on his left. "Who's a splendid dog?" asked Mr. Tarkington.

Figaro worried the question, then gave three complacent barks.

Tarkington looked serious. "What must we all do for our President?"

Figaro shut his eyes, put his front paws together and bowed his chocolate head.

"Lord have mercy on our President?" intoned Tarkington.

Figaro gave a discouraged yelp.

"Lord have mercy on all who have to put up with a Democrat?" Figaro moaned.

Tarkington looked distrustful. "Are you a Democrat?"

Two brown eyes opened and stared straight ahead.

"Are you a Republican?"

A loud bark. Figaro jumped to the floor and tore round the table.

Lunch over, Tarkington showed his guests the shore drive to Cape Porpoise via Ken Roberts' house out on the Neck. En route he pointed out Breakwater Inn. "Break-Father Inn," said Tarkington. He rode us by the pale yellow brick Wedding Cake House, trimmed with yards of white wooden lace, then chauffeur Chick turned back to Seaward and down to where the *Zantee* rocked gently at the Tarkington dock. Captain Thirkle welcomed its master and guests on board, the table was laid for tea.

How many writers do *you* know with their own dock and their own schooner and their chauffeur and captain? And never wrote a word that brought a blush. Think it over. Who was the last author you saw that had two boats, two houses, a captain and a dock and a Velásquez and a Jacobean room? Think it over.

Tarkington suggested a trip in the *Susannah* to see the school of whales. Yachting cap on, he took the wheel. Past the breakwater and the "Break-Father" Inn into deep water. Port and starboard went the *Susannah*, but never a spout.

"You can count on a dolphin or a porpoise," said Captain Thirkle, "but a whale's not reliable."

"Or a monkey." Tarkington scanned the horizon. "In Indianapolis my doctor and I like to go to vaudeville. The manager saves us front-row seats. One bill they had performing monkeys. The troupe performed with its trainer except for a small monkey who rode round and round on his bike and each time he got stage center, he looked out and glared at Dr. Page.

129

" 'He doesn't like you,' I said.

" 'It's the footlights. Bright lights make the little fellow look that way.'

"The monkey rode round again. 'I don't think it's the footlights, I think he doesn't like *you*.'

" 'A monkey's vision isn't all that sharp, the little fellow's trying to see where he's—' The monkey dropped his bike, jumped over the footlights and grabbed him by the throat."

Mr. Tarkington and Wilson finished *Bristol Glass* and sent it to George Tyler, who sent it back.

New Amsterdam Theatre Bldg.
214 West 42nd Street
New York City

Dear Tark,

I wouldn't touch it. All they go for now is bull meat and raw gin.

Sorry,
G.C.T.

"What if *we* produced *Bristol Glass?*" said Gregory. We had signed with John Golden to tour *The First Year*, but our contract let us give six weeks' notice. We could tour till we saved the money.

Mr. Tarkington said to draw up the papers, he and Harry Leon Wilson would take minimum royalties.

The show was ours and we took a partner, the manager of the Cleveland Opera House. He gave us the theatre to try out *Bristol Glass* for one roasting week. The weather was the only roast. The *Cleveland News* wrote, "Tarkington drama scores a tremendous success at Ohio where it makes its first stage appearance."

We set off on our *First Year* road tour with high hopes and vowed not to waste a cent. *Bristol Glass* would open when we saved the money. Meanwhile Tarkington's new play for Billie Burke would open the season in New York. *Rose Briar* was about a cabaret singer. Tarkington asked his Indianapolis friend Donald McGibney to compose a song for Rose.

McGibney was willing, but dubious. "Won't Ziegfeld want a song by someone *famous?*"

Tarkington reassured him and he wrote the song.

"Just right," said Tarkington and sent it to New York.

"Jerry Kern will write Rose's song," said Ziegfeld.

"Oh, didn't you get McGibney's?"

"Kern will write a good one."

Tarkington was troubled. "McGibney's is good."

Billie Burke looked unhappy. Flo Ziegfeld looked furious. "That song's a schnitzel. Kern'll write Billie a hit."

Tarkington was even more troubled. "A hit wouldn't be right for Rose's little cabaret—"

"You want Billie to sing a dud?"

"No, just something with charm, but—"

"You think this boob's song has charm?"

"I do."

Ziegfeld looked like a thundercloud, but Tarkington had given his word. "I wish McGibney could sing it for you. Do you think maybe if I—?"

"Sing it?"

"Perhaps not exactly *sing* it. Try to show you what McGibney means?"

Ten o'clock next morning in the dim, pilot-lit Ziegfeld Frolic on the roof of the New Amsterdam, Flo and Billie sat in the third row. The pianist struck up the opening bars. Overcoat draped around his shoulders like a negligee, Tarkington strolled languorously over to the piano, draped himself on it as fetchingly as his heavy coat would permit and flirted with his displeased audience behind his pink ostrich fan. "I was terrible. Oh, *terrible*. Poor McGibney, such a charming song. It needed Billie, of course. She did it with no enthusiasm at rehearsals, but I knew that in front of an audience she'd be her captivating self. I didn't stay for all the rehearsals, but Susannah and I came back for the opening. The curtain went up on Rose's shabby little cabaret. Imagine my surprise, Joseph Urban had designed it, he designs the *Ziegfeld Follies*. Rose sang McGibney's song and it was charming. Imagine my surprise, she sang a second song, it was by Jerome Kern."

By the time we played Memphis we had the money and took it to Cleveland. *Bristol Glass* rehearsed there with an all New York cast. Mr. and Mrs. Tarkington came from Indianapolis, but could stay only a day. Laurel Tarkington was ill. She'd had a misunderstanding with her mother back East and been sent to live with her father. Laurel adored her mother; she and her father didn't connect. Her shyness matched her father's. The summer that Laurel was sixteen, Maude Adams came to Seaward to talk about *The Intimate Strangers* and Laurel moved out of her room to her playhouse in the garden. She admired Maude Adams so, she couldn't bear to meet her. Was shyness why she never found the way to her father? Nor he to her. The children he understood were in his books.

Grieving about her trouble, one winter night Laurel jumped out the window. The old wygelia bushes broke the fall, but she lay in the snow. A few days after her father came home from Cleveland, she died. Was it pneumonia? Was it a broken heart?

*Bristol Glass* drew a mild press in Chicago. Nothing happened at the box office. We closed after two weeks. The New York train was ready to pull out of gloomy LaSalle Street Station. It wasn't any gloomier than Gregory. He sat looking out the window at nothing. Or was it at our troubles?

The stage manager tapped him on the shoulder. "Fred Perry didn't make the train."

"Good," said Gregory. He was a gentle person, not cut out for a producer.

*Rose Briar* finished its New York run, Billie Burke's mother died, and some people said Mr. Ziegfeld was making goo-goo eyes at Marilyn Miller. Billie decided to rent a house at York Harbor for the summer.

"She's just in *love* with Bootie," said Susannah, proud of her charmer. "And tomorrow she wants us all to come for lunch. I told her you and Gregory were visiting us and she's delighted. Do you know Glenn Hunter? He's visiting her."

Chauffeur Chick drove us through the York Harbor gate and there was adorable Billie Burke in a white wool dress edged in black at the throat and wrists, semi-mourning for her mother.

Can you remember what *you* were wearing in July of 1923? I

can remember Billie Burke wore a Panama pulled down over her famous red hair, black chiffon around the crown.

Through lunch, she talked only to Mr. Tarkington.

Well, wouldn't you?

Glenn and Gregory and I talked to each other and Mrs. Tarkington talked to Miss Louisa.

As Mr. Tarkington climbed into the car beside Chick, he said, "Excuse me for deserting you. I need a rest."

Coming into Kennebunkport, Mrs. Tarkington asked, "Did you know Weesy's decided to leave Seaward?" She gave Louisa's hand a squeeze. "Chick, we'll stop at Miss Kieffer's."

Chick turned onto a road lined with dusty sweet fern. "Isn't it charming!" said Mrs. Tarkington.

We went into a small cottage.

Mr. Tarkington had to bow his head not to hit the ceiling.

"Louisa's not as tall as you are, Bootie."

Tarkington pointed to the bed, then stretched out on it. His legs hung down to the floor. No smile from Miss Louisa. She never took to him. He put up with her. Did it stem from the day she packed his clothes for the return to Indianapolis? "She pulled a boner," said Chick. "I had to drive her down to the station where their trunks were all checked through to Indiana. Right in front of the baggage master and them waitin' for the Portland train, she had to get his pants out. She'd went and packed every darn pair."

Coffee was served in the drawing room, and before the evening drew to a close Mr. Tarkington suggested his secretary light up the Jacobean room. It was very dark, very old, very wooden. He'd had it shipped from England and loved it. His roots were Hoosier, but reached out across the water. "Of all the places I lived, I liked best my Rome apartment."

Following him down a narrow winding staircase, I seemed suddenly in another place. Mr. Tarkington, Miss Betsy Trotter and I sat and talked as if the evening had just begun. Had it?

"Do you know about Dr. Johnson's friend Mrs. Thrale?" I asked.

He nodded. "She was a fascinater."

"Could a play be written around her?"

"She was interesting."

"I think I'd be good as Mrs. Thrale, but it worries me who could act Dr. Johnson."

"It worries *me* who could *write* Dr. Johnson."

When we went back, Miss Louisa had gone to bed and Mrs. Tarkington stood waiting in the hall. We followed her up the stairs.

"*Tweedles*, formerly *Bristol Glass*, is Tarkington at his best," wrote John Corbin in *The New York Times*.

In the *Herald*, Woollcott wrote, "She has a genuine and forthright actuality and can fill the brief love scenes with—"

No May Vokes, no get off the stage and since Mr. Tarkington wrote *Tweedles* with no baby talk, no one suggested I should. May Vokes references have gone where the woodbine twineth. Goodnight May, goodnight George Jean, goodnight Heywood, wherever you are, and if you run into the Sitwells' father, tell him, without a friend I might still be getting roasted.

※　※　※　※　※

There's no business like show business and Princess Grace hasn't forgotten the lingo from the time when she played Raymond Massey's daughter in Strindberg's *The Father* at the Cort Theatre. The Princess still uses the jive.

"Did you see any shows you liked?" I asked her.

"*Butterflies Are Free. I wish* I'd seen it with a regular audience. The night we went was a benefit."

"I thought it went well," said Rainier.

"Oh no, it was a benefit. At a benefit they sit on their hands."

Nice going for a Monagasque! That's strictly show business. Did you ever hear of anyone sitting on their hands in Monte Carlo?

# Martin Beck, Dearie, Do You Want to Make Anything of It?

D o you you mind strangers backstage? I do. "Act One, please."
The stage manager knocked on my door. "I'm calling the act,
Miss Gordon."

"Thank you." At the Martin Beck Theatre the Saturday matinee
of *Hotel Universe* was going to begin. I came out of Dressing
Room Number One.

In the first entrance sat a man with a police dog. "Who are *you?*"
I said.

"Martin Beck, dearie, do you want to make anything of it?"

He had the topper. He had it through most of his life. When
vaudeville was a great industry, Martin Beck ran it, even though he
pronounced it "wardewill."

One day he thought it would be nice if Sarah Bernhardt would
do the two-a-day. He got on the old *France*, pitched for seven days
to Le Havre, whizzed through Normandy on the boat train,
dropped his bags at the Crillon Hotel, sped to Boulevard Pereire
and put the proposition to Madame.

She liked it. She agreed to tour across the country on B. F. Keith
and Orpheum time.

They agreed on terms and dates and with the lightest heart on
the boat train he whizzed back through Normandy to Le Havre.
Sarah Bernhardt in the two-a-day, what a coup! What a— Suddenly his heart missed a beat. *Two*-a-day! Had he mentioned
there'd be two shows every day?

He got his bags off the dock, took the train to Paris, didn't bother to check in at the Crillon and sped to Boulevard Pereire. "Madame," he said, "I forgot one little thing. On your tour across the country, you have to play *two* shows a day in every town."

Bernhardt nodded. "What else would I do?"

One summer weekend Mr. and Mrs. Martin Beck asked me to Elberon. Martin and I were partners in a game of bridge with Jed Harris and Louise Beck.

"No trump," she bid.

Martin and I lost.

"Four hearts," bid Jed.

Martin and I lost.

"Three clubs," bid Jed.

Martin and I lost. He wrote something on the back of the score pad and held it up for me to read.

"You can't give your partner signals," said Louise.

"Yes I can."

"No you *can't*," said the former librarian of Chapel Hill.

"Yes I *can!*"

"You can *not*, Martin. You must show us *all* what you've written."

He held up the score pad. "Ruthie, we are going to win from *now on*."

*   *   *   *   *

Do you say "Wouldn't you know this would happen to me?" Well, don't, unless it's that you won the Nobel Prize. Then it's all right to say "Wouldn't you know this would happen to me?" But if you fall downstairs or your feller leaves you or your gold turns to dross or you get the Hong Kong flu or a parking ticket, don't think of that as the natural course of events. Know that's just something you put up with and save your "Wouldn't you know that would happen to me?" till you get left a million dollars from an uncle you never knew and won't miss.

*   *   *   *   *

New subject. When he died, some people started pissing on him, but his friends took it from whence it came and noticed that from January 1943 to the close of 1970 nobody has so far taken Woollcott's place.

"He and Dottie Parker and Neysa McMein and to a slightly lesser degree Alice Duer Miller all had streaming eyes," says Thornton, "whenever the subject was animals."

Out in California where anything is likely to happen and often does, a man living on the edge of wild land had his grounds softly floodlit and after his dinner party put a big platter of cold cuts, T-bone steaks and other inducements on the lawn far from the house. Guests got binoculars and watched the deer and rabbits and a spotted lynx leave freedom and get hung up on steak.

Woollcott and Dottie came to dinner, but that night nothing showed up.

"It has only happened twice before," the host apologized. "Please come once more, I can't account for tonight. It won't happen again."

Woollcott and Dottie made a second visit. Again nothing came out of the wilderness. At eleven-thirty they gave up.

"Oh, I don't understand it," moaned the host. "How could it happen?"

Dottie shook her head in amazement. "I thought we'd at *least* get the after-theatre crowd."

❊ ❊ ❊ ❊ ❊

In London a good place for the after-theatre crowd is the Savoy Grill. Oliver Messel entertained eight of us there. Oliver is a with-it guy, I thought the others would be too. Did you ever misjudge the company? That night I wasn't the only one. The chef did, too. Someone sent back a dish. That cued me in. "I went to a luncheon that Zoë Akins gave for Lady Mary Birley. Zoë lived over in Pasadena, but gave the luncheon at her friend Jobyna Howland's house that Frank Lloyd Wright had designed for her.

"Sitting at Joby's right was her treasured Pekinese and after her butler served the guests, he served the treasure. 'Have this?' he inquired, putting down some cold meat.

"The Peke sniffed.

" 'Innocente,' boomed Joby, 'get him something he can *eat!*'

" 'Yes, Miss.' Innocente hurried out and came back with a dish of cold chicken.

"The Peke turned away.

" 'Get him something he *wants*,' roared Joby.

" 'Yes, Miss.' He came back with a dish of salmon.

"The Peke disdained it.

" 'Innocente, will you get this poor creature something he can *eat!*'

" 'Yes, Miss.' He ran back with a bowl of corn flakes and cream. 'You no eat this, you eat *shit.*' "

Did you ever have a story bomb? Oliver's party lapsed into silence and soon found it was time to go. Only Berners felt compassion. "When Adele Cavendish comes next week, shall we have supper?"

"Please."

Adele put off London and he asked me for a weekend at Faringdon House. I arrived as he was giving tea to his other guests. Between him and Castlereagh stood Berners' white horse enjoying a biscuit.

Berners greeted me and introduced me to the Castlereaghs.

"The horse?" I asked.

"Ah yes, he likes his tea. How do you take yours?"

"Please take his picture."

Some things must be on film to be believed.

✳   ✳   ✳   ✳   ✳

The phone rang. "What're you doing?" asked Billy Wilder.

"Did you ever hear of St. Jude Thaddeus?"

"Was he in *The Matchmaker?*"

"No, I'm doing a piece for Diana Vreeland and he's in it."

"Goodbye."

St. Jude Thaddeus. Do you take from him? A month before the Oscar I went into Le Dernier Cri to buy Garson a shirt. One of the owners threw his arms around me. "You're going to win," he shouted and reached in a small cupboard for a flask and put four drops on my forehead. "Take this." He thrust a white paper tract into my hand. "Never go anywhere without it. It's the wish beyond the wish."

On the cover was *Helper in difficult and desperate cases.* It curled into my evening bag, it displaced my powder puff, it went next to my money in my street bag, it went in the pocket of my Hermès traveling bag where the passport goes. It went with me to Gristede. It went with me to Cartier. It went with me to Paraphernalia. It went on TWA to New York, Boston and on the *Islander* to Edgartown and back to the Ahmanson Theatre and I won the Oscar. St. Jude Thaddeus brings the wish beyond the wish in "difficult and desperate cases." Look in your pocket book. Throw out stuff and make room.

❀ ❀ ❀ ❀ ❀

If the fire got close to your house, what would you pack? Janet Gaynor packed the stills from her old movies.

What else! She has lots of money to get more jewelry and clothes, but where could she get her old stills?

❀ ❀ ❀ ❀ ❀

If *you* have money and enough drag to lunch at Grenouille and aren't shunted into the Ketchup Room, look at Mainbocher. He's at the grand table having a grand lunch. Does he look as if he ever had a worry? How do you think he looked the day his workroom finished a beautiful wedding dress and the model caught her finger on a pin? What color was his face that day when blood spurted onto the white satin? How would *you* look? Well, that's how he looked, only more so.

Draw the veil.

"Fetch the linen thread," said Mainbocher's great fitter.

Manageress Baker's jaws unclenched just enough to murmur, "Wouldn't a Curad be better?"

139

"Linen thread," repeated Bridget and a minute later her skillful hands started unreeling and unreeling, then rolled it into a ball.

"Chew this."

"What?" said the white-faced model and Bridget thrust it into her mouth.

"Chew," she commanded.

Main went whiter. Not only was the dress ruined, but his great fitter had gone round the bend. She held out her hand. "Drop it out." Out came wet snarls. Bridget passed it over the bloodstained white satin. Bloodstains vanished, the white satin was pristine. "It has to be the spit of the one that bled," said Bridget. "Is the length right, Mr. Bocher?"

Is the *length* right! *Everything* was right. God bless the Irish and if you've got any doubts, draw some blood and chew some linen thread, but remember the words of Bridget the great, "It has to be the spit of the one that bled." Go!

\* \* \* \* \*

Remember the first dirty joke you ever heard? Was it a drunk standing out in front of the Catholic church that asked, "Is mass out?"

"No, but your hat's on crooked." Circa 1912. It blew my mind. 1912 to 1970. Is *that* ever a long time!

\* \* \* \* \*

They were sitting around knocking President Roosevelt. "He's his own worst enemy."

"Not while *I'm* alive!" said Jules Bache.

That's another long time.

# Dame Ede

IT WAS a Monday. Dress rehearsal in the morning, one in the evening. Notes and changes after the first one, the next one we went through like a performance. Was the audience cold? The audience was Mrs. Gilbert Miller and Mrs. Syrie Maugham huddled in the first row, an auto robe over their legs. The furnace had broken down and mid-October on the Waterloo Road is penetrating. It penetrated the cast, Oliver Messel's satin dresses swept through their scenes, his fifteen sets including the Mulberry Gardens and Mr. Horner's lodgings flew up to the flies, flew down to the raked stage, everything working perfectly, and down came the final curtain.

"Curtain calls will be rehearsed tomorrow afternoon," announced Tyrone Guthrie. "Four o'clock on stage for an hour. Curtain at eight for opening night. Goodnight."

We hurried along the stone passage to the dressing rooms. Someone had opened a window on the stairs. Was it colder outside or in? Mrs. Richmond was waiting, second floor, first door to the right, to get me out of my stylish pearl-gray satin. First door to the left Potter was getting Edith Evans out of her golden brocade. "Mrs. Miller will be in to see me," said I.

"Very good, Madam. Should I go down and show them the way up? The Vic isn't an easy place to find one's way."

"Yes, please." Had we been good? It had been smooth, but had we been *good?* Would we be good tomorrow night?

"Sorry, Madam, but no one's come round."

I went down the hall and knocked on Edith Evans' door. "Did Mrs. Miller come to see you?"

"No." Edith studied my troubled face. "Would you like a bite of supper?"

"Yes I would."

"What a good idea! Let us go round to the Café Royal. That'll cheer us. Potter, tell George to fetch a taxi and book a table."

Edith Evans never goes out to a café, but kindness took her that night. White wine and chicken-something for her, I had a rarebit and beer. She didn't drink. I didn't, but that night we did. "I'll ride you back to your hotel," she offered.

The Café Royal doorman called a cab.

"Here, get under my coat." Under Edith's muskrat we rolled along to Claridge's. And why part at Claridge's? "I'll just look in for a minute. You all right? I expect they were getting a chill out front and had to look after it. At least *we* had the lights on us—"

A letter slid under the door.

"It's Thornton."

"Thornton!"

"I'll read it. 'Tonight or tomorrow or one of these evenings soon, you and the great Edith will—'"

"Oh, he didn't say that, where is it?"

I held the letter out.

"Oh, what a duck!"

"'You and the great Edith will bring glory to the stage and in the wings watching and approving will be Dora Jordan and Mrs. Bracegirdle and—'"

I wish Blanche du Bois could have known Thornton and Edith, but she's also right about strangers. They are OK, too. Plenty of kindness from those opening-night ones. I see what you mean, Blanche. Do you dig *me?*

The world is full of wonderful actresses, Edith is the greatest. Like Charles, she didn't *learn* how, she makes her own rules. "When I'm acting, I don't have tea with Madam Pandit Nehru. When I'm *not* acting, I have tea with Madam Pandit Nehru."

(*Players' Guide*, copy.)

People don't wait for her to act in a theatre, they ask her to act anywhere and they bring the book along with them. Over supper at Sardi's, Peggy Webster brought out *The Importance of Being Earnest*, turned the pages. "Dear Edith, please read Lady Bracknell."

Very pleased, she chose to bridle. "I can't do it *here*, dear. You're *mad!* Where is it?"

Lady Bracknell was where *she* was, on a banquette at Sardi's, across from "John Golden's Table."

Another evening. "Please just read us Millamant's poetry speech." The book was put in her lap. The greatest of Millamants described how she hated letters, but "They served one to pin up one's hair." When asked if she pinned up her hair with all her letters, she replied, "Only those in verse, I never pin up my hair with prose. I fancy one's hair would not curl if it were pinned up with prose. I think I tried once."

In London when she'd played *The Way of the World*, they formed the Millamant Society to worship her and remind each other of her performance. And let's hope they reminded each other of Congreve who thought up the curling papers. Would curling your hair be all that interesting, even with Edith, if he hadn't known how to tell it? Goodnight, Mr. Congreve, wher*ever* you are, thanks for writing all those good parts.

Edith went up to meet Edward Sheldon. Blind and on his back for twenty years, Ned, the handsomest man in town, was still a dazzler. He had charm for everybody, with enough left over to pass around. Black satin mask over his eyes, he lay on the high narrow bed in the beautiful stately room in his penthouse in the East Eighties. "Dear Miss Evans, how good of you to come." His voice would melt the heart of an anchorite, as Congreve said so beautifully. "Dear Miss Evans" when she came in, but when it was time to go it was "Dear Edith."

"Ned dear, I'll be back." And between all that was dinner at a table beside his bed where the guests ate and he talked. "Dear Miss Evans, will you read me Millamant? I have it marked in the red book next your table." A lot of his other books were marked, too.

She filled the room with beautiful words. Among them, "Dear Ned." Not one who found it easy to express herself, she hovered beside him.

"Dear Edith." Two people fell in love. Romance had come back to the man who'd written it. He wrote it for Doris Keane, the love of his life, and *Romance* had been the rage of Broadway. Tonight had he found it again? Doris needed a theatre. Edith needed only a listener.

Sitting up in bed in my 12th Street guestroom, surrounded by her "Lesson for the Day" and Mrs. Eddy's *Science and Health*, she looked troubled.

"What's the matter?" I asked.

"I don't *know*," she grumbled. "I feel like flinging m'milk and biscuits around."

(*Players' Guide*, note the following.) "Smile, dear, it doesn't hurt to smile, dear," Ellen Terry whispered, then looked up brightly at daughter Edy who was directing her for a turn in the halls in "Great Scenes from Great Plays."

Edy looked away and her Mom whispered, "You can be a great actress and still smile," then asked her daughter, "Where would you like me to stand for my 'Quality of Mercy,' dear?"

(*Players' Guide*, Edith says work on

> *Then hear me, gracious sovereign, and you peers,*
> *That owe yourselves, your lives, and services*
> *To this imperial throne. There is no bar*
> *To make against your highness' claim to France*
> *But this, which they produce from Pharamond,*
> *"In terram Salican mulieres ne succedant,*
> *No woman shall succeed in Salique land":*
> *Which Salique land the French unjustly gloze*
> *To be the realm of France, and Pharamond*
> *The founder of this law and female bar.*
> *Yet their own authors faithfully affirm*
> *That the land Salique is in Germany,*
> *Between the floods of Sala and of Elbe;*
> *Where Charles the Great, having subdu'd the Saxons—*

The Archbishop of Canterbury has plenty to say and says it. "Work over *that* speech," says Edith, "and if you can say that one, you can play Shakespeare."

And don't forget to smile.)

Edith's yardstick for a night in the theatre: "If you don't walk a mile in the wrong direction, you haven't really enjoyed it." Of course, to do that in New York you'd be out of your mind. Also out of funds. The *best* that could happen would be they'd take your pocketbook. I guess New Yorkers'll have to settle for *feeling* like a mile in the wrong direction.

John Gielgud asked Edith to play Lady Macbeth.

"Oh no, dear."

"Why not? It's such a great part and you've never played it."

"No."

"But *why?*"

"Well, dear, I can never reconcile Lady Macbeth's behavior with a Scottish sense of hospitality."

I asked her if she'd really said it.

"Oh, I may have."

"But you've played all the others, why don't you play Lady Macbeth?"

She bristled, "Well, ducky, if I come to the theatre, I don't like to sit for three quarters of an hour in m'dressing room! I like to be on stage *doing* something."

A chum took her to see London's new sensation. After the matinee they got into a taxi and were riding toward Edith's Halkin Place flat. She hadn't said anything about London's new sensation.

"What do you think of her?"

Edith looked out at Hyde Park. And beyond. "Clever actress, wouldn't want to see her *again*."

At a rehearsal the Old Vic apprentices laughed a lot at me in the letter-writing scene. Edith looked surprised and a little frosty. "Mind you, I knew Margery Pinchwife was a *good* part, but after this I shall read the whole play."

Thirty-four years later she was waiting for me in the Savoy Grill. Suit by Hardy Amies, hat by some other genius. Everybody recognized her. And not one that didn't admire her. "I'm eighty-three, dear," she said accusingly, "and I need a vacation. I haven't stopped for two years."

"When do you finish?"

"I'll stop shooting next week. I believe they'll go on a few days longer. Albie Finney plays Scrooge, you know." Spirit of Christmas accepted the menu. "The music's by Leslie Bricusse. Shall we order? I think I told you I'm due at the Lane at two-thirty. I'm on the board of governors for the Actors' Orphanage and we're having a jolly big meeting."

We ordered, then I asked which she liked, films or the stage?

"I like them both, dear."

"Film acting is easier, don't you agree?"

She looked challenging. "Why is it?"

"On the stage, you have to hold on to the audience. You have to control a thousand people. They have to *laugh* on the same line and they mustn't laugh when you don't want them to. If they come in late you have to time it so the rest of the audience won't miss what you say and you have to do all that *before* you even start to act. In a film you just give your performance. If anyone laughed, they'd be fired."

Dame Ede looked contemplative. "I believe I *like* to control an audience."

Lobster thermidor suited her. Cold salmon with cucumber salad suited me. "Do you still like to act? I don't mean do you like to be paid, but do you still like *acting?*"

"Oh, yes," she said, surprised. "To get a good scene to play? Oh, yes! Oh, I enjoy that very much."

Eighty-three by her own count, looking a vision and tucking into lobster thermidor, when she started out it was as Cressida in William Poel's production that gave working people something to do with their evenings. Making up at the long table, word passed from girl to girl, "George Moore's out front."

"I didn't know who George Moore *was*, but I said to the girl next me, 'George Moore's out front.'

"After the performance Mr. Poel came back and introduced Mr. Moore. 'I'd like you to be in my play,' said Moore to Cressida. 'They're doing it in the West End.'

" 'Oh, I shouldn't be able to.'

" 'Why not?' asked Poel.

" 'I'm a milliner's apprentice. It cost my father money.' "

Poel said he'd arrange that and cleared the way for the greatest actress to one day play Millamant and leave millinery to others.

"There are a lot of ways to learn to speak Shakespeare and one is to talk French. The French use vocal muscles that are different to the ones we use. To be understood in Shakespeare you need everything. French muscles, English muscles, the lot!"

(*Players' Guide*, did you get that?)

The summer before the war, she came to spend July at my 60 West 12th Street house. Over on 14th Street we browsed around Hearn's Department Store. They were having a sale on straw hats: ALL HATS $1.00. The erstwhile apprentice chose several. "At a *dollar* if they blow away, we won't have to chase them." She eyed herself in the mirror and was pleased with the effect. "Have one on me!" she said.

The weather got hotter. We went up to Best's for her to choose some off-the-rack cotton dresses.

The salesgirl looked at Edith. "That one's too tight. You're big around the hips."

Edith could have replied. Instead she looked at me. "*Tell* her I have the most beautiful body in London!" Why did her voice remind me of the great Lady Dedlock?

She was reading *The New York Times*. "It's very odd in your country, you call so many people first ladies. I read that Helen is. I read it's Kit. Then Lynn. You must feel like you're in a relay race. Who's ahead now? In London we don't *have* a first lady," said the first lady of the London stage.

During July an actor can run short of money. That can happen in both countries.

"You look worried," said my houseguest.

"Well—" Could I tell her I had to get out and make some money? She'd come over to spend a month.

"Tell me. Maybe I can help."

"Well."

"Just tell it."

"Well, next month *Atlantic Monthly* will pay me. That'll tide me over till I get in a show, but right now—"

"You need money, dear? Let me—"

"No," I said. "But if I go up to Stockbridge I can get a week up there and the week after at Westport."

"But you *must*."

"Yes, but that's your last week here."

"I'll do fine," she said. And did.

I came back solvent. She had sailed for home. On Jones' dresser was an autographed glossy of Bill Robinson.

"Where'd you get that?"

"He's great. Edith and I went to the Cotton Club and he came over to the table and introduced himself to us and gave me this."

He was great and so was Edith. Why sit home when you can go to the Cotton Club? Jones is good company and in three months he was going to be ten.

"I've agreed to do the outdoor scenes from *As You Like It* at Ellen Terry's barn at Hythe. Michael will do them with me," she wrote me, "and you'll get an idea of what we did at the Vic."

Her father came over from Hastings where nothing much is going on since 1066 and all that. Edith had arranged for Mr. Evans to go with me and saw to it our seats were dead center in the second row of lawn chairs in front of Ellen Terry's barn. The performance was for a charity and Ellen Terry's daughter ran it. Why did she look so balefully at us two unknowns sitting in the enviable seats? "Who are you?" she asked.

"I'm—"

Mr. Evans leaned across me. "I'm Edith Evans' father," he said as clearly as though he'd boned up on the Archbishop's speech.

Edy Craig glared at us, but just said "Oh."

Mr. Evans nudged me. "I guess that'll hold her."

Is there no justice? Two minutes later Edy Craig motioned us out and ushered in two county folk in flowing dresses. Pray, what does the man on the woolsack say about *that*?

At the Vic *As You Like It* had followed *The Country Wife*. Their opening night, I was on the boat train pulling out of Waterloo Station and Edith was making history down the Waterloo Road.

"I was dreadfully nervous," she wrote. "I'm usually m'self on opening night, but I don't know what was the matter with me, I couldn't get started. At the end of Act I, I went down to George's booth and rang up my practitioner. We talked for a good five minutes. Act II went off a perfect treat. [*Players' Guide*, what do you think?] Oh, Rosalind is a lovely part! You *must* play her."

If she made a slow start, it didn't show in the reviews. The critics said Shakespeare's work was all very well, but Edith Evans was *great*. They flung in all the adjectives.

The Orlando was Michael Redgrave. "Did you ever forget your lines opening night?" he asked me.

"*Don't!*" I said.

"We were playing the picnic scene, Edith got up, did a dance around the stage. I knew we'd not rehearsed *that*. But she flitted here, there, then over to the prompter's side of the stage, fluttered for a moment, swooped back and down onto the grass mats. 'Were e'er the trees thus green?' she said, and we were back in the scene."

Once in *Hay Fever* she dropped off during a scene. Her cue came, she dozed on, then silence woke her. "Whose turn it it?" she asked.

The guest of honor at London's Soviet Embassy reception looked surprised. "Have you ever *asked* to come to the Soviet Union?"

"One knows it's not possible, but you people come over *here*. Why won't you let *us* come and see you?"

A week later there arrived a letter from Moscow.

"I got on the plane to Prague and *there* I was met by two strangers who steered me onto another plane. 'What am I *doing?*' I said to m'self. 'Who *are* they? What plane *is* it?' But before I decided what I should do, the plane took off. I was there for ten days, ducky. They gave me a dear little thing for an interpreter that never left m'side, I was shown anything and everything. Fancy! Only because I asked why they didn't let us. Coo!"

She was in Hollywood to be in Dick Van Dyke's picture.

"Do you like him?"

"Oh, very much."

"What have you seen since you've been here?"

"I saw *The Sound of Music*."

"Like it?"

"*Oh* yes."

"What else?"

"*Hawaii.*"

"Like it?"

"*Oh* yes. Very beautiful scenery."

"Working in a picture, how do you have the time?" asked Garson.

"Might I have another slice of that beautiful bread?"

La Rue's waiter offered some.

"Thank you. Well, I *make* time. I've always thought *art* should be what's left over from life."

Shaw wrote *The Millionairess* for her, but instead she chose to act for a season at The Vic. He came to see the first matinee of *The Country Wife*. Outside on the newsstands the papers were full of praise. Inside, the packed-out matinee roared with laughter.

Potter knocked at my door. "Mr. Shaw is visiting Miss Evans, Madam. Will you come in?"

"I didn't laugh once," he said. "No. Once. It made me laugh when Sir Jasper Fidget said, 'Oh thou libidinous lady.' The rest was a waste of time." He glared at me. "The audience didn't laugh because you were funny, they laughed because you were sensible."

It's tough to write Epifania for someone, then have them rather play Lady Fidget. Goodnight, Mr. Shaw, wher*ever* you are. I'm glad you told Edith, "When you play an intellectual part, make sure you wear beautiful clothes."

(*Players' Guide* and *Women's Wear*, copy.)

"They want me to play *Heartbreak House*, but it's too heartless for these times. They're doing all me old roles at the National. *The Way of the World, Beaux' Stratagem, Portia.*"

"We went to *Back to Methuselah* last night."

"That's one of mine. Shaw wrote the Serpent for me. I've played them *all*, dear."

She was off to visit friends in Toronto. At London Airport the man on the *Daily Express* was surprised to see Dame Edith's ticket was for Economy Class. He spoke to BOAC.

"Ah yes," they said, "Dame Edith's *ticket* is 'Economy Class,' but on BOAC *she* is first."

"I'm coming to the Haymarket tomorrow night, shall I come back and see you?"

"Please."

"I never *do*, you know."

"Then I'll come out front and see you."

Flying from L.A. to Kennedy, the pilot announced he was having trouble with the landing gear, they would come in on foam rubber.

"He made a beautiful landing," said Edith. "I was lost in admiration at his feat. I wish I could have told him so and I felt I couldn't get off the plane and not mention it. 'Didn't he make a remarkable landing!' I said to a pretty young stewardess.

"She looked at me as though I was balmy. 'That's what he's *supposed* to do.'"

When you learn to say the Archbishop of Canterbury's speech, does that mean you can learn to say no?

"Come to see my house in the country," said Edith.

So far, so good.

"Take the train at Charing Cross to—"

"Oh, I think I'll get a hire car."

"No, dear, take the train at Charing Cross, get off at Tunbridge Wells."

"Wouldn't it be simpler to get a hire car?"

"My chauffeur will have the car at Tunbridge. I shall cook the dinner. I'm a very good cook, you know."

Why don't I say I want to hire a car?

"I learned how during the war. We *all* did."

"Are you sure about—"

"Yes, dear, certain. Take the eleven-one from—"

"I will."

Next evening she rang up. "I went to Charing Cross m'self and took the train. It's quite a comfortable trip."

It was. Her chauffeur was waiting and we rolled through lanes and green spring woods and meadows where Kent skirts Surrey. Her house was a beauty and dinner was the best. The best roast beef. The best Yorkshire pudding. The best rhubarb tart. After dinner, the rain started to splash the windows, we had coffee in the sitting room before the fire. "Put your feet up, dear."

I did. "Why don't we snooze?"

"*Do*, dear, if you like."

"Wouldn't *you?*"

"Oh no, I've never learned to nap, I'll sit here and think."

Why did my neck hurt? I had fallen asleep. "Edith, I'm sorry."

No answer.

"Edith?"

Feet up, clever Edith had learned how to nap.

✻　✻　✻　✻　✻

Thornton Wilder's father told him never to tell a story against himself. And don't *you*.

✻　✻　✻　✻　✻

Mary sang it, then Julie, "These are a few of my favorite things." Round the revolving door at La Pace came Christian Dior. I was just going in the door. "I love you," I said.

"Oh no!" he said and recoiled.

A week later at Brasserie Lipp someone opened *L'Intransigeant*. DIOR EST MORT screamed the headline.

This is *not* one of my favorite things.

✻　✻　✻　✻　✻

Ever happen to get with anyone on the slow side? "Have them tell the story of their life," advised Woollcott. "That's a subject everybody's good on."

A new boy joined the company. We made no headway. "Bert, sit down and tell me the story of your life."

"Oh no," he said, "it's so uninteresting."

"There must be *something* interesting."

"No," he claimed. "Nothing."

"Bert, there has to be." I trusted Woollcott. "Sit down and start from the very beginning."

"It's so dull," he moaned.

"Let's not give up. Where were you born, Bert?"

"In the Gotham Hotel."

How many people *do* you know were born at the Gotham? Bert, you were wrong and you were right, Alec. Goodnight wher*ever* you are.

\*　\*　\*　\*　\*

In the drugstore in Washington across from the Treasury Building, Garson asked, "Do you sell glue?"

The man behind the counter went on the alert. "What do you want *that* for?" Was he faced with two addicts?

"What do you want that for?" Garson asked me.

"To glue the sole of my shoe on."

"To glue the sole of her shoe on."

The man looked us over, then shoved a pad and ballpoint forward. "Write down your full name and address and age."

Drugstores in our nation's capital have to know if it's for a sniff or a cobble.

\*　\*　\*　\*　\*

The only fortune-teller I ever went to said, "Ruthie, why don't you be smart?" Did he say the same to a Worcester priest?

When *Time* Magazine started, it didn't find it so easy to get going and once offered a lifelong subscription for a hundred dollars. There weren't too many takers, but one hundred dollars came in from a priest in Worcester. He received *Time* for the rest of his days. At the fortieth birthday party, Harry Luce asked him to stand up.

Guess who stood up. Cardinal Spellman.

\*　\*　\*　\*　\*

Do you think anybody's going to leave you something? I expect a million from a man in Streator, Illinois. Would he be around ninety now? It may be any minute. He was going to kill himself, but before he did he went to see *Fair and Warmer* and laughed so, he cheered up and made a fortune, so in his will he'll want "a million to go to that adorable actress who played Blanny in *Fair and Warmer* at the theatre in Streator, Illinois, on the night of January 16th, 1917." And that's me.

(Streator, Illinois, paper, copy.)

# Mr. Sampson

M R. SAMPSON didn't leave me a million. He left me some treasured books on the theatre and left seventy-five thousand to
his wife. William Sampson was never a big earner and the reason he
had the seventy-five was that he never was a big spender. His highest salary was when John Golden paid him four hundred dollars a
week in *The First Year*. Then he took sick and had to give up the
part. I wanted to bring him something special. Florida berries were
just on the stands and Dean's, opposite the Cathedral, was serving
fresh strawberry ice cream. "I'll have a pint," I said and brought it
to the Hotel Seymour. Up in his apartment Mr. Sampson was sitting
in the streak of sun that a half an hour in the afternoon slanted
across the courtyard into his sitting room.

"Thanks," he said and ate it, putting each strawberry to one side.

Why hadn't I gotten coffee or chocolate or vanilla? "I'm sorry
you don't like strawberry."

"I do." He looked over at Mrs. Sampson. "Mary, give me the
cream and sugar." He sugared the berries and poured cream over
them.

We had admired his acting in *Bought and Paid For* and *Be Calm,
Camilla* and *Polly with a Past*, but we never met him until rehearsals of *Piccadilly Jim*. James Bradbury had turned down the part
and someone said William Sampson is available. " 'About as welcome as an ice cream freezer to an Eskimo in—' Oh, I couldn't say

155

that." Mr. Sampson handed the new lines back to Guy Bolton. Was he going to leave?

Guy Bolton cut the line out and Mr. Sampson went on. He was small, had smooth gray hair, a warm color in his face, wore a beautifully tailored suit, was a perfect actor and looked like people.

What brought him to the stage? His grandmother was an Indian from Oldtown, Maine, and all his forebears were Yankees. Mary Webster Sampson towered a foot above him, but he ran things. "Her father's president of Kidder, Peabody, but we live on my salary."

When the will was read, leaving Mrs. Mary Webster Sampson seventy-five thousand, it was the spring of 1923. The last part he played was the father in Frank Craven's *The First Year* at Mr. Winthrop Ames' Little Theatre.

Frank and Roberta Arnold took two weeks' vacation and Gregory and I took their place. Mr. Sampson was ailing, but he rehearsed with us. The last night of his long career was the first night of our engagement. Afterward we walked him home to the Hotel Seymour, which had a spare entrance on 44th Street.

Loath to part, we stood awhile. "You have to talk louder," he said to me.

"You don't think they heard me?"

"They heard you, but that's not enough. They have to hear you without trying to."

Was that something he learned at Daly's Theatre when he played second-character parts and Willie Collier was the call boy who called the act for Ada Rehan and John Drew and the kid from Wauseon sat up in the gallery? After their New York season, the Daly company sailed on the White Star line for their London stand, followed by an appearance in Paris, where Rehan and Drew captivated the Continent as easily as they had London. Was it winning the British and the French over that taught Mr. Sampson how to be heard? Actors' knowledge isn't all in books or classes, it's passed on, walking home. It's handed down over a beer at Mock's or Sardi's.

(*Players' Guide*, copy.)

*The First Year* was our last show with Mr. Sampson. The first was *Piccadilly Jim*, opening Christmas week in Wilkes-Barre, Pa. What a Merry Christmas!

The next stand was New Year's Eve at Atlantic City's Globe Theatre down by Hackney's on the Boardwalk. What a happy New Year!

In the layover between trains, Mr. Sampson and Gregory and I left our luggage in the checkroom at North Philadelphia and gave ourselves the pleasure of lunch at Philadelphia's Ritz, mecca for elegant Main Liners and Chestnut Hillbillies. Was there ever a better dining room? Or a snootier?

We reserved our table in advance, so what could the captain do but look dismayed to have to seat three nobodies? Our elegant waiter took it for granted we couldn't read. "Poulet rôti aux fines herbes?" he suggested. "Steak au poivre? Red snapper grillé? Homard à la—"

"We'll pick out our *own* food," said Mr. Sampson.

The waiter heard *him* without trying to.

Goodnight, Mr. Sampson, wher*ever* you are, they can hear me now. In London the organization called the Gallery Gods gave a supper and one said, "Madam, I've sat in the gallery all my life and you're the only one I heard every word."

※　※　※　※　※

Monograms, goldfish, blisters, criticism, pink Christmas trees, bookends, funerals, gazpacho, string, silver jewelry, limes, lead pencils, not being heard, these are a few of my *un*favorite things.

※　※　※　※　※

How did you do on the last bissextile? Did you propose to anybody? Did you get any acceptances? Or maybe you didn't know it was on. Start reading the *Farmer's Almanack*

FOR THE YEAR OF OUR LORD

1970

BEING 2ND AFTER BISSEXTILE

OR LEAP YEAR AND (UNTIL JULY 4)

194TH YEAR OF AMERICAN

INDEPENDENCE.

Next year maybe they'll add

AND FIRST YEAR OF
WOMEN'S LIB.

\* \* \* \* \*

"Look where you're going," counseled my father. He was probably right.

\* \* \* \* \*

Isn't it great when somebody comes at you with a question and you have the topper? At *Time*'s fortieth birthday party, all the guests had had their picture on a cover. That covered just about everybody except Clare Luce. Harry said they'd agreed not. I guess they didn't agree not to have Harry's on, or how would they have got in?

During cocktails everybody tried to guess who everybody was. A small man saw us speak to Hedda Hopper. "I'd love to meet her," he said.

"Hedda, someone would like to meet you."

"Hello," she said to him, "are *you* on a cover?"

"Yes," he said, beaming.

He was so short. Was he a jockey? "What did *you* do to get on a cover?" questioned Hedda.

"I won the Nobel Prize."

Joe E. Lewis sings, "It's tough to get stuff," but Shortie had it! Goodnight, Dr. I. I. Rabi, wher*ever* you are, you topped that conversation.

# That Beautiful Girl Pearl

W HEN ARNOLD ROTHSTEIN DIED, Herbert and Pearl discussed sending a message. "He was useful to you when you could use it," she said.

Swope thought.

"Don't think, send it."

Swope did.

At the Swopes' house, people could have tea if they wanted it, but Pearl Swope favored afternoon coffee. She served it in the big room at Great Neck, along with thin thin sandwiches, lacy lacy cookies and memorable cakes. Who asked Dr. Devol to drop by? And who asked him to bring Bishop Trexler?

"Well, Miss Gordon, when are we going to see another of your in-teresting representations on the stage?" gargled the Bishop.

Few among her following ever saw Pearl Swope look startled, but that did it. She stopped pouring and F.P.A. hurried from the room, followed by others.

"Well, Miss Gordon, when are we going to see another of your in-teresting representations?" The Swope household didn't let me forget that.

Summers were spent at the great sprawling Lottie Blair Parker house looking across Manhasset Bay at Sands Point. When school started, the Swopes moved back to their two-floor apartment at 135 West 58th Street. Whether it was West 58th or Great Neck, it was like Proust's Verdurin circle. What Pearl did, the circle did. Her tailor was Sklar and Wagner. Sklar and Wagner fitted the ladies of the circle. When Swope bought her a new eight-skin sable stole, I bought her *old* one. If Pearl wore a double-breasted black velvet suit with a sable scarf, Bea Kaufman, Peggy Leech and I wore one, too. If she said "schlemiel," we did. If she went to Madison Square Garden to see the hockey games, we went. If she got a ruby necklace, we wanted one. Did she serve runny Camembert with the salad? So did we. Beside each Lowestoft place plate she had a small silver dish of salted pecans. Did we? We did.

If one evening we couldn't show up, for what reason I can't imagine, we gave references or got excused. If the Swopes were going out, we came in later or at the usual time and Mae served coffee, tea, cocoa, liquor, Ovaltine and sandwiches till Herbert and Pearl got back.

To get in was obligatory, to get away took skill. "Sit down," roared Herbert, no matter what time anyone stood up to leave. Bedtime was unpredictable. Never before three o'clock. "Sit down," roared Swope at Alice Longworth. "Sit down, Joe," he roared at Captain Patterson, Ruth and Raoul Fleischmann, F.P.A., Sherwood, Edna Ferber, old Mrs. Cornelius Vanderbilt to whom Ruth Hale was showing her naked portraits.

Josh Cosden and Nell stood up to go. "Sit down," roared Herbert, "and that goes for you too, Bernie, Al Barach, Neysa, Jack Baragwanath, Gerard Swope and his Mrs., St. John Ervine, Ralph Pulitzer, Sonny and Marie Whitney, Mortie and Adele Schiff, Nelson and Patty Doubleday, Ring Lardner, Birdie Vanderbilt, Peggy and Harold Talbot, Irving and Ellin Berlin, John Balderston, Cissie Patterson, Elmer Schlesinger, Harrison Williams with or without Mona, Alicia Patterson, William Bolitho."

The regulars knew how to time things. They were Broun, Ethel Barrymore, Peggy Leech, Gerald Brooks, Charlie Schwartz, Harpo, George and Bea Kaufman, Woollcott. We showed up every night. Where else was better? Where else was as good? At Swopes' you belonged. If you didn't, you didn't get in twice.

There were few outsiders. Everybody in was tough. Everybody could take it. And did. And everybody could give it out. And did.

"I'll see you home," outsider Arthur Brisbane said to me. "Where do you live?"

"Around the corner on 59th Street."

"Oh. I'm going *down*-town."

The circle liked that. "I'm going *down*-town" got into their language. If you weren't tough, keep away from 135 West 58th. If you got your feelings hurt, go elsewhere.

"How'd you like to play squat tag in the asparagus bed?" asked Pearl to let you know she didn't like you.

One Sunday afternoon at 58th Street, Swope made plans to go out.

Pearl didn't think so. "You don't have to go out, Herbert."

"I beg to differ with you, my dear, I *do* have to."

"Where are you going?"

"I'm going to—"

"Herbert, you're lying."

"I'm not lying." He started out to the hall.

"Herbert, where are you going?"

The elevator came up in the Swopes' hall and he got in. Pearl got in with him. From the elevator well rang out, "*Where* are you going, Herbert?"

Glued to the window, we could see Herbert stride out of 135 and down toward Sixth Avenue. Beside him strode Pearl in hand-painted white crepe pajamas, the pants and sleeves edged in white ostrich.

Swope was a gambler, but at Sixth Avenue and 58th he turned back. He knew when he was winning and he knew when he was a loser.

"Want to go to Palm Beach?" Pearl asked me. "He makes me sick."

A day or so later I asked, "Where will we stay?"

She gave me her opaque look. "Don't you like Jamaica? It's better than Palm Beach."

A day or so later I asked, "Where will we be in Jamaica?"

She wore her hard-to-get look. "The weather is better in Nassau. You don't want to go where it's rainy, for God's sake, do you?"

For a day or two I didn't inquire.

She brought up the subject. "Why don't we go down to Bernie's at Hob Caw?"

A day or so later I asked if Bernie would be there.

"You'd *loathe* South Carolina. We could go to Washington. Cissie has a house on Dupont Circle."

Where we did go was Manhasset in time for dinner at Ralph Pulitzer's on a Saturday night and came home after dinner Sunday and Swope came with us.

Pearl and Herbert were giving a dinner party for the Count and Countess of Vallombrosa. The Countess had been Ruth Goldbeck, a beauty, with a chiseled face, brown silk hair cut straight in flat silken folds around a perfectly shaped white face that framed gray star sapphires which were Ruth's eyes. She was beautiful and clever and smart and said sharp things that were true. Her stab was like Zen where the arrow wants to hit its target—hers did. Was she in love with Vallombrosa? Was she in love with the European society his title placed her in? Whatever the answer, it wasn't Ruth who would tell. She must have heard Fanny Brice's oft-repeated warning, "Never tip your mitt, kid." Or maybe Fanny heard it from Ruth. They both knew how to be smart and what it was all about. Pearl admired Ruth.

Dinner was elegant and better than anybody else's. No New York table had food like Pearl's. Always just what you wanted, always perfectly served. Mae had trained her flock of handmaidens like Freddie Ashton trained the swans in *Les Sylphides*.

Place cards, small silver dishes with pecans from Vendôme, sweet butter from Zabar's on upper Broadway where Roy took Mimi to choose it. Smoked salmon from Barney Greengrass where Roy took Pearl's mother, Mimi, to select it. The blue limousine with Holmes was for Pearl and Herbert. The Buick was for Mimi, and Roy was her jehu. He drove her to Fulton Market for the Restigouche salmon in the late spring. For months with an *r* he drove her to Fulton Market for Chincoteagues. To butcher Tingaud for the roasts and poultry. To Washington Market downtown for Jersey corn and early everything.

The Swopes' dinner came from all directions. Bribes and threats and endless phone calls had aided car and chauffeurs and assistant chauffeurs, but when stately, stoic Mae in black taffeta, with real-lace-trimmed collar, cuffs, apron and cap, opened the sliding doors between the dining room and the silver drawing room, perfection had taken place.

Vallombrosa sat at Pearl's right, Ruth at Swope's and between them intellectuals, members of the Four Hundred, celebrated actors, actresses, journalists sat and ate off the Lowestoft that had worked all summer in Great Neck and come back to 135 for the winter.

The table was agleam from the Waterford candelabra and George III silver candlesticks. "No electric light," decreed Elsie de Wolfe and painted the walls spinach green. Candlelight sprang away from the greenness as if it had been a dell up the Hudson at Averell Harriman's Arden.

Through the Barney Greengrass smoked salmon, conversation was between individuals. It always started so, then whatever it was that Swope was saying to Ruth or Birdie Vanderbilt had the table riveted.

If Ruth said, "What do you know about Captain Dreyfus?" If Birdie said, "Is Ellin going to marry him?" If Ruth Hale asked, "Can Doheny explain Teapot Dome?" Swope knew the answers. Wasn't he the best reporter ever known?

Vallombrosa turned to Pearl. "I'm trying to follow Herbert. Where is he?"

She listened. So did everybody.

"When they closed in on Harry Sinclair, he invoked—"

"He's at Teapot Dome," said Pearl. "That's this country's Cloaca Maxima."

Bernie Baruch beamed at Herbert as though he had created him.

Leonard Replogle pointed to Bernie. "He loves Herbert."

"Yes, he loves him," said Pearl. "Herbert has all the things Bernie wants, *except* money, but if Bernie helped Herbert get really rich, Bernie wouldn't have anything on Herbert."

Herbert had made a point and the table laughed. Bernie put his hand on Pearl's slender arm. "Did Herbert capture you as quickly as he has this company?"

"Horsefeathers!"

"What?" Bernie was deaf.

"You heard me, Bernie. Horsefeathers! What would Herbert be doing *capturing* me, for Christ sake, I wore him *down!*"

"How did you?"

"We went to the races at Havre de Grace and he left the room to do something. The phone rang, it was that son of a bitch of a rich widow in San Francisco. I said, 'He's out, thank God.' "

" 'Who is this?' she asked.

" '*Mrs.* Swope.'

"When Herbert came back I told him.

" 'That's cut me off from my last sure thing,' he groaned. 'Come on, God damn it, let's get married.' "

Mae offered the fresh strawberry mousse, perfect as always. Pearl took a token helping.

Mae offered the mousse to Vallombrosa. Behind Mae was Lydia with the big silver bowl of yellow hand-whipped cream from the Walker Gordon Dairy, sent fresh each day from the farm near Princeton and dated so there'd be no mistake. Pearl helped herself to a token. Lydia offered the bowl to Vallombrosa. He scooped the ladle into the cream, then the ladle slipped. It hit his shoulder, coasted down his dinner-jacket sleeve, dropped under the great Chippendale table and there came a yelp. Amy, the dog that Dorothy Parker had rescued from a beating on Sixth Avenue, had chosen the Chippendale as the place to rest under for that evening and the ladle woke her. Amy jumped to her four mongrel sheepdog feet, squeezed out between Vallombrosa and Lydia, cream on her fur, gave herself a shake that splattered cream up and down and all over Vallombrosa's trousers and Elsie de Wolfe's spinach-green walls.

Pearl stared at Vallombrosa. "Paul, are you sure you were born to the purple?"

"Pearl has a point," boomed Swope. "Our Amy had a breakdown, and you've probably sent her into another. I'll expect your check erev Shabbos to defray Amy's analyst bill, plus the dry cleaner's. Off the record, Paul, are you sure you're Vallombrosa or Count Screwloose of Toulouse? All I need are the facts and I'll be glad to head your most loyal opposition."

"Ah yes," said Vallombrosa, "Count Screwloose, I read him every morning! 'Keep an eye on me, Iggy'? No?"

"No. 'Iggy, keep an eye on me.'"

Mae brought a velvet smoking jacket of Swope's. "Let me take your jacket, sir. We'll set it right."

"A work of supererogation, Mae, unless you get the Count's pants."

Mae bowed and left with the Count's jacket. Lydia offered a bowl of cream to the Count.

"Dare I?"

"It's a challenge," declared Swope. "'None but the brave deserve the fair.'" He kissed Ruth's hand.

"Horsefeathers!" said Pearl.

Vallombrosa helped himself successfully.

The table applauded.

"Pearl," said the Count, "why don't you and I leave the world behind us? Come away with me, Pearl, do!"

She looked him over, with her American Indian look mated to Far Rockaway.

> *"I've a penny in my pocket*
> *And my eyes are blue,*
> *So ferry me across the river*
> *Do, boatman, do!"*

"What's Pearl saying?" asked Herbert.

She looked up the table at her guests, eyes guarding her distrust, "I said, 'Hand-kissing is unsanitary.'"

Jane Swope's horse had won a second. Is that an orange ribbon or a red? At any rate, Lady Mine didn't win a blue. The guests congratulated Jane till they noticed Pearl staring at them. "We know what's the one to bring home and it's not *this.*"

Mimi gave her granddaughter a bracing thump. "What do *you* care? You're a beautiful girl."

In the big kitchen at Great Neck, Jane and her grandmother were having a before-bedtime snack. "Is this clean?" asked Jane, holding up a teacup.

"Certainly it is. Wash it out."

The dirt road from Great Neck circled Manhasset Bay's sedgy shoreline, then ducked under the Long Island Rail Road's impromptu-looking trestle. Just before that, the Swopes' croquet lawn came in sight. Beyond, perched on a lower slope was the big white Lardner house with Ring and Mrs. and the Lardner boys, who later turned out to have names, but to their neighbors were the Lardner boys.

Under the Swope roof lived sixteen people before a guest was invited. Weekends, add four to eight sleep-in guests and a steady pour-through for lunch, tea, croquet, dinner, supper and poker. Among them was everybody anybody wanted to meet.

Sunday was the peak. For me it began with Mae bringing breakfast to me in bed, then Mimi looked in, since I was the only one awake. "Got everything you want? I been to church." She sat on the end of the bed. "Loveliest service. I wish you'd come some Sunday. If you come, maybe I could get Pearl to. Herbert never will, of course. But I tell you, Ruthie, I don't know what I'd do if *I* didn't go. Y'know? After all the crazy people round here and I don't mean *you*— Where's the damn sugar?"

"I don't use it, darling. Did you always go to church?"

"My God, *no!* In the old days I didn't have time to. Oh, back in Rockaway I had to earn my living. Well, you know. My husband died and left me with that beautiful girl, Pearl, and that dear little baby, Bruce, and that son of a bitch, Kenneth, I didn't have *time* for church. Y'know what I mean, Ruthie? Get married. If a widow waits over two years, then they never get married. That's what I did, waited two years. Then of course I just kept on waiting. Ruth, you get married again *right away*."

"First I have to find someone, darling."

"There's a lot of swell fellers around. You can have your pick. I mean *now* you can, but don't wait. I better go if I'm going to get that eleven-ten. I'm going in to the Capitol, they've got a good picture. I forget what it's called."

"Isn't it hot to go to New York?"

"Oh, I'm not going to New York, I'm going to the Capitol. The Capitol's cool. And it's restful. I like to get out from under these big weekends. It's all right for you. And Pearl. And big Herbert likes it, but it just gives me a pain in the ass. The Capitol's quiet and I get a good rest there and take the train back when they're all gone. That Kenneth! Oh, *God!!* He found some loose cat outside the Texas Guinan Club and decided to bring it home. Don't you think he knows as well as I do big Herbert has cat asthma? But last night he sneaked the damn cat in the house. And just now I came home from church and the damn thing was runnin' round the upper hall? Herbert'll sneeze his head off all day, mark my words. Well, I took the damn cat and opened Kenneth's door—sound asleep, the lazy thing—and I tossed that cat right in his face. Woke him up. I said, 'Here's your cat.' God, he was livid! The idea of him doin' a thing like that. Young people don't appreciate anything any more, Ruthie. When *he* has to get out and pay for a roof over his head and support a family someday, he'll appreciate how they all lean on big Herbert. Well, they'll— Who's that up? Oh hello, Heywood."

"Hello, Mimi." Broun continued down the hall.

Mimi lowered her voice only slightly. "You know, he's down for two weeks this trip. And when Mae unpacked his suitcase—he only brought *one* for the whole two weeks—and all that was in it was some books and one hand towel! All the linen we have here and he lugs along a towel! What's the matter with people anyway? No underdrawers! Nothin'! Big Herbert says Heywood gets the highest pay of any newspaperman there is. Y'know what I think? People *like* to be crazy. Everyone around *here* is. They enjoy it. Wish you could meet my friend Mrs. Donald Bishop. So normal and sensible and ladylike, it's a real rest to meet her. Y'know, Pearl used to be a lovely sensible girl? But Swope gets her jangled. Why, when they only had Swope's hundred-a-week salary, she was calmer than now. With all they've got and all their society friends, don't let anyone tell you money brings peace and happiness. Pearl had a better time in that off-Riverside-Drive-at-140th-Street apartment— What time is it?—than she has now with her ruby necklace and furs and being intimate with Birdie Vanderbilt. Of course, she'd never admit it. Well, I'm off. I'm going to get Roy to drive me to the station before Pearl gets up and makes me stay home." She went.

Trays were being carried down the hall. Breakfast was served in bed or the dining room or the veranda or where anyone said they wanted it at any time till any time. Pearl rang for hers and Herbert's and they had theirs in bed with any or all the guests looking on. By three o'clock when people drove down from New York or over from Oyster Bay or Glen Cove or across from Locust Valley or up from Smithtown or around from Sands Point, the host and hostess and houseguests were mostly awake. Lunch was at the great oblong Chippendale which every summer traveled from West 58th Street to the Great Neck dining room. Chairs upholstered in white leather made personal noises as guests rose from their places. New guests blushed at the sound sometimes made after Hungarian goulash. At the Swopes' it was the white leather. Pearl said she'd have them re-covered except she'd bought them from Doris Keane "who soaked me such a helluva lot." In the Swope household there was no such word as economy, so that was Pearl's excuse. Why spoil the pleasure of seeing a new guest wince and turn the color of a beet?

The Sunday after the Chicago Dempsey-Tunney fight Swope had invited thirty-five for croquet, tea and the long-count film. "Quinn Martin will get the fight pictures out of Jersey City and bring them over in the afternoon," announced Swope to the green lawnful of croquet players and kibitzers. He, partnered with Charlie Schwartz, Gerald Brooks partnered with Kaufman and Harpo partnered with Alice Miller were bitterly at play.

Mae came out on the lawn and waited, white organdy ribbons floating in the Manhasset Bay breeze. Kaufman made his wicket and shot his ball over to Brooks.

"Mr. Swope," said Mae.

Alice and Harpo didn't look up. The next play was Harpo's and they talked strategy. Kaufman and Brooks also held a consultation.

"Goddammit, Mae."

"Mr. Swope, Mr. Martin got arrested getting the picture out of Jersey, but he can fix it to be here by nine tonight."

"Goddammit, Quinn's ineffectual!"

"Yes, Mr. Swope." Mae bowed and took off.

Swope watched his opponents concentrating on strategy and Charlie Schwartz looking livid. "That goddam ineffectual movie critic has been stupid enough to get arrested," he announced. "And after I fixed it all the way! He'll get here with the fight pictures at nine. Until then he's the guest of Jersey City, where he will come out of jail as ineffectual as he went in, if that is not a work of supererogation. Everybody stay to dinner. Harpo, your play, if you're not too busy goosing Alice Duer Miller."

Pearl looked at me and took off. I followed my trim pink-linen hostess into the house and up the broad mahogany stairs. She turned right, went into her and Swope's bedroom and sat down by the bay window in the Elsie de Wolfe upholstered chair.

"What are you going to do?" I asked, aghast.

She gave me her Indian look and rang for Mae.

I sat down in the mate to Elsie's chair. What was there to say?

Mae, looking stoical, came to the open door. "Yes, Mrs. Swope." Mae's normal look was stoical, so this was no change. Had she looked stoical before she went to work for Pearl and Herbert in the off-Riverside-Drive apartment twelve years ago when Herbert, Junior, was under way? Had that twelve years changed Mae's looks? It changed her name. Whatever if was off-Riverside, it was now Mae Swope.

"There'll be thirty-five extra for dinner, Mae."

"Yes, Mrs. Swope." She looked stoical and left.

"What do you suppose she's going to do?"

Pearl looked at me with her never-saw-you-before look. "I haven't the *faintest* idea."

Down the gravel drive went the Buick in high. Roy was driving like Reggie McNamara making a sprint at the Garden. Mae beside him, her black straw "day-off" hat pinned over her organdy cap, the organdy streamers flying in their own breeze. Roy turned out of the driveway on two wheels, Mae hung on to the side of the car. They headed for Port Washington. Some people's address book is for friends, Mae's was for the tradespeople's home addresses. She was off to rout butcher Hewitt from his Sunday afternoon nap and help him open the store.

At nine, guests took their places on the gilt chairs at the small tables with the beautiful handmade cloths that fell to the floor. The houseguests, plus the weekend guests, plus the thirty-five extra, sat down with Herbert and Pearl and nibbled pecans from Vendôme in the small silver dishes beside each Lowestoft place plate and at the point of each George III pistol-handle silver knife, beside butter balls, beautifully paddled and resting on delicate Lowestoft bread-and-butter plates. Serving expertly in sparkling white uniform came Mae and Dorothy and Lydia and Elsie and Roy and Constance, the Swope permanent staff. Pearl had changed from pink linen to amber-colored Fortuny and was composure itself. The only one not astonished was Swope, he hadn't noticed anything unique. "Sit down, Quinn, and eat something," he advised. "You've got jail pallor. Tomorrow call up Morrie Ernst and sue Mayor Hague for damages. Ask for his last week's profits, then do me a favor and retire."

Almost every week night there was a knock on my door and Pearl, in white Chinese silk pajamas, looked in. I got out of bed. I was in my pink Chinese silk pajamas. Had I been asleep an hour? Or two? In the hall closet we got polo coats and let ourselves out the front door. Roy had left the new blue Dodge Charlie Schwartz had given Pearl. Charlie was on the board.

We drove up the back road, winding through the pine woods, past sleeping Great Neck houses, down into the closed-up village. When we got to the one bright spot, the Great Neck Long Island Rail Road station, it was five past three A.M. Pearl drove under the trestle and pulled up at the platform down the track. Swope was always on the last car.

Soft salty air off the Sound. No one on the platform and being down to the station in sleeping pajamas lent a dash. Lights showed under the bridge from Bayside, there was a rumble, more of a rumble, then came the engine with a line of bright empty cars. The conductor got off, then Swope. He strode down the platform, all the morning papers under his arm, a magazine or two, elegant light brown felt hat set on his red hair at just the right dazzling tilt. Blue shirt, with its gold collar pin, Sulka tie tied just great, dashing chalk-striped blue suit or dashing some other one, elegant polished brown made-to-order shoes, he strode along swinging a stick, as though it were mid-afternoon. He kissed Pearl and me, then climbed in back.

"Want to drive around?" asked Pearl.

"Sure. Where does Leslie live?"

Pearl headed under the trestle down Middle Neck Road.

"Kings Point?" asked Swope.

"Are you mad? Leslie Howard wouldn't spend money to live in a decent place."

"What do you mean! Leslie's one of the highest-paid—"

"And one of the lowest spenders. Herbert, because *you* think things don't have a price *doesn't* mean it's true. Want to drive through Arthur's?"

"Yes." Pearl drove into a driveway. Lawns on either side led to a large sprawling gray clapboard house, all lights out.

"Who's this?"

"Arthur's. We're just driving round for the hell of it."

"Arthur's got a nice place."

"Very."

"I like Arthur. I wonder why he married Eva."

"Because she was Bronson Howard's girl and Bronson told Arthur he'd write a play for him if he took Eva."

"I never heard of Arthur doing a play Bronson Howard wrote."

"He didn't. Here's Leslie's." She stopped in front of a small two-story shingled house on a pocket-handkerchief lawn.

"Leslie lives *here?*"

"Want to bet?"

"What would that rent for?"

"I hope I never know. Want to play squat tag in the asparagus bed?"

"Who says that?"

"It was in the *Follies of 1912*, Nicky Arnstein sang it with Fanny."

"No. Somebody says that. Who is it?"

"Mary Baker Eddy."

"Who?"

"It's Christian Science. 'There is no evil. God is love. There is no pain. Believe in the Mother Church.'" She turned the car onto the dirt road. "Let's go home."

※　※　※　※　※

Ever have a day when you don't know what to do with yourself? Look at yourself as though you were in a book. Are you somebody you want to read about? Are you interesting? Have you got courage? Courage is appealing. Have you got anything interesting to say? Think it over and make up something. They write books about most anybody, would you like the one about you? If not, what about a rewrite? Think it over.

❊   ❊   ❊   ❊   ❊

Did the Bible goof? It gives threescore years and ten for a life span, but I saw Eva Le Gallienne make her debut blacked up as the maid in *Mrs. Boltay's Daughters* and in *Move* I saw Elliott Gould piss in his sink. From blackface to bareass is only threescore years and ten?

# Elliot Fighting Pirates

I N THE SUMMER, my mother and father and I went to Christmas
Cove for two weeks. Sometimes we stayed at French's boardinghouse and sometimes at Brewer's. When Gregory and I got married we went for the summer, but we stayed at the Holly Inn. Then
twenty-six years passed before I came back. "Does Elliot Brewer
still live over there?" I pointed to the clump of spruce and balsam
that sheltered Brewer's.

"Yes, he does. Winters he's up to Augusta at the state insane asylum."

"Oh." New Englanders understand reticence.

I walked down the path beside the petunia bed sunning their soft
colors. Up the slope, Elliot was rocking on the piazza. He was gray-
haired, heavier than I remembered him, but had the same sweet,
calm face. I thought of Augusta—should I turn up the path? "Elliot, this is Ruth Jones."

He stopped rocking and leaned forward. "Yes," he said.

"Mama and Papa and I used to come and stay here. Do you remember?"

"We won't talk about that now. We'll arrange all that later."

"Do you remember me, Elliot?"

"I guess I do. I remember all those good days gone." He looked
at me intently. "You're not Ruth Gordon the actress, are you?"

"Yes."

"Well, I know *you*. I kep' track of you, Ruth. Come, we'll go in."

It was a bright blue Maine day, the sky was blue, the cove was blue, the air alive with pine and salt breeze, indoors it was brown and musty, wallpaper the color of a mushroom, furniture gone from the parlor. Elliot led me down the hall to the kitchen. The windows were closed and the coal stove was aglow. "Sit down," he said, "find a chair. Sit down, Ruth, and we'll talk of old times." I sat down in a big rocker beside the kitchen table. Elliot drew up a straight chair and sat opposite.

"I haven't been here for twenty-six years, Elliot."

"Ayuh. Well, we won't talk about that. We're here now and we'll remember the old days." He was beaming.

"Are you still in the real-estate business?"

"I *can* be," he said. "That's not important. I don't stay here winters. I'm up to Augusta to the asylum. I leave here when it gets October and that old pirate up there couldn't stop me! He thought he could, but he didn't. 'Y'can't and nothin' can,' I says to him. He was a fierce old pirate. *Now* we have the sweetest soul ever drew a breath, but that wasn't then. *Then* we had that pirate, but he found out he couldn't and he didn't and I saw it, Ruth, *Abe Lincoln in Illinois*, and nothin' that old pirate could've done would ever have kep' me from seein' it."

"You knew I was in it?"

"Why, of course I knew, I read all about you. Did you ever see the Jitney Players, Ruth? They were *fine*. I just pray the Lord lets me live long enough so I can sit down and see them once again."

"I've never seen them, but I hear they're fine."

"Fine! I should say they are, they played two pieces, I dunno what they were, but they were great!"

"I don't think the Cove has changed much."

"No, they tried to improve it and tried to, but I guess by now they just about gave up. They couldn't. So now it's just the same's it ever was."

"Captain Wells' store is down."

"Ayuh, *that's* gone."

"And Sands French's store is the Candle Beam Gift Shop."

"*Nicest* one runs it! *She's* the best of the lot. They all took a hand at it. She's the *best!* Why, she'd send clear to Boston to get a young one somethin' he could blow up bigger'n what anybody else had. Remember Aunt Flora Gammage? She's gone, dear soul. I'll get some pictures to show you. We'll just talk about old times." He opened a cupboard. "Oh, here," he said and tossed an old autograph album into my lap. "Get this over. Write a bar or two of music or anythin'. *I* don't care."

"Well, I don't write music."

"I didn't say y' did. Write 'Ruth Gordon, Captain Jones' daughter.' Here's a picture of dear old Uncle Wilbur Thorpe. Dear soul, *he's* gone."

"Was he Bert Thorpe's father?"

"Of course he was. *Bert's* gone. And here's Will Gammage. The needle grass got *him*. Couldn't swim a stroke."

"What's going to happen to the Miles house?"

"She went this *spring*."

"Yes."

"And he's gone."

"Yes. The house for sale?"

"I dunno. They can do anythin' they want with it. I dunno, don't ask *me*. They had a private sale up there. *I* went. I don't know what was private about it, but that's what they called it. I said to the feller, 'I got ten cents. I'm goin' to *buy* somethin',' and I'm goin' to show you, Ruth, what I bought. And if it ain't worth ten cents I'll eat it. You look at this and be the judge." He handed me a brown ulster, old-fashioned in its voluminous cut, but fine material.

"That must have belonged to Mr. Miles."

"I dunno. Belongs to *me* now."

I looked at the dim label under the collar: 10 Chaussée d'Antin, Paris. "Why, it came from Paris!"

"I dunno where it came from, but it's worth ten cents."

"Is the house for sale?"

"Nobody'll ever *buy* it. Fred Kelcey has the keys. He'll never *sell* it. Who's goin' to? Swimmin' pool caved in, the tower isn't steady."

"Do you remember Dennis Little? Used to be the gardener for the Miles'."

"*He's* gone."

"And his brother, Wilbur Little that ran the Christmas Cove House?"

"Sweet soul. He was a sweet soul. *He's* gone."

"I didn't see the Christmas Cove House as I came along the road."

"Burned down. Burned down *years* ago."

"That was a nice place. My uncle's camp was close to it on the cove, my uncle George Gage."

"That's right. Your uncle and your aunt, Mrs. Gage. Now where are *they?*"

"They're gone."

"Dear souls, I'll never forget them. Let's just sit and talk about the old days, Ruth, and not bother. Here ya are, here's a snapshot of Judge Parker doing his jig. His wife's here at her house. That was next to your aunt's camp. That old pirate Coggin got your aunt's camp. They were lovely people, your aunt and uncle. That was Judge Parker's second wife. You know the Holly Inn burned down?"

"Yes." I looked over at the stone foundation.

"Burned down three times. I dunno's they'll build it up again anymore. *I* wouldn't. Where's your father, Ruth?"

"He's gone."

"Ayuh. Well, I *remember* him. We'll just talk about the *old* times. You wrote in my book, didn't you?"

I showed him and he put the book away.

"Do you remember the Watermans?" I asked.

"Now *that's* funny, you askin'. I saw Mrs. Waterman, oh, I dunno just when it was. And we talked about old times. They're still in the *gruesome* business. Funeral parlors all over."

"And Mae Chapin?"

"Here's a card from her somewhere. Where is it? Here, look through these pictures, I'll find it for you to see. Where'd that card go?"

"And her aunt?"

"Had a card from her, too."

"You mean Miss Chapin's alive?"

"Of *course* she's alive. Why *wouldn't* she be? I had a card from her. Look at that picture of Aunt Flora Gammage. Dear soul. She's gone. You look at this and I'll look for that card for you."

"You remember Tommy Russell?"

"I should think I *did!* You know a strange thing, Ruth? You know how he was always making gin in the bathtub down in the Holly Inn cellar before it burned down? And forever wearin' those dirty old khaki pants and goin' round in that motorboat of his? *He* said he was the original Little Lord Fautleroy and I never believed him. Why would I? Then I read it in the *Saturday Evening Post,* I don't know when it was, but sometime. I dunno where that card is and I had it in my hands not later than yesterday. I can hear him tell me so, but, Ruth, I didn't believe it. *He's* gone, I s'pose you know. Know who this is?"

He handed me a blue-finished picture. "Larry Chittenden. You remember him. He always said I'd be in his will and they all said I wasn't, so I went right up to the Court House up to Newcastle and made 'em give me a copy. Here it is. *That'll* interest you. It's a copy of his will. I knew I was in it, because he said I was. And I *was!* Two hundred dollars. Well, you *read* it. What's it say there? Two hundred dollars."

"Why were you in his will, Elliot?"

"Because he hated me. Just *read* that. It'll interest you. What was I lookin' for now?"

"Mae Chapin's card."

"Oh, so I was."

I took out a cigarette. "Is it all right if I smoke?"

"If you want to. I'll have one, too. Do you remember Dr. Gehring?"

"Yes."

"They're gone, of course."

"What kind of a doctor was he?"

"Oh, I dunno. Something. Had all millionaires comin' here. Remember Mr. Bingham?"

"Yes."

"Had 'em all out in the woodshed sawin', I don't know what *for.* 'Exercise,' *he* said. They might just as well been out on the golf course. I don't know why they didn't."

"Didn't they move to Bethel and have a sanitarium there?"

"*I* went up. Hottest place you ever saw. An' I said, 'I want to see Mr. Bingham,' and that old she-pirate, she said I couldn't. 'Why,' I said to her, 'I don't care if you're his nurse or not, you tell him Elliot Brewer's come to see him and I'm goin' to,' and that old she-pirate had to tell him. He might just as well have been out of doors as not."

My cigarette ash was getting long. "Where can I put this?"

"Just knock it into the stove. You remember Ethel Bridgman? *She's* still around. We'll talk about the old days, Ruth."

"Elliot, I have to go," I lied, "I'm expecting a phone call." The kitchen was getting too warm.

Light faded out of his face. He drew a curtain.

"I'll be back soon."

"Well, I dunno."

"I shan't let so much time go by again."

"Well."

We were out on the piazza. "Goodbye, Elliot dear."

"Goodbye," he said distantly and sat down in his rocker. His sweet, calm face stared across the cove.

*        *        *        *        *

At the Sporting Club, Art Buchwald came up to Willie. "Mr. Maugham, may I come over to Villa Mauresque tomorrow for a half an hour?"

"By all means." Then as an afterthought, "If you think it would be worth your while."

# Via Woollcott to
# Somerset Maugham

D ID YOU EVER TRY to tell a story to Frank Sinatra? If you do,
he's apt to interrupt: "Is this going to take long?"

In the twenties, Alexander Woollcott and Harpo Marx rented a
villa in Antibes and invited me to join them. Does it seem long, so
far?

Earlier in the summer there had been hostesses, but by the time
*King's X* folded in Atlantic City, hostess Kaufman had sneaked
back to New York to hold George's hand during his first directorial assignment, *The Front Page*. Hostess Alice Duer Miller had left
for Cairo as houseguest of Pearl White, whose invitation concluded
with "P.S. I think you ought to know I am living with an Egyptian
prince."

With such diverse inducements, Villa Ganelon lost its ladies and I
was stuck with Woollcott and Marx.

Stuck with Woollcott had its advantages. He knew everybody
everywhere and they were glad when he called up or wrote. His
note had brought Bernard Shaw and Mrs. to lunch, not once but
twice. A phone call from Woollcott and we had high tea with
Frank Harris in his apartment up in the Cimean Hills at a place
called the Jersey City Pension, where tea and jelly roll competed
with the names of Oscar and Beausy and G.B.S. and Mrs. Pat and
"the Incomparable Max."

An invite from Woollcott and his dinner guests at the villa were

179

Otis Skinner and Otis' former leading lady, adorable Maude Durban, long since become Mrs. Skinner and mother of illustrious Cornelia. They arrived as Harpo came down the stairs on his way to a costume ball, dressed as the Spirit of Toilet Paper. Around his waist a chain, the handle marked "Tirez" was where his belt should have been if he'd been wearing pants. I came a step behind him dressed as a Pregnant Doll.

Mrs. Skinner raised her lorgnette and murmured, "Ve-ry int-er-esting." Was that where "Laugh-In" picked it up?

Host Marx and I went on to the ball and host Woollcott was left to continue.

At one time or another the whole Côte d'Azur dropped in. Louise Groody on leave from *Hit the Deck*, which, unlike my show, didn't fold, showed up with a Newport Goelet. Woollcott took an equal dislike to both.

Elsa Maxwell sat on our terrace singing her scatty version of the new hit: "There was I was with all my britches burned—"

"That would be the biggest conflagration since the Chicago fire," exclaimed Woollcott.

Elsa never noticed a knock, but settled back on our cushions and sold Cole Porter. "He's *not* a dilettante, he's a serious talent!"

"If he's so serious, what's he doing with the Princess Jane Faustino and the Duke of Alba and the King of Spain? If he's so goddam dedicated, why's he giving Red and White Balls in his and Robert Browning's palazzo, décor by Oliver Messel?"

"Listen to this!" she shouted and shoved us into our drawing room. "Listen!" She took over our piano. "Let's Do It" she followed with "What is this thing called love? This funny thing called—"

What did *you* think the first time you ever heard Cole Porter? Friend of Duke or Princess or King, I wanted to hear some more.

"Wait till the season *starts!*" roared Elsa. "Ray Goetz is putting on *Fifty Million Frenchmen*. There'll be a line down 42nd Street to the ferry. You call *that* a dilettante?"

Across the lawn each morning strolled Saratoga's Charlie Brackett, summering in the next villa. He went to the parties, too, but said he liked hearing us tell about them better.

A petit bleu from Woollcott and Ellen and Phil Barry petit-bleued from Cannes, "Dine with us." After dinner instead of a nightcap, we went in, starkers, off the Barrys' own gravelly plage. Drying off, Phil promised me the script of his new play *Holiday* to take back to Ganelon, but before I had time to read it, it was time to go to lunch with Sara and Gerald Murphy, the Dick Diver in *Tender Is the Night*, and best friends of Scott and Zelda.

Hostesses Kaufman and Miller were not too much missed and one afternoon whizzing along the middle Corniche toward Cap Ferrat I was pleased they weren't there. What was wrong with being the only girl with two fellows going to meet Somerset Maugham?

I'd worshipped him for a long time and as early as 1916 knew how to pronounce his name. On a two-week guest card to a snippy club called the Gamut I listened to talk about new painters, new composers, new authors, and over bouillon and saltines Miss Helen Ingersoll spoke about a new author whose name was spelled M.A.U. G.H.A.M., which he was said to pronounce Morm. It brought a cultured laugh and someone hazarded, "Perhaps he pronounces S.O.M. E.R.S.E.T. Smet."

My guest card ran out and I thought no more about Maugham-pronounced-Morm, until *Of Human Bondage* rocked the cultured and uncultured and lashed me to Morm's mast. Now I was bowling through the gates of Villa Mauresque.

"This is Ruth Gordon," said Woollcott. "This is Harpo Marx." Mr. Maugham shook hands with us and didn't give a damn whether he met us or not.

Feeling rejected, Harpo and I took a terrible dislike to him. Harpo picked up *Variety* from the terrace reading table and while the rest of us drank tea or Dr. Pepper, read *Variety*, page one to the end. Minnie Marx hadn't brought him up very well, because when he reached the back page, he tossed Maugham's *Variety* on the terrace floor.

Maugham got to his feet, picked it up and said, "I'll just put this away." I thought a man that cares for his *Variety* can't be all bad.

That was the twenties. The thirties weren't any better. Alice Astor von Hofmannsthal gave a grand party in London and sometime during the evening Mr. Maugham came across the ballroom heading for me. "Miss Gordon," he said, "my play *The Constant Wife* is being revived in Brighton. Your friend Miss Ruth Chatterton is starring in it. Will you meet me in Brighton tomorrow night and see if you can do something about her performance?"

I didn't like him any more than I did before, but if Somerset Maugham invited you to meet him in Brighton, what would *you* do?

After the performance Mr. Maugham said, "Well?"

"Well," I said, "I think Ruth Chatterton is fine. But I think your play has gotten old-fashioned and you should do something about *it*." This brought us no closer together.

It was the forties when we fell in love. I was playing Chicago and staying at Ernie Byfield's Hotel Ambassador East. One morning the phone rang. "Miss Gordon, this is Somerset Maugham, I'm stopping at this hotel and should like to see something of you."

"Would you like to come to the theatre tonight? It's a celebration of my having been on the stage twenty-five years. Alexander Woollcott is doing a radio broadcast after the second act."

"Delighted," said Maugham.

I was delighted, too, and the press agent went right around the bend! After the performance Ernie Byfield gave a beautiful party at the Ambassador East, with my name frozen in silver ice, and silver twenty-fives all over everything but the guests. Mr. Maugham signed everybody's napkin and dollar bill and program, waiters' paychecks and I liked him very much! It still wasn't love, but I liked him.

A week later Alfred Lunt and Lynn Fontanne opened in Chicago. My phone rang next morning. "Darling." It was the celebrated voice of Lynn Fontanne. "Darling, Mr. Somerset Maugham is staying in our hotel."

"I know," I said.

"Darling, tonight is New Year's Eve and Alfred and I think it would be a good idea to have supper up here in our apartment and invite Mr. Maugham. Will you come, dear?"

"I'd love to, but I have Jones and my secretary and—"

"Bring them and you ring up Mr. Maugham."

"Me?"

"Yes, darling. Ring him up and invite him."

"But, Lynnie, let's be practical. We stand a much better chance of getting him if you or Alfred ring up."

"Well, perhaps you're right, darling," and she rang off.

I told Jones and my secretary of the great event and rushed to the beauty parlor in the lobby. Several hours later, drowsing under the dryer, I felt a tug at my arm and a phone thrust at me. "Darling." It was the celebrated voice of Lynn Fontanne. "Darling, I've been trying to ask Mr. Maugham, but I've taken a fright! I can't get up the courage. I've met him, of course, but it was so long ago he may not remember me. *You* do it."

"But, Lynn, it's after three o'clock. Anybody as celebrated as Mr. Maugham must be *booked* for tonight."

"Don't give up so easily, darling! Alfred and I *both* say *you* should ask him," and she rang off. I got out from under the dryer and rushed up to my room, reached for the phone, then thought, "If Lynn Fontanne is scared to, why aren't I scared?" And I was. So I wrote a beautiful letter, sent for a bellboy. "Take this to Mr. Somerset Maugham's room," I said. "Do *not* leave it at the desk and here's a dollar." Now, a dollar in 1941—and I'm not a mathematician—but wouldn't a dollar in 1941 be the equivalent of four hundred and three tax-deductible dollars today?

Pleased with myself, I lay down to wait for Mr. Maugham to call *me*. An hour passed. An hour and a half. I got up and went down to the lobby. "What is the number of Mr. Somerset Maugham's room?" I asked the clerk, and the silly man told me! I looked in his letter box and *there* was my letter. That beast took my dollar and didn't deliver my letter! Well, Chicago's a rough tough town.

I returned to my room. "Operator," I said, "connect me with Mr. Somerset Maugham." A charming British voice replied.

"Mr. Maugham, this is Ruth Gordon."

"My dear, how nice of you to call."

"Mr. Maugham, Alfred Lunt and Lynn Fontanne hope that you will have supper with them tonight in their apartment here in the hotel and celebrate New Year's Eve."

"Alas," he said, "I'm going to the opera with Mr. Byfield and going on to his party at the Opera Club."

"Oh dear," I said. "They will be so disappointed. And so will I. It's been a sort of horrible mix-up. Lynn was to phone you earlier, but she got scared you wouldn't remember her—"

"I'm old, but I'm not in my dotage," he said.

"No," I said. "Lynn *wanted* to ask you, but she was too frightened. But happy New Year and it's been lovely to talk to—"

"Miss Gordon, I've changed my mind. Please tell Mr. and Mrs. Lunt I shall be delighted to take supper with them."

That evening he charmed us all. Alfred, Lynn, Dickie Whorf, Sydney Greenstreet. Lynn said he was the sexiest man she knew, save for Alfred. With me it was true love. The evening ended at two A.M. when Mr. Maugham crossed the Lunts' sitting room, bowed to Jones, eleven years old, and said, "I think all of us under sixteen and over sixty should now retire."

The next morning there was a letter from him, delivered by a *good* bellboy.

Dear Miss Gordon,
    You are as sweet as you are good and kind. Happy New Year.

                                                 W.S.M.
                                                 1 January, 1941

Did that take long?

※　※　※　※　※

"Where are the snows of yesteryear?" I don't know where all of them are, but some drifted into this book.

# *Godchild*

M ARY DRIFTED into my room and picked up some pearls. "Are these yours, Ruth-Gordon?"

"Yes," I said.

"Aren't they my mother's?"

"No."

She started swinging them.

"Put them down, Mary."

She just looked out the window and swung them some more.

"Mary, put them down. I mean it."

Those big forget-me-not eyes looked baleful. "I'm going to tell little Irving Thalberg on you," she threatened and left the room. *With* the pearls.

When Mary was four, Charlie MacArthur moved his family into a big white house on Broadway. This Broadway was in Nyack where Charlie's father preached from time to time and had moved his family while he went off and preached. One fine summer morning Charlie's Helen and Mary were going to walk downtown.

"Be sure and get a birthday card," said Charlie's mother-in-law, Brownie.

Helen nodded. "We will."

"Mary?"

"Uh-huh."

"Mommy forgets things, Mary. You remind her."

185

"Uh-huh."

"Helen, write it down, dear, so you'll remember."

"Oh, I'll remember."

"Whatever present you buy, it makes it nicer if you write a nice birthday card to go with it."

"Yes," said Helen. "Ready, Mary?" They strolled down the drive.

"Hold Mary's hand crossing the street," called Brownie, "and remember the birthday card."

"We will."

Mary started to skip. "Let's see how *you* skip, Mommy." They skipped down Nyack's Broadway to the village. What a good village, they found just the right present. Helen thought so, Mary thought so, and now they came skipping into the drive.

"Did you get the birthday card?" called Brownie.

Helen's heart sank, then rejoiced.

"They didn't *have* any more," said a firm voice. Helen looked adoringly at Charlie's child.

The MacArthurs had had a quarrel. It lasted. Helen stayed on at their apartment at the Waldorf which was only supposed to be for between matinee and night or for the night before a matinee. Then when she stayed Charlie stayed, too. But Helen had stayed not only the night before the matinee, but the night after the matinee and the next night. Charlie felt miserable. He drove in from Nyack with little Mary. Room service sent dinner up and the MacArthur family sat around the table. Who was going to forgive whom? Helen had certainly fixed herself up to look adorable. Abashedly, Charlie twisted his forelock, which he did when he didn't know what to do next. Neither ate much, but little Mary did. It was great to have a turkey drumstick, cranberry jelly and, right on the same table where you could see it, pink ice cream under glass in a bowl of ice. It wasn't only pink, it had pleated pink paper around it and a cookie with red sugar and a cookie with a chocolate four-leaf clover. Wait till she got back to Nyack and told Bunny and Jay about *this!* What a way to live!

"Is it lovely at Nyack?" asked Helen, a little reminiscent of Jane Austen.

186

"Not as lovely as when *you're* there." Charlie came on with his "wish-they-were-emeralds" look.

Helen looked even prettier. "Did you decide on the redwood poles, Charlie?"

"Oh, we'll do without." Was this what the fuss was about?

"Oh, Charlie! You wanted the redwood."

"Mom," said little Mary.

Helen leaned toward Charlie. "I don't think five hundred dollars a pole is much. They'll last and you want them. Please, Charlie."

"Mom." Little Mary's voice was louder.

"Charlie darling, it's our home we love and nothing's too good for our home."

"Mom." Little Mary's voice was not only loud but unromantic. "Mom."

"Don't call me Mom!" said Helen sharply. "Charlie darling, you adore the redwood. It's your idea and only you would think of redwood poles to hold up Nyack tennis nets. And Charlie darling, it'll make Ben so furious!"

Charlie laughed, then twisted his forelock some more and looked lovingly at Helen.

She looked adoringly back.

"Mrs. MacArthur," said a little voice.

Both Helen and Charlie turned around startled. A third person was dining with them?

"Mrs. MacArthur, *now* can I eat my ice cream?"

Helen's arms were around Mary. Charlie's arms were around them both. "I didn't mean for you not to call me Mom, darling, it's just that I'm trying to be like somebody in a storybook, but, darling, I *am* Mom and please don't *ever* call me Mrs. MacArthur."

"Awright. Can I eat the ice cream?"

Down in Maryland at Mr. Brown's house, Helen and Mary were having a fine time. "Let's go across this field," said Helen. Hands full of wild flowers, they were nearly across, then a bull came out of the foliage. "Run," said Helen. They ran for the stile. Heart in mouth, Helen stood back for Mary. Mary chose that moment to turn around and stare at the bull. Her mother pushed past her and was over.

"I gave her first chance, I honestly *did*, but when she didn't take it, *I* took it. How could I *do* that to my own child?"

Well, that's show business. Give someone a chance and if they don't take it, you do. Somebody has to take the lead.

Have you got a goddaughter? Mine was Mary MacArthur. I owe that, not so much to Helen and Charlie although without them there'd have been no Mary, but Ned Sheldon was the one who insisted on a christening. Helen is Catholic and Charlie was himself, so Mary was five and no holy water. Ned arranged for the ceremony in his big stately room where he could feel sure it had been done. An altar was arranged, white flowers were everywhere, the minister wore his white muslin tunic over a black midi-length. Helen, Charlie, Brownie, Woollcott, Ned's sister and mother, I and of course Mary assembled around four o'clock in his room.

Mary MacArthur Sheldon was godmother and the godfather was Woollcott. After a hurried conclave with the preacher, Helen and Charlie said to me, "Would you oblige?"

The service called for only one godfather, but two godmothers there must be or nothing doing. I was proud and happy and as the ceremony progressed I was also a little anxious. Woollcott and I stood together on one side, Helen and Charlie on the other. Mary stood in the center, solo. The thought struck me, could this be a practical joke of MacArthur's and I would wind up married to Woollcott? Were Charlie and Helen giving me away and Mary acting as bridesmaid?

I was wrong, it *was* a christening. And every so often out there in the number-one spot, Mary looked around at her folks, scared. The preacher rambled on. Did she think he was scolding her? She looked back at Helen anxiously. Mrs. Brown, who had had the presence of mind to put her daughter on the stage, now rallied to the next generation. "Helen," she said louder than the preacher, "can't you step forward and *stand* with the child?"

Coming home on the *Aquitania*, Helen and Mary and I shared a cabin. After the Captain's dinner Mary's mother and godmother brought their paper hats to the room and left them on the table by her bed.

I woke up and in the gray light of early morn I saw a big gold

Halloween witch's hat perched on long blond hair, sitting at table dealing two hands of cards.

"Mary, you ought to be asleep," I whispered.

She shook her head and dealt on.

I went back to dreamland. Who was that whispering so sweetly? "Ruth-Gordon."

"Yes?"

"I won."

❋ ❋ ❋ ❋ ❋

At the Christmas party everybody was giving their presents. "Oh, Jones, this is beautiful," said Adolph Green. "Oh my God, it's too much, I didn't give you *anything* any good." Adolph looked dismayed and handed Jones a present.

It was a wallet. " 'Who steals my purse steals trash,' " said Jones Harris.

❋ ❋ ❋ ❋ ❋

Do you get many Christmas presents? Constance Collier did. She'd been made welcome in Hollywood. At the grand Christmas party for her, everybody was there. Mrs. Pat Campbell came up to greet her. Mrs. Pat wasn't doing well. "Have you had a lovely Christmas?" she asked.

"Oh, my dear, it has been perfect."

"And did you receive some lovely gifts?"

"I did indeed."

"And who sent you them?"

"Charlie and Paulette."

"How lovely. And who else?"

"Mary."

"Ah! And anyone else?"

"Sam and Frances."

"Any others?"

"Helen and Charlie. Norma and Irving. Joan and Douglas."

"Ah."

189

"And did *you* get lovely ones?"
"Alas, no. I got none."

※　※　※　※　※

When there wasn't a word for it, Mrs. Pat made one up. She
went to see Katharine Cornell in *Lucrece*, and was describing it.
"Who was in the cast besides Kit?"
"Joyce Carey was in it. And Bob Loraine."
"Was it an all-English cast?"
"No. Blanche Yurka was yurking around."

※　※　※　※　※

"If there's a collision at sea, people rush to the spot," my father
told me. Was that just a sea yarn?
Crossing the Channel on a pea-soup day, a whistle whistled close
by, then came closer.
Ours screeched and screeched, but where did everybody rush?
Where the whistle was coming at us. A freighter loomed out of the
fog and rammed us where everybody had collected. Everybody but
me. I remembered and clung to a pole mid-deck. Do you know
what is the longest that knees can knock? Mine knocked till Dover
and from time to time on the boat train. By Victoria they'd stopped.
My father knew about where to go in a collision, because he had
one with his family and ran away to sea when he was eight. He
shipped out of New Bedford as a cabin boy on a vessel bound for
Barcelona. His only previous trips were from his birthplace in Col-
chester, Connecticut, down to a Boston boardinghouse where his
mother, with a new baby and him aged four, had been deserted. She
couldn't face such problems and killed herself.
My father's second trip was to Orleans to live with his great
aunts Jerusha and Reliance Rogers. It was rough going. Little Ste-
phen died, but Clinton cut out in the dark of the night and signed
on for Barcelona. When he was twenty, he had sailed round the
world three times and felt the need for more formal education.

Why did he choose Elmira, New York? The school plumbed his learning and put him in the fourth grade. His room at the Rathburn House was cold, so he took his homework to the Y.M.C.A.

Samuel Clemens dropped in and got talking to the young man struggling with the fourth-grade lesson book. Mr. Clemens invited him to bring his books and come over to his warm house.

"Give us a glass of whiskey, Mother," he told his wife.

"I won't give a young man liquor."

"Hell, if he can go round the world three times, he's old enough to drink liquor."

My father's education began and ended in the fourth grade. Was it there he learned everyone is entitled to a chance? He hoped I'd become a physical-culture instructress, but staked me to a career on the stage. I left home August 1 and was still unemployed in mid-September. He wrote, "Any profession that didn't offer me a berth in six weeks, I would not continue in."

Are you careful not to take advice?

In that Elmira fourth grade did he study *As You Like It?* Or did he read that going around the world? My cook served vanilla ice cream. My father accepted some. My cook passed the hot chocolate sauce.

"No, thanks, Sarah, 'Good wine needs no bush.' " Does that sound like Elmira or the Straits of Singapore?

# Fond Cousin

48TH STREET was full of cars. At the Vanderbilt Theatre, people were pouring in to the first night of O'Neill's *Anna Christie*. In Atlantic City it had been called *Chris Christopherson* when George Tyler produced it with Lynn Fontanne. At the end of a week it closed on the Boardwalk and Tyler put Lynn in something called *Maid of Money*. Draw the veil. Arthur Hopkins took over and *Chris Christopherson* became *Anna Christie*. Arthur engaged Pauline Lord to play Anna. To see Pauline was to admire her, but most people hadn't. She was always in something where she got rave notices and the show closed that Saturday night.

The curtain went up on Robert Edmond Jones' barroom. Back in the dim light, someone strayed on, so unimpressive, so faded, so rumpled and indistinct it was as though she wasn't there. At the end of the evening there was no one there except her. The frail girl in the worn brown velvet dress made theatre history when she dropped down on the bar chair and, in a discouraged murmur that could be heard in the back of the gallery, asked for a whiskey.

We filed out onto 48th Street and knew we'd been in the presence. Great writing, great acting!

Only Grace Filkins was battling the past. "A whore in brown velvet? A whore must wear red."

But that was for De Wolf Hopper's aunt's scrapbook. After Pauline's brown velvet, a whore could wear any old thing.

So could Pauline. At Guthrie's, Ruth Chatterton tossed her soft, thick mink coat on the hall chair. Pauline looked at it and deflated. She muttered, "Where'll I throw *my* horse blanket?"

New York was hers and so was London after she played *Anna Christie* there. They asked her to go with Dame Ellen Terry to welcome Duse, arriving from the Continent on the Golden Arrow. First the Lord Mayor would board the train, then as he led Duse out onto the platform, Pauline and Dame Ellen would present her with a bouquet. The train approached Victoria Station, the guard opened the gate for the welcoming party, Pauline beside Dame Ellen's wheelchair followed the Lord Mayor. The train stopped, the Lord Mayor went in, Dame Ellen touched Pauline's sleeve. Pauline bent down to hear. "Who are we welcoming, dear?"

Ben Winter let Pauline have the place at Ellenville when they divorced. She lived up there with one servant, the black chauffeur. "We look at the Sears Roebuck catalogue nights and pick out things to order," she said. "That's how I keep him, he hasn't got much sense. Getting ready to come to New York to do *Ethan*, I told him to get the phone cut off. He picked up the library scissors and cut the wire."

At my house on 12th Street we were trimming the Christmas tree. The doorbell rang, I opened the door.

"Von Cuzzin live here?" asked a chauffeur.

"No." I closed the door.

The bell rang again.

"They don't live here," I said.

The chauffeur looked troubled.

I went back to trimming the tree. Five minutes later I went through the hall and the chauffeur still stood on the steps. "They don't *live* here."

"Von Cuzzin?" he pleaded.

"Give me that." I grabbed the beribboned Christmas package. The card read "Fond cousin, from Pauline." When Zena Frome sent for Mattie, she described her to Ethan as her only cousin she was fond of.

"Von Cuzzin?" her chauffeur asked. If *your* name was Ruth Gordon, would *you* think that package was for you?

193

Pauline sat in her dressing room at Philadelphia's Grand Opera House where the *Ethan Frome* dress rehearsals were under way. "Jesus Christ," she whined, scraping her nail file over the toe of a made-to-order I. Miller cloth-topped kid boot. "I may go back in stock." She pulled the emery board back and forth over the cloth top where her ankles would rub. "With this goddam management I have to work harder over my wardrobe than I work over my part. In stock if you wear old shoes, there *are* some. Why does Max Gordon have to have them made to order?"

We were dismissed till the night's dress rehearsal. Guthrie was focusing lights on the flower-like face of eighteen-year-old Sylvia Weld standing in for Pauline and me. "She looks like an orangutang!" moaned Pauline loud enough to scare everyone. "Why don't you light *us* like you light Kit?" She continued up the aisle and out into the lobby, leaving an expression of horror on the flower-like face of eighteen-year-old Sylvia Weld. I wonder what expression was on Guthrie's face. He had his hat pulled down.

When she felt like acting, she was the greatest, and she felt like it opening nights. She felt like it again when someone she knew was out front. Other times she felt like it when she felt like it. When she didn't, it was startling. Too discouraged to care, she hurried through or gave up altogether. "I told Jotham to hitch the horses. I got to get over to Bettsbridge and get me that new Energex Vibrator. The pains in my legs are getting something awful and—" She was too discouraged. "Oh Jesus Christ," she groaned, opened the door and disappeared. She hadn't even given that dreadful threat that she would spend the night in Bettsbridge. Some nights she filled Mattie and Ethan with dread and some nights Massey and me.

"Tell me when anybody's out front," she said.

"You really want to know?"

"How else do you think I give a performance?"

"Woollcott's coming a week from tomorrow."

"Oh, thanks."

That night she gave a lackluster performance. Just ran through the lines. Didn't she like Woollcott? He didn't like her performance and wrote her so. "The way you played Zena made Ethan and

Mattie look like Judd Gray and Ruth Snyder."

After the final curtain call, Pauline asked, "Did you know Woollcott was out front last night?"

"I told you he was coming."

"When!" She suddenly was in a rage.

"A week ago."

"Well, Christ! What good is *that?* When anybody's out front, God damn it, you *tell* me! Then *keep* telling me, God damn it! *Tell* me till the day after they come, for Christ sake!"

Ruth Chatterton said that her mother and Pauline would sit for hours and talk and smoke. As they finished a cigarette, they'd put the butts on the mantel, then when the pack was empty they'd start smoking the line of butts. Ruth said if she came in, Pauline and Tilly clammed up. She'd leave and conversation buzzed again.

Pauline was a good laugher and liked to. She was also easy to put on. "Max Gordon has a new play for me," I said.

Her look grew melancholy. She didn't care if Max had a new play for *her*, but she didn't want him to have one for me if he didn't have one for her. "What is it?"

"It's *Rebecca of Sunnybrook Farm.*"

She looked horrified. "Are *you* going to play Rebecca?"

"That's what he wants," I said. "And he wants you to play Uncle Jerry Cobb."

The sun shone. It's a relief when someone else *isn't* offered a play.

"Jesus Christ! Will you stop that sighing!" Pauline's soft indecisive voice rang out firm from Dressing Room One at the National.

"I didn't know I was."

"Well, cut it out! It means somebody's walking over your grave. Jesus Christ! I hope I never get in a show with you again. What do you *sigh* about?"

Once when I hadn't seen her for a long time, at the Guaranty Trust we were each cashing a check. "I'm leaving for Baltimore," she said.

"Are you playing there?"

She looked discouraged, then nodded. "I'm in another turkey."

"When do you open?"

"I don't know. Some day next week."

"What is it?"

She raised her eyebrows. "You tell *me!* The name of it's *The Late Christopher Bean!*"

"Is it good?"

She looked past the bank toward the general direction of Betts-bridge, shrugged her shoulders and moaned, "If Lord's in it, it'll be a turkey."

*The Late Christopher Bean* and Pauline made history at the Henry Miller Theatre.

On a rainy Wednesday Pauline's funeral was held at noon at the Little Church Around the Corner, named so from the day Grace Church refused an actor a funeral service. "Try the little church around the corner," they said.

Pauline's was on a rainy Wednesday. Too bad it was a matinee day. Too bad more people didn't go. Empty seats up and down the side aisles and empty rows at the back. The only one there that I knew was Guthrie's manager, Stanley Gilkey. We had sat around together during *Ethan Frome* rehearsals and today we sat together again. The service was short. Impersonal. It could have been for anyone. It was for the great Pauline. "Lord's in another turkey," she'd said at the Guaranty Trust.

# You'll Fracture 'Em, Sweetheart!

AL WAS A JA-SAGER. And stagestruck. He named his theatre the Eltinge. Some people named theirs for a street. Not Al. He was for people. What did the name of a street ever do for business? It's *people* who get people into a theatre. Some theatres got named for the place the Pilgrims landed. Some got named for a saint named James. Al H. Woods named his for Julian Eltinge, star of his big money-maker, *The Fascinating Widow*. Mr. Julian Eltinge, as virile as anybody virile, made his contribution to the gaiety of nations by playing fascinating widows more fascinating than if fascinating real widows played them. "Sweetheart, you're a big money-maker for me," Woods told his star, "and I'm going to name my theatre for you." And he did.

Hot summer nights Al sat out front of the Eltinge watching 42nd Street go up and down and into his theatre, his chair tilted back against it, a Panama to keep the electric lights out of his eyes, one of which was markedly cocked.

"Have a beer, Mr. Woods?" asked his doorman.

"When the house gets in, sweetheart." Hot evenings his Savile Row jacket was missing, his fine lawn shirt sleeves were held in place by blue satin garters that matched the blue smoke of his Havana cigar. He had come a long way from the ten-twent'-thirt' days of Woods, Sullivan and Considine. Nobody knew where Sullivan and Considine tilted their chairs, but Times Square knew

197

Woods tilted his against his own theatre.

In the mid-twenties he built a second one. In Chicago, corner of Randolph and La Salle. The Loop traffic clanged around it and Woods never felt friendly enough to it to tilt his chair against it, although he named it the Woods. It was just another acquisition; the Eltinge was where he tilted his chair. On the top was where he kept his office. Up there, bookkeepers totted up all the money that flowed in. Casting was done by his waggish brother, Martin Herman. "Nothing today," Herman would roar happily and wave the job hunters back into the elevator. Next stop would be Sam Forrest at Cohan and Harris and after *that* "Nothing today," next stop would be George C. Tyler for a "Nothing today" at Klaw and Erlanger.

The H. in Al's name was for Herman. Woods he added on for his nom de théâtre. Woods sounded better and Al wanted the best. His office walls were covered with pale blue silk damask, the walnut furniture was from the Rue Jacob, Paris, his desk was a museum piece. The only inappropriate note was Al, his shirt sleeves gartered, his gray hair as unruly as if man had not invented the comb. His non-stop Havana cigar matched his tough persuasiveness. "Sweetheart, here's the play I seen in Paris. You'll fracture 'em, sweetheart, read it. Or sign here and don't *read* it, just fracture 'em. Compared to this, sweetheart, the other shows are just a bowl of cherries."

Al's fortune was made with melodramas and farces. *The Fascinating Widow* and *Parlor, Bedroom and Bath* and *Getting Gertie's Garter* kept his bookkeepers busy. Al had all the money he wanted, but he was stagestruck and the play he wanted was a play all Paris was flocking to, *Mozart*, with Yvonne Printemps as the adorable young Mozart and Sacha Guitry as Baron Grimm. Al Woods didn't understand French, but he understood show business and was bedazzled. The hitch was, Sacha Guitry was not bedazzled at the thought of an ocean voyage. Only rarely would he leave Paris and then it was to go to Deauville or to play a brief London season at His Majesty's. Sacha Guitry not only did not like to travel, but a fortune-teller had told him to beware of boats or he would end up in a watery grave. To cross the English Channel was as risky as Guitry would consider.

White damask and silver gleamed on the table laid for supper in the Guitry suite at London's Savoy. A frosty silver bucket cooled the Widow's beverage. Guitry made it clear to the interpreter that the answer was still no.

"Sweetheart, you'll have New York at your feet." He beamed at Guitry and prodded the interpreter, "Tell him, sweetheart."

Guitry was more interested in the oysters. "Nobody could afford it. The whole company? There would be no profit."

Woods didn't know French, but he knew a turndown. "Tell him go in that corner, sweetheart, and write on a piece of paper what he'll come for. I'll go this corner and write what I'll pay."

The interpreter gave the message. Guitry's valet handed him a thin blue sheet of Savoy Hotel stationery, Al plucked a crumpled letter from his pocket.

Guitry waved his paper, Al waved his crumpled letter. The interpreter collected Guitry's thin blue. "Twelve thousand dollars a week."

Silence to pay respect to such a sum.

The interpreter looked at Al's crumpled envelope. Guitry listened. The interpreter moved closer to the light. "One thousand dollars a week more than what you have wrote, sweetheart."

New York was at the Guitrys' feet. *Mozart* crowded the Music Box for its limited engagement and Al Woods enjoyed every performance. One more day and it would be over. Tuesday next the *Ile de France* would sail. Nobody talked about it, because Guitry went white at the thought.

Just before the Saturday matinee curtain, a pink leather box arrived from Cartier. Inside was a crystal watch as thin as a sheet of Savoy Hotel paper and outlined in a wreath of diamonds. The card had Al's scrawly handwriting on it. "Goodbye sweetheart (over)"

Guitry turned the card.

In Cartier's engraving. "This watch guaranteed to go under water."

Al came to the pier to see the Guitrys off and couldn't bear to part with them, so he sailed, too. He kept a suitcase on the *Ile de France*, the *Majestic*, the *Aquitania* and the *Berengaria* for such emergencies.

In the early thirties he was co-producer of a play I was in. Wil-

liam A. Brady, the other producer, was at every rehearsal, but Al
never came around. They said he was in London. They said he was
in Paris. But wherever he was, he was never at Mr. Brady's Playhouse on West 48th Street, New York, where the houseboards
read:

A.  H.  W OODS  AND
W ILLIAM  A.  B RADY
P RESENT
A  C HURCH  M OUSE

At the dress rehearsal, word went round that Al Woods was out
front with Mr. Brady. The curtain fell on Susie in the Baron's arms.
"Take it up," roared Mr. Brady from the back of the house.

Al Woods charged down the aisle, anxiety wrinkling his face.
"Sweetheart," he said to the Baron, "I seen this play in Budapest,
Vienna, London and Bridgeport and *you're monotonous.*"

Al was rich. The Eltinge Theatre, New York. The Woods, Chicago. Big stock-market holdings. And a million dollars in cash in his
safety deposit box. That million had brought Al through the 1929
stock-market crash. Now came 1933.

Everybody panicked. Everybody was overextended. Everybody
played on margins. Everybody's holdings plummeted. Show business went to hell. Al didn't enjoy it, but he had his million in his
safety box. Al lit a fresh Havana and strolled over to the bank.
"Hello, sweetheart. Hello, sweetheart." Al knew everybody. He
went downstairs to the vaults. "Hello, sweetheart." The box was
empty. Nothing in it but a blond hairpin. Al had held the box
jointly with his wife.

Al went upstairs and out onto the street. That was it. If you had a
million in cash you were O.K. If you had a blond hairpin, then that
was it. And that *was* it. Everybody liked Al, everybody wanted to
help, but everybody was overextended. The Woods empire went
down like a house of cards. The Eltinge Theatre passed into other
hands. The Woods, Chicago, changed owners. Al's blue silk and
walnut office closed up. He moved out of his suite at the Hotel
Marguery and took a room at the Alamac. He read plays. The Shuberts staked him to put one on. It didn't go. He read some more. He

sent some to stars who had starred for him, but show business isn't run to help someone back on his feet. You help somebody back when he has a good script and a good script didn't come along.

One evening my cook handed me a large brown envelope.

"A man brought it to the kitchen door."

"Did he say who he was?"

"No. I said you were at dinner. He said. 'Give it to her after.'"

"Didn't he leave his name?"

"No. He said, 'Don't bother her. Give it after dinner.' He had one eye that looked off to the side."

Inside the envelope was a script with a purple cover, nothing on it. On the title page, in scrawling handwriting:

This will fracture them, sweetheart,

Al.

Hotel Alamac

Nobody knew where Sullivan and Considine tilted their chairs, but until the blond hairpin Woods could be found of an evening, his chair tilted against the Eltinge. In a good year, before the crash, he had bought the big Paris success *Jealousy*, a melodrama with only two characters. Fay Bainter's name went up in lights, but who would play her lover? The *Times* announced, "Al H. Woods has engaged Guthrie McClintic to direct and co-star with Fay Bainter in the great Paris hit *Jealousy*."

Everybody knew Guthrie McClintic was a celebrated Broadway director, but who knew he had come East from Seattle with a suitcase full of *Theatre Magazines* and old playbills of the Charles Taylor Rep Company to be an actor? Who knew he had graduated from the American Academy of Dramatic Arts and had once been engaged to play small parts with Grace George at Mr. Brady's Playhouse?

*Jealousy* opened out of town in some strange place for a play to open, Greenwich or South Norwalk. Final curtains clanked from stage right and stage left and theoretically came together at stage center. We praised Fay. Friends told Guthrie he was great. Then Guthrie and I and Stanton Griffis drove back to Stanton's house in Greenwich and next day Al fired Guthrie.

Guthrie sued Al, but Al closed *Jealousy* and engaged Jack Halli-
day to replace Guthrie when Jack would be available, which would
not be until the next season. While waiting for his lawsuit to come
up, Guthrie accepted the directorial job of Maxwell Anderson's
*Saturday's Children,* a fine play with a rakish management.

At the final rehearsal Guthrie said, "I know you don't like visi-
tors, but I'm going to invite Stanton Griffis to the run-through, so
don't be disagreeable, we have to get money or we won't open in
Stamford Tuesday."

"Do you like this play?" Stanton asked me. His voice let me
know *he* didn't.

"What did he say?" Guthrie asked.

"He didn't like it."

Guthrie took a swig of his rehearsal flask and looked as though
someone had walked over his grave. "Come home to supper," he
said. Home was 23 Beekman Place, where Guthrie and Katharine
Cornell lived and were looked after by their maid-cook-best friend
and sometimes-banker Emma Wise, who never called her employ-
ers anything but "Hon" and "Shug."

"Nobody got four hundred dollars on 'em Sunday, Shug, try a
popover." Emma Wise put one on his plate.

"Stanton carries cash, but he doesn't like the show."

"Think of *somebody*, Shug. Tomorrow I'm booked to go up to
Boston to the Mother Church." She disappeared through the swinging door.

"Swope always carries a ten-thousand-dollar bill, but he's in
Palm Beach."

Guthrie's face looked dark as an August thundercloud. "Who
*has* got it is Al."

"But you're suing him."

"Yeah."

We sat and glared at supper. The popovers cooled and sank. Out
in the kitchen Emma Wise clattered pans and sang anything that
happened to come into her head.

"Goddam it, I'm going to."

"Can you ask him, if you're suing him?"

"Goddam it, yes."

His rehearsal flask helped him to the kitchen phone. "Hotel Marguery? . . . I want to speak to Al Woods. . . . Al, it's Guthrie, I need four hundred dollars in cash now. . . . What? . . . Yeah, I'm still suing you. . . . I'll be there in five minutes." He hung up. "Go home, I got it. Al's going to meet me Park Avenue side of the Marguery and give it to me. I'll go down to Grand Central and get tomorrow's tickets and pay for the baggage car. Al's four hundred will get the scenery to Stamford."

Al's one room at the Alamac Hotel looked out on Columbus Avenue where it crosses Upper Broadway. He read plays by new playwrights that nobody knew yet, and old playwrights that people had got tired of. When a play struck him, he delivered it to an actor, or an actress, or a director, and got a phone call or not. But Al knew that if you're making out, you get phone calls. If you're not making out, *you* do the phoning. And the script gets sent back, or it doesn't. And you go get it.

He read scripts, drank coffee. Read *Variety*, drank coffee. Delivered scripts, drank coffee. Thought about things, drank coffee. But when you don't have a place to tilt your chair, or a show that could fracture 'em, twenty-four hours are a lot of hours. And one day he died. Marie Doro paid for the services. Marie Doro may have been the most beautiful actress that ever lived and she and Al had been friends. When times changed, any bill that Al couldn't take care of, Marie Doro could.

The funeral parlor's small room was large enough. Not much of a turnout. Marie Doro looked after the bill and told the Alamac they needn't send their bills any more, Al H. Woods was giving up his room.

❋   ❋   ❋   ❋   ❋

"And that's the way it is," says Walter Cronkite and most of the time we hope it isn't.

❋   ❋   ❋   ❋   ❋

Did you grow up? It's not easy. They wake you up and put a dress on you, hand you a zonking piece of pink cake that has had a candle burning on it. And cold pink stuff. Cold but good. And there are a bunch of people with new dolls that squeak and pee. Everybody has paper hats on and things go bang-bang and you think things have taken an upturn. Then next day you wait for that dress bit, for the pink stuff, for another doll. Nothing. You cry and they say it's a safety pin. Why is it a safety pin? It's where's all that yesterday's junk. Forget it. They won't come on with it till another year.

Same thing with the day with a tree. Trees are all outdoors, then one morning there's one in the front room. Pretty! And more of the stuff under it. They pass you some more good-good food. Then what? The trees are all outdoors again. You cry. The safety-pin bit or they bat you one and say you have to learn. "You're a big girl now, behave like one." Why don't *they* learn? No wonder Thornton said, "Ruthie forgave her family so beautifully" when he read my play *Years Ago*. Well, didn't we all? I mean, so long as there are families, what can you do but forgive them?

❧   ❧   ❧   ❧   ❧

Micah Dow's shoes were lost. Had Sophie left them in Peoria last night? Tonight was only Bloomington, but even on a one-nighter Micah Dow had to have his shoes. The ten-year-old son of Rob Dow, a nonconformist in the parish of Galishiels, was played by Gladys Gillen, who passed *her* tenth birthday eighteen years ago. Would a Galishiels lad wear Cuban heels from Chicago's O'Connor and Goldberg's?

Sophie ferreted in the *Little Minister* wardrobe cases and costume trunks and brought forth a pair of low-heeled kid shoes. The toes were square with small crumpled black bows. "Try these," ordered Sophie. Gladys' foot slid in.

Sophie took her big shears and cut the toes to look like a poor boy's or at least like a poor boy if he was in a Charles Frohman play by J. M. Barrie.

"Those are pretty," I said.

"I should say they are!" snapped Sophie. She cut a hole on the side.

"What show were they in?"

"They were hers."

"Whose?"

"They're the Lady Babbie shoes she wore the first time she ever did *The Minister*."

"Sophie, how can you cut them up like that?" screamed Gladys.

"Micah Dow has to wear something, don't he?"

Well that's show business. Not only the show must go on, but the shoes.

\* \* \* \* \*

Did you see *Rosemary's Baby*?

"Let's get a baby carriage, Ruthie, and you and I wheel it up South Water Street." (Mia Farrow in Edgartown. Circa 1968.)

That is "a few of my favorite things."

\* \* \* \* \*

I graduated from Quincy High in 1914. Quincy gave me my opportunity, Boston theatres gave me my inspiration, New York is where I became an actress, California is where I became a success. If I think of myself as a permanent transient, why am I buying a house in Edgartown? After threescore years and fourteen am I looking for roots?

# The Former Miss Duer

C HARLES LEDERER had Cartier mount a large A made of square
rubies on a pin and presented it to Alice Duer Miller. He'd
just finished reading Hawthorne's *The Scarlet Letter* and liked the
idea that Hester Prynne had been made to wear a large A for adul-
tery. He wanted to see what a scarlet A looked like. He offered it to
Alice with no implication. "It must have looked pretty on Hester
Prynne, and I'm sorry it caused her mortification. Perhaps it'll help
the score if another lady wears it with pleasure."

When Moss invited Alice to dine with him at the Colony, he sang
a song from his childhood:

> *Alice, come out with me,*
> *Come out with me*
> *And dine—*

Over on East 52nd Street beside the East River they were building the Campanile. Alice bought two floors. The Campanile is the
apartment house across from the River Club. Woollcott urged her
to choose a low floor. "If you're going to be on the river, be as close
to it as possible."

Alice bought the second and third floors that hung over the
river. Her big drawing room looked across to whatever is across.
And also down the river.

Woollcott wanted to live there, too, but you had to buy two

floors. "What do you want with two floors, Alice?" he asked. "Cut off some measly something for me." She did. His sitting room looked across the river, too. His bedroom looked into the River Club. He could drop in next door at Alice's in pajamas and robe for a fast game of cribbage or a hand of bezique. That was the year bezique was in.

In Alice's drawing room, tea was brought in on a silver tray placed in front of Alice for her to preside. Blue blood ran in her veins, formal upbringing had been hers, what a lesson to see her handle the Sèvres teacups, pour the George III hot-water pitcher, offer the Duer ancestral sugar and creamer, pass round the Boston revolutionary Hewes' silver spoons! It *needed* know-how to drop as many things off a tea tray as Alice Duer Miller could. Her lovely long fingers could let a cup slip and drench the Persian carpet. What a field day for the dry-cleaner when the former Miss Duer slid tea sandwiches into the guest's lap! "Oh dear, I am so sorry," she murmured, quite used to it. Though sorry, she more or less expected it and hoped *you* did. "Have another cup?"

"In the hand, please, Alice," suggested Woollcott, "the floor is getting swampy."

Her carpet was Persian and so was her brindled cat. Julian the Apostate watched events with guarded amber eyes. No one knew what Julian thought of Alice at the tea tray, but it was noted he kept his distance.

When Prince Andrew of Greece was in New York, Alice gave a dinner in his honor. Her butler was English and impeccable, but, still, with royalty? Alice liked protocol. "When His Highness comes, address him as 'Your Highness'—'Yes, Your Highness,' 'Thank you, Your Highness,' 'What will Your Highness have to drink?' "

"Yes, madam. Thank you, madam."

At eight o'clock the doorbell rang. Alice stood at the drawing-room door to receive her guests. The drawing-room door was in full command of the front hall.

Farnsworth opened the front door. "May I take your coat, Your Highness."

"Yes, thank— Why, Farny! Why, Farny! *Is* it you?"

"Yes, Your Highness."

"Why, Farny, old cock, think of seeing *you.*" Prince Andrew flung his arms around Farnsworth and gave him a hug. "Alice, darling," he called, "think of Farny looking after you, we went through the war together! What a lark to find him again."

At the Millers' dinner parties Harry Miller ate his own menu and drank his own wine. While you were served roast capon, he was served meat loaf. You were served hot house asparagus, Henry had boiled beets. You were served Nesselrode pudding, Henry was served apple pie. "Have some?" he asked his vis-à-vis. "Or do you like company victuals?"

Alice had an Italian chauffeur, who drove her as if he were winning a perpetual Memorial Day Classic. Stately Alice felt perfectly relaxed if Ceppetti was at the wheel. He knew what he was doing and she never gave it another thought. Whether it was on the long straight highway or the twisting Vermont roads, she felt comfortable with Ceppetti. To go to the Island, she and Woollcott took a drawing room on the New York Central, as far as Saratoga, took rooms at the Grand Union Hotel for the night, then early next morning Woollcott and she and whoever got in Alice's car and off sped Ceppetti. He passed the green meadows so fast you couldn't tell a sheep from a daisy. New York to Saratoga in the drawing room was practical, the time could be used to play cribbage, bezique or backgammon, then upstate, revert to nature.

Alice's titles were *The Charm School, Come Out of the Kitchen, The Reluctant Duchess, The White Cliffs of Dover.*

As Miss Duer, she'd taught math at Barnard before she married Henry and they went to live on a coffee plantation in Cuba. She loved and admired her only son, Denning. She was patrician, she accepted it and never let it get in her way. She'd enjoyed the old school, but chose the new. The raffish Island bunch were her chums and when Princess Alice and Athlone came down from ruling Canada, she gave them a dinner party and invited Lederer and Harpo. She was at home everywhere except behind a tea table. Even there, her beauty made you put up with being scalded.

When cousin Ellin Mackay eloped with Irving, she told Ellin's irate father that it was a good match and congratulated both bride

and groom. When Clarry Mackay accused Irving of being a dope
fiend, Alice told him, "What nonsense! People in society may have
time to take dope, but how could a hard worker like Irving?"

\* \* \* \* \*

Where did you spend *your* honeymoon? Nat Goodwin spent his
with his beautiful Maxine at the Grenoble Hotel on Seventh Avenue across from Carnegie Hall. Nat Goodwin was the flawless co-
median who was so skilled that no one could figure out how he did
it. Maxine Elliott was "the most beautiful woman I ever saw," said
Ethel Barrymore. She was the turn-of-the-century's reigning
beauty and like Nat Goodwin she was a star, but the notices dwelt
on her beauty. Her acting? One isn't supposed to have everything.

The Goodwins passed their honeymoon at the Grenoble, a
brown brick Gothic-trimmed hotel where today rears 888 Seventh
Avenue, next but one to the Studio Bar. The "but one" is an arch, a
brown brick fragment of the Grenoble.

Down on West 39th Street there's not even a fragment of the
Maxine Elliott Theatre. It used to be between Broadway and Sixth
on the uptown side of the street. When it was being built, Mr. Lee
came by to see its progress. A lofty column was being derricked
into place. Who else was watching? Nat Goodwin stood, hands
behind his back. "See that marble column?"

"Yes."

"That's only half as hard as her heart."

The honeymoon was over.

If you're going to play the emotional scene, take a leaf from Nat
Goodwin. He sat in a box at the old Hollis Theatre in Boston. A
comic from Weber and Fields was making his debut in the legit.
"He'll never make it," whispered Goodwin.

"Why?" whispered his companion.

"He hasn't laid down the preparation."

Whether it's a scene in a show or a scene with your wife or your
husband or lawyer, lay down the threads for the big moment. In
*The Matchmaker*, billed as a farce, Thornton Wilder wrote a moving soliloquy near the end of Act III. It comes in the midst of high

jinks with fellows dressed as ladies, a grande dame offering to scrub them and general red-wigged hilarity, but early in Act I Wilder laid down the preparation. He wrote a scene where Dolly Gallagher Levi asks Mr. Vandergelder for a loan.

"You could get laughs in that scene," they said to me.

"Did you ever have to ask for a loan?" I asked. "It's not funny. In this scene I lay down 'the preparation.' "

Nat Goodwin's knowledge outlived both him and David Warfield. "The gossamer thread," Felix Frankfurter called the things that aren't written down anywhere, but go on and on and become part of life.

*   *   *   *   *

Do you eat the sour ones and save the ripe for the finish? Do you wear your old sable coat and save your new? If you do, you're an optimist. A ja-sager. And so is a lady I know who at eighty-nine bought a summer home and had it all done over.

"It'll take a year and a half," they warned her.

"I'll do it," she said, "or I'll wind up playing bridge at the Harbor View."

She did it and when she went into the Martha's Vineyard Hospital she said to the President of the Board, "Cash this *today*." It was a check for ten thousand dollars and that night she turned in her chips. How nicely she turned them in!

(Ja-sagers, take notice)

# That's Nice

ON THE SLEEPER from Denver to Chicago maybe Selena felt like telling the time she and Miss Miller fished Don Alvarado's diamond bracelet out of Miss Miller's Savoy Plaza toilet. Or after we bombed at Princeton and were in my room at the Nassau Inn, with a comforting bourbon and ginger ale, maybe she'd tell how Mr. Ziegfeld set up a soda fountain backstage at the New Amsterdam for hot nights. "Well, he was just as lovely, doncha know. Of course, in the *Follies I* looked after Miss Ray Dooley and Carrie was with Miss Miller. Carrie went with Miss Miller right after Violet that had been with her since the Five Columbians, doncha know, left to marry a feller in Washington. Violet always called Miss Miller 'Miss Baby' because in the beginning Miss Miller was billed as 'Mlle. Sugarplum' and both Miss Miller and Violet cried so hard, Mr. Errol had to send out for a champagne cocktail for Violet. Well, he was always just as nice, doncha know. Did I tell you Carrie went to Paris with Miss Miller? They always went to the Ritz and one time Carrie went downstairs to pay the bill and Miss Miller was going to look after the jewel case, but somehow they got to the station and Carrie noticed no jewel case. So she left Miss Miller with a lady going on the boat train and took the taxi back to the Ritz and they were already cleaning the room up, but Carrie got down and looked under Miss Miller's bed and there was the jewel case, doncha know, and she got back to the station in time."

When Selena first came with me, she'd only been with musicals. There were a lot of costume changes in *The Country Wife*, so we didn't talk much, but the next show was at the Central City Festival up in the Colorado Rockies.

"I'm going to do *A Doll's House*."

"That's nice," said Selena.

Was it? Nights when *A Doll's House* had a night off and the company took the scary road down the Rockies to Denver, Selena and I sat on the bench in front of the Teller House watching nothing go by. Was that nice?

"Madam, it's just like being in jail."

Selena had never been to jail, but Carrie had. "When Carrie decided to go in the business, she went with a couple whose act was booked on the Orpheum. Carrie worked one show, then her people were handed a summons and had to go to jail. Carrie didn't *know* Chicago, doncha know, and thought maybe they might need her, so she went, too."

"Does Carrie like being with Miss Lawrence?"

"Oh, yes. She's just as easy, doncha know, likes tea first thing she wakes up in the morning. Carrie thinks she's a real star. In *Tonight at 8:30* she has a quick change right down to the skin. They make it in the wings, of course, behind a screen in the entrance and Carrie has the dress on a hat pole and her shoes. And while Miss Lawrence is making the change she all the time has to keep talking to Mr. Coward, doncha know. He was on stage and one matinee the zipper stuck. Miss Lawrence just kept on talking, got down on the floor, lay the dress out flat, kept talking to Mr. Coward, got the two sides of the zipper together even, went on talking, put the dress on, zipped it and went on on cue. Carrie says Miss Lawrence *should* have her name in lights."

(*Players' Guide*, what is your definition of a name in lights? Mine is, fix a zipper.)

Carrie and Selena were born in Virginia. Mr. Randolph and his wife had twelve children. The oldest was named Honor.

"Honor Randolph. I think that's a beautiful name."

"Well, that's nice, the youngest was named Peachie, doncha know."

Central City's festival was over. On the sleeper from New York to Toronto, I couldn't sleep and Selena climbed down from the upper. "They sell Leichner's in Toronto, should I get some?"

"Please do."

"Miss Miller couldn't ever have played some matinees without Leichner's. Don Alvarado would paste her one, doncha know, and I'd have to make up the black and blue with Leichner's Number 5 and 2. Black and blue is hard to cover, but Leichner's will. They sell it at the drugstore across from the Royal Alexandra."

"I get it in London."

"That's nice. Do you know up in Toronto if they still have the Fritz-Carlton Hotel? The *Follies* didn't play Canada, but Carrie came there with Miss Lawrence and she and Miss Lawrence stayed at the Royal York where we're going to, but it made Carrie laugh because on the callboard the hotel for the crew to stay was the Fritz-Carlton. It made Carrie laugh because she and Miss Miller stayed at the Ritz-Carlton in Boston and the Ritz in London and Paris, doncha know."

The night Tony cabled that the Old Vic's Lilian Baylis died, Selena walked me back to Milwaukee's Hotel Schroeder. We passed a window full of fur coats. Selena wanted to distract me. "You like that one?" she asked.

"Yes. What about the white one?"

"That's not fur. That's ur."

Every Sunday was spent in a drawing room.

"Wouldn't you hate to live here?" I asked as a town slid past miles from anywhere.

"Oh, they prob'ly find lots to do. Was Mr. Jaffe late for the finale last night?"

"No, he made it. This show's going to be a hit, Selena."

"That's nice. Mr. Jaffe's number goes well."

His number was when Krogstad comes to the Helmer house and threatens to expose Nora.

"At the matinee Bill didn't hear the warning and I had to run get Mr. King or he wouldn't make the finale."

"Another openin', Another show," sang the maid in *Kiss Me, Kate*.

I came back from the London engagement and called up Selena. "We're going to open in October. I hope you'll come with me."

"That's nice."

Before New York *The Matchmaker* played Boston. Selena had a room overlooking the garden at Mrs. Brown's boardinghouse. She said Mrs. Brown would like to see the show. That was an honor. Mrs. Brown could go to all the shows and she selected ours.

"My house seats for Mrs. Brown," I wrote on a note to the company manager. "Please hand them to Selena." Mrs. Brown wasn't somebody who stood in line at the Colonial Theatre box office to pick up gift seats. Mrs. Brown could go to every show, but didn't care to. Once in a while she'd tell Carrie she'd go to see Gertie or tell Evelyn she'd go to see Kit or Priscilla she'd go to see Helen, but most of the time she didn't.

The evening she came to *The Matchmaker*, she paid me the compliment of coming backstage. She didn't say she liked it, she just said she was pleased to meet me. Tall, dark-complexioned, she dressed like all Back Bay ladies. No particular color, no particular cut, but good material that could be made over and sponged down and not be for one, but for many a winter.

The night after her visit Selena brought me a daintily packed box of fried chicken. "Mrs. Brown wants you to have this," said Selena as though handing me the Nobel Prize. She was right. It was the Nobel award of the fried-chicken department. "Mrs. Brown always sent Miss Miller some. I *told* you she liked you, doncha know."

※　※　※　※　※

Are you good in a hurry? Laurence Olivier says, "When I have to hurry, I put on after-shave. Why is that? I never do if I have plenty of time."

# The Smallest Hamlet

W AS IT 1966? Whenever it was, at the first rehearsal of *A Very Rich Woman* the company was seated in a half circle on stage at the Belasco Theatre. Ernie Truex got up and went stage left, studied the floorboards, then planted his feet. "Here's where I stood rehearsing *A Good Little Devil* the day Belasco told me I was going to be a success."

"Move over," I said. I stood there and so did everybody.

Around Denver ten-year-old Ernie Truex did recitations for parties and banquets, spoke a piece in church at Easter and Christmas and was in the school show. It put ideas in people's heads. One idea was to star him as THE SMALLEST HAMLET. He toured successfully for several months.

When he was eighteen, a call came from the musical stock housed in Boston's old Castle Square. It was his first time East and he liked it. And he liked the ingenue. Young Juliet Day was pretty and talented as well as thoughtful. "After rehearsal Sunday we'll get Papa to drive us around in his taxi."

They saw Beacon Hill and Bunker Hill and Concord and had a trip through the Fenway and past the swell homes in Brookline.

"Is the ocean around here?" asked the Denverite.

"Why, sure."

"I never saw one."

"You didn't!" Juliet and her papa were astonished. "I'll drive you out to Revere," he said and stepped on the gas.

The ocean was even better than Ernie thought it would be. "I'd like to send some to my grandma."

"*She* never saw it, either?"

"No," said Ernie. "I'd like to send her a bottle."

They found one, filled it with Boston Harbor water and shipped it out to Denver.

In Wollaston I could see the ocean, but what I liked to see was *The Theatre Magazine*. I read every word, then read it over again, until the Thomas Crane Library got the new one. One issue had a picture of Ernest Truex playing the boy in *The Dummy*. He was in a scene with a golden-haired little girl who also made a hit. She didn't care so much about that as she cared about Ernie. "I'm not a little boy," he told her.

Little Joyce Fair didn't even listen. She was *really* ten years old like the part she was playing, but Ernie, playing the fourteen-year-old, was a grown man.

"Ernie, I love you," said little Joyce.

"I love you, too, dear, but I'm married and have a baby."

Dramatists' Guild, would you say it was *Lolita* in reverse?

What would *you* say, little Joyce Fair? You ought to know. After all, you wrote *The Women*.

When Ernie was Mary Pickford's leading man in *A Good Little Devil*, at a final rehearsal Belasco stood in the first entrance with a log and pounded out the pace he wanted the actors to speak at. "Thump, thump, thump," reported Ernie. "Then a more exhilarated set of thumps, 'Thump-thump-thump.' Then came Mary's emotional scene. 'Thump (pause) thump (pause pause) thump.' " Belasco did it right through all the acts. Was that why at the close of *A Good Little Devil* America's Sweetheart went back in silent films?

Talkies took over the silents and Sidney Kingsley took over Ernie's Bucks County farm. "It's beautiful. How could you part with it?"

"Roll 'em," said *Bachelor Mother*'s assistant director.

The scene started, but when his cue came, Ernie didn't speak.

"Cut," called Garson. "Ernie, where *were* you?"

"In New Jersey," he said wistfully.

At the same Belasco where *A Good Little Devil* had played, *A Very Rich Woman* was closing. Ernie walked down the flight of iron stairs from his dressing room, gave the brim of his hat a tug, looked around him. "Well," he said, "it was first class all the way." It was his farewell to Broadway. The smallest Hamlet decided to retire. He went back to his ranch in Fallbrook, California.

On New Year's day I rang him up. "Happy New Year, Ernie."

"It certainly was. We had quite a New Year's out here."

Sylvia got on the extension. "Oh, Ernie, you're *not* going to tell *that*."

"Sure I am. The Fallbrook Country Club—"

"Ernie, I'll never speak to you again."

"—where we play golf has a big do New Year's Eve—"

"Ernie, you're not going to tell Ruth that."

"Why not? And you know out in Fallbrook they look on me as some kind of a celebrity—"

"Ernie, you're *dreadful*."

"—so they said would I speak to them."

"Oh, Ernie."

" 'Sure,' I said. It was quite a stylish thing, y'know—"

"I should say it was till *you* got going."

"—everybody in black tie and the ladies all gotten up, but I stood up and I said, 'Did you ever hear of Gary Cooper?' "

"Oh, Ernie."

"Well, of course, that was no more than they expected, that I know all the big shots. 'Well, *did* you?' I asked.

" 'Yes,' they all shouted.

" 'And did you ever hear of the Countess di Frasso?' Well, no, they hadn't, but they enjoyed hearing a grand name. Well, y'know Gary Cooper was a tall tall tall hunk of man and the Countess was a little little little lady—"

"Ernie, *don't* go on."

"And they were romancing each other. Only Lupe Velez didn't like it, because she and Gary had been *also* romancing, so Lupe says very simply, 'Countess, what's the idea?'

"And silent Gary just stood there. I guess the Countess thought he'd vouchsafe, but he didn't and there was Lupe practically thumbing her nose at the lady, so the lady said, 'He's my lover.'

" 'Well,' says Lupe, 'look out, Countess, you don't get your hair ribbon caught in his fly.' "

"Ernie just wrecked the whole evening."

"I did not! *Lot* of 'em said I brightened it up."

What else from THE SMALLEST HAMLET?

❃   ❃   ❃   ❃   ❃

In opera they said Geraldine Farrar could not only sing, but could act. Sam Goldwyn brought her to Hollywood to do *Carmen.* "I'm going crazy," she told Ned Sheldon. "How do actors act without a *beat?*"

Too bad they didn't send for Belasco and his "thump, thump, thump" log.

❃   ❃   ❃   ❃   ❃

How are you going to feel when you drop dead?

Embarrassed is how I will.

# The Good That Men Do

"THE GOOD THAT MEN DO lives after them." That's a quote from myself. I know the correct one, but I don't think so. I think the *good* lives after. The evil gets accepted or forgotten. Or becomes hearsay. The *good* lives on and does us all some good.

Are you lucky? I am. A December evening in 1915 I came home to the Three Arts Club from a day of "Would you have any part in a play I could do?" and in my letter box was "Be on the stage of the Empire Theatre Sunday at 11." I still have that slip of paper. Wouldn't *you?*

Sunday at 11, Three Arts girls marked time at All Souls Episcopal, West End Avenue, or St. Malachy's West 49th Street or Columbus Avenue Second Baptist or washed their hair or knickers, but you know where *I* was.

Miss Maude Adams told Mr. Homer Saint-Gaudens to try me out for the part of Nibs. She also told him to try out two other girls for the same part in her revival of *Peter Pan*, opening on that same stage four glorious days before Christmas. The tryout wasn't to find if we were wonderful actresses, but were we up to Nibs' pillow dance?

Miss Maude Adams left to bedazzle our capital with *The Little Minister* and *Quality Street* and Monday I showed up at the Lyceum Theatre, West 45th Street.

"Come to the Lyceum Theatre," Mr. Homer Saint-Gaudens had said.

Wouldn't *you* try the stage door?

The stage doorman said I couldn't come in. "Ask out front," he mumbled and returned to his own pursuits.

Out front wasn't too clear to one lately from Wollaston, but I went around to the lobby. The box office had a long line buying for the holidays. "Excuse me." Nervous prostration set in, but I squeezed up to the window. "Excuse me, where is Mr. Homer Saint-Gaudens?"

"Rehearsal hall. Next?"

Is rehearsal hall all that clear?

In show business either you know where to go or you don't, and when you find out, you're a professional. I spun around the lobby until Box Office took mercy. "Up those steps. Next?"

Up those steps was clear. Up those steps was an elegant carved wooden door and as I was going to knock, the door swung open and a tall tall, elegant man in a tall tall hat stood in a small small elevator that framed him perfectly.

Worry overwhelmed me. "I have to go to where Mr. Homer Saint-Gaudens is rehearsing and I don't know how to." An asinine tear fell down my nose and dropped onto my blue winter coat my mother had made me, buttonholes by Mr. Will Cohen, Wollaston's tailor. My buttonholes may have looked professional, but I looked ridiculous.

"Step in," said the tall tall elegant man. "I'll take you." My mother had warned me never to follow strangers, but who was thinking about their mother? Up we creaked till we swayed to a stop. "There you are." He opened the door. "Good luck."

The door opened into a long narrow room, snow pelting against two sooty skylight windows, the piano player running over the dance music.

"Couldn't you walk up?" snarled the stage manager. "Did you have to get Mr. Daniel Frohman to run you up in his elevator?"

Mr. Daniel Frohman had helped me find the rehearsal! Mr. Daniel Frohman of the Lyceum Theatre had said "Good luck" to Ruth Gordon, born Jones!

"Got your bloomers on?" The piano player went at the pillow dance and so did a Dorothy, a Mabel and a Ruth.

"Can you kick any higher?" asked Mr. Homer Saint-Gaudens and waved his own long leg in the air, but he was six foot something and I was five foot nothing, emphasis on the nothing. That night a Ruth went to bed discouraged.

"Telephone for Gordon."

Into my lavender Japanese wrapper Mrs. Wetmore had given me as a going-away-to-become-an-actress present and into my lavender going-away bedroom slippers my mother had made me to go away with Mrs. Wetmore's lavender wrapper and up the hall to the wall phone.

"You're the worst dancer, but you got the job," said beloved stage manager. "The salary is thirty-five a week."

"Thirty-five *dollars?*"

"No, pinhead, thirty-five doughnuts! Rehearsal hall, ten A.M. and *don't* bother Daniel Frohman, simp."

"Good luck," said Mr. Daniel Frohman one day and that night I was an actress! My father had given me fifty dollars to pin inside my dress, my mother had done sewing to provide me with extra, but Mr. Daniel Frohman had said good luck and tomorrow I was going to rehearse in his Lyceum Theatre where there'd been a Dorothy and a Mabel and tomorrow there'd be just a Ruth.

Daniel Frohman had a right to wish people good luck, he had it to spare. He wanted to be in show business and was. He wanted to be a manager and was. He wanted to own a theatre and did. He wrote a book about how he felt.

## CHAPTER ONE

I used to come to New York once or twice a season from my youthful wanderings about America as advance agent of a "one-night-stand" show. Theatrical people are fond of the theatre, so on these homecomings, I spent my evenings watching the splendid performances of Palmer's Company at the Union Square Theatre and those of Lester Wallack's Company, then at Broadway and 13th Street—

That's how he began his book. No boring "I was brought up in Sandusky, Ohio—" His "homecomings" were not to Sandusky.

221

Home to him was Broadway and Union Square to see what Lester Wallack and Palmer's Company were doing. Dan Frohman's book doesn't bother with where he was born, he was in show business and Sandusky, Ohio, was a one-nighter you played and got out of and came home to Union Square. Sandusky, Ohio, he and his brother put up with until Dan could be an advance agent and lease and own theatres and his brother Charles could become New York's and London's most admired manager. Did his book mention their boyhood? It didn't even mention a brother till the end of Chapter One. "I little thought then that I should pay E. H. Sothern fifty thousand dollars a year and later Charles Frohman would pay him one hundred thousand. And for two years." Was Charles his younger brother? His older? Did it matter? Why write stuff like that? What mattered was a manager paid a star a hundred thousand dollars a year for two years.

Union Square, Broadway at 13th Street, the Madison Square Theatre were home. The only other home he was interested in was the Actors' Home, founded by the Actors' Fund of America in 1882. Some of the profession held a meeting on the stage of Wallack's Theatre. Joseph Jefferson showed up. And William J. Florence, A. M. Palmer of the Union Square, Nedda's father Edward Harrigan—a lot of fine people. Wallack was elected president and Dan Frohman was elected secretary. "Everyone knew the secretary would have to do most of the work, so I was unanimously elected. The Actors' Fund of America was incorporated and James Gordon Bennett of the *New York Herald* gave ten thousand dollars and opened up his newspaper to aid our plea for subscriptions. Al Hayman gave ten thousand, my brother Charles gave five thousand and the players and managers all contributed. Times weren't good and too many actors had to come round to the stage door to ask for a handout. That doesn't make *anybody* feel any good."

That was the start of the Actors' Home, but Dan's home was the Madison Square Theatre which he'd been engaged to run. And later the Old Lyceum which he leased and in 1903 the New Lyceum which he owned. At eighty-nine he died in his rooms in a hotel. It was only a place he went till time to come back to his beloved 45th Street Lyceum.

From time to time he also had a theatre in London "where the critics would sometimes say praiseworthy things, but nobody brought home any money."

Even the great Booth noticed it. "Did anybody ever know an American actor to bring home a profit?"

Not John T. Raymond, the famous "Colonel Sellers" who said to his Shaftesbury Avenue manager, "Gillig, how do you send money back to America?" But after he opened, he whispered to the same Gillig, "How do you get money sent *from* America?"

Dan Frohman wrote his book about things of interest and it didn't interest him that he was born August 22, 1850, but it did interest him that you could get a great notice in London and come home with no money.

Some people enjoy going to a theatre, some people enjoy working in a theatre, some people enjoy leasing a theatre. Dan Frohman leased the old 23rd Street Lyceum and before he found a play for it, engaged an actor. Who better could the actors have elected for their Fund's secretary?

The actor he hired was young Sothern, appearing in Miss Helen Dauvray's company which Frohman had booked into his Lyceum till he could find a play to produce. Miss Dauvray's season closed in the early spring and Dan Frohman said to his actor, "I'd like to keep the house open till hot weather, but I don't have a play." Young Sothern said his father left him some and had the old theatrical trunks sent up.

"We found one that appeared attractive," writes Frohman. "It was called *Trade*." He scratched out the title and named it *The Highest Bidder*. To stage it he engaged young Dave Belasco of San Francisco. Rehearsals didn't look promising, but the first night surprised everybody. "At least we had a right to be hopeful."

The end of the first week Frohman and Sothern were having dinner at the Ashland House across from the Lyceum when Sothern pointed at the theatre. "Look!" he said excitedly. "There's a speculator!"

Two weeks later they were playing to crowded houses and he and Sothern had dinner at the Ashland again. "Can anything be done to stop those infernal speculators?" asked Sothern. Dan Frohman ended Chapter One with that. Chapter One doesn't tell us where he came from or if his brother was older or younger, but it tells us he knew a tag when he heard one. When his leading man asked, "Can anything be done to stop those infernal speculators?" he knew that was the laugh.

*The Highest Bidder* was a hit, but what Dan Frohman wanted for his Lyceum was a splendid company in residence, like Wallack's or Palmer used to have. He engaged a company, then hired two authors. "Write a good part for everybody," he said and gave them the list of actors that were to make his old Lyceum Stock Company theatre history.

Like Rose Trelawny in *Trelawny of the Wells,* he "loved the players." For fifty-one years he would occupy himself with the problems of their Home and their Fund, so why wouldn't the new lessee of the old Lyceum order "good parts for everybody"?

"Everybody" was Herbert Kelcey, the perfect actor, who later on was to star.

DAVID BELASCO

PRESENTS

HERBERT KELCEY AND EFFIE SHANNON

IN

YEARS OF DISCRETION

Herbert Kelcey was hired first, then Henry Miller. Miller was the Lyceum's leading man. Matchless actor, matchless director and so successful a producer he was able to build his own theatre on West 43rd Street, legacy to his son Gilbert.

For character parts, there was no one to equal Charles S. Dickson. Later generations saw him listlessly wave his palm-leaf fan in *The Great Gatsby* to temper the heat as he drove a knife into Gatsby's future. Dan Frohman sought the best for his new stock at the old Lyceum and Charles S. Dickson was the best.

Another of the troupe was Grace Henderson. Near the end of her theatre days someone asked her, "Was it true you acted with Lionel Barrymore?"

"Acted with him, I *slept* with him," she said, contemptuous of modern ignorance.

To play old ladies, Dan hired elegant Mrs. Thomas Whiffen. Henry Miller must have admired her, too, for when he put on *Just Suppose* at his own theatre he engaged her for the grand lady of Virginia who welcomes the Prince of Wales and his friend Bubbles, acted memorably by Leslie Howard making his New York debut.

Playing second fiddle to Miller at the Lyceum was William Faversham. Some years went by and Dan Frohman's second fiddle became the town's acknowledged matinee idol. Elegant, handsome, charming, he filled Charles Frohman's Empire. Its red velvet boxes and orchestra seats rustled with taffeta to see the dazzling Faversham.

Henry Miller, starring up the street, came backstage after a matinee. "Favvy, dear boy, such a good performance. What was it you were referring to in Act Two when you pointed to the panela?"

"Why, the panela, of course," said Faversham.

"Ah yes, but what are panela?"

"Oh, you know—" An elegant gesture.

"No, dear boy, I don't."

"Well, dammit," said Faversham, "I don't either."

"But I mean, what do you *point* to?" asked Miller, the realist.

"The panela. What it says in the script. 'The marvelous old panela.' Actually now you ask me, I don't know what I *do* point to."

The stage manager found the line. "The marvelous old panela."

"I told you so," said Faversham.

Miller looked thoughtful. "I believe that's a typographical error, dear boy. I believe that should read 'panels.' "

They had played the play half a season and no one had questioned 'panela." But panela or panels, Faversham, the matinee idol of New York, had once been Dan Frohman's choice for second business and understudy. In the end he was again beholden to Frohman. When Favvy retired, it was to the Actors' Home.

"Write a good part for everybody." And he had the company who could play good parts. The writers were Henry De Mille and Dave Belasco. Belasco had directed *The Highest Bidder* and would also direct this new one. "A society comedy would be good," suggested their producer.

De Mille and Belasco must have liked the theatre as much as

Frohman, because where they chose to write their society comedy with a good part for everybody was on stage, after or before the performance. Their method was as unique as their locale—they wrote their play without dialogue.

"Putting in the dialogue was the most difficult part of their labors," writes the new manager of the Old Lyceum Stock Company. "And when their play got the dialogue in it, Belasco would direct. He had never been further east than Sacramento, but I heard about him at San Francisco's Baldwin Theatre and brought him to New York."

At the Baldwin, Belasco's job had been prompter, actor, director and author. Around the Baldwin, they said Dave Belasco could make a play out of the "synopsis of scenes" from a theatre playbill. He not only could, but did. On a week when a play wasn't forthcoming, their bright boy wrote one that often resembled some current New York success.

"Young, ambitious and hot-tempered," remembered Frohman, "once he brought his fist down on an iron safe with such violence, he had to direct with one hand for a week." But one hand or two, Dan Frohman saw he had a director. He figured if De Mille was the literary man, Belasco was the dramatist. "Belasco would act all the parts of their new play, making up words appropriate to their dialogueless scene, and at the same time he would time it, so that De Mille, setting it down, wound up with the play cut to measure." Dan Frohman had an eye for talent. They opened on schedule with a dialogueful modern society comedy which De Mille or Belasco or both of them named *The Wife*. That title was a lot better than *Trade* and Dan Frohman saw no reason to scratch it out.

On the evening of November 1, 1887, the curtain went up, but the legendary company's beginning didn't meet with the success expected. The critics praised the players, but found the play not consistently good.

Years later George S. Kaufman, stung into criticism of the critics, inquired, "Ever go to a dinner party that didn't somewhere let down? Ever sit around with a friend and have some moment less than sparkling? Ever take a trip and not have the scene drop between Niagara Falls and Grand Central? You think notices don't have dull moments? Why must only a *play* be expected to never let down?"

If Dan Frohman had those feelings, he didn't reveal them. He told his authors to get back to work. His book doesn't tell us if he ever went to school, but it tells us, "By excisions and revisions, the authors got the show into more attractive shape. Acts I and II became Act I. The role of the veteran who limped was deprived of his wound, and his scenes, like his game leg, ceased to drag." The bright boy of Baldwin's, or the literary De Mille, or the lessee of the Old Lyceum knew what made show business and the play ran for a year. "The first week of the run, my old friend S. S. Packard of Packard's Business College bought three hundred seats as a Christmas present to his pupils." Dan Frohman's book never mentions that he married the fascinating actress Alison Skipworth, then later the beautiful Margaret Illington, who made her name up out of her birthplace Bloomington, Illinois, but he tells us he had a friend who bought three hundred tickets for a play that got poor reviews. How about that, Sitwells' father?

His cast was praised, his play, with its excisions and revisions, ran through the season, his friend bought three hundred tickets, Dan Frohman could enjoy his stationery.

LYCEUM THEATRE, 4TH AVE. AND 23RD ST.
DANIEL FROHMAN, LESSEE

When things are going well, one's name in print is enjoyable, and soon after *Peter Pan* opened I called on a printer and parted with some of my thirty-five dollars. Fifty professional cards were mine.

RUTH GORDON
THE MAUDE ADAMS CO.
CHARLES FROHMAN MANAGEMENT
EMPIRE THEATRE

In the same lobby where I'd been so distracted, I offered the company manager my name in print.

RUTH GORDON
THE MAUDE ADAMS CO.

227

CHARLES FROHMAN MANAGEMENT
EMPIRE THEATRE

I used the lingo, "Do you honor the profession?"

He did and I enjoyed Ethel Barrymore's Thursday matinee of *Our Mrs. McChesney* in Daniel Frohman's Lyceum Theatre, where the stationery read,

LYCEUM THEATRE, WEST 45TH ST.
DANIEL FROHMAN, OWNER

All that came twenty-eight years after the Old Lyceum's *The Highest Bidder* and *The Wife*. And once again Frohman told Belasco and De Mille to get busy on another. They did and made the secretary of the Actors' Fund indignant. "You can't leave the leading woman of the company out of one whole act!"

Back to work went the authors. "They remembered *David Copperfield*," writes Dan Frohman, "and borrowed the idea of Dora and Agnes and turned in their play with *two* leading ladies, both in every act. That wasn't just like *David Copperfield*, but it gave them the clue," writes tactful Frohman.

When Daniel Frohman set down things, he did not include the fact that his father was Henry Frohman and his mother was Barbara, but he knew a father and mother were what you had to have. He bought the London hit, Pinero's *Sweet Lavender*, for his Lyceum Company and felt confident. On his New York opening night it did not seem as though the London success was in the cards for the old Lyceum. "The first-night patrons were startled to find that the heroine was an illegitimate child." Startled first-nighters were not what Dan Frohman was after. He cabled Pinero to rearrange the parental relations. Pinero grudgingly consented, while expressing a dim view of the New York public.

"The revision made it run a season," writes the lessee of the old Lyceum, "and two companies toured it." Henry Miller played an Englishman and the part of an American was acted by the only Englishman in the Lyceum Stock Company, Herbert Kelcey. The Actors' Fund secretary not only "loved the players," but didn't practice type casting.

The years went by. Fourteen of them. Dan Frohman's first actor, whose play came out of his father's trunk, alternated his New York engagements with the Stock Company. "When Sothern held the boards at the Lyceum, the other organization toured." And while one played and the other toured, Dan Frohman found time to nurture the Lyceum School of Acting, now the American Academy of Dramatic Arts which in the years to come nurtured Spencer Tracy, Grace George, Garson Kanin, Mary MacArthur, Grace Kelly and yours truly.

The Ohioan whose "homecomings" bypassed Sandusky for New York could see what was going to help the actors not only for *his* season, but for all seasons. Teach them how to act, get a good part for everybody and the leading lady to appear in every act and a place where beginners could learn how to do it.

If you can get past the moment, things shape up. Success mollified *Sweet Lavender*'s author, he forgave the New York public and offered Dan Frohman his new play, *The Second Mrs. Tanqueray*.

"Do not dare present so frank a play in the evening bill," Frohman cabled, "but would like to produce so fine a work at series of matinees."

Pinero trusted him again, but Frohman didn't produce it after all. He ceded the American rights to the celebrated English couple, Mr. and Mrs. Kendal. "*The Second Mrs. Tanqueray* was regarded as exceedingly strong meat, although in San Francisco where a play like that *should* find favor, *Mrs. Tanqueray* fell flat. The explanation was that the play carried no illusion for the Golden Gate audiences, the city was full of Mrs. Tanquerays, but Philadelphia loved it and requested a return engagement."

After *The Wife* came other plays, all with fine titles—*The Maister of Woodbarrow*, *The Dancing Girl*. And more players were added to the company. For the new ingenue, Dan Frohman engaged the enchanting Effie Shannon, later to star with Herbert Kelcey for Dave Belasco whose stationery was to read,

BELASCO THEATRE, WEST 44TH ST.
DAVID BELASCO, OWNER

In the lean years, after Herbert was gone, Effie Shannon played on into her eighties. Then she went blind. Time to retire to the Home. The Home was ready to welcome Dan Frohman's Old Lyceum ingenue and considered how might they make her feel comfortable. Her theatre maid had stayed on with her, even after there were no more engagements. The Home wondered if Miss Shannon would like to bring her maid with her. Miss Shannon was pleased. Arrangements were made, then Effie died. With her went the love, admiration and respect of the profession.

E. H. Sothern had always played in comedies, but Henry Arthur Jones' *The Dancing Girl* was a drama, the great role in it was the Duke of Guisebury. Sothern was dubious.

"I urged him to switch to serious acting," writes Frohman, "I had invested five thousand dollars."

Five thousand dollars was a lot of his friend's money. Sothern took the flier into drama. (Sitwells' father, don't skip anything.) *The Dancing Girl* and E. H. Sothern, as the Duke of Guisebury, were a hit. And what a good thing for forty-one players listed. The Actors Fund secretary loved the players and put on plays with lots of them in it. Nor did he stint on the scenes.

| | |
|---|---|
| Act I. The Beautiful Pagan. | Scene—The Isle of St. Endellion (Scilly Island.) |
| Act II. The Broken Bowl. | Scene—Villa at Richmond. |
| Act III. The Last Feast. | Scene—Guisebury House, St. James' Park, London. Two years pass. |
| Act IV. The Desired Haven. | Scene—The Isle of St. Endellion. |

A hit, a merciful hit! "Good luck," he said and had it to spare.

Well, he was eighty-nine and he died in a hotel. And he wouldn't think that worth remembering, but what is, his Lyceum he built on West 45th Street still has an out front and a stage door and probably somebody is trying to get in it and somebody not letting them. And out front there still is a box office and more often than not the box-office man is saying "Next?"

The steps are there and the elegant carved door. And the small small elevator. Let us hope somebody is telling somebody to get in and wishing them "Good luck."

The Lyceum is there, packed to the flies with memories. Daniel

Frohman's wonderful Lyceum Stock Company have all "joined the majority," but another legendary company called the Lyceum Theatre home. And after they toured across the country, looked forward to *their* "homecomings" where they trod the boards of Daniel Frohman's West 45th Street new Lyceum Theatre, become the A.P.A.'s old Lyceum.

They've moved on, too, but that's show business. *Borstal Boy* moved in and won the Critics' Award for 1970! Who's the lucky one to open there this season? And next? And so on? The *good* that men do lives after them. Who cares what's interr-ed with their bones?

※   ※   ※   ※   ※

"I am I," said Gertrude Stein, "because my little dog knows me."

Well, fine, so far as it goes, but I have no little dog. I have to be I because *I* know me. Dog is man's best friend, but in a pinch who would you count on, you or your best friend? Now that I'm in the movies, everywhere I go people know me. Isn't *that* better than my little dog? If I sit down at Hamburg Heaven in New York or Hamburger Hamlet in Beverly Hills, someone talks to me. Sometimes they say they love me. Can my little dog say as much?

※   ※   ※   ※   ※

Gladiolas, calves' brains, birds, upside-down cake, fat, cameras, the one about the two ostriches, these are a few of my *un*favorite things.

※   ※   ※   ※   ※

On Super Chief the man asked, "Are you a full-blooded Indian?"

"I'm not an Indian at all."

"Why, I'm surprised!" he gasped. And looked surprised.

"No," I said.

He seemed so let down I said I was sorry.

"Why, I could have sworn you were a Cherokee!"

231

"No," I said. "I'm not."

"I can't be sure you're full-blooded, but I'd take an oath you're part Cherokee."

"No, my real name's Jones, not that that proves anything."

He was still dubious.

Why did I look like an Indian? I had on a Hattie Carnegie dark blue suit and a dotted Swiss blouse from Lanz.

# Kit

K IT was the first ecologist in show business. She was one all day
at Sneden's Landing, in the evening she played *The Green Hat*.

"Isn't it a long ride after the show?" I asked.

Kit shook her head. "Always be a place where your feet can
touch some earth. You have to connect with the soil."

On Sunday at Sneden's we connected with a lot of pancakes for
breakfast. They sloshed around in country butter and Vermont
maple syrup, then we took a lazy walk to the waterfall, then played
bridge. The way *we* played was restful. No mean looks. You didn't
get your partner's signal? OK. You had a good hand and won? That
was nice. The only jarring note was when Kit reached toward the
box of Fannie Farmer chocolate creams.

"Don't, Kit!" pleaded Guthrie, thinking of siren Iris March.

Kit swallowed the gorgeous bitter chocolate with the thick white
center. "It's only sugar and water," she said, reassuring him. "Now
whose turn?" No mean looks. No tension. No hurry. No cue. No
precision. Sunday at Sneden's was a day to do what you felt like at
any particular time. "Sunday," said Kit, "is the day when you can
get as tired as you want to by nine in the morning."

Stroll to the waterfall? Don't stroll to the waterfall. That's what
Sundays are for.

(*Players' Guide*, copy.)

233

Why didn't Guthrie think she was right for *The Green Hat?*

Kit did. She had the idea and stuck to it. She got it made into a play. She got Al Woods to back it. Al didn't think she was right, either, and Mrs. Woods said she'd be no good.

"Kitty, *how* are you going to say those lines?" asked Guthrie. "*How* can you say those *lines?*"

Kit, never too sure of herself, got courage from somewhere. "I'll know how," she said.

"But *how?*" he pleaded. "Tell *me* how."

"There's a way."

"But before I sign a contract to direct it, Kitty darling, I've got to know *how* you're going to say 'Boy Fenwick, he died for purity.' Kit, *how* can you say that?"

"I will."

"But, Kitty, tell me *how.*" He could see disaster.

"Iris March thought purity was ridiculous, so I'll say it as though it's in quotes. 'He died'—then I'll laugh, then I'll say—'for purity' in quotes."

Anyone know a better way?

Guthrie signed to direct it.

"Mrs. Woods refused to believe I could play it. She'd seen me only in *Candida.* But it wasn't only Mrs. Woods," said truthful Kit. "Nobody thought I was right.

"All during rehearsals, Guthrie wasn't convinced either, but he directed it as though he was and called down Leslie Howard because he was kidding the lines. 'Do it as though you believe it, Leslie,' Guthrie told him, 'or get out.'

"We opened in Detroit and opening night Jeanne Eagels was out front. When I saw her in the front row, I dried. Of course I knew why Al had her there. Well, the only thing I could do was get on with it."

She got on with it and stood Chicago on its head.

"Al came back excited. 'You're great, sweetheart.' *Mrs.* Woods never did think I was right, but Al did. 'You're great,' he said, 'but we gotta get rid of that Leslie Howard.'

" 'Leslie *is* Napier, Al. He's *perfect.*'

" 'No, sweetheart, he leans on the furniture.' "

Kit looked to see if I was following. "You know? Like Leslie always did in real life? Leaned on women and furniture?"

I nodded.

"Al said, 'We gotta get you a new man.'

" 'Al, we open in New York with Leslie or you don't have me.' I thought about Jeanne Eagels out front and Mrs. Woods thinking I was wrong, but I *said* it. I really did."

"Who made your wonderful green hat?" I asked.

"Oh, that was one of Guthrie's I twisted into shape. You know how you're proud of something that probably no one ever notices, but you're proud of it? In *The Green Hat* I was proud of one thing. I don't know if you remember, but in the play I didn't smoke or drink. Not that it was important, but you know how once in a while you like something you do? Well, I liked that. I didn't want to *do* things, I just hope I *was* Iris March. In London, Tallulah smoked and drank and the play didn't go. Guthrie saw the first night over there and cabled me, 'Hat worse than I hoped.' "

Over at the Empire, *Casanova* was having its opening night. Katharine Cornell was Casanova's dazzling prey. Lowell Sherman, elegance itself, maneuvered her toward the boudoir door. Three steps up and he would have his way.

She looked at the steps, then into her future. "Three little steps, where will they lead me?"

"To Cain's Storehouse, dear," whispered Lowell in her upstage ear.

He was right. That season Cain's Storehouse did a great business and Kit rose to stardom on failures. She was in three and dazzled New York critics with her versatility.

Some years went by and once again it was dress rehearsal at the Empire. Kit was playing Edith Wharton's wayward Ellen Olenska, heroine of *The Age of Innocence*.

"Miss Cornell says to hold the curtain," said the stage manager.

Could Guthrie believe his ears? He tried to remember when she'd done that. Not even at Jessie Bonstelle's stock where she was the leading lady and he was the director and they got engaged in a Detroit park. *When* had she held a curtain?

When she came onstage, she was worth holding a curtain for.

Formal curls piled high shaped her head above the white neck with the string of square emeralds curving out of strawberry silk by Worth of Paris who knew what to show and what not to. What a pity the strawberry silk and the emeralds would go to Cain's, too, but it would leave the ascendant Katharine free for yet another critical triumph.

# A Gentle Man

MR. CLINTON JONES
NIUMALU HOTEL
HONOLULU T.H.
AM MARRYING GREGORY KELLY SUNDAY WRITING LETTER VERY
HAPPY. LOVE,

RUTH

Do *you* count the words? One, two, three, four, five, six, seven, eight, nine, ten. *Over* ten is extra. How remarkable to be able to buy ten words to say that on a certain day, at a certain hour, in a certain minute, my life had changed.

"You can have Edna's two ginghams and her yellow straw hat for five dollars." That was the minute. That five sent me on my way. That five opened up a new life. It didn't get me far with Stuart Walker, but it got me Gregory Kelly.

"They want a blonde, dear." Austa Mason ran Packard's Theatrical Agency and liked me, but what could she do if they want a blonde?

"But what if they don't *get* one?"

"Well, they're lookin', dear."

"Do you think they *might* consider me?"

"Blonde, they said, only blondes, dear."

"But I'm not *dark*."

237

"But you're not a blonde."

"Well, how long do you think they'll look?"

"Till they get one. They're seein' tomorrow at eleven." Did she get sick of me? "Go," she wrote on a slip.

I put on Edna Hibbard's gingham with the brown pin stripe and the buttercup cartwheel hat and looked the best I ever looked. To keep cool I walked up the shady side of Seventh Avenue. The entrance to the offices in Carnegie Hall was on the corner of 56th opposite the Grenoble Hotel and when that elevator went up and came down, my life had changed. It was changing when the big fat girl in the outer office said, "Mr. Walker and Mr. Kelly will see you."

Mr. Walker sat behind the desk. Mr. Kelly sat in a chair tilted against the wall. Neither stood up. Well, that's show business.

"Thank you for seeing me, I know you want a blonde, but I guess Miss Mason couldn't listen to me any more and gave me this appointment, please forgive me."

"We will," said Gregory. He was adorable. Dark hair and wearing a nifty gray flannel suit.

Stuart Walker was dark-haired, too. "I'm from Kentucky," he said. He seemed to be pushing elegance. "What have you done?"

"Last season I played the Madge Kennedy part in *Fair and Warmer*."

"What company were you in?"

"The third," I lied. "Madge Kennedy was in the first, Francine Larrimore was—"

"Did you play Indianapolis?"

"Did we?" I pretended to think. "I *think* Edna Hibbard played Indianapolis. We were Detroit and St. Paul and Minneapolis and so on." I hurried off this phony route. "The year before, I was with Maude Adams in *Peter Pan* and *The Little Minister*."

Stuart Walker fixed his peepers on Gregory. "I'd love to see you do Peter. It doesn't *have* to be a girl you know. Let's try it, Greg."

"Think it might be a little chaotic if I ran down to the foots and asked, 'Do you believe in fairies?'"

Stuart Walker laughed and looked back at me. "He's always right. I'm sorry, Miss Gordon, but we do want a blonde. The girl

238

who played the Baby Talk Lady when we tried it out this summer in Indianapolis acted it very well—very well, indeed—but she was quite wrong for Mr. Tarkington's description of her. Agnes Rogers is very dark and not at all an ingenue, but a very accomplished actress."

"I think Miss Gordon would be good," said Gregory.

"We'll let you know."

"Thank you."

Had Edna's dress and the yellow hat changed my life? Three days went by. Sitting out on Martin Theatrical's front steps, I thought a lot about Gregory Kelly. Across the street, people went into the Booth Theatre and I wished Gregory Kelly would go in.

"For you," screamed Mollie from the switchboard.

"Hello."

"It's Gregory Kelly. I'm sorry, but Stuart chose somebody else."

That evening sun turned black and went down fast.

"I'm disappointed," he said. "*I* think you'd be fine."

In two days it would be September, the road companies all cast. Broadway shows were in rehearsal. From where did courage well up? "I hope you have a big success, Mr. Kelly. It's just a wonderful book and you'll be *great*. I certainly wish I could play the Baby Talk Lady, but as long as I can't I wish whoever got it well and I know *you'll* have the biggest success."

All the tears aren't cried on stage, there's many a soaking wet pillow.

"Call for you," screamed Mollie.

"Yes?"

"I let the girl go that Stuart engaged," said Gregory Kelly. "I want you to play the Baby Talk Lady. Can you come up to the office and talk to our manager Harold Holstein?"

"Can I come right now?"

"Let's make it eleven tomorrow morning."

"Oh, thank you." And thank *you*, Edna Hibbard, and goodnight wher*ever* you are!

Rolling along the old Boston Post Road, Mr. and Mrs. Gregory Kelly's second-hand Peerless stopped rolling. Gregory got out and looked at the gas gauge. It was in the rear and it said "No more."

We'd been admiring Rhode Island and, unlike Lot's wife, forgot to look back. We got out and pushed our five-passenger open touring car. It wasn't easy, but the road wasn't hilly the way it would be when we got into Massachusetts.

We rolled past fields of Bouncing Bet that some people say is a weed and some people say is allergic and some say is pretty. Past the high blueberry bushes was a garage. Two sinister men stood in front of it. "Want any help?"

"No, thanks," said Gregory and rolled on.

It was getting darker. "Shouldn't we stop?"

"I don't like their looks."

You've got to love such a feller. No one could say to Gregory, "O ye of little faith."

We rolled on and the true believer was rewarded. A good garage with a good man stood waiting for someone to roll their car down the road. God not only had his eye on the sparrows, but on our Peerless.

We got past Boston and into Maine and Gregory was looking for a place to park. On Damariscotta's Main Street was an empty lot with a high board fence. Gregory backed in. I directed. "All right," I said.

Gregory backed toward the board fence.

"All right."

He backed.

"All right."

He backed.

"All *right*," I said.

Bang!

"You said 'all right.' "

"I said 'all *right*'!"

What a darling feller, all he said was "What a time for an inflection!"

That's all he said in Damariscotta, but there was a time "an inflection" became a harrowing thing.

"A jolly room and a *good* floor," said Gregory.

"No, Gregory," sighed Harrison Gray Fiske. "Try it again, Gregory."

"A *jolly* room and a good floor."

"No, Gregory."

"A jolly room and a good *floor*."

"No, Gregory. Go out and make your entrance again."

Gregory walked between two kitchen chairs that served as the future door to the future ballroom.

The future Lady Keynes gave him his cue.

Gregory sauntered on, looked around, looked at the future Lady K., née Lydia Loupokova, and said, "*A jolly room and a good floor*."

"No, Gregory." Harrison Gray shook his boring head. "*How* can such a good actor not say a line right?"

Goodnight Harrison, wher*ever* you are, good!

Mrs. Fiske told Gregory that she and Elbert Hubbard were on a train waiting for it to pull out. On the station platform stood Hubbard's nineteen-year-old son, who'd come down to see them off. "Elbert Hubbard's son was handsome. His profile was chiseled perfection," said Mrs. Fiske. "We sat waiting for the train to start and I looked admiringly at the handsome young man. 'What do you suppose he is thinking about, Mr. Hubbard?' I asked.

" 'Madam, not a God damn thing.' "

When Mrs. Fiske played Tess in *Tess of the D'Urbervilles*, Gregory said that acting changed from grandiose to real. After Tess killed Angel Clare, she came back to her own room, picked up her hairbrush and brushed her long hair. She brushed and brushed, then brushed it harder. And after a time, down came the curtain. Before that, nobody ever saw anybody do anything like that.

She made theatre history again when she played Becky Sharp. In the house in Mayfair, Rawdon Crawley returned unexpectedly and surprised his wife with Lord Steyne, then she was left alone. "She dropped down awkwardly on her fashionable, unpaid-for carpet," said Gregory, "and sat in a tangle of satin skirts saying, 'I'm done for. I'm done for. I'm done for,' in a voice like a metronome."

When John Cope acted with her, she thought his tempo too slow. As Cope talked, Mrs. Fiske tapped her foot rhythmically. "Please. Please. Please," she said in a quicker tempo than Mr. Cope was speaking.

"Please *what*, Mrs. Fiske?" asked Mr. Cope.

Though she never directed, she was a director. Her ideas come down to us through actors passing them on. "After you've played a play, Gregory, do you notice some nights it doesn't go as well?"

He had come to see her in *Mis' Nelly of N' Orleans.*

"When that happens, Gregory, try cutting out the pauses."

She told him, "Always save the cream of your energy for the performance. *Nothing* can surpass that. Talent? Skill? Experience? It's the cream of energy that tops them all."

She was Gregory's idol. If I saw someone in an old-fashioned long skirt and long coat and nondescript hat and veils, I'd say, "Oh, here's Mrs. Fiske."

"Don't say that," said Gregory. "Be respectful to an actress that you nor anyone can ever be—"

"Grrrrrregory!" said the long coat and veils. It was Mrs. Fiske. "Grrrrrregory, how lovely to see you, my child." She was between engagements, enjoying San Francisco where so often they'd enjoyed her.

A place we didn't enjoy was South Carolina. Ever hit Barnwell?

The hotel clerk took against us. Actors? People named Kelly? Northerners? Get 'em outa here. He gave us a room not made up.

We went back to the lobby. "May we have a room that's made up?"

"Your room's the one I gave you."

All along the hall, doors opened on made-up rooms. We went in one. It had bedbugs. The unmade one didn't, so we moved back.

"Now you're charged with *two* rooms," raged Boniface.

Our character man who had starred in *The Prince of Pilsen* and now was playing Mr. Sampson's part on the tour asked, "Is there a Catholic church?"

"We have a Methodist, a Presbyterian, a Congregational, and the Ku Klux Klan," said Front Desk.

As though everything else wasn't the worst, the theatre was the Vamp. During the performance who was stumping down the aisle? The hotel man. He opened a door under stage center and stoked the furnace while the former Prince of Pilsen talked above it. " 'Mr. Thomas Tucker has sold his piece of land in Joplin,' " read Mr.

John W. Ransome from his morning paper. He raised his voice louder over the rattle of the furnace. " 'Mr. Tucker was paid one hundred and fifty thousand dollars for—' Well, you picked a fine time for a fight with him."

The furnace door slammed and our hotel man stomped up the aisle.

At five-fifteen next morning we paid the bill for the two rooms and got into the station bus. "We'll throw the room key away the first decent place we play," said Gregory.

Four months after, we dropped it off the bridge over the Chicago River by the Tribune Building. Was the water still running in Barnwell? We'd put the plug in the bathtub and turned on the faucet, locked the door and brought the key with us. Was there a flood in Barnwell? Circa 1923?

Do babies still have the croup? Gregory *had* it when he was two. The doctor looked at him, then rushed to his office and came back with a gold tube he slid down baby's throat. Gregory stopped strangling and two years after made his debut as little Minna with Joseph Jefferson. He never forgot Mr. Jefferson waking up from his twenty-year-long nap, looking out at the audience and saying, "I guess I got de rheumatics"; then noticing the gun beside him, he picked it up and it fell apart. Mr. Jefferson looked back at the audience. "I guess my old *gun's* got de rheumatics, too."

From *Rip Van Winkle* to *The Butter and Egg Man* was the span.

Way back in when was it? And are dates of any interest? Way back in whatever it was, things were on the calm side in our tenth-floor front at the Algonquin, then George Kaufman dropped in and said, "Going to write a play for you, Greg."

The world shook and gave a whimper. Across the street, the Hippodrome disappeared, Woollcott writing his Sunday piece on the second floor never was and all the Seeing Eye dogs in Morristown, New Jersey, couldn't have found him. On the tenth floor we clung to Frank Case's furniture as we got used to the fact that George Kaufman had said, "Going to write a play for you, Greg."

Does stuff like that happen to *you?*

A few months later he sat in our armchair and George began to read out loud. "*The Butter and Egg Man*, Act One." What a title!

243

What an afternoon! What a George! What a hit! What a— What the hell was *that!*

George was tough, funny, sharp until he got to Gregory's part, when he lisped and simpered. What the hell was *that?*

"Curtain," said George, and we swung in the expected "Oh, yes!" "Oh, boy!" "Oh!"

Off went George, and two shaken Kellys stared at each other.

"What the hell was *that?*"

"What do you mean?" As though I didn't know.

"What does he think I *am?* A fairy?" Gregory was staring out the window past the Hippodrome to where?

"Oh, he doesn't think *that,*" I said, with no conviction.

"He thinks I'm a fairy!"

We went for a peach of a walk. Then—well, what would *you* do? When George S. Kaufman writes a play, would *you* turn it down?

Rehearsals got under way and after a day or two—a nervous day or two—Gregory's non-lisp, non-simper performance seemed to strike George as OK. It encouraged Gregory to open up. "What the hell were you doing, the way you read *my* part?"

"Oh, I can't do *you.* You've got a style of your own."

"What does that mean?"

"Gentle."

"Oh?"

"Unique."

"Oh?"

"Kind of persuasive."

"Well, in *that* case, thanks."

High hopes and pretty soon the calendar got to opening night. Bea Kaufman, a cool head and a loving heart, believed in it. George did, too. For one of the rare times, he threw caution to the winds and admitted it had a chance. Word around was great. Woollcott invited Charlie Chaplin to be his opening-night seat-mate. The word was *right.* Messrs. Chaplin and Woollcott laughed hard and so did the less talented. *The Butter and Egg Man* and Gregory were a hit. A big fat socko hit! The only play George S. Kaufman ever wrote alone and did he know how to write it! And did Gregory know how to play it! Goodnight, Mrs. Fiske, wher*ever* you were, I wish you'd been at the Longacre.

When Gregory and I got married I wore black. I thought it was very New Yorky. First I got my dress made, then I got married, then I wrote my father.

Dear Papa,

I guess you think I dropped off the face of the earth, but not quite that bad. We were married on Monday the twenty-third at 10:30 and left on the 11:08 for Balt. We were married at St. John the Divine, a Catholic Church. My religion doesn't bother me and Gregory's doesn't either, but we both felt we would like to be married by someone we knew rather than a stranger and Father O'Connor was an old friend of Gregory's. We found we had to have two witnesses after all, so we had Gregory's mother and Stuart Walker who has been perfectly wonderful to us. The service was lovely and very impressive in this great huge church with only five present. I wore black broadcloth trimmed with ermine and a large black hat from Giddings, a stylish Fifth Avenue store, and I carried a wonderful bridal bouquet of lavender orchids.

My wedding ring is a beautiful thing, a platinum band set with square diamonds all the way round from Tiffany's. For Christmas Gregory gave me a gorgeous full length beaver coat which cost five hundred dollars at Giddings. It is so nice and warm.

We opened in Baltimore that night. Of course I will keep on being on the stage and we intend to play leads together. Gregory gets two hundred and twenty-five a week and a percentage which comes anywhere between a hundred and three hundred weekly. He has given me my salary as an allowance for clothes or whatever I want to spend it for. Seventy-five a week is a pretty good allowance and I have quite a lot of clothes so I have been adding to my personal account at the bank. I have never been so happy.

Love,
Ruth

# God's in His Heaven, All's Right on Temple Place

D O YOU BELIEVE in God? I do. And He not only watches when a sparrow falls and a Peerless fails, but He watches where those five-dollar bills go. Walking along Temple Place, Katherine Follett said, "Oh look," and right in front of Thayer, McNeil and Hodgkins she picked up a five-dollar bill. I thought she'd offer me half, but she put it in her pocketbook and we went round the corner.

"Two in the gallery," I said.

"You're too young," said the Tremont Theatre box-office man. "Next?"

If *Damaged Goods* didn't want us, Drury Lane's spectacle, *The Whip*, did. It wasn't the same thing as *Damaged Goods* and my mind wandered. Why didn't Katherine give me half? I had twenty cents in my bag and she had at least five dollars.

That was 1914. I wondered about splitting the five for years, then I got the message. I think of Katherine with gratitude. Why had *she* saved up fifty cents to get to a matinee? *She* wasn't going on the stage. Why wouldn't her fifty cents have done better to buy a "blue ribbon to tie up her bonny brown hair"? Did God think so, too? Did He send us via Temple Place? That five dollars staked Katherine to not only Drury Lane's *The Whip*, but Annie Russell's *She Stoops to Conquer*, Marguerite Clark's *Prunella*, Ethel Barrymore's *Tante*, Eddie Cantor, Bert Williams and Ann Pennington in the Ziegfeld *Follies*, Billie Burke's *The "Mind-the-Paint" Girl* and *The Amazons*, José Collins in *The Merry Countess*, Joseph Santley in *When Dreams Come True*, Julia Sanderson and Donald Brian in *The Sunshine Girl*, Robert Edeson and Anne Meredith, the future chatelaine of Knole, in *The Indiscretion of Truth*, George Arliss in *Disraeli*, Olive Wyndham in *What Happened to Mary* and the Actors' Fund Benefit that ran for five hours. Now I think of it, Katherine is still behind. Lord, keep Your eye on the ball and if anybody drops a dollar and a half, Katherine lives at 6 Presidents Lane, Quincy, Mass., as You well know. What am I doing telling You!

# Provident Loan

RUTHIE FORGAVE HER FAMILY so beautifully," said Thornton. He was talking about the play I wrote about my mother and father and me when I was seventeen. He was talking about that and maybe about all of us, but a family I *couldn't* forgive was the Felix family. When the greatest of all French actresses died of consumption at only thirty-seven, her family put all her things up at auction. If you read the catalogue for the auction of "Choses Personelles de Rachel," notice the item "Lingerie." Would you forgive your family if they auctioned *your* underwear?

And why *did* they? Did they need money? My father knew *I* would and gave me fifty dollars and his spyglass to take with me to New York. "Take it down to Captain Forbes, the foot of South Street," he said, "and he'll give you a hundred for it. Or if he's off on a voyage, take it to any reliable pawnshop."

"Papa!" I gasped. "I'd rather be *dead* than go into a pawnshop."

My father looked at me with the eyes of experience. "If you're going to be an actress," he said, "you'll be in and out of a pawnshop all your life."

The first time I went in, I looked up and down Madison at 28th Street to make sure no one saw me. I went in, hand shielding my face. At a window I offered my square-cut. It was as dignified a transaction as one could wish, a paper was offered me, I signed "Ruth Kelly" and was out on Madison with the money. Thornton says, "Nothing more dignified than making money." Does that include hocking a ring?

In time, a play came along and after a few paychecks I was flashing my square-cut. Then a lean season again. Again I scanned Madison, again the dignified transaction, Ruth Kelly handed over her square-cut and went to the bank with the money.

"In and out of a pawnshop" was accurate and after a number of ins and outs I didn't bother to check Madison and 28th. I went straight to my favorite window.

"Hey, where y'been?"

"Around."

"The show didn't go?"

"Not this one." I handed over my square-cut and the diamond bracelet from Spaulding's that Gregory bought me when we played *Clarence* in Chicago and my diamond engagement ring he had made at Cincinnati's Ratterman's.

"*This* one I always like, that's a beautiful setting." He shoved the paper, "Ruth Gordon," I wrote, counted the money, "Be seein' you."

"You bet." They were a nice bunch at the Provident Loan. Goodnight, wher*ever* you are, it's been a long time.

※　※　※　※　※

Shakespeare died when he was fifty-two. If *I* had I'd never have been in *The Matchmaker* or met Mia or been on the Joey Bishop Show or flown sixty-seven times across the country or won an Oscar or eaten papaya or been robbed of all my jewelry or seen *M\*A\*S\*H* or *Where's Poppa?* or Don Rickles.

It's good Don Rickles saw Helen Hayes or he might never have made it. He was in Mary MacArthur's class at the American Academy and planning a career in the legit. He made no noticeable stir around school till he started doing takeoffs of Helen Hayes to cheer up himself and several other unfortunates.

"Rickles, I understand you are making fun of the first lady of the theatre," said headmaster Jehlinger.

Rickles died. "Oh *no*, sir."

249

"I hear you *are*."

"No, sir."

"For class today suppose you do an impersonation of Miss Helen Hayes. I'm ready, Rickles."

There was no exit. Don did his stuff. Jehlinger looked thoughtful. "I believe that's where your talent lies, Rickles. Follow your bent, son, you might make it."

❄    ❄    ❄    ❄    ❄

That's where Don learned what to do. From time to time I go to *my* fount. Mine is the paperback portable Emerson, and what is a card from Montgomery Printing Co. doing between pages 193 and 194? "Telephone Main 8677, 22 Columbus Street, Seattle, Wash. E. J. (Ted) Brabyn."

Do you find things like that in your fount?

# Dead at 34

JEANNE EAGELS took my arm and walked me back and forth across the stage. "Your part can be awfully unsympathetic, but it needn't be. The key is to *listen*. Listen to Cora Witherspoon tell you what to do. Listen *hard*. Let *her* be the unsympathetic one and you blindly follow her instructions." Jeanne and Zoë Akins had come to see the tryout in Stamford of Anita Loos and John Emerson's *The Fall of Eve*.

"I thought I *did* listen to her."

"You do, but the way *you're* doing it, you listen and make it *your* idea. That makes you as big a cheat as Cora. You do it as if you could have thought of that yourself."

"And how should I?"

"Well, *first* thing, do it as though you're *pretty*. Not a battle-ax like Cora. Act as if you're *terribly* pretty and trying to remember what homely *Cora* said. And after she says it, don't be too sure what she meant. The audience will laugh and adore you."

Jeanne Eagels was the most beautiful person I ever saw and if you ever saw her, she was the most beautiful *you* ever saw.

Coming back from the country, the car radio droned out the news. "Jeanne Eagels died today at a midtown hospital. She was thirty-four." Thirty-four. All that talent, all that beauty, all that destruction was ended.

After *Serena Blandish* she came back to my dressing room.

251

"How's the picture?" I asked.

"Mad about it, they have to do exactly what I want." She was gleeful. "You know the chord in my voice?"

Who didn't?

"When they do something I don't like, I use it and it breaks the microphone." Destruction enchanted her. So beautiful, so gifted, why did she love to destroy?

She'd gone into pictures because she had missed so many performances. Her understudy went on several times each week. Equity Council took the matter up.

"Jeanne is a tightwad. Fine her," I suggested. "She'll think twice before she pays out money."

There were other ideas. Council chose the one that banned her from the stage for six months.

"That will only hurt Equity members," I said. "Jeanne can always be in a show, then actors are employed. She's rich, she doesn't have to work and Famous Players is begging her to give up the stage and do a film in their Long Island studio. Fine her. If she misses a performance, make her pay a forfeit, she'll think a *long* time before she pays out money."

They took the vote and banned her from the stage for six months. She told Equity to go to hell, signed for films at a fabulous salary and our loss was Famous Players' gain. I got sore at everybody but Frank Gillmore and resigned from the Equity Council. Jeanne was gleeful at so much destruction.

"The man who plays Lord Ivor Cream, who's he?"

"Henry Daniell."

"What's he like?"

"What's anybody like?"

A look went across her face. "I'd like to see more of him."

If she'd like to, she would.

In my dressing room was the last time I ever saw her. The first time was in Cincinnati.

"That's the greatest profile in the world," said our company manager and pointed across the Sinton dining room. Jeanne Eagels was having dinner alone. She was George Arliss' leading lady in *Hamilton*, opening at the Klaw and Erlanger theatre next day. To see her was worth double the price of dinner.

Harold Holstein called for the check and since he was company manager of *Seventeen* took no time to figure out what was my share plus half the tip. I paid up, he paid out and went his way, I took the elevator. In the elevator stood Jeanne Eagels. Since waiting beside Maude Adams in *Peter Pan,* I'd never been so close to a famous actress.

"Five," I said. The elevator stopped and she got out. How did I remember to?

She walked down the Sinton's dark brown hall, I followed. What could I do? That was the way to my room. "In Chicago Mr. Bruce MacRae and I came to see you, you're very good." She was talking to me. "Mr. Bruce MacRae thought so, too."

On a Sunday night in Cincinnati *Jeanne Eagels* spoke to me. Or did I make it up?

"What did Jeanne die of?" I asked Kit Cornell.

"Nobody loved her."

I thought about that. "What did the hospital say?"

"Something. But that wasn't it."

Had Jeanne worn out everybody? Destroyed them? She married Ted Coy, then destroyed him.

"You can't go on living if nobody loves you," said Kit. She didn't sell it, just said it.

Jeanne was playing *Her Cardboard Lover* at the Empire. Driving back after a performance, she decided she'd give a party on her birthday. She and Ted stopped off to tell Fay and Reggie. Fay Bainter and Reggie Venable lived in the rented cottage on Jeanne's place. They'd gone to bed, but got up and dragged out a quart of scotch, which got finished planning the party. Jeanne thought it would be good if Fay arranged about the refreshments, because Fay's play had closed and hers was still playing. Jeanne said she'd get out the invitations and there'd be seventy-five. Ted said he'd order the band. He didn't know how big a one, but to leave it to him.

Two days passed, then Jeanne called up from New York and said a new set of bedroom furniture was on its way out. Would Fay help arrange it?

253

She would and started to order things for the refreshments. That same night, coming home from the theatre, Jeanne and Ted dropped by the cottage. Fay and Reggie were entertaining Holbrook Blinn and Ruth. Hal Blinn was starring in *The Play's the Thing* and their house was a short distance away in Croton. Hal loved a party and when Jeanne asked the Blinns to hers, Hal said yes and "Ruth makes a delicious potato salad."

"Bring some," said Fay and as they polished off the quart of scotch, Jeanne was reminded she'd sent out the invitations. A hundred and fifty. That reminded Ted he'd engaged a twenty-piece band.

Next morning Fay put on a bungalow apron and kept it on till Saturday. The party was Sunday, but the houseguests would arrive Saturday night. Jeanne said she'd invited Ethel Barrymore, Zoë Akins and her co-star Leslie Howard and his wife and me.

Fay's phone rang. "Hello."

"The new bedroom furniture makes the curtains look faded, could we all drive down to Ossining to pick out some material for new ones? Also something to cover the lampshades? If you help with the lampshades, I'll make the curtains."

Jeanne cut them out, but cut them wrong, then had to leave for the theatre. Fay told her she'd make the curtains and Jeanne left, fairly cheerful.

During the Wednesday matinee Jeanne phoned. "I bought a new set of porch furniture. I bought it wholesale and unpainted, which makes it cheaper. Would Reggie help Ted paint it? Also would it be nice to have a canoe on the pond?"

Reg rented one down in the village, loaded it on the roof of the Ford, launched it and in no time it started to sink. Reg had been an admiral in the navy, so he knew what to do. He loaded it back on the Ford, drove to town and rented another.

The porch furniture didn't get delivered till late Friday. Ted and Reg had to sit up most of the night painting it for the next night's guests. Reg was glad to get out of the cottage because Fay was in the kitchen boiling hams to serve cold, frosting six birthday cakes with "Happy Birthday, Jeanne," and cutting three hundred and fifty sandwiches, two apiece for the band and guests with a few spares, in case.

Besides porch furniture, Jeanne forgot to say she ordered a few chairs, two tables and a couch to pick up the downstairs. Most of Friday and Saturday the dirt road off the main road from Ossining was full of trucks. Before leaving for the matinee, Jeanne ran over to Fay and Reggie's. "The weather's so lovely we must light up the grounds with Japanese lanterns."

Reg headed the Ford for Ossining, sucked on Life-Savers to keep awake and came back with two hundred lanterns. He and Ted strung them up all afternoon, and when they finished, dark clouds were bearing down from the Catskills. Around six the clouds opened up and Fay left her hams and cakes to help get the lanterns down. The paint on the furniture hadn't dried and they dragged it indoors. Ted put on all the electric lights to dry it quicker.

The phone rang. Fay dreaded answering it, but it was only that Fay better bring the liquor over to her house because Ted was apt to take too much when he got tired and she didn't want him drunk for the party.

Fay sent Ted off to fill all the vases with all the flowers she'd ordered and she and Reg carried the liquor home.

Hal Blinn rushed through *The Play's the Thing*, stopped off at Croton to pick up Ruth and the potato salad which they delivered in a baby's bathtub. They both said the house looked lovely and Hal helped Reg bring back the liquor, because now they could all guard it till Jeanne arrived.

A car drove through the rain. Jeanne at last. Reg had a champagne bottle ready to pull the cork. He filled their glasses, then he and Fay and the Blinns went out on the wet piazza, glasses raised to sing "Happy Birthday."

Jeanne stepped out of the car, a half-empty bottle of champagne in her hand. "What the hell is *this?* I told you *not* to open the liquor." She turned her back on them.

The Blinns and Venables were so astonished they couldn't say anything. Jeanne ordered the chauffeur to drive her back over the road to look for Leslie, who'd been following.

The chauffeur told Jeanne he wouldn't go out again for anybody, so Jeanne got into her Nash sedan and drove down the dirt road herself.

"I don't know what anybody else is going to do," said Reg, "but

I'm going home." Hal said they'd go, too. Ted said he couldn't blame them and watched them walk the back way to avoid Jeanne.

"What'll we do for tomorrow?" worried Fay. All the hams and cakes and sandwiches had been taken over and she hadn't bought anything for home. The same with the Blinns, they had nothing over in Croton. While they thought what to do, Reg opened a quart of scotch.

Fay decided to sneak back for a cake and a ham. Hal went with her for his salad. They stood back in the shadows as Jeanne's Nash stopped, Leslie's car right behind. He got out, looked at the house, then told his wife, "Don't take the bags out until I see what's going on."

After his hard work and sobriety, Ted was finishing the birthday champagne. Jeanne tossed some of hers in his face and told him to get out, too. Leslie and Mrs. Howard she told to go to bed, then disappeared upstairs.

The Howards got back in their car and took off. Ted wandered over to Fay and Reggie's.

"What the devil do *you* want?" asked Reg.

"Jeanne put me out, I have no place to go."

Reg said he didn't give a damn. They had no extra room, as Ted damn well knew since Jeanne owned the cottage.

"Could I spend the night out on the porch?"

"I don't give a damn where you spend the night."

Ted settled down on a damp Gloucester hammock till the Blinns went home and took him with them to help eat their potato salad.

Sunday Fay and Reg joined the Blinns and Ted and when the band and guests drove through the rain up the muddy road, Jeanne didn't open the door.

The season she played *Rain*, Jeanne wore the same dress to every party. Every night all season at every party there'd be an electric moment and it would be Jeanne in that slim black satin sheath, low-cut neck, low-cut back, pearls, diamonds and a quart of champagne under her bare arm. It was Prohibition and she brought her own special vintage. Would you say *she* was a special vintage?

Do you think she *did* throw the string of pearls off the boat deck of the *Aquitania* that trip with Nick the Greek? Was that legend? Or was it Jeanne in love with destruction?

Ted Coy was the idol of football fans when he led the Yale squad to victory. Before their marriage ended, it was awful to see a man so cowed. He was a polite man, and up against Jeanne he didn't stand a chance.

When Clifton Webb invited us to the Sixty Club, Gregory couldn't believe he would actually meet the great Ted Coy. It was a supper party for Freddie Lonsdale and his daughter and Jeanne and her fiancé. In the end, Ted quailed before Jeanne's destructive powers and lost, but some saw what might befall them and escaped.

Joseph Hergesheimer was asked to 38 West 59th. Every night after the theatre Clifton, Zoë and Joby, Fay and Reg and Gregory and I were invited, too. At Jeanne's the entertainment didn't vary a lot. She liked a game of forfeits. We all slipped off a ring, a ribbon, a something, handed it to Fay. Fay stood behind blindfolded Jeanne.

> *"A forfeit, a forfeit,*
> *A very fine forfeit.*
> *What shall the owner*
> *Do to redeem it?"*

Fay held the ring or the ribbon or the whatever over Jeanne's blond head.

"Male or female?"

Fay said which. Then Jeanne told what the owner must do. Not as inventive at forfeits as she was in her acting, the forfeits were mostly the same. Fay held up Mr. Hergesheimer's gold watch. "Male," she said.

"He must take his trousers off and hang them on the chandelier."

Mr. Hergesheimer did, got them down again, put them on and returned to West Chester, Pa.

Was that appointment in Samarra? His career waned. That couldn't have been Jeanne, could it?

"*None But the Brave.* How could they discard that beautiful title and call their play *What Price Glory?*" scolded Jeanne. When *she* said it, *None But the Brave* sounded great. *Was* it a better title? It certainly described Jeanne's friends.

✻  ✻  ✻  ✻  ✻

Do you know what you're doing? Or do you just act as though you do? Sometimes that works, sometimes not, but it works a lot better than floundering around waiting for someone to tell you how.

✻  ✻  ✻  ✻  ✻

The New York phone book has five Ruth Gordons. Not so many in Los Angeles. I wish my mother had let me take Fentress Serene Kerlin for my stage name. I bet there'd be only one of those.

✻  ✻  ✻  ✻  ✻

I'm lucky. I've been in every state except Montana and Oklahoma and Arkansas and I never saw bedbugs but twice.

✻  ✻  ✻  ✻  ✻

The property man for *A Doll's House* had been Mrs. Fiske's property man when *she* played Nora. "Before Mrs. Fiske went on to play the tarantella scene, I gave her a glass of champagne. She never took anything before any other scene and I was with her nine seasons, but before that tarantella she had me stand with that glass in my hand and she drank it and went on."

(*Players' Guide*, copy.)

✻  ✻  ✻  ✻  ✻

Lionel Barrymore stood in the wings watching the incomparable Bert Williams. "Isn't he great!" said Lionel.

"Yes," agreed the manager of St. Louis' Orpheum. "He's a good nigger and he knows his place."

Bert walked past. "Yes," said Bert, "he's a good nigger and he knows his place and his place is Dressing Room Number One."

258

# Boston Guide

Do you dress in Number One? Is your show going to play Boston? Well, wherever you dress, do you know what a fen is? It's where Jude the obscure walked, wrote Thomas Hardy. Back of Back Bay's Kenmore Hotel where the ballplayers stay is called the Fenway. It's where Mrs. Jack Gardner invited Edith Wharton when her Florentine palace was ready for a housewarming. "Come at eleven minutes past eight tomorrow morning," she wrote.

"I wouldn't come to see *myself* at eight-eleven," replied Mrs. W.

When you play Boston, walk out around her palace, why don't you?

Do you know where to stay? If you don't dress in Number One, take a room in a roominghouse on Commonwealth or Beacon or Marlborough. A lot of them still have trumpet vines and blue morning glories. If you dress in Room One, write the Ritz. Say to put you on Eric's floor, he's been floor waiter since the old days. Ask for the corner suite that looks over Commonwealth Avenue at the Charles River and M.I.T. in Cambridge and across Arlington Street to the Swan Boats in the Public Garden. And if you want to look like you know what you're talking about, don't make it plural and don't call it the park. Massachusetts thought a park sounded royal. They don't even call Massachusetts a state. They're a commonwealth and they have a Common and the Public Garden.

In your suite do all your phone calls in the middle room. If it's the fifteenth floor, it's number 1504. In 1503 they can hear it across the hall and through the bathroom in suite 1501 and 1502. If you phone in 1505 they can hear it in room 1506. That's the room beyond you and they can hear it better than who you're telephoning can.

From the window of the sitting room look at the house on the corner of Commonwealth and Arlington Street. It was the great Sears mansion. Over in the Fenway at the Fine Arts hangs the Sargent painting of Mrs. Sears and little Helen painted in their drawing room where you're looking. Theirs looks out at the Public Garden, too. I wish Sargent had also painted Mrs. Sears and Miss Helen receiving in the jardin d'hiver at the head of the stairs. The society page reported, "For her debut, Miss Sears wore pink tulle and a pearl necklace, Mrs. Sears wore a white satin ballgown by Worth of Paris and her black diamonds." Zap! Wouldn't you like to see *that?* When *I* saw the jardin d'hiver, there was only a potted palm. The Ursuline nuns occupied the house. The nun pointed to a portrait. "That's Cardinal Cushing. This was the Sears' reception room. In there was their library. It had seven thousand books."

How many times have you looked out a window at a house where the family had seven thousand books?

We went up a flight. "That mantelpiece over the fireplace is pink Parian marble," said the nun. "This was Miss Helen Sears' room." Pink tulle, pink Parian, I guess Helen's color was pink.

Down a hall was the ballroom. "The floor doesn't work now, but it's still on springs." Talk about the light fantastic! There must've been plenty of that on Arlington Street, corner of Commonwealth.

Are you playing the Shubert or Colonial? Whichever it is, it's "Pull up your tights, girls!" Over at Searses' they were doing it on springs.

"After Mr. Paderewski played the organ up here in the music room at the top of the house, Mrs. Sears locked it up. It was never played again."

Whose organ do you know is locked up?

I marveled at what a lot of help they must have had.

"Thirty-two and a Chinaman," said the nun.

Speaking of help, if you don't know where to get a great dinner, go to Anthony's on the pier down past the South Station and off Atlantic Avenue. Have a bucket of steamed clams, a couple of steamed baby lobsters, popovers, of course, and look out the window over Boston Harbor while you wonder if you've got room for blueberry pie. Does that big freighter look like it's heading for Anthony's? Sit there! Don't ask for your check, it'll dock across the way. Is a voice over the loudspeaker telling you "The *Star of Gibraltar* hailing from Yokohama carrying a cargo of toys for the Christmas trade is now docking at Pier Four"?

In a week or two when things go great and you get Sunday off, don't fly to New York, you've been there. Drive forty minutes to Concord. If it's autumn you'll pass cornfields stacked, with piled-up pumpkins scattered around. Look in at Mr. Emerson's house across the road from where Louisa wrote *Little Women* in the Alcotts' house.

At Mr. Emerson's, notice a fine chair in his front hall, made for him by his hired man. He made it with a drawer to keep his Sunday gloves in, just under the seat. By the way, where do you keep *your* Sunday gloves? Henry Thoreau thought a drawer in the hall chair was a good place.

Well, even if you don't go, you'll know it's there. And has been for a long time. Don't ask me why, but knowing that makes you feel different when you're making up over at the Colonial. Or is it the Shubert?

Rehearsing and playing, you need to pack-in a lot of energy. Do you like a great homemade brioche with some last-summer raspberry jam? Look out the sitting-room window that looks out across the Public Garden to the low red brick building on Boylston Street, then follow your look and go there. It's the Women's Industrial Union, where if a woman wants her little girl to take piano lessons, she brings in some brioches she baked. Or if a woman wants her boy to get a dancing lesson, she brings in a coconut layer cake for you to buy and *she* gets most of your two dollars. That's how I could play "The Keys of Heaven" in Booth Tarkington's *Seventeen* and do Nibs' pillow dance at the Empire when Homer Saint-Gaudens asked could I dance? Why couldn't I? My mother had baked a lot of good cakes. Think it over and get one at the Women's Industrial Union.

Could you take a five-minute stroll? Make it ten and go up on Beacon Street and look at what Homer Saint-Gaudens' father made. He didn't make any cakes for the W.I.U., but he made the Robert Gould Shaw Memorial for the spot right across from where Bulfinch made his building with the gold-leaf dome. Boston's always liked show business and young Robert Gould Shaw left an estate that gave a million dollars last year to Harvard to fix up their theatre collection. What are you and I going to leave them? Think it over.

"My father died in Boston."

"We died there, too. Where was your father playing?"

That's the old vaudeville wheeze. Lotta Crabtree did die in Boston and at her own hotel opposite where the Touraine was, and her fortune, that started with golden nuggets tossed at her feet and nursed into millions by her ma, is now the Lotta Crabtree Estate and giving away her millions from the Washington Street office. Look it up in the phone book under Lotta Crabtree. How many show folks do *you* know whose former nuggets rate a phone number?

There's no business like show business and now is a good time to think it over.

Do you go for hot-fudge sundaes? Have the goodness to post a notice on the callboard that at Bailey's, West Street, hot fudge runs over the edge of the silver dish. It still glonks on the saucer the way it did when I had it after the *Follies* matinee at the Colonial Theatre, still swooning over Eddie Cantor, Bert Williams and Ann Pennington, and had heard every word they said where now they can't hear you till they turn up the microphones. Put Bailey's, West Street, on the backstage callboard even though it's nothing to you. "The star of a show is not just some stuck-up shit-heel, he has to look out for the troupe," Guthrie McClintic told me or words to that effect. He gave me that note after the first performance in Stamford of *Saturday's Children*, when I wanted to go back to the hotel and cry, because the audience laughed twice on lines they weren't meant to. Guth said to go to the company party, because if I didn't they'd think I had some inside info that the show wouldn't get to New

York. "A star is the captain," he said, "and looks out for not only themselves, but also the troupe."

Think it over.

✳   ✳   ✳   ✳   ✳

Did you know "the Halcyon days" aren't just in poetry? They're in the *Farmer's Almanack*. They're definite. Like the dog days. "The Halcyon days," says the Farmer, "begin December 11 and there're fourteen of them. The Mediterranean at that time of year is usually pretty calm after some blustering winds. They're called Halcyon or Alcyon."

Is that if you are or are not a cockney?

A Halcyon day just before *A Doll's House* opened in New York, young Lorna Lynn ran into trouble. Three years old and had played *A Doll's House* in Central City, Toronto, Detroit, Madison, Chicago, Minneapolis, St. Paul and Cincinnati, then the Gerry Society went for her. "A three-year-old child cannot be on the stage."

"Why?" asked Jed Harris.

"It endangers her health."

"Did it endanger Maude Adams'? She went on at six weeks. Did it endanger Lillian and Dorothy Gish's? Did it endanger five-year-old Helen Hayes Brown's who left home to act in *Old Dutch* down at Weber and Fields'?"

Everybody got worked up and the mayor said he'd see what *he* thought. Three-year-old Lorna and thirty-eight-year-old Jed were ushered into the mayor's office.

The mayor greeted Harris and lifted Lorna onto his knee. "How old are you, dear?"

"Three."

"What's your name?"

"Lorna."

"What's your other name?"

"Lynn. What's yours?"

"La Guardia. Do you like to be in the play?"

"Yes."

"Why is that, dear?"

263

"They're nice."

"Who is?"

"The people."

"What people?"

"The people in the play."

"Where did you play the play?"

"Oh, Chicago and Toronto and Cincinnati and—"

"What's Cincinnati like?"

Lorna looked surprised. "Don't *you* know?"

"I don't see it's done her any harm," said La Guardia. "Let her play the show."

On the way out a reporter asked Lorna, "What do you think of the mayor?"

"Very cute," she said.

*    *    *    *    *

Boston or New York don't have nicknames, but a name like Philadelphia is asking for it. Philly, for a lot of us, but not everyone. "Where do you open?" Sherwood asked Jane Cowl.

Jane looked pensive. "Philamadelphums."

*    *    *    *    *

"Be a ja-sager," says Thornton. Maybe you already are. Test yourself. Do you believe the ass may speak? Our founder was the first guy that did. He *had* to. He was sentenced to death. "Please, sire," he said to Louis XV, "do not condemn me. If you let me live, I'll make this ass speak," and he pointed to his stupid-looking, long-eared beast. What a donkey was doing in the courtroom has not been explained. "Please, sire, you'll be the only ruler who has such an animal in his kingdom."

"I'll give you six months," said the fifteenth Louis.

"Oh, thank you, sire."

"But if in six months the ass fails to speak, you will be beheaded."

"I shall not fail, sire."

Court was excused and he and his friend led the ass away.

"What good is *that?*" asked Downbeat.

"I have six months."

"But in six months you'll be beheaded." (Let's get rid of *him!*)

"Maybe not."

"How so?" (*He* was no ja-sager.)

"Because in six months the king may be dead. Or I may be dead. *Or* the ass may *speak*."

Let's hope he had a good third act.

\* \* \* \* \*

Lloyd and Kathryn Lewis wanted a house.

"Give me what you're going to spend and *I'll* build you one," said their friend Frank Lloyd Wright. He built it at a pretty address. Little St. Mary's Road, Libertyville, Illinois. Remind you of something by Charles Ives?

It nestled under the trees, beside the Des Plaines River. Woollcott looked at it and said, "It looks like a cross between something out of *Swiss Family Robinson* and a sandalwood fan."

It was the first house where the kitchen and dining room were one. "Food and you should be no secret," Frank Lloyd Wright said. "It's all part of the same act." Or words to that effect. The heating pipes were under the floor.

"What will I do if anything goes wrong?" asked Lloyd.

"It won't," said Frank.

For all the years Lloyd and Kathryn lived there, it didn't, then Lloyd had a check-up, ate a big piece of layer cake at his sister's, had indigestion but wanted to get home, so they drove back to Little St. Mary's Road and before the doctor got there Lloyd died.

The heating pipes were still fine when Kathryn sold the house and moved into Chicago's Marina whose heating pipes are also hard to get at.

\* \* \* \* \*

I don't know where Holbein put the pipes at Wilton Castle when he designed it for the Herbert family, but they seemed to keep warm enough. Mrs. Duke didn't complain about feeling cold when Lady Juliet Duff was showing her the great double-cube room with the portraits of the Herbert family painted by Van Dyck in that same room. Mrs. Duke was interested in paintings. She was buying some for her own collection. They got to the hall. "This tapestry was a gift of Henry the Eighth to the Herberts," said Juliet.

"I'm not interested in textiles," said Mrs. Duke.

# Indelible Impression

W HO FIXES UP your place? You or a decorator? The first one was Elsie de Wolfe, later become Lady Mendl. Before all that, she was a stage star.

"What was she like?" I asked John Emerson.

"More a personality than an actress." John had been a stage star, too, before he and his wife wrote all the terrific silents that Constance Talmadge acted in. Then Mrs. E. looked into her crystal ball and, seeing Women's Lib, she got her own pen and paper and wrote *Gentlemen Prefer Blondes*.

John was the only one I ever knew who saw Elsie act, but all of us saw the rooms she decorated. Her first big chance was a house up Fifth Avenue for a Pittsburgh tycoon named Frick. Elsie worked out her design and presented it. Mr. Frick looked long and carefully, then said, "I like it very much, Miss de Wolfe, and I would like to see a second choice."

Elsie told us that was the moment when her fate was in the balance. "Mr. Frick," she said, "when I design a house, there *is* no second choice."

Time stood still. Mr. Frick thought.

You can bet Elsie thought, too.

"Go ahead with your plans, Miss de Wolfe."

That was the moment for Elsie. For Mr. Kellogg, his was Corn Flakes. For Mr. Ford, his was a Ford. For Mr. Heinz, his was 57.

For Mr. Bergdorf, his was Mr. Goodman. When yours comes, take a position.

Elsie believed in position. "Will you come for dinner Sunday night? Before you reply, I think I should tell you the dinner is for my dear friend Mike Romanoff."

"Fine."

"I've been told that if I give a dinner for him every door in Beverly Hills will be closed to me. They said that in London when I was doing something or other. 'Every door in London will be closed to you,' they said. I told them, 'The only door I care about being closed to me is my own.' "

At her house in Benedict Canyon, dinner was served in the orchard. The table was set on the turf and surrounding us were pear trees strung with heavy white silk rope, their leaves shining through white silken loops. It was lit by a treasure she'd known in Vienna and when he came as a refugee to our country Elsie set him up in business. Did you know it was she that first thought of lighting gardens at night?

Something else she thought of was to send furniture to her cabin when she sailed. Also linen sheets, pillows, pillowcases, towels, napkins and blankets. Walker-Gordon sent their unpasteurized milk on board and eggs marked E. de W. in indelible ink. She made an indelible impression on a liner. She made an indelible impression everywhere. Goodnight, Elsie, where*ever* you are, who got the gold unicorn? Do *they* keep a white camellia beside it?

# Mr. Lee

I DON'T KNOW if Al Jolson was a ja-sager. One year his Yuletide message in *Variety* was "Merry Christmas to all except one."

Does that make him an optimist? Merry Christmas to everybody but one is a good percentage. The Broadway grapevine said the "one" was Lee Shubert, who'd first brought him to the Winter Garden, then named a theatre the Jolson.

Well, that's show business.

Pass 2
Lee Shubert

wrote Mr. Lee in the Livre d'Or at the Hotel de Paris, Monte Carlo.

"Lee wants you to come to Monte Carlo with us." Marcella was on the phone.

"Love to. Jones is with us and Garson's mother . . ."

"Just a minute . . . Lee says bring them. We'll drive over and pick you up at seven and . . . What, Lee? . . . Lee says bring your passports for when we go in the casino or they charge three hundred francs."

Mr. Lee was good at trimming the budget.

A little before seven when I went downstairs, a chauffeur was wandering around the big hall.

"Que voulez-vous?" I asked.

"Pardon. Est-ce que Monsieur et Madame Kanin demeurent ici?"

"Oui."

He hurried off and a minute later a big black limo drove up. "Lee sent the chauffeur in to ask," said Marcella. "He took a look at the place and told me I had the address wrong. 'The Kanins don't live in a place like that and I don't want to get thrown out.'"

We rented Les Rochers from Peggy Singer. It had been built by Paris Singer for Isadora and just before he had had the sixteenth-century apothecary shop installed on the third floor and the thirteenth-century chapel anchored just above the waterline, the lovers had a quarrel.

Pass 2
Lee Shubert

he wrote with his stylo, but no principle was involved, the Livre d'Or was so heavy no one would show up with *that* at the door of the Broadhurst and expect two, gratis.

At the Casino we presented our passports and saved three hundred francs each, then Mr. Lee bought us each a stack of blue ones. I lost mine and went over to where Mr. Lee was standing, looking at people. "Don't you ever play?" I asked.

"No, Ruthie. If I won, it wouldn't mean all that and if I lost, I'd feel bad."

Marcella and her sisters came from Worcester, Mass. In a *Passing Show* at the Winter Garden, do you remember a blonde beauty? That was Marcella.

Once she showed up in a play. How inappropriate can a black dress and white cap and apron look? That's how they looked on Marcella.

When *we* met her it was at Mr. Soulé's Pavillon. "This is my wife," said Mr. Lee.

Her Paris dress was appropriate.

"Why don't you get somebody to give you a hundred and fifty thousand dollars?" asked Mr. Lee. "That's what Eben Jordan gave Richard Mansfield."

Mr. Lee had plenty of hundred and fifty thousands, should I get it from him? We were standing on Tremont Street in front of the Majestic. "Is this your theatre? I saw Forbes-Robertson play Hamlet here."

"Come in, we've done it over. Come see it, it looks beautiful."

Did you ever enter a theatre with Mr. Lee Shubert? Did you ever enter Balmoral with Queen Victoria? I imagine it was one and the same.

The theatre was dark, the stage brightly lit.

"Oh, they're having a rehearsal," I said and drew back.

"Come!" he beckoned.

"We'll disturb them."

"Who is in here?" he asked a bowing silhouette.

"The Theatre Guild, Mr. Lee."

"Put some house lights on." He walked down the center aisle. "Come with me," he beckoned.

"Hello, Mr. Lee," said Terry Helburn, sitting where Elliot Norton would sit opening night.

"Hello, Mr. Lee." Lawrence Langner sat across the aisle in Elinor Hughes' seat.

Onstage, little groups were talking.

"See how it's all redone?" said Mr. Lee proudly. A rehearsal was *their* business, his was his beautiful theatre.

I pointed to the gallery. "I sat up there to see Olive Wyndham in *What Happened to Mary*. It was in the back benches and I saw it for only a quarter."

"They're scaled higher, you got to get more than a quarter or they think the show's no good. Get somebody to back you. That's how Richard Mansfield got started, the money came out of this town. You know Jordan, Marsh's department store? That's where the money came from. Eben Jordan. He gave Mansfield a hundred and fifty thousand and Mansfield put on *Arms and the Man* and some others. *Devil's Disciple*. Well, some of them did OK."

If you don't like somebody, can you tell a story about them the same as if you liked them? Arthur Hopkins told how Lee Shubert referred to Duse as La Dooze and when Nazimova was brought up from Second Avenue, Mr. Lee called her Madame Moozie and called *A Doll's House*'s author Isben. That's what Arthur said, but when Mr. Lee told us about booking her into one of their theatres he didn't call her Madame Moozie, he said her name right. I don't know how he said Ibsen. At our Lindy lunches the subject never came up, but I bet Mr. Lee said it right. Anyway, when Arthur

Hopkins died, some of his friends thought the Shuberts should change the name of the Plymouth Theatre to the Arthur Hopkins. I asked Mr. Lee if he was going to. He said no.

"Why?" I asked.

"Because I don't want a house called the Arthur Hopkins."

He said that name right. He didn't say Hokpins, so why would he say Isben?

I phoned the Carlton Hotel. "Can you come to dinner? We're having Somerset Maugham."

Mr. Lee and Marcella were going to Spain, but postponed it. "I'm not going anywhere till I meet Somerset Maugham," said Marcella.

After dinner at Les Rochers we strolled down to the big tent set up at the port to celebrate the Fête of St. Jean. As we neared the box office, Mr. Lee went ahead and bought tickets. Marcella, Mr. Lee, Maugham, Alan Searle, Garson and I took our places on the backless benches.

Mr. Lee bought us each a bag of sweets, then bought six more.

"What are those for?" asked Marcella.

Mr. Lee pointed to where the tent canvas hit the ground. Children had poked their heads under to see the show. Mr. Lee bent down and put a sack of candy beside each head.

"Shouldn't we buy them some tickets?" asked Garson.

Mr. Lee froze. "Never give away free seats," he counseled. "That sets a *bad* precedent."

Some people speak French, some speak Spanish and some speak the language of money. Mr. Lee wanted a piece of land the Astor estate owned. They offered it for a lease of eighty years. "Nothing doing," said Mr. Lee. "Ninety-nine-year lease or nothing doing."

"The Astor estate leases land for eighty years only."

"I don't give a snap for the Astor estate! Ninety-nine years or nothing." *He* was eighty.

His office on top of the Shubert Theatre was oval and painted light pink. As we were ushered in, he looked at us suspiciously. "What can I do for you?" he asked. Where were the laughs of half an hour ago? Half an hour ago at Lindy's, Mr. Lee got up from the table and said, "I have a date."

"So have we," said Garson. "It's with you."

"Yes," he said, all smiles and friendly. What changed the man in the pink room?

Garson plowed ahead. "There's trouble about Donald McClellan."

"He's very good."

"He wants fifty dollars more."

"That part won't pay fifty more."

"We'll lose McClellan."

"Well, find another actor."

"But he played the week at Westport and he's very good. You just said so."

"He *is* good, but he's not worth fifty more." Mr. Lee sat and looked at us. "You think fifty dollars is a small amount?"

"No, but—"

"You think the play will be a success?"

"Yes."

"You think maybe it'll run a year?"

"I hope so."

"Maybe two?"

"Maybe."

"Maybe tour?"

"Yes."

"Then you're not talking about fifty dollars, you're talking about seventy-eight hundred."

After years in the theatre we brought Mr. Lee and Cole Porter together. Cole asked Garson and me to lunch at Mr. Soulé's Pavillon. I put on my new Mainbocher.

Cole ordered. "Jambon de Bayonne, grilled sole, salad." He turned to us. "I need your help. I notice you have a good many friends and I want you to help *me* make some."

Would that remark rivet *your* attention?

"I'm getting bored with all mine and they're getting bored with *me*."

Would that? It may be the most surprising thing ever said in Mr. Soulé's Pavillon.

We made boring protestations, but Cole, accustomed to his own way, continued. "I'd like you to think of some new people. I can do a very good dinner for eight. Eight's a good number to get acquainted with. I'll give a series of four dinners. Shall we make the first one two weeks from today?"

Phones rang. Cole's Mrs. Smith took messages and gave them to Cole when he was out.

"Margaret Truman?"

"Delighted," said Cole. "I may not vote for *him*, but I'd like to meet *her*."

"Damn it," said the President's daughter. "That's the night I'm on a damn radio show. Do you think he might ever ask me again?"

"Put her name on the next dinner list," Cole told Mrs. Smith.

"How about Lee Shubert?" asked Garson.

Cole suddenly looked astonished. "Do you know I've never met him? My shows play his theatres, but we've never met."

Garson rang up the Ritz Tower. "Marcella, will you and Mr. Lee be free for dinner at Cole Porter's a week from Thursday?"

"My God!"

"Can you come?"

"We certainly can!"

"Waldorf Towers at eight."

Garson hung up and our phone rang. "Listen, Lee says will you pick us up? It'll be better if we go in with *you*."

"Ten to eight we'll be at the Ritz Tower."

Cole was delighted. "I've asked Anita and Sturges, just to give me confidence." Sturges' other name was Howard. He was Cole's oldest friend and they and Anita had been clubby since before *Gentlemen Prefer Blondes*.

"Marie Doro?" asked Garson.

"My God! Would she come?"

"Let's ask her."

"My God! At Yale I fell in love with her twenty-four sheet. It was a line drawing of her profile. My God!"

"Delighted," said Marie, "what shall I wear?"

"Informal, but terribly pretty." Could Marie Doro look anything else?

On the day of the event Marie rang up.

"Don't tell me you're dropping out!" I warned her.

"No, no, I've bought some new shoes for it, and I'm resting, but would you pick me up?"

The phone rang again. It was Marcella. "Informal or formal?"

"Informal, but look terribly pretty!"

"And you'll pick us up?"

"Better make it *twenty* to eight, Cole says we must be punctual and we're picking up Marie Doro. We'll get you first, then drive to the Volney."

"Marie Doro!" screamed Marcella. "Lee'll go out of his mind, he *loves* her so."

At twenty to eight, we drove up to the Ritz Tower. "They're not answering their phone," said the clerk.

We got in the elevator, rode up high in the tower, a maid opened the door and looked surprised.

"Mr. and Mrs. Shubert?"

She just looked surprised, so we walked past her into the big drawing room that looked out in all directions, but we looked in only one. Through the French doors to the dining room we saw Mr. Lee and Marcella and two guests being served a soufflé.

"Marcella!"

She turned around and did a double-take. "Not *tonight?*" she gasped.

"Yes, *tonight!*" said Garson. "Right *now!!*"

"It's *tomorrow,*" wailed Marcella. "I called you up about what I'd wear *tomorrow.*"

"*Tonight!*" said Garson.

Mr. Lee reached in his vest pocket and brought out four theatre tickets and handed them to his guests. "You must go to the opening without us. It's at the Golden, we'll meet you afterwards at '21.'" He turned to Marcella. "Are you ready?"

Marie Doro, Mr. Lee, Marcella, Garson and I walked through Cole Porter's door as the clock struck eight. "Don't tell him," whispered Marcella. We never did.

Mr. Lee, eighty-one years old, who had just eaten his own dinner as far as the soufflé, ate Cole's dinner from soup to nuts. You've got class or you haven't.

❋   ❋   ❋   ❋   ❋

Zoë Akins had it. She came from Humansville, Missouri. At least,
that's what she said. I could never find it on a map, but I hope
there's such a place. She called a pillow "a pill-yo." She called millions "mi-we-yuns," maybe everybody in Humansville did. She
called her friend Ina Claire "Eena." That wasn't how we knew she
had class. When her husband died she brought back the canvases
that Hugo had painted away at till something better came to fill his
time. The widow Rumbold shepherded them through customs.

"Value?" said the man on the dock.

"Five thousand dollars each," said Zoë.

Zoë Akins wrote *Déclassée* for Ethel Barrymore. It was a triumph for them both. She wrote *Morning Glory*, it won Katharine
Hepburn her first Oscar. She wrote a play for Laurette and Elsie
Ferguson and Marjorie Rambeau and another for Ethel that Spencer Tracy had a small part in. She wrote *Papa* for Mr. Ames' elegant Little Theatre and *A Texas Nightingale* starring Jobyna
Howland. Zoë had talent as well as class.

❋   ❋   ❋   ❋   ❋

The Playwrights' Company had talent, but did they have class?
They booked the first performance of Robert E. Sherwood's *The
Rugged Path* into a theatre in Providence that could do seven thousand dollars a night. Opening night Garson and I stood at the back
of the 43rd row.

"Which is Spencer Tracy?" whispered people. Even *with* the
scorecard, you couldn't tell the players.

People will put up with a lot, but not three Rhode Island toughies.
They left their seats in the outfield, strode toward the stage and sat
crosslegged on the floor by the front row. They came to see Spencer Tracy. Wouldn't *you?*

❋   ❋   ❋   ❋   ❋

"It's tough to get stuff," sang Joe E. Lewis. It certainly is. And gets tougher and tougher. When he sang that at the Copa, was the great Joe E. a prophet? He was certainly great. Both on and off. When the boys came to cut him up in Chicago, they said, "Joe, we hate to do this to you," but they did it. It took him about a year to recover, then he went back. What do you think he sang about? "Poor Little Feb." Other months had thirty or thirty-one days, poor little February only had twenty-eight, or twenty-nine just once in a while.

❋　❋　❋　❋　❋

Do you feel strongly about Verdi? In Montecatini *don't*. We were rolling along the fine road to Viareggio, Thornton in front with Silvano, Garson and I in what C. N. and A. M. Williamson always referred to as "the tonneau."

"Scusa," said our chauffeur and asked if we'd like a look at Puccini's house.

"No, I'm a Verdi man," said Thornton, kindest of men, *but!*

Silvano drove us to Viareggio. And back. And wherever else we told him for the five days of our stay, and during all five he never spoke a word. His rigid back was in front of us, his rigid arm opened the door, his rigid expression looked past us and his rigid lips never spoke to us. Sorry about that, Silvano, and goodnight, wher-*ever* you are. And that goes for Signor Verdi. Goodnight, wher-ever *you* are.

❋　❋　❋　❋　❋

Are you popular? You should have caught me in Philadelphia before they tore down the Ritz. My phone never stopped!

"Roof Garden?"

"No, Ruth Gordon."

❋　❋　❋　❋　❋

277

Anybody know the one with the tag "I ain't even *been* yet, let alone went"?

❊   ❊   ❊   ❊   ❊

Old Mr. Webster was president of Kidder, Peabody. I was having lunch at his house on Commonwealth Avenue, across the green trees from the Vendome. Mr. Webster was in his eighties and Mrs. Webster only a year younger. She said, "I've just taken up piano and after lunch I expect teacher." With that for a hint, we didn't dawdle.

"Did you always live in Boston?" I asked Mr. Webster.

"No. I came down from Providence. I sold wallpaper in a store there."

"How did that prepare you for State Street?"

"One day I showed a tough customer every roll of paper in the store. I lifted rolls off top shelves. I got some from down cellar and finally I satisfied him.

" 'I'll have four of this.'

"I got down three more. The end of the third had a two-inch tear in it.

" 'Give me a roll without a tear,' he said.

"This was the last roll in that pattern. 'Let me take this up in the loft to make sure I match the pattern,' I said.

"He was agreeable to that and I took the roll with the tear in it up the ladder, cut off the damaged two inches and came back."

"What would you have done if he'd asked to see the roll you took up with the tear in it?" asked Mrs. Webster.

"I shouldn't have made good on State Street and *never* would have won you, my dear."

❊   ❊   ❊   ❊   ❊

Who Billy Wilder won was the singer with Tommy Dorsey's band. They got married and lived happily ever after in California. One morning outside their Wilshire Boulevard window up on the twelfth floor, there was a funny noise that interfered with the

278

Dodgers game. "What's that, Aud?" asked her husband and turned up the TV.

Audrey looked out on the balcony. "My God, there's an owl out there."

"Get rid of it," said Wilder.

(Paging Women's Lib.)

❋ ❋ ❋ ❋ ❋

Never give up! Windy didn't. He loved to ride in the station wagon. He'd get under it and wait for hours if it meant going for a ride. He was in it when they went to buy the firecrackers and near home it crashed. Everybody got out, but the station wagon was a wreck. Windy came up the hill to the house, hair still smoking from the firecrackers.

They towed the wreck up the hill to see if it was worth the repair. Toward evening I walked to the garage. In front of it was the station wagon, lopsided, hood crushed in. Under it Windy was waiting.

❋ ❋ ❋ ❋ ❋

Facials, a New York taxi, tapioca, a seat on the side in the last row, maraschino cherries, these are a few of my *un*favorite things.

# Cher Maître

"I NEVER SHOULD have given up opium," said René Clair. "*Sous les Toits de Paris, A Nous la Liberté, Le Million* were all made while I was on it. I never should have lost the habit."

"How *did* you?" I asked.

"When I went to England. It's too hard to get it there. *The Ghost Goes West* finished shooting the same time as my supply of opium, then I had to stay and cut the film. I should never have given it up."

"But when you came back to Paris?"

"Oh, I'd lost the habit."

"Didn't you think of taking it up again?"

"Well, yes, but I was doing something and you know how it is, your attention wanders, then fastens on something else. Merde," he said ruefully, "I should never have given it up."

The war was everywhere and as many people as could squeezed into Washington to help, to hinder, to make something, to give something, to write about it, to enjoy it, to see the results. Among others were René Clair, Robert Sherwood and Madeline and Garson and me. Was it the war? The Salle de Bois ran into a snag with its seafood. We took a clam off the shell, chewed, spit it out, buried it in the ice and tried another. René looked around at us bashfully burying them. "Should we have a clam-spitting contest?" he suggested.

In St. Tropez we were celebrating Jeanne d'Arc Day. Mme. René Clair asked Yvonne and Olga and Frédéric Chaix to walk with us to the port, have a glass at the Bar de Lys and go across the street to see De Mille's *The Greatest Show on Earth*. Mme. René Clair walked the road to the port between Yvonne and Olga. She led Bijou on the leash. René walked with me, Frédéric Chaix walked alone. "Come with us," said Mme. Clair.

"Je vous suis."

At the Bar de Lys, Yvonne, Olga, Mme. Clair, René sat at table and drank a glass. Frédéric sat at a table by himself.

"Frédéric," called Mme. Clair.

"A votre santé!" He lifted his glass.

"Sit with us, Frédéric."

"Suis content, Madame." He'd been the Clairs' gardener for fourteen years, but he was a man who sat alone.

Just the opposite was Bijou. The Clairs' big black poodle was born in Los Angeles, but she was also a born traveler. Super Chief knew her, so did the Twentieth Century, so did the *Ile de France*. As a passenger next to Mme. René Clair on the front seat of the Renault, she'd enjoyed St. Tropez, St. Jean–Cap Ferrat, St. Jean de Luz, crossed the Alps from Cortina d'Ampezzo, seen Mont Blanc on a clear day and been over the Brenner Pass to St. Moritz for a summer cure. Such a traveled dog liked to drop in at the Cinema and see *Les Actualités*. Up on a chair in the loge, Bijou watched. Sometimes she gave a low bark. *Les Actualités* over, Bijou studied the feature a minute, made sure it wasn't part of the newsreel, jumped off the chair and curled up under it for a snooze.

What was Bijou's attraction to money? René and I were breakfasting on the Train Bleu. Bijou stayed in the compartment with Bronia. I finished first and went back. Bronia went in to breakfast and I sat with Bijou. Bijou barked.

"No, Bijou." We were whirling through no place to be put off.

Bijou barked louder. The Blue Train tore through Sens at how many kilometers an hour? Bijou barked and turned round in circles like a London taxi.

"Bijou, tais-toi."

A louder bark.

"Tais-toi, Bijou darling."

Bijou knew when a "darling" was phony. She put her ears back and let out an unearthly whine.

Why did I open my Hermès bag? Did I think there was a piece of chocolate in there? There never had been. Why did I? I took out a fistful of franc notes to see what I'd find. Suddenly Bijou wasn't barking. She was staring at the franc notes, attention riveted as if it were the newsreel.

I put them on the seat beside her. She jumped up and lay down with the franc notes.

René and Bronia came back.

"She was barking, then she quieted down when I got out the franc notes."

"Yes," said René. "She loves money."

She'd have loved Mrs. Violet Trefusis. I never knew her well enough to love her, but I loved her name. If you'd been born Jones, you'd have to. Violet Trefusis? Shades of Pinero and Ouida! I got a bang out of it. She came with George Cukor, who came with us, who came with René and Bronia to the Marché aux Puces. René and Bronia made it every Saturday morning. "Wear old clothes," commanded René. "Otherwise they will cut off our balls."

George Cukor said he would and did, but Mrs. Violet Trefusis, in her claret-colored limo driven by claret-liveried chauffeur, came richly turned out by Dior when Dior was Christian Dior.

Disgruntled, but a good sport, René led us through the mazes. "We won't buy anything, because they'll double the price."

"Nonsense," said Mrs. Violet Trefusis, then haggled and underbid and harried the flea merchants till her claret-liveried chauffeur could carry no more and George Cukor risked backache carrying his friend's bargains.

Just because people are rich needn't mean they haven't got plenty of talent. Goodnight, Mrs. Violet Trefusis, where*ever* you are. What a smarty! If we have to give up opium, should we take up Mrs. Trefusis?

Beverly Hills Social Note: The welcome parties for René Clair and Madame were beautiful. After a while we noticed they were thinning out. "Announce we are leaving," directed René.

There was an immediate whirl of invites. "Farewell dinner for the René Clairs."

"Ah yes," said René, "but now the only thing we can do is leave."

※　※　※　※　※

Jones says, "Did you ever notice in all second-hand books there is a bus ticket?"

※　※　※　※　※

Do you want to be a star? How old are you? If you're over four, it may be too late. If you're four, start now. Curve your family into line. Be sure the whole house revolves around you. Rich, poor, beggar, thief, doctor, lawyer, merchant, chief, make sure *you're* the center of attention. At four if you start knocking on it, you've got a great chance. *A Star is Born* was the movie, but that's fiction. A star is *not* born, a star makes himself or herself a star. If you're four, don't let the grass grow.

※　※　※　※　※

Remember the grand blonde girl in Renoir's paintings? That was Gabrielle. When it was all over, she left Cagnes and wound up in Westwood. After a high tea she asked if we'd like to see her husband's paintings. We followed her to the garage. She waved her hand toward the walls where Mr. Slade of Boston's pictures were hung and burst into laughter. Mr. Slade smiled, too. He was a kind, dignified man with a beard, who understood that once you'd been with the master, other pictures were for a laugh in the garage.

Gabrielle and Mr. Slade and their son lived in Westwood, but Gabrielle never learned English. She went to Farmer's Market, traded at all the stores, had long talks over the fence with her neighbor who spoke only Hungarian.

"What do you talk about?" asked René.

Gabrielle shrugged. "Everything."

She didn't speak English and she didn't pick up California ways. After a grand dinner at Carmel Myers' new house, the hostess took her guests on a tour. After each room Gabrielle waited behind the others and turned out the lights.

In a thrifty family like Renoir's, the model was also the nanny. Gabrielle was Jean Renoir's. You've seen them in several portraits.

After this and that, Jean Renoir wound up without a painting by his father. One Christmas on Orange Drive, Gabrielle kissed him on both cheeks and thrust a rolled-up canvas into his hands. She thought Jean should have a painting by his father.

Speaking of hands, Jean held out his to her and Gabrielle washed them. She could also cook him calves' liver the way the master loved it. Sitwells' father, was *she* a mistake?

❊   ❊   ❊   ❊   ❊

*God rest ye merry gentleman,*
*Let nothing ye dismay—*

You think you're the only one that feels dismay? That song about it has been a standard for years.

And Ben Franklin got the message. "Be not disturbed by trifles, or accidents common or unavoidable," he wrote in his *Saturday Evening Post*. If I'd been around then, I'd have asked what's unavoidable?

Dizzy Gillespie wondered about that, too, that time he tried to tame a snake. He was in India giving concerts and got watching snake-charmers. At the tootle of flutes, big cobras would peek out of their baskets and listen. Dizzy thought if they went for that, he'd *really* entertain them. He got out his horn and blew. A big cobra cocked his ear or whatever he cocks to listen with. Dizzy made a beautiful sound. The cobra looked astonished and rose up out of his basket and looked as astonished as a cobra can with what he's been given for features. Dizzy blew and the cobra started to sway. He reared up, swayed, reared. Dizzy really went and the cobra rocked. Dizzy got a little anxious, the cobra was about twelve feet up in front of him.

"Don't stop, man," his friend warned.

Dizzy knew that was for sure. Now he played soothing rhythm, but the cobra kept on rocking.

"Don't stop, man."

Dizzy played as soothing as he could.

The cobra swayed.

Dizzy was getting beat.

"Don't stop, man."

The cobra swayed and writhed.

"Don't stop."

The cobra wove and lilted, twelve feet up in the air.

"Don't stop, man."

Dizzy blew, but his wind was going.

The cobra stopped.

Dizzy's heart did, too, but he kept blowing. Soothing, soothing—

The cobra reared back, let fly his yellow venom. Spewed it over Dizzy's face and trumpet. Just spewed. Didn't attack, just spewed and spewed.

Dizzy's face and trumpet dripped. Then the cobra wound down twelve feet and collapsed into his basket. He'd shown what he thought of American jazz.

✿  ✿  ✿  ✿  ✿

That was India, but in Concord, Mass., they showed how they felt, too.

"Would you walk with me?" asked an acquaintance of Thoreau.

"There's nothing so important to me as my walks. I have no walks to throw away on company."

That's how Thoreau cooled it.

# You're the Top

A T YALE I was on the debating society. 'Is Parcel Post Here to Stay?' was the subject. I took the negative side and won," said the rich boy of Peru, Indiana.

Cole Porter came from Peru, Indiana. It was a one-nighter and I played there. I asked him where he got all his grand ideas.

"From the Peru Opera House curtain. It was a painting of a palazzo on the Grand Canal. Every Saturday matinee I sat admiring it. 'Someday I'll live in one,' I promised myself and when I married Linda we bought Robert Browning's. His was even grander than the one I loved at the Pee-Roo Opera House."

I turned a corner of the Piazza San Marco and ran into Howard Sturges. "Show me where Cole's was."

Howard hailed a gondola and we poled up in front of a beauty. "Closed For The Day."

Soft words and lira were exchanged and we were in Robert Browning's and Cole and Linda's palazzo. Howard looked around him and his face lost its New England façade. "It was so beautiful. Think of Linda's beauty here! It was not to be believed. Once Cole gave a red-and-white ball. Can you imagine it against these gray stones? It was of a beauty! In this open courtyard look high up. Poles were placed across and acrobats performed. The guests watched or didn't. I can't tell you why, but it was perfect. Oliver Messel did the décor. He said there must be movement and engaged the small acrobat troupe."

In London, Cole admired Oggie Lynn. He wasn't the only one. All London thought she was terrific. Cole offered to launch her in New York. The date was agreed. Cole would pay for her and her accompanist and put her up at the St. Regis. Where would be the ideal place for her to sing? He could engage a theatre, but a theatre wasn't intimate enough. He went to see Mrs. Cornelius Vanderbilt and asked if Oggie Lynn could sing in her ballroom. Mrs. Vanderbilt was delighted and Cole invited a hundred guests, all opinionmakers. White tie for the gentlemen and every lady in her finest. Cole sent Oggie the money for *her* finest. He met the boat and installed her in the St. Regis suite, then took her to see the ballroom at Mrs. Vanderbilt's.

Limos rolled down Fifth Avenue to 51st Street. The weather obliged by being perfect. At the appointed hour a hundred guests sat in a hundred gilt chairs. Polite applause for Oggie's accompanist. He took his place at the newly tuned Steinway and looked toward the door. Oggie came through it in the beautiful dress. White-gloved applause. The pianist looked at Oggie. She didn't nod. A moment passed. He kept looking.

"I don't feel like it," she said. And didn't. What did Cole do? He laughed.

"Have you been invited to Cole's new apartment?" asked a wide-eyed Moss Hart. "Wait till you see it! Even his accountant's room is better than any place you or I live."

On his Waldorf Towers dinner table was a plate of fudge. Not grand like on the Boardwalk or Schrafft's, but shapeless. Unpretentious. A lady in Peru made it and Cole's order was for one box a week, year in, year out.

Trouble with the bad leg and Cole was up at Harkness Pavilion. "Come and see me," he said.

We got out of the elevator at the fifth floor and a man in morning clothes met us. "Good afternoon, I'm one of Mr. Porter's valets." He led us down the hall to Cole's.

How many valets have *you* got? And do they bring your Baccarat glass to the hospital?

"One of Cole's valets poured tomato juice for us and served pâté and biscuits.

"What's going on?" asked Cole.

"Dick and Alan are working on a musical about the life of Chanel."

"You can't make one," said Cole.

"You can't?"

"No."

"Why is that?"

"Chanel was never in love. You can't make a musical about *that*."

❊   ❊   ❊   ❊   ❊

Are black cats superstitious? I hope so. I only crossed their path once. An adorable black Persian kitten followed me. I kept telling it to go back, but it jumped up and down with pleasure and nipped right ahead. "Go home," I urged. What wisdom! But the foolish kitten took no heed, went with, nay, ahead of the stranger. Our lease said "No animals." I closed the door and the black kitten roamed the lawn. "Go home," I called out the window.

The kitten sat under the big pine and from time to time wailed, but sat on.

Frances said, "I'll take it in until you do something." She took it into her cottage by the gate.

We walked back to where I crossed the kitten's path. Some houses didn't answer. Some did, but weren't missing a kitten.

"There's a kitten here," I told the SPCA, "and I don't know who it belongs to. I'll advertise if you'll keep it."

They drove up and away.

"Your black cat has 'cat fever,' " said a voice on the phone.

"Oh? It seemed to be fine."

"Very contagious. We'll have to put it away."

"Couldn't you keep it and cure it?"

"Incurable."

Goodnight, black kitten, wher*ever* you are. I'm sorry I crossed your path.

# St. Moritz Guide

EVER GO to St. Moritz? In a car? In November? Don't. The Alps get larger. Then they get larger and larger. Past Chur the roads get snowy. Very snowy. And go straight up. Ever have a car start to slide? Ever sit and look over a drop off the road? Thornton, Garson and I sat and shivered. Garson started the car again. Again a slide and the car turned sidewise. A car passed by in the deep part of the snow. Garson maneuvered ours toward the deep part and we start down the hill. At the first auberge, Thornton asks La Patronne if there's much snow up the hill. She nods and we go cautiously back to Chur. The car goes in the garage, we go to the hotel for the night and book seats on tomorrow's train. Where did I lose my eyeglasses? What do I care? Have a night of comfort and next day look for them. They're at the railroad station and for fifty cents they give them back. Why fifty cents? The Swiss charge for everything, but they do find your glasses.

Lunch on the train. It starts to climb. Curves. Precipices. Very high now. The train halts. Lower the windows and see what's wrong. Goats on the track. The engineer blows his whistle. The goats look terrified, but keep chewing. They step off our track cautiously. My father would have approved of them. *They* certainly looked where they were going.

Lavender houses pass by. And pink. And yellow. And fierce green mountain brooks. Everything else is white. Trees. Mountains. Roofs. Everything except the bright blue sky. Tall trees. No trees. Avalanche prevention. Here we are at St. Moritz. No blue sky. Thick snowflakes. A sweeping white curve of road from station to the village. Our luggage goes in a red sleigh. Thornton says to stop for a hot chocolate at Hanselman's.

At Hanselman's whose St. Bernard is waiting for who to finish?

At the hotel we meet a lady with two French poodles en route to Bombay, a Venetian Countess and her little boy passing the weekend before she leaves him in school, a couple from Brooklyn, honeymooning.

At night we walk to the Suvretta for dinner. We arrive with ice-coated eyelashes. The Suvretta is bedded down for the night, but the very correct maître d' produces hot drinks in front of the fire. Ranged in the foyer are the guests' coats and overshoes. Why does it remind me of *Wuthering Heights?*

In the mornings we write. The heights give me melancholia. A Scorpio doesn't go for heights. I picked a fine place to be a Scorpio. (I'll have another martini.)

Tonight shall we take a sleigh ride?

In the sleigh our faces ice over. "Grüss Gott" even from strangers. At the bistro, La Patronne plays a game of patience with her mother. At one table is the dwarf that runs the shoe store. He is knitting a gray wool sock.

For lunch to where they serve the cheese fondue. The big earthen skillet bubbles and we poke our bits of bread in on forks with long handles. The first time I ever had cheese fondue was when my father came back from Wiscasset, Maine, and told my mother how a French girl made it. My mother made some and I liked hers better than at St. Moritz.

In the morning, children come up the hill to school dragging their sleds so they can slide home on them. They carry sealskin bookbags, with straps their arms pass through, then they sling the bags across their shoulders. Some kids wear sealskin shoes.

Every morning, men come up the hill carrying big uncovered cans with milk slopping out. I can see them out my window. And I can see Dr. Gut's clinic. Sometimes there's a lighted window at night, sometimes not. Why do I think of *Wuthering Heights?* A woman shovels the snow. She's husky, wears a blue apron and dark hug-me-tight. People go in. Why don't people come out?

Up here some men go about with no overcoats, just a muffler round their neck. At the cinema there's never anybody there. They show *Stage Door*. Next week they show *Carrie*. Next week a dire Italian film. November isn't the season. The Engadiner Kulm and the Palace aren't open. The Mercerie is run by Paravicini. Any relation to Liza Maugham's first? The trees are all covered with ice. An old fille tells us her lawyer will only let her travel in Switzerland or Holland. Thornton takes a slug before and we try the Alkohol Freies Restaurant. At our Neues Posthotel the tall skinny maître d' looks like a high-school principal. Late Sunday afternoon the week-end skiers ski home to their own villages. They make a sharp curve coming down the main street. The cars follow them off to Italy, full of smart Italian women.

At Hanselman's the fat woman and her fat husband drink iced chocolate. Thornton invites Cooky from Sils Maria for luncheon. At the next table are two American soldiers on leave from Germany. Why is the St. Moritz Post Office the essence of modernity? Why are the houses ugly? Why, if it's so healthy, is the store window full of cough cures and bronchial cures? Why does the tower lean? Why does the man water the ice? Why is it so monotonous? Why does Roman Polanski come here? He and his friend Jerry are skiers. On their last day, Roman picked up his skis, waited for Jerry. Jerry said, "The last day you break your leg." He wouldn't come.

Roman went off, had a beautiful day, came back, Jerry went out to meet him, slipped on the sidewalk and broke his leg. Off to Dr. Gut's!

Roman went off to Paris. I mean, after he stopped laughing.

# He Should Have Stood in Bed

D ID YOU ever have anything go wrong? I did. The year was 1946. A letter came from Mr. Homer Saint-Gaudens. He'd heard about my success in *Over Twenty-one*. He wrote, "I was in love with you. Did you know that?"

On my Cartier paper with "Ruth" engraved in silver in a circlet of buttercup yellow, I wrote how thrilled I was to hear from him. Did he ever come to New York? "My husband, Garson Kanin, and I would love to have you dine with us, please let me know. Much love and gratitude, Ruth."

Love and gratitude I should hope! Hadn't he given me my first job on the stage?

Yes, he'd have dinner. Great excitement, a table booked at the Pavillon, Mr. Soulé told that our guest was head of Carnegie Institute Art Museum and had given me my start.

Garson, moved by the coming event, asked, "When was the last time you saw him?"

"1916. In the spring. He left the Maude Adams Company on its tour, enlisted and went to Plattsburg."

Thirty years had passed and now here we were at the Pavillon, well ahead of time, we waited at table. Then there he was, looking thirty years older and yet somehow the same. He was moved too. Thirty years with all the people missing? All the things that had happened? All the things that had gone?

We ordered and Garson chose a superlative wine. We talked. We reminisced. Mr. Saint-Gaudens was deaf, so we talked louder. He was here to look for pictures for Carnegie Institute.

"Have you found any?" asked Garson.

"What's that?"

"Have you found any pictures?"

"No, I've been damned unlucky."

"Have you seen Henri Bernstein?"

"What?"

"Have you seen Henri Bernstein?"

"No."

"He has two for sale."

"He has?"

"Yes. At his suite in the Waldorf. Beautiful."

"Which ones are they?"

"Manet's portrait of Bernstein as a small boy. And Lucien Guitry and Jeanne Marnier acting a scene, by Renoir."

"My God!" exclaimed Mr. Saint-Gaudens. "And he wants to sell them?"

"Yes," said Garson.

"Why don't you buy them and keep some Jew from getting them?"

Martin poured the wine, dishes were whisked on and off, Mr. Saint-Gaudens enjoyed things. He addressed remarks to Garson. Garson nodded or looked dubious, but didn't open his lips.

"Hey, are you always this silent?"

We drank the coffee, had a brandy, Garson paid the check, we were on the sidewalk, "Goodbye," I said.

"Goodbye," said Mr. Saint-Gaudens.

Garson took my arm and I was in the limo.

Do things like that happen to you?

✢   ✢   ✢   ✢   ✢

"It's as warm as a chicken," said Mia.

"What does that mean?"

"You know. Warm."

"Yes?"

"Like a chicken."

"Oh."

✻　✻　✻　✻　✻

The gossamer thread showed up on 45th Street at Irving Berlin's
Music Box Theatre. Soon after *Over Twenty-one* opened, the
doorman said, "Remember Cohen the tailor that made the buttonholes in your blazer?"

"Yes."

"I'm his boy. You and your mother brought it into the shop."

A boy from Newport Avenue was stage doorman at the Music
Box where the girl with the blazer was acting in her play.

Our season at the Music Box ended and we were going on tour.
Willie Cohen brought me a scarf for my makeup table with
OVERTURE embroidered on it and a pink crocheted envelope that
folded and snapped with three snaps. In it was a slip of paper with a
drawing of a horseshoe turned up, so the luck wouldn't fall out, a
four-leaf clover, a heart with LOVE printed across it on the bias, in
the corner was: "1944 May your earning years be full of sunshine,
happiness, success and good health. Trust in God for He is Good to
bring your loved one back after this war. God will help you to fill
this little boodle bag to overflowing and your overtures will never
cease. From a friend of Will Cohen, Gerry Decker."

All my jewelry got stolen, but not my scarf that says OVERTURE
and in the drawer where I kept the jewelry is the boodle bag, the
pearl and diamond heart got stolen out of it. Goodnight, Willie
Cohen and Gerry Decker, where*ever* you are, and God *did* bring
my loved one back and *did* help me fill my boodle bag and after it
got stolen we all lost interest.

# *And One Was Out in the Cold*

W AS IT the gossamer thread that led me back to the American
Academy of Dramatic Arts?

Mr. Worthington Miner stepped to the dais. "The final award to
be given today goes to a vivid and colorful figure in our American
Theatre. What sets Ruth Gordon apart is her ability to make an
audience share her unquenchable joyousness in doing what she is
doing. I talked with her for half an hour on the phone the other day
and there was such zest for life on the other end, I said to myself as
I hung up, 'If that girl has celebrated her golden jubilee in the theatre, I'm Neanderthal.'

"But let no one confuse joyousness with a lightheartedness toward work. Ruth Gordon taught the workhorse what it means to
be in harness. Hard work is her caviar. I've known her for forty
years, I've worked with her, and I've directed her—just once—but
no one I've ever met has equaled her capacity to drive and drive
and never give up, until she's achieved that exultant moment when
she is able to say to herself: 'That's it, I've got it!' There's been a
golden jubilee of sweat and tears behind Ruth Gordon's triumphs,
but the end has been a contagious sense of sheer exuberance. May
all of you graduating here today achieve this same exuberance, for it
lies at the heart of every performance you may give, whether it be
in *Hamlet* or in *Plaza Suite*.

"I've no intention of reading Ruth's full roster of credits as actress and playwright—from Nibs in *Peter Pan* to Cass in Brian Friel's *The Loves of Cass McGuire*—we'd be here till May. I do want to point out that, for all her irrepressible spirit, nothing was ever handed her on a platter. She had no Barrymore tradition behind her to open doors. She was a little girl out of Wollaston, Mass., who had to struggle for every break she got. After all, she was not a type. Was the Baby Talk Girl in *Seventeen* the actress you'd choose for *Ethan Frome?* Was Susie Sachs in *A Church Mouse* the woman you'd select for Mrs. Levi in *The Matchmaker?*

"All of which implies a daring and a courage. These characteristics are epitomized in Ruth's determination to play the lead in *The Country Wife* —and to play it, of all places, in London. The British have claimed Restoration Comedy as their own private preserve —it's been a form of theatrical apartheid. Nonetheless, this girl from Massachusetts dared throw this challenge into the faces of a London audience and a lion's den of London critics. Their surrender to her imagination and outrageous vitality was complete and abject.

"Always Ruth's finest achievements have been off-beat and unpredictable and yet she has found a way again and again to make each performance sing to her commanding tune. In view of her vast energy and volatile mind, one well-nigh unrecorded performance stands out for me as a measure of her basic integrity. In *Action in the North Atlantic*, a World War II film starring Humphrey Bogart, she was asked to play the relatively colorless part of a sea captain's wife. And yet in those tiny moments with Raymond Massey she struck a note so simple, so honest, so humble, it remains in my esteem the ultimate measure of the true artist.

"I'm proud today to present the American Academy's Award of Achievement for 1968 to a figure of courage, of imagination, and of joyous gaiety, which represents everything this school stands for and respects—Miss Ruth Gordon."

Well, I always knew stuff like that would be said about me, but Tony was right, nothing *was* handed to me on a platter. Especially at the American Academy of Dramatic Arts. Especially in the spring of 1915. For the end-of-the-year examination the Academy cast me in John Galsworthy's play *Joy*. I wish he'd stood in bed. I wish Joy had stood in bed, too. Joy was the part I played and they told me I wasn't suited to the stage and not to come back.

I didn't, till the afternoon Tony made that speech.

I held up the flap of an old envelope. "We'll be out of here in no time," I said, "here are *my* notes." They knew we spoke the same language. " '1725 Green Valley Road, Haverford, Pa.,' " I read off the flap. "Does that ring a bell? It does for me. This morning I was walking down Fifth Avenue and a girl came rushing up. 'Miss Gordon, I read that you went to the American Academy of Dramatic Arts and I've got to go to the American Academy of Dramatic Arts and I have to have a letter *recommending* me and, Miss Gordon, would you write a letter?' She tore off this flap of an envelope and wrote her address.

"Before I came here today, I wrote the letter, because when *I* was frantic to go to the American Academy of Dramatic Arts, I didn't happen to run into any actress, so I wrote a letter to the leading lady of the Castle Square Stock Company. 'Dear Miss Doris Olsson, would you please write a letter recommending me to the American Academy of Dramatic Arts. I am frantic to go to the American Academy of Dramatic Arts and if I don't, I will kill myself.' Well, she wrote the letter and I *did* come to the Academy, so we'll be out of here in no time, because if *I* were listening to my speech I would wish it would be over and we could get to the question-and-answer part. *My* question would be never mind advice, theories and ideals, do you know who does the casting for David Merrick? And is it better to write or drop in?

"Well, if I knew, I'd tell you, but what do you think of this? After we *do* find out who does the casting, and after we find out whether to write or drop in, there come those terrible moments—just terrible—when you sit around and you wonder. And you worry. And you try to ferret out what does it *take?*

"They say it takes talent. They say it takes looks. Personality. You shouldn't be too tall. You shouldn't be too short.

"I sat around until I came up with I don't think so. I think those are trivialities. I think what it takes is *don't give up!* DON'T GIVE UP. Just don't give up and that sounds like a put-down, but it isn't. And it sounds as though it's easy and it *isn't.* DON'T GIVE UP. I learned that at the Academy, and it was all I did learn. It wasn't what my father paid four hundred dollars for, but it may be the best lesson I was ever taught. DON'T GIVE UP! The class I was in had sixty of us. Sixty students, sixty! Well, who's standing here today?

"1914 is when I came. The president was Mr. Sargent. He welcomed our class to the Academy, then said 1914 was a very bad year to go on the stage. He said it was unusually bad, and of course it was, but I guess *every* year somebody says it's terrible. '1914,' Mr. Sargent said, was really 'an *unusually* bad year to go on the stage.' Well, what could we do? We'd spent our four hundred dollars. What could we do? Mr. Sargent said, 'We will study hard here, and by the time we learn it all, probably the war will be over.' "

That brought down the house!

" 'Here in the Academy,' he said, 'it'll be like a nice, safe retreat.' Well, as it turned out, it wasn't so safe for *me*, because at the end of the year, he said to me, 'Don't come back.' He said, 'You don't show any promise.' Well, I hope that's never said to anybody here. That's *terrible*. But what is even *more* terrible is, he was right and I knew it and so did the whole school. And do you know *why* I didn't? I was scared. I was scared I wouldn't find out how to be an actress because in that year the school hadn't taught me. I'm smart and I can learn, but the school hadn't given me a clue. Four hundred dollars and all I got for it was fright, because even to *myself* I didn't show any promise. 'Well, don't come back,' he said. 'Don't come back.' That's a terrible thing, you could drop dead."

They laughed.

"You could kill yourself."

They laughed.

"You could give up. You could go back home and settle down with some nice man."

They laughed, but the laugh had changed. All show business, even beginners, know that fear.

"You could give up and become president of Macy's."

They laughed because we were on the same side.

"Or you could *learn* something. Isn't that what we came to the Academy for? So I learned something and what I learned here was and *is* DON'T GIVE UP. So some rainy afternoon, when somebody says to you, 'You're not pretty enough,' 'You're too tall,' 'You're too short,' 'Your personality's not what we're looking for,' DON'T GIVE UP! And not only *that* rainy afternoon, but all the rainy afternoons of all *seasons*. Think it over. And while you're thinking it over, stay stagestruck. That's the most!'"

※ ※ ※ ※ ※

Garson said why would I tell a bunch of kids that aren't even started not to give up?

Because that's when you *do* give up. In the beginning you're scared and think you're the only one. Later you find out everybody is, at the start. You don't know that and that's why people quit. If you've been at it a long time, you've got a big investment! Could *I* give up? But just starting, what if I had?

Draw the veil.

※ ※ ※ ※ ※

When you have a long career, after a while people give you honors, you go to a lot of funerals, you like a lot of things you didn't used to, you hate a lot of things you loved and you go to your 50th high-school reunion.

At ours, the class of 1914 elected Garson an honorary member. He made a speech of acceptance, then said, "Though so recently accepted, may I make a suggestion? I've been listening to arguments whether or not there should be a reunion celebrated every year or should we wait till our 55th? I suggest we hold one on our 55th and not in Howard Johnson's Banquet Room, let's hold it in a nudist camp."

Silence. Then laughter.

We held it at Hugo's in Cohasset. Could it be on our 60th we'll take the new member's advice? It's Massachusetts, remember, and even on June 25 we'd have to hope for a break from the weather.

When Maude Adams staged *Joan of Arc* at the Harvard Stadium, she took the trouble to ask the U.S. Weather Bureau when there'd be a nice day three months later. They wrote her a date and she wrote it to Harvard Stadium. It was a nice day.

If our class president writes, they'll tell *him*.

(Harry Burr, make a note.)

※ ※ ※ ※ ※

But what about Garson's idea? They're doing it on the stage and in pictures. In *Rosemary's Baby* Roman asked me to, but I thought no friend of Helen Keller should go bareass, but is that the way an actress should think? They gave me a muumuu, but was that what Minnie Castevet would have worn at the witches' meeting?

If David Merrick does his next version of *Hello, Dolly!* at the Harmonia Gardens Nudist Colony with Mr. Vandergelder and Mrs. Dolly Gallagher Levi starkers, are you going to be troubled? Isn't it "What do they *do* on the treadmill?"

If Thornton had written *The Matchmaker* with a situation that called for me to come on in the altogether, should I have turned down the role? Should Carol? Or Ginger? Or Phyllis? Or Betty? Or Martha? Or Pearl? Or the great Ethel?

Until I hear from them, I'll say we shouldn't.

※ ※ ※ ※ ※

Where do *you* go Sunday nights now there's no more Lindy's? Mrs. Ed Sullivan and Mrs. Jesse Block used to have dinner together there when Ed was working and Jesse was at the Friars. The helpings were big enough for a family, but that's the way Mr. Lindy liked it. He liked to see a heaping plate. He was a small, thin man, but admired a groaning board.

There was always a lot left over and Eva Block and Sylvia Sullivan are light eaters. "Wrap this up for my little dog," Eva told the waiter.

Time passed. The waiter looked out the serving-pantry door. "Would your little dog like some pickles and pumpernickel?"

※ ※ ※ ※ ※

300

"Il est né gai," said Louis XVI about his son and I guess Bob Garland's father said the same.

Bob reviewed the stage show at the Capitol. "Then Mr. Block and Miss Sully came on, or is it Miss Block and Mr. Sully? Mr. Block, or is it Miss Block, sang and then Miss Sully, or is it Mr. Sully, did a routine. Following Miss Block, or is it Miss Sully, were—"

Next day came a wire.

MR. ROBERT GARLAND
NEW YORK JOURNAL AMERICAN
NEW YORK
IT IS MR. BLOCK AND MISS SULLY MR. GARLAND OR IS IT MISS
GARLAND?

JESSE BLOCK

\* \* \* \* \*

John or was it Joan, the Gishes' parrot, laid an egg. It was hard on the Gishes because their parrot had been John for years, so to say Joan wasn't easy.

In the days before the egg, John or was it Joan and the Gishes lived at New York's Hotel Ambassador. It was summer and John's or was it Joan's wings had been clipped, so he or was it she was allowed out of the cage and bounced from floor to chair to table and, before anyone could stop him or her, bounced out the open window. Down, down, down went he or was it she, flapping her or his wings and crying "*Oh* dear! *Oh* dear! *Oh* dear!"

Traffic waiting for the light to change stood still and Joan or was it John lit on the back of a truck still saying "*Oh* dear! *Oh* dear!" as the Gishes screamed out the window a few oh dears of their own.

Thanks to an ad in the paper, John or was it Joan was returned and lived for a lot more years with the Gishes and never gave cause for any further oh dears, nor laid another egg.

One night Lillian had George Jean Nathan and Jed Harris and me for dinner. Coffee was served in the sitting room, then Lillian left to play *Uncle Vanya*'s beauteous Elena and I left to play Dorothy Parker in *Hotel Universe*.

301

Over the coffee cups George told how terrific *he* was and Jed did his long-play how *he* was the greatest. When they left, John or was it Joan said, "Well, well, well."

Lillian and Dorothy came from Massillon, but they'd dropped their Ohio accent, except when they weren't thinking. John or was it Joan dropped it too, except when the phone rang. Dorothy or Lillian would answer, then rush out and as the door slammed, John or was it Joan, in pear-shaped tones, said, "Hello? . . . Hello? . . ." Then in Massillon-ese, "Be ri' down."

*       *       *       *       *

Do you notice the gossamer thread turns up when you least expect it? Laurence Olivier was at the wheel of the Bentley. I sat beside him. In the back seat, Garson held hands with Vivien and we set out from Edinburgh for our drive to Newcastle-on-Tyne. The sun was out, the sky was blue, there was a crackle in the air. "We have a great deal of time," said Larry. "Everyone may choose a side trip."

"How will I know where I want to go?" I asked. "I've never been in Scotland."

"You'll know," said Vivien. "I choose Melrose Abbey."

"What's that?" I asked.

"It's where they treasure Robbie Burns' heart."

Larry speeded up. "Puss has chosen. Now it's you, Ruthie. Then Gar."

"I won't know any."

"You will."

"How will I?" A sign pointed left. "Stop!" I cried.

"Where?" asked Larry.

"Left. Go left."

"Galashiels?"

"Galashiels." Could I believe my eyes? Galashiels was where Barrie's little minister had preached. I'd seen Galashiels on the stage of the Empire, at Philadelphia's Broad Street Theatre, in Easton Pa., Lancaster, Allentown, Reading, Harrisburg, the Atlantic City Boardwalk, in Connecticut's Bridgeport, Middletown, New Haven, South Norwalk, at Boston's Hollis Theatre, Detroit's Opera

House, Chicago's Blackstone, in Hancock Michigan, Iowa's Mason City, Omaha's Brandeis Theatre, in St. Joe Missouri, Ishpeming, Madison, Bloomington where the bedbugs were and Fall River, Mass. where Lizzie did or didn't murder her folks and where *The Little Minister* didn't sell out. *Now* in Laurence Olivier's Bentley I was driving through the streets of Galashiels via the gossamer thread.

❉   ❉   ❉   ❉   ❉

"Don't never act in no place where they serve hard liquor," was my father's advice the August 1st I left home. He'd given his consent to my going on the stage, but it turned out I had to have something more. I had to get hired and nobody hired me till mid-December. For a time, it was as if my father had said "Don't act in *no* place." I was down to thirteen dollars, owed the Three Arts Club seventy-two dollars, which meant I hadn't paid my board bill for nine weeks, but just the same I knew my father wasn't with it when he wrote me, "Any profession that didn't offer me a berth in six weeks I would not continue in."

Goodnight, Papa, wher*ever* you are, I'm glad I didn't take your advice.

❉   ❉   ❉   ❉   ❉

Have you got a lucky piece? I wear a gold four-leaf clover from Natalie Wood, a gold ruby-eyed baby given me by Mia, a gold miniature Oscar given me by Gregory Peck, a gold St. Christopher "Look at me and be safe" given by John Golden, purple beads Lucy Saroyan strung for me and I'm lucky.

Well, that's show business.

❉   ❉   ❉   ❉   ❉

When you go, do you really go? We kept our buckwheat batter warm all night in a big bowl under an old blanket back of the coal stove. Will Bull sent our maple syrup when they tapped the trees at Bomoseen, the Newport Sausage Company of Medford, Mass., put some on the New York, New Haven and Hartford's Boston-to-Washington train and someone threw them off at the stationmaster in New Haven where Chapman was waiting to drive them the eighteen miles over the Danbury highway up the dirt road to Faraway Meadows. *Who's Who* doesn't list this as one of our accomplishments, but I think it is. Mrs. Robert E. Sherwood thought so, too. She won first prize for putting away thirteen buckwheat cakes and her full share of Newport Sausages. Goodnight, Newport Sausages, wher*ever* you are. Too bad you joined the snows of yesteryear.

※　※　※　※　※

At Faraway Meadows, food was a feature. "We're having caramel ice cream," I announced.

"Oh," said Isabel.

Said Thornton, "That's a very　　　　　　flavor."

What adjective did he use? It was the perfect description. *The* perfect.

Later Garson said, "What was that Thornton said about caramel ice cream?"

We tried to think what he said. Then we asked Thornton.

"Yes, what *was* it? It was rather good. Isabel, can you remember?" She couldn't.

Would you believe four smarties agreed it was *the* perfect description and not *one* could remember the word? Praise the Lord and pass the caramel ice cream, see what that'll chalk up.

※　※　※　※　※

What do *you* do to get talked about? Gertrude Stein says you only have to reach five hundred people, but those five hundred must be opinion-makers. In Wollaston I didn't know any opinion-makers, but I got myself talked about. You think that's easy? Ruth Jones, 14 Elmwood Avenue. Nothing inflammable in the way of personality or looks. What could I do to hold interest? I persuaded my girl friend to walk to Boston. You're let down? Nobody ever did it before. A walk from Wollaston to Boston is seven miles and even today it's got a lot of bezazz. *Endless* talk before you do it. *Endless* doubts whether you'll do it at all. Then the discussions. Would it rain? Would it shine? Would we do it rain or shine? Already people were talking and I hadn't spent a nickel. Did we *really* know the way? Did we *really* know what we were doing? What if a white-slaver put us to work in South Boston?

"It takes you through one of the *worst* sections of Dorchester," warned my mother.

"Mama, I can look after myself."

"It takes you through one of the *worst* sections of Boston."

"Mama, I'm seventeen years old, don't you *trust* me?"

We did it and didn't wind up in the white-slave trade. We didn't even get accosted. All the worst sections turned their backs on us. Was that a knock or a boost? But we did what we set out to do, people talked. "Ruth Jones and Kay Follett walked to Boston" is still in the jive.

❊   ❊   ❊   ❊   ❊

Another way to get talked about is to get nominated for the Academy. When you do, do you think about what you're going to say when you win? Do you ever write a speech? "Draft for an Oscar Speech," I wrote, then added, "Just in Case." That was clever, because sometimes you're nominated and they call out someone's else's name. Did that happen to you? That's a horrible feeling. Peggy Wood was straightening her back hair and I was smoothing my dress and they called out "Shelley Winters."

Draw the veil!

Then another year came along and I wrote another "Just in Case." I wrote, "People ask me what *Rosemary's Baby* looked like. It's too bad, but it looked like its father. But Mia didn't go for that, so she booked it on a few commercials and with *that* money had them do a plastic job. Horns, tail, everything. Now every day the baby is looking more like Mia. But what interests me even more than that, if you can believe such a thing, is that I won the Oscar.

"And I'm pleased I won it in the category of a supporting actress

305

because that means I'm not only good for myself, but good for our producer Bill Castle, our director Roman Polanski and our star, wonderful Mia Farrow. Thank you all who voted for me, and all you who didn't, I'll try to get you in the next round."

By the time I got nominated, I got sick of it, so I wrote, "I can't tell you how encouraging a thing like this is. The first job I ever had, I was an extra in a movie in 1915 and now it's 1968, I don't know what took me so long. Anyway, thank you Bill, thank you Bob, thank you Roman, thank you Mia and thank you all who voted for me and all you who didn't, excuse me." That one came in handy.

To me and to Laurence Olivier.

DARLING RUTHIE, CAN YOU EVER POSSIBLY FORGIVE ME. I HAVE DONE THE MOST IMPOSSIBLE UNPARDONABLE THING STOP I USED YOUR ACCEPTANCE SPEECH WHEN I GOT THE ENGLISH AWARD FOR BEST SUPPORTING PLAYER STOP CAN YOU EVER FORGIVE YOUR REPENTANT ADORING

LARRY

I did.

What he said that was really useful was that "Stop." At his age and mine shouldn't people be supporting *us?* Think it over. It could happen again. This year?

✳   ✳   ✳   ✳   ✳

Are you against stealing? Not me. It helped me through some hungry days. Anyone who's flush enough to leave a dime on the bureau wouldn't miss it and a dime paid for a bowl of Child's vegetable soup. Why would I be against stealing? Always leave a quarter on your bureau, the price of soup's gone up.

And speaking of stealing, what was *your* robbery like? At our house we had professionals. It was October, of course. After all, I'm a Scorpio and if you're a Scorpio, October you go! And maybe some of your things.

*The Matchmaker* went great. Sometimes a Saturday-night audience liked a rougher show, but this Saturday was bull's-eye. "The arrow likes to hit its mark," say the Zen people. It did.

After the show, Chapman had the car at the stage door, but the night was so fine we walked. Chapman took the flowers and laundry and odds and bods and we started up Broadway to 49th.

Can you pass Horn and Hardart's? We went in, me telling how great *The Matchmaker* was, Garson telling how terrific was *The Diary of Anne Frank*.

At 242 we unlocked the door, flowers and laundry and odds and bods were in the front hall. We bolted the front door, put the flowers in water, I went in the dining room to make sure the garden door was locked, upstairs to the parlor floor, turned off a light or two, up the second flight which are circular stairs, and when I came round the bend I *did* go round the bend. On the hall floor was Garson's new gold-colored tie from Bronzini lying on the red carpet. He'd never worn it. New Englanders don't *wear* new things, but I don't care who you are, nobody throws a Bronzini necktie on the hall floor. "We've been robbed," I whispered.

"What?" Garson was coming up the stairs behind me.

"We've been robbed. They may be still in the house."

"Why've we been robbed?"

I whispered that his good tie was on the floor and to let's get out of there.

"Well, just because—"

"Garson, let's get *out*."

"But just because a tie is lying on—"

"We *don't* run a house where a new Bronzini tie is on the hall floor." I plunged down the stairs. I'm not afraid to lose my things, but I'm afraid of being murdered.

"Well, if we've been robbed," said Cool-Head, "I'll phone the police."

"No! They may still be in the *house*." I was out the front door, Garson too, but not convinced.

At Third Avenue and 49th, the Silhouette Bar was also having a good Saturday night. Now a big high-rise stands there. Thank God, it didn't that night! At midnight whose phone can you use in a high-rise?

"This is Garson Kanin, we've been robbed . . . 242 East 49th."

How did *you* feel when policemen ran through your house with guns drawn? Something! Some ran up the stairs, some ran down cellar. Aren't *they* scared of being murdered? The front man got to the Bronzini tie and whistled. Down the hall, our bedroom looked like they'd used a Waring Blender. Everything all over everything. O.N.T. thread and the Morgan Guaranty checkbook mixing it up with stork embroidery scissors and on the floor was my jewel case upside down. Was yours? All mine had left in it was an enamel Van Cleef pin sprinkled with modest diamonds and beside it a Cartier gold mirror. All the stuff that pays off at the pawn shop had left East 49th. Goodbye the seventy-five-carat emerald Garson sent me from London, goodbye Fulco's ruby cigarette case, good I stopped smoking. Goodbye, diamond heart with the stars. They got it all except Garson's Bronzini gold silk tie that Butterfingers dropped in flight. Out over the roof like Santa Claus, only they didn't *bring*, they *loaded out*. Goodbye, we never saw it again. The Chemical Squad came and squirted white powder over everything for fingerprints and people asked questions all night long and every so often I said, "Don't forget to mention *The Matchmaker*, David Merrick will never get over it if a corny jewel robbery doesn't at least use the name of the show."

When I said they better pay the insurance, they did and canceled me out for life. After seeing men run through the house with pointed guns, do I want some more jewelry? "Diamonds are hilarious," says Mia. She's right.

\* \* \* \* \*

People ask me if I like New York. Why wouldn't I? I got there in 1914 and from 1914 to 1970 is a big investment to be wrong about. Why *wouldn't* I like New York? I've cried my eyes out as far uptown as 85th Street, as far downtown as West 12th and crosstown from Second Avenue to the Hudson. Notice any tears blotting this page? *Something* must've gone right. Why wouldn't I like New York? Between 1914 and 1970 and 340 West 85th and as far east as Second Avenue and downtown to 12th I cheered up.

In California we don't cry so much. California offers a lot of comfort. Is that good? Maybe New York whamming away makes you find out how to take it.

It certainly makes you resourceful. In New York if you can't get to Aqueduct to see the horses run, *you* can run against the traffic lights, and with those turned-on taxis coming at you, it may beat being on the winner.

In California we wait for the lights. I don't know what the penalty is, but I bet even Peter Fonda wouldn't cross against them in California.

The law says everybody is created free and equal, but in New York that's not how it works out. That keeps toughening you up. In New York there's nothing free or equal, except that *everybody* has it no good. Seven people live in one room, one person lives in seven, but both ways they've got things that drive them crazy. That takes care of if one room should sleep seven or seven rooms belong to one.

Remember when the idea used to be to have a lot of diamonds? After they took to grabbing them, it became a treat not to have some. The young folk said flowers were the thing and diamonds are hilarious. (They do look kind of obsolete.)

Then fashion got the ax. The dresses and suits and coats for the lady that lived in seven rooms had to have two fittings and cost hundreds of dollars, some other people put on beads and short skirts, asked what was "lingerie," and the clothes with the two fittings looked as obsolete as diamonds and the lady with the seven rooms was buying things off the rack. Pants came to the theatre. Pants came to the Met. Satin or velvet for those places and, for the Mets, anything that was streaked. Balenciaga cut out, Bergdorf said goodbye to Miss Gertrude and showed things you stepped into. Goodnight, two fittings, wher*ever* you are.

People's hair grew as long as Samson's, the sweet smell of pot savored the Baronet, off-Broadway won the prizes and people saw Fourth Street that never had been south of "21."

On the Bowery to climb up in a loft or crawl down cellar cost eight dollars, sometimes ten. Know anybody who went bankrupt? Or who stopped going?

Everybody flailed away at *Oh! Calcutta!* Or rhapsodized, then

309

dropped the subject. Now it's taken for granted like *The Barretts of Wimpole Street* and *Life with Father*. Ever hear anyone talk about it? I notice they still run an ad.

People don't talk about *Oh! Calcutta!* but they tell each other safe streets to walk. "After the theatre walk home Seventh Avenue," said our lawyer.

"Go crosstown only on 57th or 59th," says the doorman. "On the East Side don't trod the pavements," says everybody. Didn't they shoot at somebody in front of the Plaza? And coming out of the Colony? Well, what are *you* going to do?

I think I'll keep my appointment till a bullet or a mugger or my cholesterol count says, "Knock off, this is Samarra."

❄   ❄   ❄   ❄   ❄

John Keats died when he was twenty-six. At twenty-six I hadn't written my will, let alone "Ode on a Grecian Urn."

Think it over and take care till you get something good launched off the pad.

❄   ❄   ❄   ❄   ❄

No way's a good way to go, but if I get run over I hope it won't be winter. Zap! And you're lying there, a wind blowing through 57th Street. Not 57th, Lord. And not January.

❄   ❄   ❄   ❄   ❄

Southampton can be cold, too. That's where the *Mayflower* sailed from. Is that where the Cunards got the idea? Those days the ship made a stop at Provincetown, then tied up at Plymouth. Eight years later they "hanged a witch." I'm glad they didn't hang all of them or what about Rosemary's baby? *They* might've done me out of an Oscar.

❄   ❄   ❄   ❄   ❄

Alexander Woollcott wrote in *The New York Times*, "Ruth Gordon was ever so gay as Nibs." That was 1915 and in 1970 I re-read *Peter Pan*. On page fifty Barrie writes "Tootles" dash-dash-dash "is the humblest of the band. Nibs is more gay and debonair."

Well, wouldn't you think in my *first* part I'd have read the stage description the author wrote?

And how about without reading it, I got it right! There must be *something* to me, but still it pays to be thorough. The boys in *The Boys in the Band* played *their* parts as if *they* read their author's directions.

❈ ❈ ❈ ❈ ❈

Are you settled down? I think I am, but then I'm on the move. What happens? Do I get uprooted or do I uproot myself? I make friends, I think I'm part of the scene, then the moving man's at the door. "Settle down," people say. They claim I ruin their address books. Well, write me off or get a bigger address book or buy an eraser, I'm a permanent transient.

❈ ❈ ❈ ❈ ❈

I change my address, but not my intentions. I left home to go on the stage, today people go in the theatre. Not me. On the stage is where I was going and still am if I can find it. I came to New York for some razzle-dazzle and am still looking for it. "Thank God," said Justice Holmes, watching the Old Howard burlesque show, "my tastes are low." Me, too. If I'd known I was going to be in Ibsen and Shaw and Chekhov, I'd never have left Quincy, Mass. I was hoping to get in the *Follies* or the *Passing Show* or anything that wouldn't improve anybody. Once a lowbrow always a lowbrow! Goodnight Mr. Justice Holmes, wher*ever* you are, I wish you were back.

❈ ❈ ❈ ❈ ❈

Don't let anyone ever tell you Ibsen isn't a moneymaker. All I had to do was say I was going to do *A Doll's House* and I made two dollars.

Thornton said I should tangle with the classics and I asked, "How about *A Doll's House?*"

"It'll have to be a new adaptation. No one would sit through those 'Has my little bird been eating a jelly?' versions."

"Would *you* adapt it?" I asked.

He said he didn't feel like tampering with the great Norwegian.

I asked Noël Coward, Sam Behrman, Lillian Hellman and who else?

"No," they said.

"Who can I go to?"

"Somebody or I won't put it on." Thus spake Jed Zarathustra Harris.

If I *couldn't* get somebody to adapt it, should I try to get somebody else to put it on?

Eddie Dowling's office was in the 44th Street Theatre, his feet were up on his desk. "Would you want to put on *A Doll's House?*"

"Where do I get hold of a copy?"

"Brentano's."

"Get me one," he said and tossed two one-dollar bills across his desk. I thanked him and didn't come back. Why trifle with luck? The show hadn't even opened and was already out of the red.

I called up Thornton. "I've got to drop *A Doll's House.*"

"Why?"

"Jed won't do it unless it's a new version and no one will write it."

There was silence from West 12th Street, Manhattan, to Deepwood Drive, Hamden, Connecticut.

"Will *you?*"

More silence, then a sort of sigh. Was it the wind or Wilder? "Yes," he said and stopped writing his play and tampered with Ibsen. We broke all records on top of our initial profit. And maybe those playwright courses should advise everybody to stop writing a play in the middle and do a new version of Ibsen. It didn't seem to hurt *Our Town.*

❊  ❊  ❊  ❊  ❊

Do you know anyone who lights up real candles on their Christmas tree? Do you know anybody that pops corn and strings it to toss over the branches? I don't, but a Christmas tree is a Christmas tree is a Christmas tree, what changed are the presents. How long since you found a combing jacket under the spruce boughs? Or a signet ring in your stocking? Or a crocheted boodle bag to pin on your corset? Or a raffia hair-receiver? Or sealing wax? Or a pair of stork scissors? Or a fireless cooker? Or a Kewpie doll or a Billikin? Or a fascinator? Or wristlets? Or a scalloped doily? Or a chemise or teddy bear? Or sterling silver lingerie clasps? Or a pyrography set? Or a game of Lotto from Parker and Co. of Salem, Mass., or a game of Old Maid? Or Little Red Riding Hood? Or Pit? "Three wheat! Three wheat! Three—"

"Three wheat." They hand you three cards and you give three. "Three barley! Three barley!"

"Three barley."

"Pit. I win."

Merry Christmas and, now that I think of it, is it only the presents are different?

❊  ❊  ❊  ❊  ❊

Reclining on the *Ile de France* afterdeck, I said, "Bronia is a wonderful person."

"A wife is what a husband makes her," said René.

"Is a husband what a *wife* makes him?"

"No."

All right, girls, let's go. (Paging Women's Lib.)

❊  ❊  ❊  ❊  ❊

Did your father have a short temper? Gilbert Miller's father did. Everybody who worked for him had to look out. Everybody took a lot of trouble not to get Mr. Miller upset.

313

"Get me somebody to play the boy in Act Three," he told Willard Barton, whose middle name was Thorough.

The part called for a boy nine years old. Willard Barton selected a number of nine-year-olds and advised the young gentlemen to show up on the stage of the Henry Miller Theatre at ten the following morning. Then Willard, the thorough, thought about the part some more. Maybe real boys were too rugged. Hadn't Sarah Bernhardt played young L'Aiglon? Hadn't Miss Adams played young Peter Pan? Hadn't Little Corinne played Little Lord Fauntleroy? Willard studied the casting files and interviewed some sweet little girls who could tuck their curls under a wig and wear short pants. "Come with your mama to the Henry Miller at ten," he told them and got to thinking some more. What if the play played Washington? Our capital wouldn't allow minors on the stage. Willard interviewed some midgets. "Come to the Miller at ten," he said to a few who hadn't been minors for years.

At ten on the stage of the Henry Miller waited the rugged boys, the golden-haired little girls, the middle-aged midgets. Willard Barton felt a glow of confidence. He'd covered the ground.

Elegant Mr. Henry Miller strode on stage and stopped. "Barton, what's *this?*" he demanded.

"They're here for the nine-year-old boy, Mr. Miller."

Mr. Miller's handsome face turned purple. "God damn it, Barton, I ask for a boy and you get me everybody from Little Eva to Uncle Tom!"

Mr. Miller had a house in Stamford. He thought he'd like a fine big touring car. The chauffeur went to pick it up and when Mr. Miller looked out his bedroom window, there was the new seven-passenger, top down, and in the back sat his wife, Gilbert on the jump seat, Gilbert's brother Jack beside the chauffeur. Mr. Miller groaned, "My God, it looks like a rainy matinee in Baltimore!"

꙳   ꙳   ꙳   ꙳   ꙳

Whitebait and oyster crab, stainless steel, celery tonic, spoonbread, hangnails, massage, licorice, funerals, these are a few of my *un*favorite things.

# Right in the Middle of
# His Forehead

STROLLING UP to Fifth Avenue from the Algonquin, Charlie MacArthur and Benchley waited till the cars halted for the traffic light, then both stepped forward, carefully placed something under the first car, jumped away, their hands over their ears.

People hurriedly got out of the car and looked. A policeman looked. Pedestrians looked. All that was there was city dirt and a used match from the Algonquin bar.

I met Charlie in Chicago in Ned Sheldon's room at the Presbyterian Hospital, out on Chicago's West Side. Charlie's brother Alfred had married Ned's sister Mary. That's all I knew about Charlie, except that Ned said he was a good newspaperman. In Ned's room was Lenore Ulric, starring in *Kiki* down in Chicago's Loop, and when Lenore left Ned's room, Charlie left with her. And that's all I know about that.

Draw the veil.

The next year, Charlie was around the Algonquin and everybody knew him and he knew everybody. Woollcott claimed he was going to have a great success. This was based on chemistry known only to Woollcott. It upset Swope, who claimed Woollcott was the master of snap judgments.

Sometime after that, Charlie and Ned Sheldon, now back in New York, put their heads together and *Lulu Belle* starring Lenore was Belasco's big hit at the Belasco. If you asked Swope what he thought of Woollcott's snap judgment, he was inclined to change the subject.

*Lulu Belle* was the first legit black-and-white show and was sensational. Among other wonders, Henry Hull drove a Ford around the Belasco stage and off. Lenore put on becoming mulatto greasepaint and was the toast of the town and Charlie MacArthur was in the big money and Woollcott prided himself that he didn't say, "I told you so."

Charlie's romances were unconcealed and brightened the Algonquin, the Penwick, Tony's and the Colony. Then he met Helen.

Like most everything, it started at Neysa's studio. Helen dropped in. Charlie offered her his bag of peanuts. "I wish they were emeralds," he said.

Was it love at first sight? It was for Helen. She had opened the Guild's new theatre, now the ANTA. She was Shaw's Cleopatra to Lionel Atwill's Caesar. Every night since she'd accepted that peanut, she came onstage when the act was called and looked through the peekhole in the curtain.

"What are you looking at?" asked Helen Westley, dressed as Ftatateeta but fooling no one.

"I'm looking for someone I met. He said he'd come to the show."

"But you look every night! Why don't you call him up?"

"Oh, I couldn't."

"Why not?"

"Oh, I couldn't."

"Call him! I call them till they move."

Did Helen call? Or did Charlie show up? One of them must have, because twenty years later when Charlie came back from India he offered Helen a bag of emeralds. "I wish they were peanuts," he said.

Bob Montgomery and Helen were doing a movie. Was it *Another Language?* When it was over, Bob gave Helen a fabulous cabochon-ruby-studded cigarette case. Charlie looked at it, twisted his curl. "I hope you didn't deserve it," he said.

Christmas Eve, Charlie and Helen rushed back to Nyack to trim the tree. Little Mary had hung up her stocking in front of the fireplace where Santa Claus would come down. Beside it Charlie arranged a chair and a small table, then put a cup on it.

"What's that for?" asked Helen.

"Santa. He'll like a cup of Ovaltine." Charlie poured some of Helen's into the bottom of Santa's cup, then went out to the kitchen. From the room back of the kitchen came a bark, then a yelp.

Charlie came back with two stiff white hairs from the West Highland they were giving little Mary for Christmas. "Have you got some New Skin? I want to paste these on Santa's cup."

Little Mary loved the tree and the West Highland and her stocking full of presents, but sat enraptured, looking at the cup Santa had drunk Ovaltine out of and left two whiskers on the side.

"What are you going to call your dog?" asked Helen.

"Best Whiskers," said Mary.

Things had slowed up for Charlie. Not too much was doing. He chartered a boat and rode up and down the Hudson and around by Spuyten Duyvil to Long Island, but there still was a lot of time. He twisted his forehead curl and looked off across a lot of space. "It's a charming thing to be due places," he said.

Charlie was ill.

On the radio they said it was serious. We told the driver to drive us to New York Hospital. It was almost midnight when we went through the quiet halls. The nurse left her desk and went for Helen.

"Come and see him," she said.

At the end of the hall, she opened a door into a room like something in science fiction. It was dimly lit. A nurse stood silently by. On a high bed was Charlie, a canopy over him and instruments helping him to breathe.

His face looked dark and troubled. I couldn't find Charlie. Was Helen aware of the change? She looked at him with love and hope. "It's a question now of if he can only pee."

Before the matinee I went out to the pay station by the doorman's table. "Mr. Charles MacArthur . . . oh . . ."

In the house at Nyack we sat waiting for the service. We'd been to services there for Helen's mother, for Mary, now it was for Charlie. His brother Alfred and Alfred's wife Mary had flown from

317

Chicago. And his brother John. And his sister Helen drove over from Alpine. That was all that was left of the family of the itinerant preacher and the Canadian girl.

We sat waiting in the house in Nyack, the town where Charlie came as a boy with his father and remembered it and brought Helen and Mary to this house they loved and changed and rechanged and worked in and bought the redwood tennis-court poles for and built the pool overlooking the Hudson River, then Charlie had had to order hundred-pound cakes of ice to cool it off on a summer's day. Alfred looked round him and said, "Why don't you give this place to the Actors' Home, Helen?"

Did I see Charlie twist his curl and laugh that laugh that sounded not so much like a laugh as the *end* of a laugh?

❀   ❀   ❀   ❀   ❀

Emerson writes that "Captain John Brown of Ossawatamie has a flock of three thousand sheep. He knows the face of every one of them." Do you and I know the face of three thousand anything? Emerson says, "Captain John Brown knew the minute a stray sheep entered his fold." He knew it wasn't a face he recognized.

Is *your* memory like that?

"A grazier knew every horse that came into Concord from up country. Every horse that came in town from that part of Mass."

When was the last time *you* read about a grazier? Did you ever think of improving your vocabulary? A lot of words get lost.

❀   ❀   ❀   ❀   ❀

So did André Previn's key.

André wanted to get the song finished.

"I've got it all except one line," said Alan Jay Lerner, "and I have five to choose from."

"Well, would you choose one?"

"I will."

"But I mean now." André was in his Conductor of London's Symphony Orchestra office. He wanted this song done and off his mind.

"I will," said Alan, the perfectionist.

"But when? If you've got five, choose one now."

"I'll do it, just be patient."

"When?"

"I'll do it."

"I'll wait." André threw his office key out the window.

"Oh, come on," said Alan. "I know you've got another."

"No, I haven't."

The song got finished that night. London Symphony had to make their conductor a new key.

❋    ❋    ❋    ❋    ❋

Up in Edinburgh I went to a bakeshop and cake store. On the floor above it was a restaurant. "Do you smoke?" asked the woman in charge.

"Yes," I said.

"Next floor above."

I went up another flight. It didn't look as family style as the floor below, so I went back. "I won't smoke."

She showed me to a table where sat a Scotswoman, spare, gray-haired, sweet-faced. She wore a gray-blue tweed coat and a black hat. "I'll take brown Windsor soup," she told the waitress, then turned to me. "You're an American."

"Yes."

"I'm sixty-eight, will be sixty-nine in March." She told it with pride. "I have Saturdays and Sundays off, I work at a carpet factory. Really *hard* work, I stand up at loom all day, and sometimes even after years of experience the threads break. That's, of course, when the thread is na' good. And when it breaks, then of course it tangles and has to be sorted out and re-threaded again. Tangling can be ter-rible! Saturday and Sunday I looked forward to, for Friday I work from seven-thirty in morning until eight-fifteen at night, fifty minutes off for lunch."

"Do you bring it with you?"

"A woman across the way serves the meal at her house. Soup, meat, potatoes—always a big dish of potatoes—vegetable and pudding. All different kinds with milk on. Other days than Friday I work only until five-thirty. Do you know that sometimes I make as high as nine pounds a week? Always I make eight. That's verra good."

"Do you get overtime?"

"There's na' overtime. I've been working fifty-five years and during World War One was at —"

I couldn't understand the name. The Scottish accent made it a stumper. We both laughed when I finally got it. "Bonnie Rig," I said.

"You ha' a strong American accent, but you pronounced that na' bad. Did I say it's where I worked during war? During war there was na' carpet business. At Bonnie Rig I worked at sorting out nuts and bolts. That was all right for war, but war over, I was glad to get back to loom again. In America, do you have old-age pension?"

"Yes."

"Here a woman of sixty years starts getting ten shilling a week. At sixty-five she gets three pound. At seventy, three pound ten and that is the limit. That is the most you get, but that you get until you pass on. That's verra good, though a man at seventy gets four pound, but he does na' start to get pension till he turns sixty-five. You're no eatin' your potatoes."

"I don't want to get fat."

"Oh, you'll no get fat on potato. I eat a big dish every day and I'm no fat. A nice thing to have is a big dish of potatoes mashed together wi' turnip or a big dish of potatoes and cabbage. Cabbage is very good. How old are *you?*"

"I'm sixty-eight."

"Look out for twinges of rheumatism. I had phlebitis four years ago and never ha' been quite the same. We stand up to looms and that's hard. They put in some tip-seats, but they were na' good. Too small and the seat was a hard board. They were na' comfortable. Sometimes I roll a barrel in, tip it up and I have a cushion I put on the top. It's good, but mind you don't get it in others' way. Our manager is very good. He came up from Dumfries, a young man of forty-nine. His plan was to speed us up. He was troubled at old folks working at looms. The old were troubled, as well, they felt they would be dismissed, but when manager heard, he said na' to worry. None would be dismissed for old age. That's a fine ring you have on. Was that mutton good?"

"Very."

"Is that real cream on the peaches?"

"No, but it's good."

"I thought it was na' real cream. Had it been real, they'd na' give you tha' much."

     \* \* \* \* \*

Do you like a slice of raw onion with your hamburger? Frank Sinatra knows the kind to get. At the Tamarisk Golf Club he heard me say to the waiter, "Slice of raw onion, please."

"Do you like Maui onions?" asked Frank.

"What are they?"

"Maui onions?"

"I never had any."

"George." He didn't raise his voice, he just said "George" and George Jacobs was at his shoulder. "Send for some Maui onions. Tell them to have them here right away."

The following twilight Mia and Garson and I were trying to find the road back to Cathedral City. Garson at the wheel tried this turn and that. Left? Right? Right? Left? To while away the twilight, Mia turned on the radio. "Temperature in the low desert ranging from 40° in the night to 85° by day. In the mountains 20° to 61°. That's the weather, folks. Do you like onions? Frank Sinatra does. Yesterday he had a hamburger at a country club and they didn't have Maui onions, so he phoned the island of Maui and two bushels are being delivered to his Cathedral City hacienda in time for dinner tonight."

     \* \* \* \* \*

Before there was air-conditioning, all the theatres left their fire doors open. Wander out of the Booth on a warm night and look in all the fire doors in the alley. After a scene in *Saturday's Children,*

321

step out and look in the Plymouth's fire door at Marjorie Rambeau in Zoë Akins' *Daddy's Gone A-Hunting* or see a scene of *Tarzan* at the Broadhurst. Between cues, everybody drifted round the alley, including Tarzan's moth-eaten lion. He came out to cool off, got mixed up and went back into the Plymouth and stayed to watch Marjorie Rambeau.

The act ended and the stage manager started onstage. The old lion was still watching. He ushered him across the alley into his own theatre, then knocked at Dressing Room One. "Miss Rambeau, why didn't you tell me!"

"Tell you what?"

"That there was a lion there."

Marjorie Rambeau shrugged her shoulders. "Listen, if Maude Adams comes off and says there's a lion there, OK, but if Rambeau comes off and says there's a lion, you think she's pissed."

For Marjorie Rambeau's Broadway debut, she and her husband Willard Mack were in a play he wrote called *So Much for So Much*. I was in the gallery on a pass from the Three Arts Club. Was it 1914? It was when I still thought a show was meant to be enjoyed. Passes from the Three Arts Club and the American Academy of Dramatic Arts got me in to see all that season's failures. Five that Harrison Gray Fiske directed all starred Rita Jolivet. She had gone down on the *Titanic* and come up again and wouldn't you think that was enough? No. Five shows starring her went down.

Did she get discouraged? I never saw her after 1915, but Marjorie Rambeau I did. She was the first actress that sounded like a person just saying things that happened to be in her head. Back at the Three Arts Club I tried to do it, too, but that's harder than you think.

❋   ❋   ❋   ❋   ❋

So are a lot of other things. At the Arthur Rubinsteins' I met Marcel Pagnol again after forty-one years. If it's only every forty-one years you run into someone, it takes a minute to catch up. Forty-one years ago his *Marius* and *Topaze* were the two greatest hits in Paris. "Do you speak English now?" I asked.

322

"No, but I read it. I read Shakespeare *very* well, *Variety* I *still* cannot read."

❋   ❋   ❋   ❋   ❋

Do you get frightened? Do people say not to? Do they tell you not to worry? Who *wants* to? I'd stop it if I could.

# Look Up, Pauline

E THEL BARRYMORE had a lot of things to worry about, but no one can remember that she did. Did she learn not to at Sir Henry Irving's Lyceum Theatre? She was engaged to act with Sir Henry and Ellen Terry in *Peter the Great*. Her part was one scene, but good. Opening night at the Lyceum she stood in the wings ready to go on. It got nearer and nearer to her cue.

It was Ellen Terry who spoke it.

Ethel braced herself. She was eighteen. It was her London debut. Ready. Now. What? What was she hearing?

Ellen Terry skipped the cue for Ethel's scene and *Peter the Great* was barreling right along.

At supper afterward in the Beefsteak Room, Sir Henry asked, "How did that happen?"

"What?" asked Ellen Terry.

"You missed Ethel's cue and we skipped the scene."

"We did?" said Ellen. "Oh my child, I'm so sorry."

Ellen Terry was a wonderful actress. Was she a wonderful actress offstage, too? Ethel Barrymore could never decide if Ellen Terry had forgotten, or purposely left the scene out opening night.

Well, whichever, that's *not* show business.

That was when Ethel was in her teens. When she was a little girl, the Maurice Barrymores took a house in St. John's Wood where Sunday afternoon Georgie Drew Barrymore received. The children, all dressed up, came down to the drawing room. Jack was too young to be useful, but little Ethel and Lionel passed the cakes. Ethel was shy and when there were strangers she kept her head down.

"Look up, Pauline," her mother reminded her. It was a line from *The Lady of Lyons* that Georgie Drew and Maurice had played in.

One Sunday little Ethel was passing the tea cake.

"Look up, Pauline," said her mother's soft voice.

She looked up and screamed, the tea cakes fell to the floor. She looked at a great white face framed with red hair. It was Oscar Wilde.

Young star Ethel Barrymore was playing *Cousin Kate* at Boston's Majestic. Sir Henry Irving was at the Colonial. Both stage doors opened on the same alley and when Ethel finished her matinee, she crossed over.

From the wings she watched Sir Henry, heard the salvos as the great man walked off. "Ethel, my dear! What a pleasure." He kissed her. "How is your new play?"

"The Boston critics roasted us," she said forlornly.

"But *Cousin Kate* is a very good play. It was much admired in London."

"They weren't so hard on the *play*, but *I* got it."

"Why, what did they say?"

"I traded on my mannerisms."

The great man patted her head. "Make sure they never say anything else, my dear."

Everyone was in love with Ethel Barrymore including red-haired Winston Churchill, but *she* loved Russell Colt. Mr. Colt Senior was a Rhode Island tycoon and he liked his actress daughter-in-law. "If you see a good house out in the country I'll buy it for you, if it's not just some pretty place. It must be a good piece of *property*."

Ethel thought about where would be near enough to drive back and forth from the theatre. Mamaroneck seemed a good spot.

"There's a house on Taylor Lane," said the agent.

Ethel looked at it and wrote Mr. Colt Senior, "Taylor Lane, Mamaroneck."

Mr. Colt went to Taylor Lane and bought the house. He told his daughter-in-law, "If you ever wish to give up the stage and go in the real-estate business, I'll back you," and presented her with the deed.

"How did you know a good house?" I asked. All her life she'd lived in hotels and boardinghouses, how could she know a good piece of real estate?

Ethel claimed she didn't.

"Then how did you choose?"

"It had a big front hall and I thought what a good place for a little boy to fling his cap."

She had the house on Taylor Lane and an apartment at 36 West 59th Street in New York. Then came the time when they tore the building down and built another one. The new one was called 36 Central Park South.

Walking by one day, Ethel remembered how lucky she'd been in the old building and went in and leased the eighth floor east.

From her windows she could look across the park at what used to be the old B. F. Keith's Colonial. Now Walter Hampden had his repertory there. She agreed to go over and play Ophelia to Walter's Hamlet.

That did well enough. Then Willie Maugham sent her his new play. She said yes. *The Constant Wife* had its opening in Cleveland. Ethel forgot her lines a lot and George Cukor, hidden in the fireplace, whispered them to her. Together they brought the evening to a close.

Maugham remembered, "She threw her arms around me and said, 'Willie, I ruined your beautiful play tonight, but it'll run a year.'"

It did.

They were opening at the Maxine Elliott Theatre. So much depends on the opening. How do you prepare for it? What do you do all day? Do you rest? Do you what? What do you eat? Where? When? How?

I rang Ethel up and said, "Opening night my cook will cook you dinner here." Our apartment was like hers. We were the fifth floor east.

"Lovely," said Ethel.

"What time do you like to eat?"

"Six?"

"Six. Sarah will serve you dinner."

Sarah had come up from the Carolinas. Had she ever seen a play?

"Sarah, day after tomorrow I want you to cook dinner for Miss Ethel Barrymore. She'll come down here and she'll be alone. I'll go out. Sarah, day after tomorrow may be the most important night of Miss Barrymore's life.. No matter what she does, it's *all right*. She may be nervous. She may eat or she may *not*. I'll order dinner and she may not eat any of it or maybe she will. Maybe she'll eat it all. Anyway, Sarah, whatever she does, don't pay any attention, because this is a *great* night in her life. She'll come down at six, you serve her clear tomato soup with croutons, roast chicken, mashed potato, string beans, lettuce salad, apple pie and coffee. Now remember, Sarah, she may eat only salad. Only—"

"Yes, ma'am."

A little before six I went out and didn't see Sarah till she brought my breakfast tray next morning. "Was everything all right?" I asked.

"Everything fine."

"You served the dinner?"

Sarah nodded. "She ate fine."

"Did she eat it all?"

She nodded. "We took our coffee in the parlor."

Did Ethel ask Sarah to sit down and have dinner with her? "We took our coffee in the parlor"?

What was *that!* Goodnight, Sarah, wher*ever* you are, you were nice.

Ethel's cousin Georgie Drew Mendum married an actor. "The family always referred to him as 'the lame excuse,'" said Ethel. What play was *that* a line from?

Garson and I went to see *The Two Mrs. Carrolls*.

"How was it?"

"Bergner was great."

"Great?"

"Great!"

"You must have caught her on an off night."

Ethel and Garson and I were ready to leave Fanny Brice's when Fanny rushed to the upstairs phone to get a report on the Dalton

Trumbo play she'd invested in. They'd had the opening that night in New Haven. We stood at the foot of the stairs waiting to hear.

Fanny rushed down, tripped and fell. "Honest to God, kid, it's not the money," she said as Garson helped her up. "It looks like a hit. Only the theatre seemed a little big. Next week they play Boston, at the Wilbur they'll be heard."

Ethel nodded. "The first night I was starred was in a play in Philadelphia where my grandmother had the Arch Street Theatre. I was nervous and from the gallery I heard a voice call out, 'Speak up, Ethel, you Drews is all good actors.'"

"You Jews is all good actors?" asked Fanny.

Out of all show business, only Ethel Barrymore's close friend Fanny had never heard of the Drews.

The big ANTA benefit was at the Ziegfeld Theatre. Tony Perry, Brooks Atkinson and a committee chose scenes and numbers from treasured plays and musicals. Francine Larrimore came out of retirement for *Let Us Be Gay*, Ray Massey stopped whatever he was doing and we did a scene from *Ethan Frome*. The big event was when Ethel said she'd come back from the movies and do *The Twelve-Pound Look*. J. M. Barrie wrote it and Ethel played it in vaudeville in the days when she and Sarah Bernhardt were the only greats to play the two-a-day. Whenever her Charles Frohman play closed its season and Ethel felt the pinch, she spoke to Martin Beck and charmed the B. F. Keith circuit or the Orpheum time.

The part that Barrie had written was the wife of a wealthy, mean Englishman and when he left home in the morning, his wife, with her portable typewriter, went out to earn twelve pounds toward becoming self-supporting.

Next on the program for ANTA:

*Miss Ethel Barrymore*

IN

J. M. BARRIE'S

THE TWELVE-POUND LOOK

It's a wonder the Ziegfeld didn't fall apart with all the cheers, salvos, applause. Beautiful Ethel Barrymore in navy-blue coat and hat came on carrying her bag with the typewriter.

If the theatre didn't go to pieces, the audience did. For us of the theatre, Ethel Barrymore *is* theatre. Niece of the great John Drew, granddaughter of the great Mrs. Drew, daughter of Georgie Drew and Maurice Barrymore, sister of Lionel and John, she left the films of Hollywood, rode across California, Arizona, New Mexico, Colorado, Kansas, Missouri, crossed the Mississippi to Fort Madison, Iowa, rode on through Illinois, Indiana, Ohio, cut across the corner of Pennsylvania, into New York State to play her vaudeville play for ANTA at the Ziegfeld Theatre.

Of course we rose. Of course we applauded. Of course we cheered. Of course we wept.

Ethel waited. The ovation went on. And on. She waited, then stepped forward and smiled. "You make it very tempting," she said and went into the first line of Barrie's play.

❈ ❈ ❈ ❈ ❈

Ever go behind the scenes of a restaurant? Charles Masson showed me his. One hot Sunday afternoon I was walking past La Grenouille and he waved to me from the upstairs window. He and Mme. Masson and their little girl were there doing something. "Come and see it," he said. He was wearing a crumpled blue Hawaiian shirt and I was wearing a rumpled pink Lilly Pulitzer, not right for Grenouille, but today the chairs were stacked on the preferred tables. No flowers. Everything quiet.

Mr. Masson led me through the room where they seat the people who ask for ketchup. Through a door and we were in the serving pantry. How small! How clean! *Up* a flight to the kitchen? The kitchen is upstairs?

It's no larger than our kitchen in California. In that compact spot they concoct the quenelles? The Homard au Porto? Poulet Rôti Basquais? Salade Niçoise? Ratatouille? Canard à l'Orange? Mousse, tartes, île flottante?

"Here's an oven for our soufflés," said Mr. Masson.

It looked like a steel bureau, with a drawer where each soufflé cooks. "Here are the dishes in the hot cabinet. And the cups."

How clean! And what little space! Think of dinner at Gre-

329

nouille. The precision. The style. And it's up one flight in a place with no room to spare, like the works in the case of your watch.

"Here is the wine room, this building has no cellar."

Wine is taking it easy in individual crannies.

"Here is where the waiters change."

Racks and coat hangers in a place no bigger than where the Supreme Court Justices change, but there are only nine of them.

"How can anything be so clean?"

"Every night after we close, it is scraped and blasted and washed. Even the stoves come out from the walls. Everything is on wheels. That is my own invention."

"Who comes in first every day?"

"Me. At five-thirty I choose the meat, the fruit, the vegetables, the fish, then I do the flowers."

Why do I think about Toscanini? "Maestro, how do you learn all those scores by heart?"

"I *learn* them."

Do *you?*

Think it over. When things are well done, there's usually a reason.

❋   ❋   ❋   ❋   ❋

Carol Matthau does things *her* way. And always did. In the days when Oona moved over to Carol's the rule was "Be in before eleven."

"So we had to do everything before eleven," said Carol.

It was working out, then Carol's beau had to go away for three weeks. "I want you to write me a letter every day," he said.

"Oh, Bill, I can't."

"You have to."

"But I write such dreadful letters."

"Every day." And the way he looked, Carol knew he meant it.

She wept, then she and Oona tried some. Carol was right, she did write dreadful letters.

"Jerry writes me *great* ones," said Oona. "We can get stuff out of his."

They went to work. A letter went off every day. Jerry was a faithful writer, his letters to Oona got copied and kept everything status quo, although when Bill got back, he said Carol was right.

"Was I, darling?"

"You certainly can't write a letter."

Carol looked downcast, but only momentarily, because they got married. And not long after, Oona married Charlie.

No more eleven o'clock rule, the two couples went out on Charlie's boat. Bill brought a book along. "This guy's the best that's writing today." He held up *The Catcher in the Rye*.

"You didn't *use* to think so," said Carol.

"When?"

"When you said I couldn't write letters. They were all of them copies of Jerry Salinger's."

And so forth and so on, until everybody forgave or forgot, and when Lucy Saroyan was ten, she came for dinner in a beautiful sprigged muslin bought by Bill in India and white gloves bought by Carol.

At table, count on Lucy to carry on. When a pause draws out, rely on Lucy. She'd been photographed by Avedon for his ten most beautiful women when *she* was only ten. She'd given Gloria Vanderbilt advice about trouble. She'd endeared herself to Ed Sullivan by nearly blacking out when she actually met him.

Driving to the theatre, Lucy interrupted herself as we passed the Morosco Theatre where her mother was playing in Sam Behrman's play. The car halted in the theatre jam, Lucy leaned forward and pointed to the blowups. "You see that one with the black hair?"

It was Suzanne Pleshette. Suzanne Pleshette had made the hit of the show.

"I hate her guts," said Lucy.

Well, that's show business.

&#x273D;  &#x273D;  &#x273D;  &#x273D;  &#x273D;

When I act in a movie they always get me a stand-in my age or older. In *Where's Poppa?* she was twenty and pretty and had a beautiful figure.

331

"At lunch hour could I use your onstage dressing room to sleep in? I'm up late and if I could sleep an hour, that would be the difference."

"Why don't you go to bed at night?"

"I'm in the show."

"What show?"

"*Oh! Calcutta!*"

That's *my* stand-in? Things are looking up. Then a thought struck me. If *she* can't make it to *Oh! Calcutta!* do I stand in for her? Wouldn't that only be tit for tat?

Leonard Lyons put it in his column.

"Thank you so *much*," said my stand-in.

"Why thank *me*?"

"My roommate at the show says you must have sent it in, it's too refined to come from *our* press agent."

❊   ❊   ❊   ❊   ❊

Do you know how to tip? Garson does. Only once did he feel doubtful. We had a lot of luggage we were bringing from London to Paris on the Golden Arrow. Claridge's man came down to Victoria to see our bags on the train. "At Dover there'll be a man that will see your things onto the Channel boat. Just let him know you'll look after him."

"How can I do that?" asked Garson.

"Just make the gesture." He slid his hand in his pants pocket.

At Dover, Garson called a porter, slid his hand in his pants pocket and said, "I need help with my luggage."

He got it.

You will, too. Just make the gesture.

❊   ❊   ❊   ❊   ❊

Do you know the Biltmore Theatre where *Hair* is playing? I was at the opening night of that theatre. That threescore-and-ten stuff can't be on the level! I can not only remember the Biltmore Theatre opening, but I can also remember that Elizabeth Marbury, leading play agent of her time, was there, accompanied by friends Elsie de Wolfe and Anne Morgan. She strolled down the aisle to where the usher stood with her tickets, Elsie and Anne passed to their seats and Bessie Marbury sat down on the aisle seat and went right through to the floor.

She threatened to sue, but her lawyer advised her not to. Could she swear she hadn't *asked* for a seat on the orchestra floor?

❋   ❋   ❋   ❋   ❋

Larry Olivier and Garson and I went to Philadelphia to see the first performance of *Gypsy*. None of us had ever seen a first performance of a musical and *Gypsy*'s first night at Philadelphia's Shubert seemed as perfect as when I saw it later in New York. There was only one word for Ethel Merman. Great. She played Rose, Gypsy's mother, as though she'd done it all her life. Young Sandra Church was adorable as Gypsy. In the long black dress and gloves and boa, she sang "Let Me Entertain You" as though she'd sung it for weeks. As she started the strip, the zipper of the black dress stuck. Sandra kept on singing, but slithered over to the first entrance. "Let me entertain you," she sang as Ethel's capable hand came through the black velvet side curtain and the zipper responded. "Let me—"

The show went on. Rose had given Gypsy first aid in the strip department, as she did in real life.

Well, that's show business.

# *Fanny*

WEDNESDAYS and Saturdays when she was in a show, you could find Fanny Brice after the matinee sitting at Dinty Moore's. Hers was the table around from Miss Moore's desk. On her lap was a big yellow bowl, on the table a dish of boiled potatoes to mash while carrying on a talk with her own personal Touchstone, Roger Davis. Their talk had gone on for years. "Where'd you get that, dear?" He pointed to her diamond bracelet. "Was that the one you bought at Coney Island? Emma Maloof gets all her jewelry there."

Emma Maloof had a shop on Madison offering panne velvet tea gowns to widows. Georgette hostess robes sagged in the showcase. Crepe meteor blouses on dummies, designed to conceal every line. "Emma says this year she favors only raincoats. After I wrote *As You Like It* I never went out in anything not an Emma Maloof. Did you read my notices? Nothing's ever been like them."

Roger had been in a lot of shows with Fanny. There was always something he could play. Any show she was in had to make room for her friends. So did her California house. Valeska Suratt might drift down the stairs the way she had in the *Follies*. Only then it was for a number, at Fanny's it was for dinner.

"What are you doing now, Miss Suratt?" somebody asked her.

"I'm writing the life of Lafayette."

"*You* couldn't write the life of Herman Timberg!" sneered another guest. At Fanny's the air was charged.

The great Harry Pilcer, who had been Gaby Deslys' partner and had danced on every stage in Europe, was sojourning at Fanny's. "I'll carve the roast," he offered.

Fanny passed him the carving knife and served her mashed potatoes. Harry carved a slice.

"You cut roast beef too thick," said his hostess.

"Cut it yourself!" screamed Harry and dropped the carving knife. He could live through his escape from Europe, he could put up with having no job, he could bear his hair getting thinner, but questioning his carving? He couldn't take it.

Well, that's show business.

Fanny married Billy Rose and they lived up on Madison at the new hotel, the Westbury. After the theatre everybody dropped in at their suite. Great spiced beef, great rye bread, great stories. On her dressing table was a gold plaque from her new husband. Before they were married, for propriety's sake and the children's he had to roost under the eaves at the house on Fire Island. Engraved on the gold was YOUR BOARDER FROM GOOSE HEAVEN.

꙳   ꙳   ꙳   ꙳   ꙳

Beatrice Straight sat next to me at the Running Footman with a girl with shiny, shiny hair and no hair tint.

"This is Daphne Harrington," said Beatrice.

"Hello, Daphne, how do you get your hair shiny, shiny?"

"I lie with my head over the foot of the bed and brush it."

It pays to ask. I guess it also doesn't hurt if you're an acrobat. Can *you* lie with your head over the foot of the bed and brush? And why does it make me think of Everett Sloane, who said, "Now, if they could only think of something to keep the leg makeup off your ears"? It was at a rehearsal of Don Stewart's *How I Wonder*, when Ray Massey said the lipstick came off when Meg Mundy kissed him.

"Powder down?"

"It doesn't work," said Massey. The air was fraught.

The man in Gray's Cut Rate Drug Store said, "Sta-Kiss." He

showed Garson. "Put the lipstick on, let it dry, then put Sta-Kiss on and nothing comes off."

At rehearsal Garson told Meg to put the lipstick on, let it dry, put the Sta-Kiss on, let it dry and plant one on Massey. It worked. The company stood around marveling. "Now," said Ev Sloane, "if they could only think of something to keep the leg makeup off your ears."

Did a funny guy like that have to kill himself?

✳   ✳   ✳   ✳   ✳

"The Kennedys are an engaging family."

Does that sound like Beverly Hills? Does that sound like Broadway? Or Park Avenue? Does that sound like supper on Dumbarton Avenue? Joe Alsop was entertaining Alice Longworth. Who else says a family is "engaging"?

"Jack was Erin Go Bragh. Bobby was Dark Rosaleen. And Teddy? He could be the son of Jim Farley," she said in her engaging voice.

Why shouldn't *I* say engaging? As a young lady in Wollaston, I longed for ways to improve myself. I read, "No lady would dream of carrying a parcel," so I didn't. "A lady carries nothing more bulky than a letter."

I was so intent on improving myself that I didn't notice my family much, but when my mother burst into tears, that attracted my attention.

"What's the matter, Mama?"

She threw down the *Boston Globe*. Would a lady do that?

"Oh, *poor* President Roosevelt!"

"What happened?"

"His daughter Alice was asked to leave the lobby of the Copley Plaza. She was *smoking a cigarette*."

How I wished someone would ask *me* to leave the Copley Plaza.

"How did *you* feel?" I asked her.

"Delighted." Or did she say "bully"?

# Between the Ritz and
# Providence

H OWARD STURGES had been Cole's best friend since Yale. His
family came from Providence where the New England in-
habitants have time to say Weybosset Street. Most of New England calls its shopping street Main or High, but Providence has
time.

When Howard was a little boy, Mr. Sturges called the family
into his study. "I want you to see a passport," he said. "Your
brother needs this to go to Russia. Look at it closely, children. This
is your brother's passport."

Passports were needed only for Russia. The first time the rest of
us saw one was after World War I when we needed not only a
passport but a visa, and paid for one for each country.

During War II Howard took the night shift in Penn Station.
Down on the mezzanine below the gates to trains going to Washington and Philadelphia and the South, Howard looked after anyone in uniform from midnight to five.

"Where will I find you if I want to write?" asked René Clair.

"I'll be between the Ritz and Providence."

The first time I ever heard of him, I read in the Boston Globe
that "Fashionable debutante Miss Eleonora Sears of Pride's Crossing walked from Boston to Providence with her escort Mr. Howard Sturges."

The express train took forty-five minutes, so no wonder they

337

wrote it up in the *Boston Globe*.

When Howard served his guests, he tasted the wine, then drank no more.

"When did you stop drinking?" I asked.

"When they found me lying face down in the gutter outside Maxim's, wearing a picture hat."

Howard's mother was also between Providence and the Ritz. The Paris Ritz. Howard says he and his pa were coming into the grand lobby just as his mother came toward them, majestic as only the lady of a Rhode Island first family could be. Like a frigate heading into Newport, she crossed the lobby, her train rustling behind her, and riding skillfully on it was her Pekinese.

Howard knew everybody. Grandes dames, femmes fatales, the elite and the rooty-toots. Just mention Consuelo Balsan, Katherine Duer Blake, Boston's Gladys Deacon or the Fenway's Mrs. Jack. He called *her* Aunt Belle.

He said that on Ash Wednesday Aunt Belle's coachman drove her to the Church of the Ascension, lifted out a bucket of soapy water and brushes for Aunt Belle, down on her knees, to scrub the church's steps. That was to kick off Lent.

In October she watched football at Groton. Her nephew played and some afternoons Aunt Belle came out and sat on the bleachers, her pointed black satin slippers resting on the bleacher below. On one toe shone a big ruby, on the other shone a big sapphire.

She didn't like to put up with things. If there was snow in front of her Beacon Street house, she told her coachman to drive onto the sidewalk and she stepped out onto her steps.

Sometimes she put her baby leopard on a leash and took him shopping in the fashionable Tremont Street stores.

When she wanted to go shopping for her Florentine palace, she chose a Harvard boy named Bernard Berenson to go with her. Together they combed Europe for its treasures.

I asked a ninety-three-year-old charmer who had known her if Mrs. Jack had liked Mr. Gardner.

She thought for a few minutes. "She liked his money," she said.

When Eleonora and Howard weren't walking to Providence, they sometimes went to tea with Aunt Belle. Just the three sipped tea, surrounded with treasures. On the wall hung Mr. Sargent's portrait in the tight black velvet dress with the rope of Gardner pearls round her waist instead of her throat. All Boston had been shocked. Tea was skimpy, but it was served on priceless Sèvres. On a plate entitled to a glass case over it were three Five O'Clock Tea biscuits, one with the end knocked off.

Nothing was knocked off at Sturges' Rue Monsieur apartment in Cole Porter's house. On *his* Sèvres plate was goat cheese. The first I ever had. "Goat cheese goes well with rough red wine," he said. And it did. It and the goat cheese looked beautiful on the white damask cloth with its own fringe below the broad red-and-white border. Napkins to match.

"When your mother dies, who gets her table linen?" asked Natasha Wilson, born Princess Paley, so her own table linen must have been pretty good.

When Howard died, I hope she got his.

"I'll be between the Ritz and Providence," he said. It was his best description.

✻   ✻   ✻   ✻   ✻

People lose their shirt, but do you know anybody lost their pants? Estelle Winwood did. Elegant, exciting, English, the stage manager told Al Woods that she was temperamental. He told Al Woods he had to put up with a lot.

One performance her pants started to slip down. What would you do? She moved behind the piano, never missed a line, let her pants drop off, kicked them back of a potted palm, came back to her rightful stage center and went on, elegant, exciting, English.

Back of that palm was a hole where a heavy electric cable went through to light the stage.

"Take over," the stage manager told his assistant and got a coat hanger. He poked it through the hole, caught up Estelle's wispy chiffon drawers and ran to the Eltinge where Al was enjoying the evening, tilted against his theatre.

The stage manager waved the pants at him. "Didn't I tell you she's temperamental!"

❀   ❀   ❀   ❀   ❀

Do you struggle to get things right? Anita May does. "Clarence, put it *here*," says Anita.

"Yes, ma'am."

"Clarence, when you serve a cocktail, do it *this* way." Anita shows him.

"Yes, ma'am."

"Clarence, *not* like that. Like *this*." Anita does it.

"Yes, ma'am."

The phone rang and Clarence bowed and went to answer.

"Anita, how long has Clarence been your butler?"

"Forty-seven years."

"Why do you keep at him?"

Anita looked astonished. "I'm *training* him."

Well, Anita's right. And after seventy-four years I'm taking a page out of her book and training myself. I've got a lot more to me than meets the eye. Have you? Think it over and get training. If Clarence and I are the only ones getting it right, it'll be lonely up there.

# Neysa Girl

AT HER EASEL stood Neysa McMein, her extraordinary face smudged with varicolored pastel chalk. She peered through wisps of straight blond hair at her model. Everyone dropped in to her studio and talked above the El's roar.

There of an afternoon were Woollcott and Reinald Werrenrath and Kathleen and Charles Norris and Scotti and Lenore Ulric and Averell Harriman and F.P.A. and Mrs. Raoul Fleischmann who'd lived on the right side of the tracks in Quincy, Illinois.

Neysa came from the wrong side of the tracks in Quincy, Illinois, and when she was old enough she went down to the station and came to New York. She holed up at the old Lincoln Arcade.

Was it with Solita Solano and Janet Flanner? It was where Lincoln Center now rises.

Neysa and chums had money for one meal a day only, so they ate popcorn and drank water to make it swell up and fill the aching void. A numerologist said to change her name from Marge and enroll at the Art Students' League. Pretty soon she was as sought after to do magazine covers as Howard Chandler Christy and Penryn Stanlaw. Popcorn became a thing of the past. Nobody got paid higher than Neysa girl. Her studio at 57th and Sixth Avenue with the El rattling past was the only salon in New York. Neysa and Benchley and Woollcott decided to give Irving Berlin a birthday party and not since Captain Hook ordered "a rich damp cake with green icing on it" to bring an end to Peter Pan had there been such a cake. Dean's was commanded to bake it and did, against their better judgment and only after sharp words from Alexander Humphrey Woollcott. It was a beautiful-looking layer cake with nuts and bolts baked in it instead of nuts and raisins.

Lenore Ulric's sight was rather hazy. "What's in here?" she kept asking. "Did I get a nut or a nutshell?" Or was it a bolt?

Across the hall lived Dottie and Ed Parker, and from time to time when Dottie cut her wrists, Neysa and Benchley or some other swain rushed over to stop the flow.

People eddied around the studio and talked with each other or to, or at, or about, then drifted off and were missed or not, but all the time Neysa painted. Feather Havemeyer brought her a diamond feather to be worn as a pin. Zuloaga gave her his portrait. Cole Porter loaned her his chauffeur-driven car, and so that her beautiful long legs could keep warm, Linda Cole Porter left her the mink auto rug marked L.C.P. when the Porters left for Cannes. Woollcott offered her his hand, Jack Baragwanath won hers. So inconsolable was another suitor, it seemed only human to invite him to Spain on the honeymoon. Off they went, all three.

When the old brick building got torn down, Neysa painted and entertained our bridge club at the Hotel des Artistes, 1 West 67th Street. Alice Duer Miller, Mrs. Crosby Gaige, Neysa and I played bridge, but it didn't bother us that we weren't bridge players. If one Thursday Alice went home with two dollars, next Thursday Hilda Gaige would go home with two. And so on and so forth and at four o'clock, no matter what the bid, we stopped for a collation. Out in the kitchen Neysa's secretary Rose checked cups and saucers and what other lovely things?

Neysa whispered, "Rose baked a cake this morning. She hardly ever bakes one, but she's wonderful at it. Praise it. I want to encourage her to do it some more."

"Are you ready?" called Rose.

"When you are," said her tactful boss.

Rose came out of the kitchen carrying a tray with cups, teapot, hot water, cream, lemon, sugar, napkins, plates, all centered on a big pink-frosted octagonal-shaped cake. Led by Neysa, we burst into applause and Rose stumbled and fell.

Neysa's cat, Gooseberry, fur standing on end, went screeching across the room and looked out from under the sofa. Rose lay full length in a welter of cream, sugar and dishes. The pink cake was upside down under Neysa's easel.

Neysa gave an embarrassed laugh, then remembered. "Girls, Rose baked the cake. I know you'll all want some."

"It's ruined," said Rose in tears.

"Why is it? It's just under my easel. Go make tea while I slice it." Why would a girl who'd eaten swollen popcorn waste a cake?

Some people can handle applause and some people can't, but Neysa was right about Rose knowing what to put in a cake. The Ladies' Bridge Club picked things out of the pink frosting and gave forth.

The stock market went up. Jack worked for the Guggenheims and Neysa forsook the West Side for an East 66th Street co-op. Among the dinner guests was Pearl White. Neysa packed a lot of surprises.

"How did you meet her?" asked Alice Miller, impressed.

"I've always known her."

She may have. Neysa was never held down by the truth.

The market was still booming and everybody bought a country house. Neysa's was at Sands Point. Moving out with her went Rose, Marian her cook, little Joan, and Jack Baragwanath who, after four years, Marian still called Mr. Baragander. And of course Neysa's beautiful chinchilla-colored Persian, Gooseberry. Neysa worried about Gooseberry. He was a city cat. How would he do in the country? What if Gooseberry killed a bird?

Draw the veil.

Rose and Marian and Neysa and little Joan and Mr. Baragander all made the change, but alas, it didn't work for poor Gooseberry.

Gooseberry would be eased out into the garden, only to be terrified. You could see him dash across the pansy bed, a robin in hot pursuit. The only place in all Sands Point Gooseberry felt comfortable was under the foundation where a mason left out four bricks.

Floating on her back around her Sands Point pool, Neysa watched her guests jump off the diving board. "Isn't it a great

343

board? Especially built. It has a great give to it. See how it never touches the water? I'll float under it and somebody dive."

"Don't do that, Neysa."

"It's built to. Dive." She floated gently under it and beckoned. A guest dove. Neysa girl went to Doctors' Hospital with a concussion. "It *shouldn't* have hit me," she said. "It's built *not* to."

"Oh ye of little faith" never applied to Neysa girl.

❊   ❊   ❊   ❊   ❊

Do you cry over spilt milk? It spilled over my *King's X* Act I dress that Jed Harris had okayed after I showed him about a hundred and none got a yes. I was so happy to finally know what I was going to open with, I opened a bottle of milk, but when I pushed the cardboard top down, it plooshed over my Act I dress and I burst into tears.

"My God," said Pearl Swope, "when he said yes, why didn't you take your dress off? You certainly took off a lot of others."

❊   ❊   ❊   ❊   ❊

"Know why mules don't go to college?" asks Milton Berle. "Because nobody likes a smart ass."

Well, *that's* true.

# Just People

AT DRESS REHEARSAL the night before *The Guardsman* opened, Maurice Wertheim told Alfred Lunt he didn't like him in the show. Maurice was a banker on the board of directors. *The Guardsman* was the Lunts' first play for the Theatre Guild and Lynn had spent nine hundred dollars on her Act I dress.

"He didn't like me," Alfred told her.

"He didn't like me," he said in the taxi going home.

"He didn't like me," he said as he was getting undressed.

"He didn't like me," he said as she turned out the light.

What was that noise? It woke Lynn. Was it in a dream?

It was Alfred, with his suitcase, starting down the fire escape.

If Lynn hadn't waked up, would theatre history have had a dent!

Some people know their own legends. Ethel did. So do Alfred and Lynn. Should they be backward just because they're famous? They know the legends about Ellen Terry, about Irving, about Dame Madge Kendal, why be obtuse about themselves?

"I must tell you about the *Amphitryon* opening," said Lynn.

Was I really going to hear from *her* what she'd said at their first *Amphitryon* performance? It's become part of theatre lore and now was Lynn going to tell it?

"It was in San Francisco. I don't know whether you remember it or not, but it was a difficult production. *Very* difficult. And this was our first night. No New Haven, no out of town—well, of course, San Francisco I suppose one *might* say is out of town, but it never seems so. And our first night in San Francisco is always a gala, everybody turns out. Well, in a scene with Alfred he suddenly changed all the things we rehearsed. I couldn't believe it, but he did. And he kept *on* doing it. He made odd faces that had *never* been the way we'd rehearsed it. And he did strange gestures. *Very* strange. *Pointing* at me. He'd *never* done that. Well, when the curtain came down I'm afraid I flew at him. 'Alfred, *what* were you doing? You changed completely. *What* were you doing?'

" 'Lynn,' he gasped, 'your breast is out.'

" 'Oh, *don't* tell me things like that, Alfred, until I know my words.' "

Lynn and I have known each other since 1919. Why had we never gone to the theatre together?

A vision, with her enchanting hairdo, full-length sable coat, she and I, arm in arm, were going in to see *Promises, Promises*. Alfred and Garson behind us were absorbed in their topic. As we got near the ticket taker, I slowed Lynn up. "What is it, dear?" she asked.

"Garson has the tickets."

She looked at me, surprised. "Tickets are for *other* people, dear," she said, bowed to the ticket taker and waved me through. "Tickets are for *other* people."

Woollcott came up to Boston for the Lunts' opening. There was a knock at the door. Alfred stood outside.

"Where's your wife?" asked Woollcott.

Alfred just looked at him, then after a moment asked, "Lynn?"

I was playing *Here Today* in Chicago, they were playing *There Shall Be No Night*. We rode down to the theatre in their car.

"Alfred, do you think people can be on the stage as long as we three and be as dedicated as we are and *still* stay people? Or did we give up all that?"

Alfred looked at me aghast. "Of course we're people! I say to Lynnie over and over, 'Lynnie, you *must* be more like an actress,' but look at her! She *will* be just people."

❊   ❊   ❊   ❊   ❊

I wonder if Grace Moore was just people. She loved a farm and her Faraway Meadows was going to be one. She bought the cows and sheep, but a cow kicked her off her stool while milking, so the cows went elsewhere.

The sheep didn't last either. They wouldn't stay in the faraway meadow. They strolled around the terrace, and when Grace drove up, sheep were sitting on her new white furniture. One, stretched out on her chaise longue, craned his neck to see who was making that racket. Her farmer said to wire the meadow so it would give a sheep a little electric shock if it strayed over the fence, but she said that was cruel and they followed the cows elsewhere.

When we bought Faraway Meadows, they told us about the cows and sheep, so we said we'll have pigs and chickens. Our hens wouldn't lay until Laurence Olivier studied the henhouse and said their quarters weren't cramped enough. "To get a hen to lay," said Larry, "she can't be let to move around."

As soon as we cramped them, we had eggs enough to raise all our friends' cholesterol.

With the pigs we never made it. Isn't a pig supposed to eat anything? Ours got sick of corn, got sick of apples, got sick of cake, and when they showed up as bacon, *I* got sick.

A farm is a farm is a farm is a farm, but is that show business? And never mind what Alfred says, I don't think any of us are people.

# Born in Asbury Park

D ID YOU EVER get booed? The great Laurette Taylor did. She
went to London, where the great Charles Cochran presented
her.

LAURETTE TAYLOR

IN

ONE NIGHT IN ROME

Midway in the first act, the gallery started to boo. Catcalls, whistles, boos kept up until the stage manager rang down. Mr. Charles
Cochran went in front of the curtain to address the audience. They
booed him. Consternation in the stalls as well as backstage. Consternation and amazement. How could this happen to the great Laurette? How could this happen to the great Cochran?

Everybody asked everybody the questions.

"Is it because she's an American?"

"Is it because the scenery hung low and the gallery couldn't see?"

"Is it because during the war she didn't do something or other?
Or did?"

Everybody asked everybody and nobody knew the answer.

In her dressing room a distraught Laurette received friends and
sympathizers.

"Darling, it's a disgrace."

"Oh, Miss Taylor, it's too dreadful!"

"Laurette, we're too shocked for words."

Mrs. Pat Campbell strolled in.

"Oh, Stella, what *is* it?"

Mrs. Pat looked in the mirror and applied a little powder. "They just don't like you, dear."

Laurette knocked New York sideways in *Outward Bound*. My houseguest and I went to see it at Mr. Brady's Playhouse. A lot of shows didn't appeal to my houseguest, but a minute after Laurette came on, Edith Evans looked serene.

After the show, the two sat in Laurette's room. Two equals felt at peace. Two giants felt each other's greatness. Laurette discussed the play. Then Edith talked. Then Laurette pointed out some handicaps. "Of course, *Florence* is bad," said that silken voice that carried up to the highest second balcony.

"Laurette!" I pointed to the wall behind me. On the other side of it was Dressing Room Two where Florence Reed dressed. I'd dressed there in *A Church Mouse* and knew that every word said in Laurette's room could be heard in Florence's.

Laurette looked at me questioningly.

"Florence can *hear*," I whispered.

"Oh, Florence *knows* she's bad. She knows it, but she can't help it."

The doorbell rang at Clifton and Mabelle's apartment at the Algonquin. "Oh, come in, dear. Clifton's out, but sit with me." Mabelle showed her guest into the sitting room. "I'm dead on my feet, I'm just back from the funeral. Where were *you?* Ethel was there and Jeanne and Marilyn and Zoë and Alice Brady and Helen Menken."

"Didn't he have any friends?" asked Laurette.

Chicago's Civic Theatre booked *The Glass Menagerie*. Was that new playwright going to make it? Would Laurette? Nobody greater, but was she drinking?

The advance sale was four hundred dollars. In all Chicago only four hundred dollars' worth of people looked forward to seeing Laurette Taylor in *The Glass Menagerie* by Tennessee Williams.

Opening night the assistant stage manager knocked on the door. "Half hour, Miss Taylor."

"Better hold it," called Laurette.

"Hold it, Miss Taylor?" The a.s.m. started to shake.

"Yes, hold it."

A.s.m. hurried to report to stage manager. Stage manager knocked. "Anything wrong, Miss Taylor?" he asked, voice unconvincingly casual.

"No."

"Did you say you want the curtain held?"

"Yes."

"Anything I can do?"

"Come in, I'm dyeing my Blue Mountain Casino costume. I *told* them it looked too good." Laurette's arms were dark blue up to her elbows as she dowsed her Act II Blue Mountain Casino costume up and down in the washbasin full of blue Diamond Dye water.

That night was history. Laurette. Tennessee. The play.

"Kathryn, would you mind going to the Civic Theatre again tonight?" asked Lloyd Lewis, critic on the *Chicago News*. "I want to see that again."

"Love to," said his wife.

As they drove up, Kay Ashton-Stevens stopped her car and Ashton got out. "We're coming back. Are *you?*" asked the Hearst paper's critic.

The *Tribune*'s Claudia Cassidy followed them in. For the only time anyone ever heard of, the critics came back to see a second performance.

The play was named for the glass animals that Laurette's daughter collected. The part was played by Julie Haydon, awe-struck by Laurette's great talent. At the curtain call she didn't bow to the audience. She bowed only to Laurette, then dropped down on one knee and kissed Laurette's hand.

"Don't ever do that!" said Laurette as the curtain fell.

"But you're so *great*," moaned Julie.

"Don't ever do that!"

The next night on the curtain call, Julie bowed to Laurette, dropped down on one knee and kissed her hand.

"Don't *do* that, Julie! I warn you."

"But you're so *great*," she pleaded.

"I warn you."

Next night on the curtain call, Julie bowed, dropped down on the knee and kissed Laurette's hand. Laurette gave her a one-two to the chin and knocked her out in full view of the astonished audience. The stage manager was so astonished, the curtain took longer to come down than the long count for the Dempsey-Tunney fight in that same city.

After every performance Julie stopped by Laurette's dressing room to say goodnight. "Julie, this is Mrs. Cas—"

"Oh, Miss Cassidy, *thank* you for that bad notice."

"No, Julie, this is Mrs. Cas—"

"It will help me to learn! *Thank* you for all the dreadful things you said about me."

"Julie," roared Laurette, "this is *not* Claudia Cassidy, this is Irene *Castle*."

After the triumphant run at the Civic Theatre, *The Glass Menagerie* by the new playwright with the poetic name was booked to open at Mr. Brady's Playhouse on West 48th. Great hopes, great fears. Laurette was triumphant, but with the strain of a New York opening night, would she keep on an even keel?

Opening-night telegrams, flowers, presents poured up the alley and in the stage door. Their good wishes were boundless, their hopes high. From critic George Jean Nathan came a bottle of scotch.

Laurette and the play were triumphant. The bravos went on and on, and when the crowds poured back, George Nathan was among them. Laurette pointed to the bottle of whiskey. "Thanks for the vote of confidence."

It was selling out, but some people found *The Glass Menagerie* hard to say. Our ticket broker asked us, "How 'bout two for *The Glass Me-jan-erie?*"

She was born Lauretta Cooney in Asbury Park. Her birthday was April Fool's Day. Remember when she sat stage left in her black silk dress and listened to her son up at Carnegie Hall playing *Humoresque?* I wish all of us in the profession could see her listen again. Goodnight, Laurette, wher*ever* you are, and wherever you are, you're the greatest!

※ ※ ※ ※ ※

Did you ever say a stupid thing? I said I think I'm going to live forever. Next morning I couldn't get up. A raging fever, raging sore throat and chills. I don't know when "that evenin' sun" is going down, but you can bet I know it's going to.

※ ※ ※ ※ ※

We had our feet up, the evening papers all over the floor, our maid was out, Suzanne was fixing our favorite dinner and then the doorbell rang.

"Oh, Garson," I said crossly, "I *wish* you wouldn't have the office send home things—"

"The office isn't sending anything. Why do you—"

Suzanne looked in. "It's the piano player."

"The piano player?"

"Yes."

Was it the piano *tuner* Julie Styne said he was going to send?

I looked over the stair rail into the lower hall.

"You've done it *again*," scolded Arthur Rubinstein. "You can *see* they don't expect us."

Nela looked troubled.

"It's a week from tonight," I said, "but come up."

"We'll give you a choice," said Garson. "We can go out or we can have dinner here. When we're alone we order meat loaf, beets, calf's-foot jelly made with fresh strawberry juice."

"We'll go out," said the piano player.

We went to that new Spanish restaurant. Arthur Rubinstein is a man of action, but we shoulda stood in bed.

# Friend in Fur

Is your dog bright? Ours wasn't. He was beautiful. He was good, but not bright. Which would you rather be?

Sometimes he was brighter than others. He liked watermelon. Well, that's bright. In the summer he'd go to the watermelon patch, nudge one off the vine, trundle it up a small hill with his nose, then let it roll down till it hit against a rock and burst open. Man, did he tear into that watermelon!

In warm weather a walk left him gasping. Back at the house, he rushed to the cool shadow cast by the barn. Well, that was bright. But in January he'd rush home from a walk through the snow and cool off in the shadow of the barn.

His goodness went out to everybody and everything as long as it didn't keep him from a walk with us. He lay waiting on the front walk for the door to open, when it did he jumped up and three kittens dropped out of his fur. He was their central heating.

A story conference made him happy. He could count on his loved ones not to stray. He listened and always looked at the one who spoke. When people were thinking, he looked subdued.

"I've got it!" someone shouted. Sacha wagged all over with excitement.

One day he rolled a watermelon down the hill and it missed the rock. He walked down to it and tried to fathom what happened. He looked at the rock, then looked at the melon, then back at the rock. Suddenly he dashed into the melon patch, got another one loose, rolled that one down, it hit the rock. Why isn't *that* bright? Maybe we were wrong, Sacha darling, and goodnight, wher*ever* you are.

He was named after Sacha Guitry, who was not as good or as beautiful, but brighter.

In the autumn we had the signs up, but the hunters drove right through. We were afraid they might aim at Sacha and tied a red bow on his topknot. Windy looked at him and growled. Sacha's black poodle head looked adorable with a red hairbow. Windy could foresee all the compliments. He growled.

We tied a red ribbon on Windy's silken hair. He shook it off, then came back to Sacha and growled. We had to take Sacha's off.

*Was* Sacha brighter than we thought? A marauder came and looked in the drive. A marauder in the form of a Great Dane. Sacha saw that mammoth and ran for the kennel. Windy went forth to battle. Why a stranger on his grounds? Windy was a black-and-white cocker spaniel someone in Chicago had given Grace Moore. He came with the house and decided to protect it. Poor Windy.

Hans, the gardener, drove what was left of him to the vet at Newtown. Poor Windy. He lay on a slab at the vet's. They did what they could. He was in bad shape. Next day Hans drove over to see how he was and brought Sacha with him. Sacha and Hans stood by the slab. Windy half opened an eye, saw Sacha and gave a feeble growl. Every day Hans brought Sacha and every day Windy's growl got stronger. One day Windy went back with Hans and Sacha. Windy climbed into the front seat beside Hans and growled at Sacha. Sacha hopped in the back.

\*     \*     \*     \*     \*

My mother's middle name was Never Give Up. When she lost her diamond, she found it. Is that what you do? My mother lost hers out of her engagement ring. It weighed just under one carat. She lost it in our house at 14 Elmwood Avenue. Our house had eight rooms and an attic and a cellar to look for almost a one-carat diamond. My mother hadn't gone out of the house, so her diamond had to be somewhere. She retraced all her actions and looked every place big enough to hold a diamond just under one carat. It was under the grape basket we kept potatoes in at the head of the cellar stairs. In the crack between the boards of the landing, it sparkled. With a straw from our broom she coaxed it back. If your middle name is Never Give Up, you get your diamond back.

# Marguerite's Sister

WERE YOU EVER an extra at Fort Lee? Did anything ever look colder than the early-morning Hudson River from the deck of the Fort Lee ferry?

Inside the big black limo, with a fur rug tucked around her, sat Miss Cora Clark, very upright. Marguerite's sleepy head rested on her sister's shoulder while she dozed across the cold river to Jersey.

Well, that's show business. She was a star and I was starting. She was in her limo on the way to her grand dressing room. I was out on deck on the way to look for work.

"*Over Twenty-one* gave me pleasure," wrote Miss Cora Clark to me at the Music Box. The upright lady didn't remember me on the Fort Lee ferry, but I remembered her.

I asked little Hazel Dawn about her. "She lives in two grand apartments on Central Park West."

Do you know many people who live in two?

"She's rich. Her sister Marguerite left her all her money. She has one apartment for herself and servants and one to entertain. And even her servants are different. The maid that opens the door wears a ballet dress. Mother's her youngest friend and they knew each other way back at Famous Players. *All* her friends are from the past and just about as different as she is. At dinner, one put her brocade evening bag on the table. I said, 'Isn't that pretty big for an evening bag?' She said, 'That's not my evening bag, that's my husband's

356

ashes. I never leave them home.' "

The only time *I* ever spoke to Miss Clark was the day Cole Porter was having auditions and rang up. "Can you ask little Hazel to come down to the Shubert?"

I said yes, then I couldn't find her number. I rang Miss Cora Clark.

"Little Hazel is not here," said Miss Clark in a precise, distant voice.

"Please, may I have her number? Cole Porter is holding auditions, he'll hear her if only we can find her."

"Ah yes." There was a pause. "Will you write it down?"

"Yes," I said.

"Plaza 4–9 0 4 4 2 3 2 7 9."

"Thank you," I said.

"I feel sure you'll find her there. Goodbye."

Goodbye, Miss Cora Clark, wher*ever* you are. Up there did you bring your wrong numbers?

＊　＊　＊　＊　＊

Why is "My God" such a popular expression? "My God," wailed Humphrey Bogart, "don't *you* ever make a mistake?"

"Very seldom," I said. "And when I do, it nearly kills me." I guess if you go through life thinking it's normal to make mistakes, you make them. If they nearly kill you, you don't make them so often.

＊　＊　＊　＊　＊

Louise de Vilmorin sat under trees sipping un dry. "Me, I adore Chinese food."

"Do you like it, Diana?" asked the host.

"Adore it, but where can one get it in Paris?"

"My house." Paul-Louis Weiller left his shady Neuilly garden, went in his house and made a phone call. "Come."

"You said *your* house," said Louise.

Maecenas nodded. His car drove them to another street in

Neuilly and stopped.

"Whose house is this?" asked Lady Diana.

"Mine."

Perfect servants served a perfect Chinese luncheon.

Lady Diana made an excuse to go to the powder room and went to the kitchen. Two little Chinese children played in the corner. The Chinese cook bowed and smiled.

"How long have you been here?" asked Milady.

Chinese cook smiled and bowed. "Long time."

"How long?"

"Long time. No know how much years."

Do you ever surprise your friends? Think it over. Maybe it's a good idea.

※　※　※　※　※

Theda Bara surprised *me*. She and I split up because I wouldn't tell the Theatre Guild that her nephew was a good actor.

"But I never *saw* him, Theda."

"You've met him."

"I mean I never saw him act."

"Can't you take my *word* for it?"

"I'll give him a letter, but I can't say I saw him act."

After that when I called, Theda Bara wasn't home any more. Goodnight, Theda Bara, wher*ever* you are, you gotta *see* someone to recommend him.

※　※　※　※　※

Fannie Hurst let her arm hang over the rail of her stage box and four bracelets fell off clonk, clonk on the head of the *Journal-American*'s Alan Dale. It knocked him out. Woollcott reported next day, "The evening was uneventful for the audience, but one critic was carried away, not so much by the entertainment as by Fannie Hurst's bracelets made of Portland Cement."

# Destiny's Tot

W HEN JED HARRIS produced a play, he stuck with it day and night till the day of its New York opening, then that afternoon he went to Atlantic City. This new one had been tough. Originally it was called *Norma's Affair*. That couldn't be, so Jed got George Abbott, fresh from co-writing Broadway's wowiest hit *Broadway*, to have a go at *Norma's Affair*. Helen Hayes liked George's version, Jed christened it *Coquette*, hired George Cukor to direct, then he was out and George Abbott was directing. Why was the star miserable?

Charlie and Ned Sheldon had written a play called *Salvation* and Helen wished she was in it. To make her more miserable, Philadelphia critics said it would be goodbye *Coquette* when and if it ever got to New York.

Helen begged Jed to leave it in Philly, but Jed believed in it or himself or something and booked *Coquette* into the Maxine Elliott. No matter how Helen pleaded or railed, he stuck to his guns. Stuck to them till the afternoon of opening day, then, as usual, left town.

That night *Coquette* made history. Cheers. Wild enthusiasm. Helen's performance was a peak! As the curtain fell, Dick Maney in the Maxine Elliott box office phoned Atlantic City. "It's the biggest hit in town!" he yelled.

"I don't believe it," said perverse Mr. Harris.

"Listen to *this*," shouted Dick and held the receiver out toward the audience. Cheers and whistles and applause brightened up Atlantic City's Boardwalk.

Jed Harris was born in 1900. At twenty-seven he had made a million and had three hits running on Broadway. That rattled the town. Noël Coward referred to him as "Destiny's tot." George Kaufman said, "He thinks he's Napoleon and I think he is, too."

The week before Christmas *The Royal Family* opened. This time it was Jed who called Dick Maney. "Close it."

"But it got rave reviews," pleaded press agent Maney and business manager Whit Ray.

"Close it," commanded Jed.

"But *why*, Jed?" asked Whit.

"It didn't sell out."

"But it's Christmas week, Jed, everybody's made their plans ahead. Next week we'll go clean."

"Close it," said Jed. "A show that gets rave reviews and doesn't sell out should close."

What fluke let *The Royal Family* stay open to become theatre history? Who slipped up *there?*

❊　❊　❊　❊　❊

The Kanins and the Harrimans were acquiring some jewels. Averell sent Marie a pink diamond from Russia. Garson sent me an emerald from dear old Blighty.

Marie and I ran into each other in Fulco's elevator.

Some days later Fulco showed me my emerald beautifully set in a ring.

"How did you set Marie's pink diamond?"

"I threw it away."

They had landed Ave with a phony.

Do I notice much change? people ask.

You bet. I mean, is it the belle époque when Harriman's diamond is no good and Kanin's emerald is good enough to get stolen?

❊　❊　❊　❊　❊

If your hands itch, do you reach for the zinc ointment or open a new bank account to be ready for the money to pour in? If it's the bank bit, you're a ja-sager and know that the king will die, or you will, or else the ass will definitely speak.

\* \* \* \* \*

"People say Americans are witty," says Dame Edith. "It's because Americans talk till someone laughs and when they do, they stop. If you laugh, you like to think it's at something witty."

# The Girl of the Golden West

MAUDE ADAMS was the first star I acted with and the second was Blanche Bates. Her Rolls limo waited for her on West 48th Street in front of the Belmont Theatre, now torn down. Remember it? It was beside the Bristol Hotel, now torn down, and opposite the Friars' Club, now torn down. Remember?

Blanche Bates' claret-colored limo stood out front. She was a star that had the equipment. At rehearsal if she felt chilly she reached for her sable coat that missed the floor by two inches and when she felt like nibbling on something, pulled a garlic bud out of her sable pocket and nibbled on it as she said lines.

At rehearsals Maude Adams' black toque was never off, but Miss Bates' satin turban, with bird of paradise swooping below where the garlic bud went, came off after lunch.

If your mind wandered and you didn't pick up your cue, you could blame it on her big square emerald. "Oh, excuse me, Miss Bates, I can't take my eyes off your ring. Excuse me."

Her pearls? Oysters took time to grow their own and who knew about simulated? Hers graduated from big to the size of a pea. When *Mrs. Partridge Presents* opened in Washington, our star's finery was a match for anything out front.

Blanche and her ma were products of the West. Blanche acted for the miners and Ma invested the nuggets. Belasco had known her when he and she were Coast favorites, and after he made it in New

York he starred her as Cigarette in Ouida's *Under Two Flags* and in *Madame Butterfly*. It was that production that gave Puccini the idea to compose the opera for Geraldine Farrar.

When Blanche became Mrs. George Creel, she retired to San Francisco, bore Frances and George Junior, then couldn't resist the call. She uprooted her family from Divisadero Street and with Henry Miller made theatre history in Jimmy Forbes' *The Famous Mrs. Fair*.

One matinee at the Blackstone Theatre in Chicago, after Act III Mr. Miller sent word to dismiss the audience, he didn't care to play Act IV.

"Why did he *do* that?" I asked his co-star.

"Oh dear, Henry was a difficult man. I talked and talked to him. I reminded him the fourth act took only twenty-two minutes, but I couldn't do anything with him."

"But why wouldn't he go on?"

"He didn't like the audience. Oh dear, it was a mess. On Saturday afternoon the banks were closed and people couldn't get their money back until Monday. Oh dear, Henry was a difficult man."

Her New York house was down on Murray Hill. How did she give it the feeling of Ma Bates and the West?

At the head of her table was a big rocker where Blanche sat ladling out the chowder from the big tureen, then carved the roast.

In *Mrs. Partridge Presents*, after a scene in Act I, I went off to applause. Stage custom forbade applause for a supporting player if the star was left on the stage, so when I exited Blanche Bates followed me off, waited for the applause to finish, then came back and went on with the scene.

One performance there was no applause. Miss Bates looked startled. "What!" she said in a ringing voice and behind the scenery clapped her hands. Out front the audience joined in. "That's more like it!" snorted Cigarette and Butterfly and the Girl of the Golden West and Mrs. Partridge and strode back into the scene.

Over a plate of chowder I asked, "How can you be so generous? I can understand not keeping me from getting a hand, but I *can't* understand you starting it."

Those gray eyes that had looked on miners and had dealt with

Belasco and Henry Miller dealt with me. "After you've done it awhile, that won't seem all that important."

Little George and Frances lived with her at the house on Murray Hill. George was small and slender. Frances was husky. "Meet my brakeman daughter," said Blanche.

Did Frances introduce *her* as Ma Creel?

When Ruth Chatterton and Henry Miller had their falling out, Blanche did the impossible and stayed friends with both. Ruth opened in a musical comedy called *The Magnolia Lady*, adapted from Alice Duer Miller's novel, *Come Out of the Kitchen*. The Shuberts presented it and it was the first time Ruth had acted on a Shubert stage or in a musical. Opening night Blanche Bates caused a stir when she walked down the aisle of the Shubert and was seated back of the *Times* critic.

Too bad it wasn't a better night. The musical was slow and didn't show off Ruth to her best advantage. Too bad. When you break with a fellow, it's nice to come in with colors flying. They not only didn't fly at the Shubert, but in the dance with her new husband, Ruth slipped and fell. Eyes turned to Blanche Bates. Would she tell Henry Miller?

Blanche looked straight ahead, and you can bet *me*, she forgot it. "When you've done it awhile, that won't seem all that important." Goodnight, Blanche Bates, wher*ever* you are, what a star!

(*Players' Guide*, copy.)

# Child of the Century

ANITA Loos and John Emerson and I were driving back from Asbury Park after the show. Did John get sleepy? He didn't make the turn and the car wound up in the cornfield, high stalks all around us. We got out among the alien corn, undamaged. "Oh, Mr. E.," said Anita ruefully, "you think *only* of yourself." That was the summer of 1925, I have to ask Anita what she meant. I didn't have time to ask that summer, because we went to Paris to order clothes at Mme. Lanvin's for *The Fall of Eve*. It was my second trip to Europe and my first lunch in the Ritz garden. Beautiful! The tables! The food! All the people! Maharajahs, Maharanees, all the beautiful Paris people and from home our own Hattie Carnegie. But who was that dazzler on the banquette? Was he wearing a pink shirt? Was he really?

"Who is that?" I asked.

"That's the new London star. He's written his own play and stars in it. His name is Noël Coward."

Looking across the Ritz garden, did I see Lynn's friend who'd lived down in the Village and written about a play a week during *Dulcy?*

He brought a few to Gregory. Was Gregory wrong? We thought the young playwright was nice, but how did we know he was going to wear a pink shirt in the Ritz garden and be Noël Coward?

When he wrote *Present Indicative*, he gave the galleys to Woollcott. Woollcott liked it, but said there were too many verys.

When Super Chief stopped at Albuquerque, Noël sent off a wire to "A. Woollcott, Lake Bomoseen, Vermont." The message was seventy-five verys he'd cut out of his book.

Woollcott and Kaufman wrote *The Dark Tower*. When Noël landed, he went from the dock to the matinee and thence to Woollcott's East River apartment. "It's easily the worst thing I ever saw. Now let's talk about something else."

Noël and Garson and I dropped off my old friend McDermott at the Algonquin. "Bill is the drama critic on the *Cleveland Plain Dealer*," I said to Noël.

"Then you saw Kit's *Antony and Cleopatra*."

"Very fine," said McDermott, then reached for further praise. "She's very courtly."

The car drove off. "Very courtly!" repeated Noël. "That's who we're at the mercy of when we play Cleveland?"

Princess Grace's charity was being benefited by a gala supper at the Sporting Club. "*Where or when?*" sang Frank.

> "*The smile you are smiling*
> *You were smiling then,*
> *But I can't remember*
> *Where or when . . .*"

Frank looked blank.

"*Some things that happen for the first time,*" sang Noël from our table.

"*Seem to be happening again,*" sang Frank.

I wish Noël still had Goldenhurst. From the upper windows, on a clear night you could see the lights of France.

He dropped into Western Union off Times Square, wrote out a first-night wire and signed it "Fiorello La Guardia."

The operator looked displeased. "You can't sign Fiorello La Guardia."

"Oh." Noël crossed it out and wrote "Noël Coward."

Operator looked more displeased. "You can't sign Noël Coward."

"But I *am* Noël Coward."

"Oh, you are? Well, in that case, you can sign it Fiorello La Guardia."

❈ ❈ ❈ ❈ ❈

I wish the Sitwells' father had known me. To have Helen Keller and Don Rickles for friends *can't* be a mistake.

Don was getting ready for his scene. The assistant cameraman held up the slate with the scene number on it. It was going to be a close-up of Don, and all the lights and equipment left little room for the assistant. He had to get down on his knees to hold up the slate.

Don looked down at him compassionately. "Just talk to Billy Graham, he'll have you walking in a week."

# Supporting Player

W EST 71ST STREET and the Hudson River was where Ethel
Wilson and King Calder found an apartment. You saw the
Hudson as you came in, but it was sort of on the bias. Downstairs
the lobby was dismal, but once you walked up the grubby stairs
their apartment was nice. "Come for lunch, Jessie," they said,
proud of their new home.

Jessie came in, shaking her head. "Let's have lunch and say goodbye, I get depressed enough without my ever coming *here* again."

The first show I was in with Jessie Busley, we bombed. We were
headed for Philly, but before Philly we bombed in Princeton.

"My husband—" pause "—is paralyzed from the waist down."

The Princeton men tried not to, but what could they do? They
howled.

Jessie Busley looked in my dressing room. "Don't send the laundry out."

Selena and I went back to the Nassau Inn, poured two ginger ale
and bourbons. Some of it in a glass, some of it over my new blue
gabardine shoes.

Well, that's show business. A show bombing makes you spill
stuff.

At rehearsal they gave out the notes. "Jessie, while the scene goes
on, brush Ruth's hair. Brush it a hundred strokes. You'll have a line,
but for tonight just brush. Ruth, start the scene. Jess, brush."

" 'My husband—' " pause " '—is paralyzed from the waist
down.' "

"By the way," said the author, "that 'paralyzed' line better be out."

"Now we stopped," said Jessie, "why would I brush her hair a hundred times? Won't that wear it out?"

"Oh no, it's good for the hair. My wife loves it."

"Oh yes?" Jessie went back to brushing. "Some argument," she said out of the upstage side of her mouth. "How do *I* know what his wife looks like? This show's got to close, there's no one to root for. Did I tell you I—"

"Quiet, please," said the director and went into a huddle with the author.

"What were you going to say?" I whispered.

"The day we left town—and I wish I were back there—I was walking in the Park and I noticed a lady strolling with a woman that was strolling two feet behind her. 'This'll be somebody English,' I said. Know who it was? Julia Marlowe. Her English maid walks behind her."

Director looked over our way.

"I was asking Ruth if she knew my cue to stop brushing or didn't you get to that yet?"

❈   ❈   ❈   ❈   ❈

Do you have a good memory? And is that good to have? "Children don't remember time or names of people or places. They're smart," said Margaret Fuller. She died in an Italian liner shipwrecked off Fire Island.

When told that Margaret Fuller wanted to go to Europe, Emerson said, "If she's an intellectual, doesn't she know that there is here?"

Think it over.

❈   ❈   ❈   ❈   ❈

"I'm looking out my window at Bel Air burning," wrote Doris Vidor. "Smoke and flames and houses falling down. I can't *tell* you what this is doing to my sinuses."

369

❉  ❉  ❉  ❉  ❉

Do you know any Quakers? They have their own way of getting back at people. When Lloyd Lewis was six, he got sore at his mother. He went back of the woodpile and hissed, "Monday! Tuesday! Wednesday! Thursday! Friday! Saturday! Sunday! You!! Yes sir!!!" If a Quaker says the name of a day and "you" instead of "thou" and a "yessir," look out! He's *really* raving.

❉  ❉  ❉  ❉  ❉

Jack Barrymore was the juvenile in *The Yellow Ticket*. He'd made a hit. Now would he show up at the matinee? He always did, but what if he didn't? Sometimes he just made it, sometimes he was hung over. "Get him a bowl of soup," the stage manager said to his assistant and gave him a dime and a pail. Assistant rushed back with Child's vegetable soup. While Jack slapped greasepaint on with one hand, with the other he got the vegetable soup into him with his shoehorn.

❉  ❉  ❉  ❉  ❉

Do you like to go to the theatre? Ruth Fleischmann hated it, but Raoul liked a good play, and when Ruth hated it so much she couldn't take it any more, she got down and sat on the floor. Good *that* didn't catch on!

❉  ❉  ❉  ❉  ❉

The traffic light turned red, a beggar stuck his hand in the window. "Please spare me something."

Tallulah fumbled in her pocketbook. The red light turned green. "Find it yourself, you sonofabitch," she yelled and threw her pocketbook at him.

During the war they asked her for a blood donation. "Give it to the Japs," she advised, "and we'll win the war."

370

She and Sir Francis were walking up Bond Street. Sir Francis threw himself down on the sidewalk and kissed the feet of a nun. "Oh, sister, forgive a poor miserable bugger."

❊　❊　❊　❊　❊

Mrs. Alvin Fuller came in the shop.

Nate pointed to the door. "Go home and put on something else," he said to the wife of Massachusetts' governor. "I don't want anyone wearing red to try on a hat of mine."

The governor's lady laughed.

"I mean it," said Nathan Gibson Clark. "Come back in something else. I didn't sit up all night thinking up hats to wear with red."

❊　❊　❊　❊　❊

Who was it said, "If you want to diet, don't have a choice"? If you go to a restaurant, it's "Have an appetizer. Have a steak. 'Have an egg roll, Mr. Goldstone, have a spare rib, have a—' " Thank you, Steve Sondheim, for writing that and do you know what I mean? Everybody's confusing the issue and before you get the check for what you don't want, you've put on a pound. But sit home with the low-fat cottage cheese and the unsweetened pineapple and isn't that scale pretty when the needle shows you're down ten?

A good way *not* to lose is do what every French child does every afternoon at four. Come out of the nearest patisserie with a petit pain au chocolat.

"Someday *I'm* going to have one," I said.

Bronia led me into Senequier. "Elle n'a jamais mangé un."

"Tiens." The petit pain was snatched from my hand.

"She'll heat it," said Bronia.

Back it came dripping chocolate from where a hot dog should be in our country. It's better than low-fat cottage cheese and unsweetened pineapple, but not to take off weight.

❊　❊　❊　❊　❊

371

Ottie Swope heard Rudy Vallee on the radio and said he had to meet him. The Swopes didn't take stuff lying down and got in touch with Jed Harris who'd been at Yale with Vallee. Jed phoned and put the situation to him.

Could it be that Herbert Bayard Swope, Junior, is alive and well and living in New York because Vallee gave him a saxophone lesson?

\* \* \* \* \*

Did you ever let your father down? Doris Warner decided to come to New York and be a theatrical producer. She brought her fortune with her and engaged a fine suite at the Carlyle.

Harry Warner, president of Warner Brothers, came to see her and burst into tears. "I never thought I'd see a daughter of mine live in an uptown hotel."

\* \* \* \* \*

People think daring begins with *Oh! Calcutta!* At the Metropolitan Opera the Gerry fans thought daring began when Geraldine Farrar sprayed perfume back of her ears, under her arms, then, one foot on her dressing-table stool, she leaned over and let fly with her Piver's Blue Hour up *Zaza*'s saucy skirt.

\* \* \* \* \*

On the *Queen Mary* did you ever get Fred J. Snooks for your room steward? Ursula Jeans and I did. It sounded hilarious to hear Ursula's well-bred English voice say, "Would you mind fetching me some tea, Snooks."

\* \* \* \* \*

When the phone rings and you're in the bathtub, do you get out and answer it? Neysa McMein did.

"Mrs. Cosden's on the phone," said her maid.

Nell Cosden had the grandest house at Sands Point and was hostess to the then Prince of Wales.

"If your maid had said, 'It's Mrs. Kaufman,' would you have gotten out of the tub?" asked Pearl Swope.

✻  ✻  ✻  ✻  ✻

In London everybody's name is in the phone book. Here, as soon as you make it, you cancel out. It's the yardstick. When you hit town, you use a pay station. Then with that first sweet whiff of success, you order a phone, "I'm in the book," you boast and every so often look yourself up, just to see that beautiful "Ruth Gordon, 36 West 59th Street, Wickersham 3361." How successful it sounds to say, "Don't bother to write it down. I'm in the phone book." When I read the notices for *Mrs. Partridge Presents*, I figured I was in business. "Don't bother to write it, I'm in the phone book."

In *Saturday's Children* I got such praise, there was only one thing to do: tell them to take it out.

✻  ✻  ✻  ✻  ✻

When you take the train at Victoria, do you wonder who'll get into your compartment? Lord Berners liked a compartment to himself, so he lowered the window onto the platform and when anyone approached, he leered and beckoned them in.

What would *you* do? They looked for another compartment.

✻  ✻  ✻  ✻  ✻

Gielgud invited me to supper with Peggy Ashcroft and Mrs. Pat. Mrs. Pat was telling about two friends. "They were quite unaware that they were not alone and were going at it like a pair of stoats."

"Like what?" I asked.

"Stoats," said the original Eliza Doolittle.

I had heard it, but I was forty years old and nobody had ever said "stoats" in a conversation. Now I'm seventy-four and never heard it again. Have you?

❊   ❊   ❊   ❊   ❊

Oscar Levant married a pretty chorus girl from the Music Box
Theatre and bought her a nutria coat. She loved it so, she hung it
up for the night by an open window to keep it cold. In the morning
Oscar closed the window.

"What about my fur coat?" she cried.

After a few colds and a divorce, pretty Mrs. Levant married Mr.
Loew and moved into the great Loew mansion at Glen Cove. Late
at night sometimes the phone rang. "What's playing at Loew's?"
asked Oscar.

❊   ❊   ❊   ❊   ❊

Did you get to Condé Nast's parties? I hope so. Up Park Avenue
in a big big beautiful apartment, there was dancing and there was
everybody you ever were glad to meet or hoped to. I was invited to
two before I met Condé. I didn't even know what he looked like.
How did he work up his guest list?

Fred Astaire was there, but I knew what *he* looked like. When he
and Adele were at the Winter Garden in *The Passing Show*, Fred
gave dance lessons for ten dollars an hour. I thought he was out of
his mind to charge such a price, but a few kids in the company took
from him. When I danced with him at Condé's we just shuffled the
length of Condé's floor, Fred's arm around me—is that bad?—then
turned the corner and shuffled south. He didn't put out. Was that
what he was going to teach me for ten dollars an hour?

Fred's clothes were super and so were Adele's. She had a black
velvet coat lined with ermine. Bergdorf made me one like it, but I
had them put on a white fox collar and cuffs. I didn't have Adele's
class. Hers looked like just black velvet, then she took it off and
you saw the ermine.

She was scotching a rumor. "He hasn't got a big pecker."

"No?"

"No. It just *looks* big, because his hands are so small."

\* \* \* \* \*

Ever make a mistake?

I did. I told my age.

"Don't tell your age," said everybody.

I wish I'd listened.

"Why are you so preoccupied with how old you are?" asked Thornton. "I'm sure you say to a taxi driver, 'Drive me to 242 East 49th Street and you do know I am seventy-four years old.' "

It was a mistake.

"*Don't* tell how old you are," urged Lynn and Alfred.

They were right. At seventy-four I'm getting minor raves on my looks, but I'm caught in the middle. Who knows what seventy-four looks like? Who cares? But if I'd listened to friends, I could now lie and say I'm eighty-four. For eighty-four, the way I look is spectacular. To look like this at eighty-four I could start a trend. But who likes to be told things?

Nobody. So turn the page if you're doing all right, only *don't* tell how old you are until you come up with an attraction-getter.

Do *you* pay the government or does the government pay *you?* And listen, Alfred, and listen, Lynn, and listen, Thornton, if I didn't tell my age, would my Uncle Sam send me that two hundred-plus every month?

"*Such* a mistake to have friends! " said old Mr. Sitwell.

Do *you* think so?

Not me. Rex Harrison sat on the edge of Vivien's bed. Downstairs at the party, she had turned white. "Come upstairs and lie down, darling," said Garson. He put his arm around her. She wasn't sick or anything, she felt forlorn. Lost. She, who always knew how to do everything so beautifully, now didn't know what to do.

So until she found out, she drank Pouilly Fuissé.

Garson stood by the bed and Rex sat on the edge and stroked her arm. So gently. "Darling Viv, do you pee enough?" A world of love, a world of compassion was in his voice. "You have to, darling, it's the healthiest thing one can do." He stroked her wrists.

375

Rex knew that. And so did our Mara. Cornsilk and fresh parsley tea were Mara's remedy. That's what she drank in Chile. And she drank it at 242 East 49th Street, where she did our laundry every day from eight until four. In seven years all she ever said to me was, "Hasta mañana," then smiled and went out our kitchen door.

"Hasta mañana," I said and she was gone until mañana at eight.

She didn't speak English and I don't speak Spanish or Portuguese, so all we could say to each other was hasta mañana, but I drank her tea, made from cornsilk and parsley, because Mara made us understand that in Chile they know it's good to pee.

She couldn't speak English, she couldn't speak French, but she knew pain when she saw it and one July morning our cook had a bad one. Mara went round the corner to Second Avenue Gristede's, bought ears of corn, took the cornsilk and added a bunch of parsley, brewed a tea and pantomimed, "Drink it."

Suzanne did and by afternoon felt fine.

"Hasta mañana," and the smile.

Next day Suzanne bought a Spanish lesson book. She and Mara sat across our marble-topped kitchen table and Suzanne picked up a usable language. And also picked up how to make the tea, because in Chile they know what they're talking about. Do *you*?

Jack Warner does.

One day Blake Edwards sat around his office on the Warner lot and, thinking about his own health, wondered who he knew that looked the best. He came up with Jack Warner.

"What makes you look so great?"

"I piss a lot," said Jack.

Blake pursued the subject. Was he just naturally gifted that way?

"Mountain Valley Water. Never be without it," and off went Jack, via the men's room, to play tennis.

That's how Rex and Mara and Jack feel good and another way to feel good is to get organized. We went to the Pavillon one night, the Pavillon that was where the Côte Basque now is. Always elegant, always beautiful, this night the Pavillon had a new look.

"What's different, Mr. Soulé?"

"Mr.-Mrs. Kanin. I will tell you. The business was becoming not *good*. The accountant said to me I must cut *down*. 'Business is off everywhere,' he said to me. 'And at Le Pavillon, *too*. You must cut down your *expenses*.'" Mr. Soulé moved the bowl of red and white roses a quarter of an inch toward center. "Mr.-Mrs. Kanin. I said, '*No*. I must spend more. If business is no *good*, this means I must be *better*.' You see the flowers? More *beautiful*. The waiters? There are more. The lights? Are all changed. Mr.-Mrs. Kanin, they are not more *becoming*, yes? Mr. Kanin, please to look at Mrs. Kanin. Yes? The food is *always* good. The food I can *not* improve. But the menu. Look at the menu, Mr.-Mrs. Kanin, new *dishes*. Gigot avec flageolet beans. This we did not have *yesterday*. Is very good, I give you my word, Mr.-Mrs. Kanin. Un poulet basquais. Excellent! Mr.-Mrs. Kanin, tonight Le Pavillon, I give you my word, is become vraiment excell*ent*."

"But Mr. Soulé," said Garson, "when business is bad everybody cuts back, fires the secretaries, marks stuff down, and *you* spend more!"

"Mr.-Mrs. Kanin, I will tell you *something*. When things are not *successful*, you must get *better*. I give you my word. Mr.-Mrs. Kanin, you know how I know this? Je suis bien organisé."

When things don't swing, do you blame everybody else or do *you* do things better?

It's hard to do, but it's occupying. And that's *another* way to feel good. Gertrude Stein thought so. "It must be fine," she said, "to be a miser."

"Why?" asked Thornton.

"It's so occupying."

Who likes to be told things?

Nobody, but I'll listen to Mr. Soulé and Gertrude Stein. And I'll listen to Lillian Gish: "Keep your stocking drawer straightened out," she advised Dorothy, "and everything will be fine."

Why not try it? You might wind up with a million. Lillian did. When she wound up her great starring days, she had a million. Do you think it was *Way Down East* or her stocking drawer?

Why not straighten yours out, in case of a tie?

Where do *you* go for privacy?

I run a big house, but for privacy I go for a walk. The walk to

377

Beverly Hills village is lined with white brick, white stucco, pink stucco, buff stucco, gray stucco, half-timber, modern, shingled and clapboard houses. Everything but a brownstone and all of them pretty. Beverly Hills is a pretty place. Camden Drive is shaded by magnolia trees, Roxbury Drive is cooled by elms and Beverly Drive's tall coconut palms let you take a walk in the sun. Something for everybody, but for me, privacy. Gardeners spray the rosebushes, clip the privet and arbor vitae hedge, water the lawn or tint the grass greener, but they, too, value privacy. In hello-dear Southern California, they and I do not even nod. Privacy is our bag. I walk my daily three miles and nobody looks out the window. Cars pass and mind their business. Could the last privacy in the world be a walk through Beverly Hills?

When you give a dinner party, do *you* hog your guest of honor?

We give ours the gift of other guests. On Arthur Rubinstein's right will be Edith Goetz. On his left Mia Farrow. Or Natalie Wood.

Dame Edith Evans will have other evenings to talk to Garson and me, on her right will be Gregory Peck, President of the Academy, on her left, Charlton Heston, President of the Screen Actors' Guild.

"I, too, am a president," said Dame Ede in answer to Garson's after-dinner toast. "I am President of R.A.D.A."

At our dinner in honor of Merle Oberon, where did she sit? At the head of her own Chippendale table. We rented the house from Merle.

Do *you* celebrate all holidays?

We do. How does a Labor Day dinner grab you, with Don Rickles as the guest of honor?

Assisting were Fred Astaire, Katharine Hepburn, Véronique and Gregory Peck, Lord and Lady Moore, Anne and Kirk Douglas, George Cukor, Natalie Wood, Edie and Bill Goetz, and San Francisco's Whitney Warren come to pass Labor Day in the south.

"*Who* is that person?" asked Whitney and by the time the fresh huckleberry pie was served, he urged Don to visit him at his palace on Telegraph Hill.

Do *you* like to be up and away?

With *me* it's a must. My father was eight years old when he split from his home on the Cape. I have *go* in my blood.

Are *you* happy?

Is happiness when you forget to turn on your phone?

It means you're *absorbed*. Is there anything better? Absorbed, and you don't have a worry, a trouble, sickness, money problems. How could you? You're absorbed.

Is misery wondering what to do with yourself?

How's your personality?

Do you work on it?

I began with my name. Ruth Gordon Jones, I was christened. It wasn't only the christening that left me limp, it was mostly my name. The only bright spot was, they almost named me Ethel.

Ethel Jones?

Draw the veil.

I did. And wondered what to do with what they stuck me with. In Wollaston Grammar School Third Grade I decided to become a breakthrough. "Rythe Jones, October 30, 1904" headed my spelling test. Miss Glavin marked it "Imperfect."

"My mother *wants* me to spell it like that," I lied.

Miss Glavin didn't bother to reprove me. "Sit down, R.U.T.H.," she said.

She could have gone to work on *her* name and personality, but I put up with her. She was like everybody. *I* was going to be different.

I learned a lot at Wollaston Grammar School. I learned at Quincy High, but I learned the most from Gene Tunney.

"When you start boxing lessons," he told me, "even before you learn how to put on your boxing gloves, they teach you, *never give up*."

They taught him sparring and running and rabbit punches and right hooks and left hooks and footwork and uppercuts and medium cuts and don't eat cold cuts on a hot day. They taught him everything to make him great in the ring, but the big lesson they kept knocking on was, *never give up*. It saved Gene Tunney's life. One wintry night he was walking in the woods and crunch went one foot. He had walked onto the frozen pond. Crunch went the other foot. *Never give up.* The ice buckled and broke and Gene went down under. *Never give up.* His head kept coming up under the ice. *Never give up.* He fought the dark and the cold and the black water. *Never give up.* Then his head came up free, he reached out his hand, felt the ground. *Never give up* saved Gene's life and became the keystone of mine. *Never give up,* and even without any talent, you can still make it, because so many people *do* give up.

It gets rough and they give up and get married. They lose interest and go into millinery. They inherit money and knock off. They can't get with it, they kill themselves. They don't get the job and go work in a service station or become vice-president of Macy's.

The time to watch it, of course, is when you're young. I've been practicing for fifty-six years. Can I throw that out and kill myself? Or become president of Bonwit Teller?

Thank you, boxers, and watch me! I'll probably make it in the next round.

Never mind what Jackie or Babe is wearing, how about figure it out for yourself? Mrs. Jack Gardner did and do you read the books about her? She didn't care what Mrs. Stuyvesant Fish and Mrs. John Jacob Astor were featuring in the Met's Golden Horseshoe. She took her place in her Boston Opera House box and when the Red Sox had a victory Mrs. Jack put on her diamond tiara and tied a ribbon around it that read: OH YOU BOSTON RED SOX!

Can you think of the right thing to do and say at the right moment?

Lillian Gish can.

Her lawyer, Tom Chadbourne, and his partners in the great law firm of Chadbourne, Stanchfield and Levy came up to break the news to Lillian. She'd lost her suit. She owed the government a hundred and two thousand dollars.

In cash.

In 1930!

In 1930 there *wasn't* a hundred and two thousand in cash.

"What did you say when they told you?" I gasped.

" 'Gentlemen,' I said, 'I have worked hard all my life, and I am *very* tired.' "

"Tired" is the right word, that's for sure. Could anything be more tiring?

How do you do at a party?

It's no good being shy. And no good looking no good. Today, clothes are priced right for everybody and what rips out that shy feeling is to get an OK from your looking glass, then set off for Brissons', Edie Goetz's, Douglases', Bennys', Lemmons', Lazars', Frank McCarthy's or the Gregsons' and when Theodore opens the door and Dagny is ready to take your wrap—which you are not so old-fashioned as to wear—you hear Kirk or Gregory or Alan or Jack or Freddie or Richard or Frank saying, "Do you look smashing!"

What bracket are you in? St. Laurent? Dior? Chanel? Ungaro? Valentino? Oscar de la Renta? Givenchy? Cardin? Donald Brooks? Malcolm Starr? Mollie Parnis? Will-you-come-home-Ben Zuckerman? (Never mind about Bill Bailey.) Will-you-come-home, Ben Z.?

If you're a little short on cash, don't forget Sunset Strip and curve in Suzie Creamcheese on the next weekend up in Vegas. Keep looking till the price is right. Today between couture and boutique there is something for everybody. Like a grab bag. A grab bag you don't get stung in.

The last one I grabbed was 1902 when Avis Tobey had a lawn party in her back yard to raise money to buy the Sunday school a sand map. To help them I handed Avis my nickel, then grabbed and came up with a square of gray cardboard, a photo of a cat pasted on.

"I don't care if it is for the sand map," said my mother, "it isn't worth the money."

But Dior and De la Renta and the Strip and Suzie Creamcheese *are*, because they get you to the party looking wowy. Or groovy. Or super. Or beautiful.

I said to Willie Maugham, "Why do you like society?"

"Their houses are so beautiful, dear. Millicent Sutherland receiving at the head of her stairs was well worth going out for."

Doris Stein doesn't receive at the head of her stairs, but at the head of Angelo Drive, looking out over all California among tall pines, fore and aft. They bought the house for thirty-five thousand dollars from Enid Bennett and Fred Niblo in the forties. I offered to buy it back at what they paid for it, but Jules said he wouldn't take a million. No wonder people love California. Especially people who knew the Niblos.

At the foot of Angelo, behind bronze gates, the Jack Warners drink their Mountain Valley Water and give parties.

I went to one. The food was like you imagine, the house was handsome and full of beautiful people. In one room was a three-leaf-clover seat with Hedy Lamarr sitting in one leaf and Janet Gaynor in the second. Wouldn't *you* sit down in the third?

Hedy was complaining about men, love and emeralds. "When I was married to Mandl, what did he give me for Christmas? Emeralds! He knew I hated emeralds."

Janet and I made sympathetic noises.

"And now George, he loves horses. All he *thinks* about is horses." She looked past me to Janet who knows what to do about everything.

"Hedy," said Janet in her direct, earthenware voice, "Hedy, you've got to *learn*. In love there's always one person *loves*, and one person that's loved. *One* of you has to be the one loves too *much*, and *they're* the ones get stung."

"That's *me!*" said Hedy.

Who do *you* learn from?

During *Rosemary's Baby* everybody said, "Mia must learn a lot from you."

Did she?

I admired her miniskirt. "It's great on you," I said, "but I'm too short to wear one."

Thought wrinkled up that flower Mia uses for a face, until it looked like a yesterday's pansy. "Ruthie," she said, "I think you just use that for an excuse, because you don't want to change."

I wish *she'd* been my third-grade teacher. I might now be Rythe Jones.

Everybody's too busy resting. You've got to cut it out. Or down. To really feel good, find out what makes you jump.

William James was looking for it, too. "You're out dead on your feet," wrote James, or words to that effect, "and you win the sweepstakes that pays off a million tax-free deductible dollars. Wouldn't that rest you more than a nap?" Or words to that effect.

All his life, he was trying to find the equivalent. Of course, the equivalent for you and me may not be the equivalent for Mitzi Newhouse, who couldn't be bothered with another million tax-free dollars. What's going to make *her* jump?

A play called *Saturday's Children* did it for Joan Payson. Joan came to see Humphrey Bogart and me keep house on a hundred and seventy-four dollars a month and still not get uptight over who smoked the most Camels. *Now* Joan's Mets make her jump. And a lot of the rest of us, too.

In front of Anthony's, Pier 4, I waited for George, the chauffeur, to pull the limo around. Diners were pouring into Anthony's, diners were trickling out. I felt an arm go around my waist and a shove toward the excursion boat tied alongside Pier 4. Was this what my mother warned me of? Was this some belated white-slaver?

A fine Bostonian looked at me. "Oh, excuse me," he said, "I thought you were my granddaughter."

Why did I tell my age?

Or what if I were eighty-four!

"You're different," said Truman, "You've got all that confidence."

Why I have is because I took the trouble to see that it's built in. In my business they pay people to tear you wide open, so your confidence has to work around the clock or you could get bags under your eyes from crying.

I started building mine in 1910 when the Wollaston Grammar School eighth grade was going to graduate. Mrs. Roberts, who lived in the other half of our house, hand-embroidered the panel, belt, sleeves and collar of my graduation dress. Her daughter Ellen embroidered the princess slip to go under it. My mother gave me white kid slippers from Thayer, McNeil and Hodgkins, my sister Clare gave me white Dorothy Dainty hair ribbons from R. H. Stearns, and my father gave me my confidence. He got his from the College of Hard Knocks.

"The whole eighth grade is going to march onto the stage, Papa, and I'm going to lead them," I boasted.

"Why, Snuggy!" he said proudly. "You got the highest marks?"

"No, I'm the shortest."

"Chosen on account of a deformity," he said. He prized education the more, since *his* ended in the fourth grade.

After dinner at Edie Goetz's we go into the drawing room. There are the Sisleys. The Picassos. The Monet. The Toulouse-Lautrec. And the movie, which is *our* business, just as the Sisleys were Sisley's business and the Picassos are Picasso's business.

"Nothing more dignified than making money," said Thornton. And in a room with the Picassos and the Sisleys, we admire them and also a lot of *our* pictures, which happen to be moving.

"Move the orchids, Snoogy, it's CinemaScope."

Dear Snoogy.

"The Renoirs and the Toulouse-Lautrec and the Monet look on at *Goodbye, Columbus*. Does that make it, or them, less good?

"Good evening, Shorty." Edie tells the operator to start.

Does it hurt if Picasso's harlequin and Degas' ballet girl look on, too?

"It's death," says Thornton, "for an actress to have the 'please-like-me' approach. Let the audience come to you, don't please-like-me them."

Do I do that?

Not offstage. Or I'd never say, "I have the greatest cook."

She is French. And adorable. And been with me since 1934. Shall we say I'm not troubled with that "please-like-me" attitude? If anything will make people turn on you—and some things will—it's to say you have a cook. To say you have a *great* cook cuts your public in half, and to say you had her since 1934? Draw the veil.

I don't know how long Rhode Island's Governor Beekman kept his help, but Howard Sturges said that one day the Governor walked down to the beach and looked out over the North Atlantic that favors Newport. "Who's swimming out there?" he asked his gardener.

"Mrs. Beekman's maid, sir."

"Tell her to come out, Mrs. Beekman wants to go in."

In the Ambassador Club at Kennedy I heard, "We don't have

any children, so wherever we go, we're not far."

Is that freedom? Or loneliness?

Kitty Hart thought she and Moss should have another baby.

"What are you thinking of?" asked Moss. "Chris and Cathy are growing up, we're only a few years from room service."

Where are the snows of yesteryear?

Some of it is in the Veranda Grill on the S.S. *United States*. The Firestones had the corner table and laughed hard at something.

Sitting next to us was Newport's Mrs. Forsythe Wicks telling about beautiful Katherine Mackay and the days one walked a mile across the decks of Newport yachts.

The Firestones laughed again.

"Don't be cheap," called out Mrs. Forsythe Wicks in the same clear voice that had called across a mile of yacht decks and could still reach the Firestones.

Mrs. Wicks disapproved of a lot of things. "She was an *actress*," she said with a look.

"I'm an actress, Mrs. Wicks."

"I know," she said forgivingly.

Are *you* forgiving?

I forgave my family when I was six because I knew my mother wasn't with it, and was careful to tell her only non-essentials.

"Never speak to strangers," she warned me, "and never accept anything from anybody you don't know."

Could *you* follow that advice?

What if I hadn't picked up Thornton Wilder in front of the Booth Theatre? What if I hadn't had my picture taken with Garson Kanin before I ever met him? Advice is like what Mrs. Pat said about money. "It's for those who need it." You have to know if it's for *you*, and if it's not, find out what *is*. My mother's advice wasn't for *me*. There's nothing new in the generation gap.

"Horses sweat, men perspire, ladies glow," instructed my mother. She never did a TV show.

On a TV show, horses, men *and* ladies sweat. What was going to happen to my groovy Christian Dior? I rang up Natalie Wood.

"For TV use Mitchum's. But that's for special. For every day, Dry Mist."

Thank God for *Inside Daisy Clover*. When Natalie Wood

nodded her pretty head, I was hired and if she'd said no, *who* would be responsible for my groovy Dior dress?

Do *you* face the facts? My cousin Edith just rose above them. Her last name was Boozer. Could she help it? She fell in love with a guy named Boozer. Could *he* help it? But when Cousin Edith's little girl was born, she *could* help it. She named her Lady.

Lady had lots of beautiful dresses and one day during spring cleaning her mother came upon forty she'd forgotten that Lady had. In my family everything was colored by economy, but Cousin Lady Boozer's forty forgotten dresses gave me something to aim at.

Now I have forty dresses, but my ambition wasn't to *have* forty, but to forget forty and not miss them.

Is your pelvis dropped?

Pick it up.

At Peter Glenville's dinner party. A dazzling lady on *Vogue* said, "Most people age and their pelvis drops, but Ruth Gordon's is right in place." She stood up to illustrate.

"When you get old, your pelvis drops, but Ruth Gordon's is right up there," and she showed what she meant.

Thank you, Françoise, that's praise indeed, from one whose pelvis is also right up there. And thank your husband for thinking up such pelvis-lifting creations.

People used to get praised for a well-turned ankle, an hourglass form, une belle poitrine, small feet, tapering fingers, and in *Love for Love* Congreve praised a lady for "the jut of her bum." I'm glad praise got around to my pelvis.

I haven't been in the park at night since I was at dramatic school in 1914. I went in with Marian and her beau and our class mate Oscar Johnson. Even then the park was dangerous. We settled down at a place that looked like a small crumpled castle. It had something to do with the waterworks. Marian and her beau did some kissing and hugging, but Oscar never laid a glove on me. Not that I wanted him to, not that I wasn't prepared to wrestle, but not to *have to* could break your spirit. The park has always been dangerous.

Do you know what you like?

Corn on the cob, pink blotters, brooks that freeze over with grass sticking up through the ice, David and John Anderson gingham, hand-whipped cream, woodbine, West 45th Street, Quincy High School Class of 1914, sealing wax, Atlantic City Boardwalk, money in my purse, Edgartown, ribbon, the east wind, sunflowers, the Côte Basque Restaurant, old musical comedies except one, rain, Mia Farrow, lobster salad, peonies, sneakers, no underwear, La Grenouille Restaurant, a full moon, Dressing Room Number One, peanut butter, a large house, these are a few of my *favorite* things.

Do you know what to do if you catch your hand in the electric fan?

Olga didn't. And it left her hand with a bad bruise and a cut.

Olga had been a grand lady's maid at the Grand Hotel, Rome, and Bronia Clair brought her back to Neuilly and to Miremer in St. Tropez, for her personal maid. Olga was flawless and the Neuilly and St. Tropez households fell in love with her. Especially Frédéric Chaix, gardener, boule player, repairman, shopper and friend for twenty years.

Frédéric, a shy man, lost his Tropezien heart to Roman Olga. Olga thought Frédéric was nice. And that was that.

The day Olga caught her hand in the electric fan, Frédéric put down tools and took off for the mountains back of Grimaud. Four hours later he was back, carrying three flowers wrapped in damp leaves. He put them on Olga's hand and tied a linen handkerchief over them. That evening the pain was gone. The next morning there was no bruise, the cut was healed.

"But Frédéric," said Bronia, "you went so far to find the flowers, why did you bring only three?"

"Three would heal her hand."

"But suppose you lost one?"

"Why would I do that?" asked Frédéric.

He, also, had built-in confidence.

Anybody who's gone steady with Thornton Wilder for forty years must have something to recommend them, even if it isn't the fabulous beauty of Lynn Fontanne.

What did she do to cherish it?

I heard she drank tea made of parsnip greens.

I've known her since 1919 and thought maybe the time had come when I, too, should drink parsnip tea.

"How do you make it?" I asked.

She'd never heard of it. It was one of those legends. But she said, "When you come to visit us in Genesee Depot, I will tell you all my secrets. All, except two."

Ruth Chatterton told me *her* secret. I was staying with her and nothing was going right for her. Or me. Her love life had gone to hell. Mine, too. Her finances had gone down the drain. Mine, too. *We* had to call our agents. And we weren't getting any younger. But on the surface there was style.

In a corner cabinet was ruby glass that Ruth had sent an expert to England to find. Her drawing-room walls were walnut boiseries that would bring pride to a museum. The gleam from the Waterford chandelier was welcome to pretty ladies.

In the morning her secretary, Rita, knocked on my door. "Ruth would like you to come in."

Looking beautiful in any light, sun or Waterford or Welsbach, Ruth sat up in her beautiful, lonely bed, wearing a beautiful bed jacket, and on the beautiful counterpane dealt the cards in a game of chain solitaire.

I exclaimed over her bed jacket.

"Hitrova," she said and shuffled the cards.

" 'Rue du Quatre Septembre.' Pearl Swope gave me that address. I got one nightgown there."

"Show her mine, Rita."

Rita brought in a dozen Hitrova bed jackets just out of customs.

Ruth dealt a hand, talked, to me or on the phone, got ready for her horseback ride, or her lesson to pilot her Stinson, and every morning and evening there came a phone call, "Oh hello, darling, I'll call you back."

"*Take* it. I'll go out," I whispered.

"No, no," she said and hung up.

"Ruth," I said, "give me a nod and I'll go."

"It's not what you think."

"What do I think?"

"You think it's a fella. It isn't. But I know *you*. You'll think it's silly."

"What is it?"

"It's this terrific man. He tells me what's going to happen. He guides my whole life. Two months ago he told me I would hurt myself and I shut my hand in the car door. Now he says I'm going to sign a contract and can go to Seville for the Easter bullfights. It wouldn't hurt *you* to talk to him."

Next evening after dinner Ruth showed me into her upstairs sitting room. There sat a small, wiry, gray-haired man in a blue serge suit, white shirt and a bow tie.

"This is Dr. Harris."

He pointed to a chair.

I sat down facing him. He stared at me, and not knowing what to do, I stared at him. He must have stared at me for five minutes. "Ruthie," he said at last, "why don't you be smart?"

That was it.

And I never forgot it. In a tight squeeze I think of Dr. Harris. "Ruthie, why don't you be smart?"

Why did he think I wasn't? I was born in the part of Quincy called Wollaston. That was smart. I went to Wollaston Grammar School, I was smart there. I graduated from Quincy High and in Quincy, life was such, I was given the opportunity to become what I sought to become.

Quincy gave me my opportunity, Boston theatres gave me my inspiration, Boston money earned by my father at 41 Central Wharf bought me a ticket in Boston's South Station to come and tackle New York. Last October 30th I was seventy-four. I can't fool you and say eighty-four. Anyway, it's just numbers. What I care about is, I don't want it to stop. It's been awful and great and hair-raising and beautiful and side-splitting and terrifying and unbelievably groovy and I wouldn't live over one single day of it, but will I ever hate to see that evenin' sun go down!